I0245516

BEATLES

ARCHIVES VOL 1

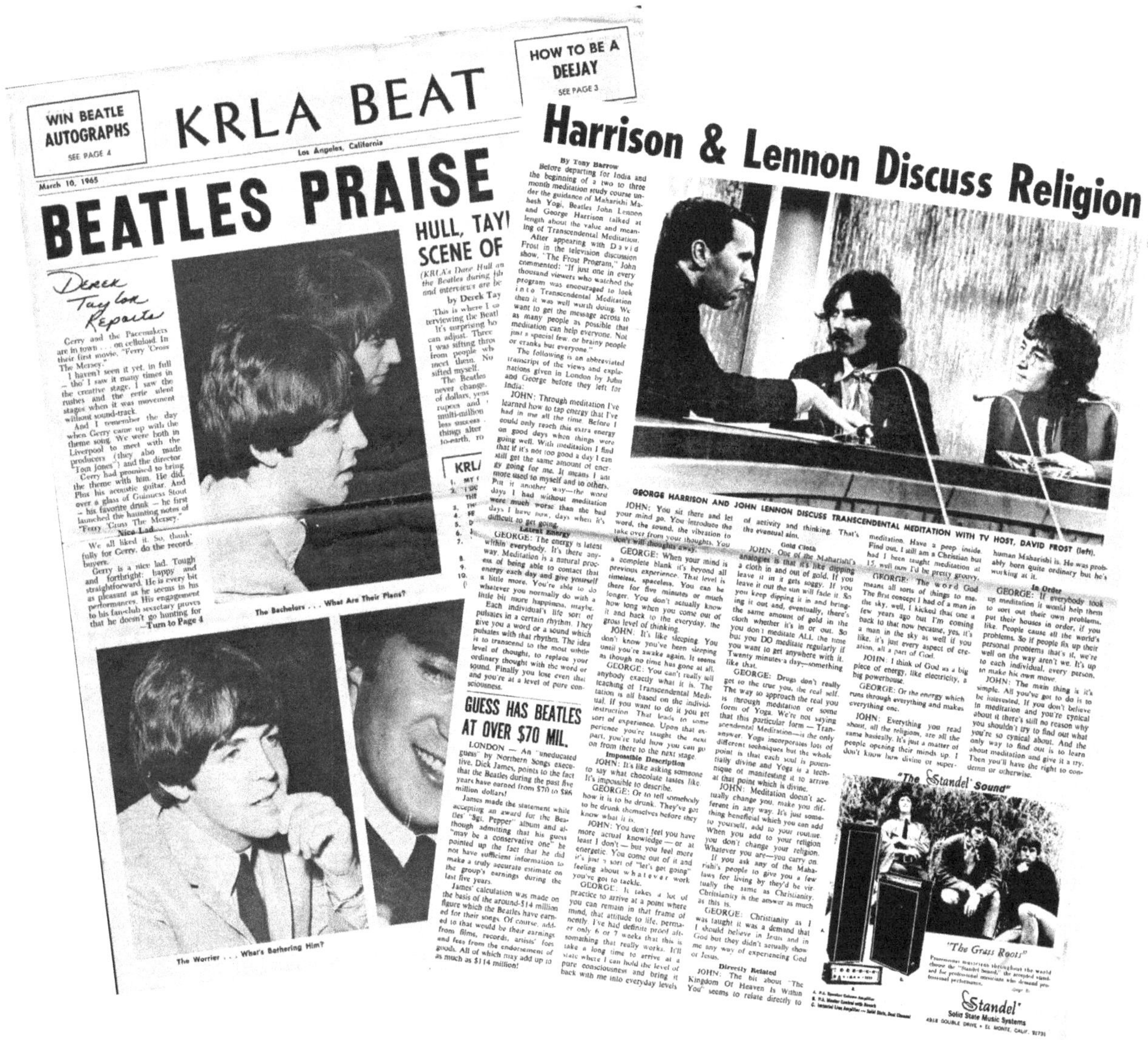
WIN BEATLE AUTOGRAPHS
SEE PAGE 4
KRLA BEAT
Los Angeles, California
March 10, 1965
HOW TO BE A DEEJAY
SEE PAGE 3
BEATLES PRAISE
HULL, TAY
SCENE OF
Derek Taylor Reports
Nice Lad
Turn to Page 4
The Bachelors . . . What Are Their Plans?
The Worrier . . . What's Bothering Him?
GUESS HAS BEATLES AT OVER $70 MIL.
Harrison & Lennon Discuss Religion
By Tony Barrow
GEORGE HARRISON AND JOHN LENNON DISCUSS TRANSCENDENTAL MEDITATION WITH TV HOST, DAVID FROST (left).
Latent Energy
Impossible Description
Gold Cloth
In Order
Directly Related
"The Standel Sound"
"The Grass Roots"
Standel
Solid State Music Systems

White Lightning Publishing

Copyright ©2016 White Lightning Publishing

This volume reprints artifacts related to the Monkees. Through research, we believe that all pieces to be in the public domain. If you hold valid and current copyrights presented, please contact us at WhiteLightningPublishing@gmail.com with proof so that we can remove materials on future printings.

BEATLES ARCHIVES 1

JOHN LENNON coming to America?

RINGO now friends with the Richard Burtons

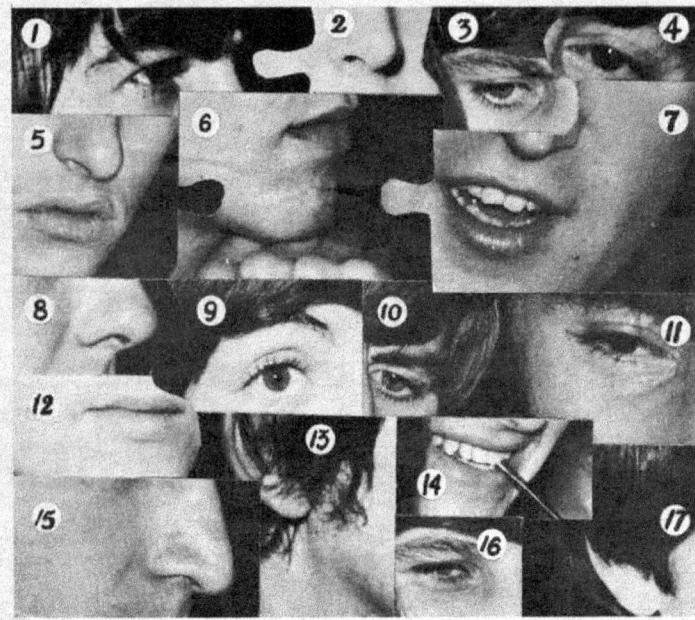

Beatle Scrambled Features Contest

My Answers to the Beatles Scrambled Features Contest:

Mail Entry to:
KRLA BEAT
6290 Sunset Blvd., Suite 504
Hollywood, California

Name
Address
City
State
Phone

Test Your Beatle Skill – Autographs For The Winner

ATTENTION Beatlemaniacs: Here's the contest you been asking for . . . The Beatles Scrambled Features Contest. And the grand prize is something out of this world – An Autographed Picture of the Beatles!

Derek Taylor and Dave Hull are bringing back the prize when they return from Nassau – personally autographed by John, Paul, George and Ringo. If you know the Beatles as well as you think you do, then you may be the winner. And the owner of one of the few autographed pictures of the Beatles in the entire world!

Look at each of the scrambled features in the picture layout to the left. If you think that's Paul nose in No. 2, then write his name beside that number on the entry blank below.

When all the blanks are filled, send in your entry and wait for the results to be announced in the KRLA Beat. You may enter as many times as you like. All entires must be postmarked before March 15, 1965, and in case of a tie, the earliest postmark wins. Good Luck!

ADVERTISERS
For rates and information call the KRLA BEAT at 469-3641.

KRLA T

1. (1) MY GIRL
2. (14) I DON'T WANT TO S
         EIGHT DAYS A WEE
3. (6) THIS DIAMOND RIN
4. (8) FERRY ACROSS THE

Scene and Heard

Ringo Starr becomes the first Beatle to make a solo guest appearance in a TV variety show. He's scheduled to duet with songstress Cilla Black in her new BBC Television series February 6 and has been rehearsing his part in a comedy routine with her for the same program

Vacation for Lennon

Lightning six-day vacation in Casablanca, Morocco, for John Lennon and his wife Cynthia when they decided at the last minute to accompany actor Victor Spinetti to North Africa . . . John Lennon's brilliantly painted Rolls Royce (the one the newspapers love to call "psychedelic") shipped to New York for possible touring use by the Beatle in America later in the year. However, he has no immediate plans to cross the Atlantic as the Rolls could be in storage for quite a long time!

During Rome shooting of the movie "Candy," Ringo and Maureen Starr became very friendly with Elizabeth Taylor and Richard Burton . . . Estate Duty Office in London declared an estate of just over one million dollars (gross) left by Brian Epstein who died last August without making a will. But the gross total does not include a yet-to-be-agreed valuation of his major business interests.

Beatles Coming, $100,000 Going

The Beatles are coming to Los Angeles again this August and they're planning to take a good deal of money with them when they leave.

They've been set for one evening performance in Dodger Stadium Aug. 28. Tickets will be the same as last year, $3 to $7, but the when, where and how they may be purchased, has not been announced yet.

The Beatles themselves have been guaranteed $100,000 against 65% of the gate. The $100,000 guarantee is a record for any entertainment act here in Southern California.

It's nothing for the Beatles though, who are sort of used to breaking records. They received the same amount last year from appearances in New York's Shea Stadium and the Kansas City Athletic's ball park.

Last year the Beatles received $45,000 a night for their two performances in the Hollywood Bowl.

Although they'll only do one show this year, more fans will actually be able to see them since Dodger Stadium holds over twice as many people as the Hollywood Bowl. The Bowl holds just under 20,000 while the Stadium holds 50,000.

This is actually a feather in Dodger Stadium's cap. They've been trying to lure in more entertainment acts since the L.A. Angels moved to Anaheim.

BEATLES ARCHIVES 1

WIN BEATLE AUTOGRAPHS SEE PAGE 4

KRLA BEAT

HOW TO BE A DEEJAY SEE PAGE 3

March 10, 1965 — Los Angeles, California — Ten Cents

BEATLES PRAISE L.A.!

Derek Taylor Reports

Gerry and the Pacemakers are in town . . . on celluloid. In their first movie, "Ferry 'Cross The Mersey."

I haven't seen it yet, in full — tho' I saw it many times in the creative stage. I saw the rushes and the eerie silent stages when it was movement without sound-track.

And I remember the day when Gerry came up with the theme song. We were both in Liverpool to meet with the producers (they also made "Tom Jones") and the director.

Gerry had promised to bring the theme with him. He did. Plus his acoustic guitar. And over a glass of Guinness Stout — his favorite drink — he first launched the haunting notes of "Ferry 'Cross The Mersey."

Nice Lad

We all liked it. So, thankfully for Gerry, do the record-buyers.

Gerry is a nice lad. Tough and forthright; happy and straightforward. He is every bit as pleasant as he seems in his performances. His engagement to his fan-club secretary proves that he doesn't go hunting for
—Turn to Page 4

The Bachelors . . . What Are Their Plans?

HULL, TAYLOR VISITING SCENE OF BEATLE MOVIE

(KRLA's Dave Hull and Derek Taylor are on Nassau, guests of the Beatles during filming of their second movie. Their reports and interviews are being broadcast daily over KRLA.)

by Derek Taylor

This is where I came in. Interviewing the Beatles.

It's surprising how soon you can adjust. Three months ago I was sifting through inquiries from people who wanted to meet them. Now I've been sifted myself.

The Beatles are fine. They never change. Their millions of dollars, yens, kroners, marks, rupees and pounds — their multi-million fans, their ceaseless success . . . none of these things alter their basic down-to-earth, rough-and-ready ap-
— Turn to Page 4

KRLA TOP TEN
1. MY GIRL
2. I DON'T WANT TO SPOIL THE PARTY - 8 DAYS A WEEK
3. THIS DIAMOND RING
4. FERRY 'CROSS THE MERSEY
5. DOWNTOWN
6. JOLLY GREEN GIANT
7. YOU'VE LOST THAT LOVIN' FEELIN'
8. KING OF THE ROAD
9. BOY FROM NEW YORK CITY
10. RED ROSES FOR A BLUE LADY

(Complete Listing Page 4)

by Dave Hull

Hi, Hullabalooers!

Right now Derek and I are relaxing beside the pool here at the beautiful Balmoral Country Club after our first get-together with our hosts — four fellows named George, John, Paul and Ringo.

You probably never heard of them, but they're singers. Also movie actors. Their group is called . . . let's see, is it the Bugs? No, that doesn't sound right. Maybe they're the Insects. No, that's not right either. Surely I haven't forgotten.

Here it is . . . I wrote it down so I wouldn't f o r g e t. THE BEATLES! Isn't that a funny name? They couldn't amount to much with a name like that. They're nice boys, though.

Seriously, it was a great thrill seeing them again after their visits to Los Angeles last summer.

They said to tell all of you hello and that they were looking forward to their next trip to Southern California Aug. 29 and 30. They regard last year's
— Turn to Page 3

The Worrier . . . What's Bothering Him?

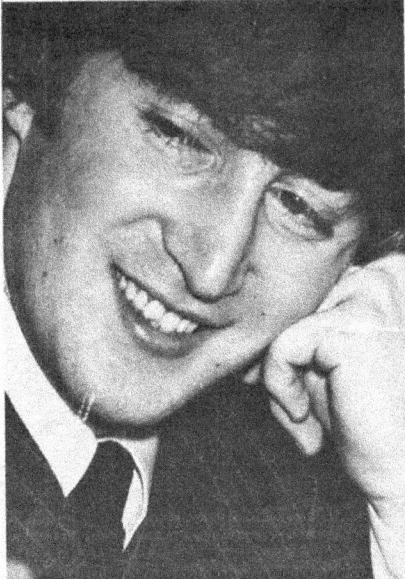

The Married Men . . . Check Ringo's New Ring

BEATLES ARCHIVES 1

KRLA BEAT

Volume 2, Number 23 — September 10, 1966

Beatle Box Score: 14 Hits, One Error

Lennon: 'Sorry About the Mess'

With religious groups still condemning them and teens greeting them with mixed reactions, the Beatles are concluding their U.S. tour amidst apologies and attempted clarifications of John Lennon's statement on the condition of Christianity.

Lennon continually apologized for the furor caused by his statement that "the Beatles are more popular than Jesus," but insisted that he did not mean for his comment to be anti-Christian.

The intellectual Beatle said he merely was attempting to show that Christianity was on the decline — not that the Beatles were above Christ.

Losing Contact

"I do believe that Christianity is shrinking, that people are losing contact with it," he said at a recent press conference.

"However, I didn't mean it the way it sounded," he added. "I was using the Beatles as an example because that's what I'm most familiar with. I could have just as easily used cars or television."

Lennon said he was as surprised as he was worried when the statement had allegedly been taken out of context and printed in an American magazine.

"When I first heard of the uproar that the statement had created I didn't want to come to America at all," he said. "Then we decided we had better come and try to straighten the trouble out.

"I'm sorry about the mess it made."

Lennon said when he made the statement he never considered the way it might be misconstrued.

When asked if he was a Christian, Lennon replied that although he was brought up as one, he wasn't a practicing Christian. "But I don't have any un-Christian thoughts," he quickly added.

True Test

Meanwhile, teens across the nation continued to be violently divided on the Beatles' status in the world of rock.

The Beatles' tour however, rolled along without major incident. It was met by the customary hoardes of screaming teens who continued to proclaim the Britons as their idols.

And this, it is said, is the only true test of their popularity. So once again, the Beatles may be the first family of rock.

Home After Stormy Tour

England's all-star infield is back home after its blustery U.S. road trip — but not without the 14 consecutive victories skeptics said would be impossible.

After drawing the greatest mass reaction ever given a pop group, the Beatles capped their third tour of America in "the only state we really looked forward to," and the results must have been gratifying all the way around.

The Beatles frenzied near capacity crowds at Dodger Stadium and Candlestick Park — ending what some say will be their last U.S. visit — and it looked like a scene from the past.

For about an hour on their final stops they were the Beatles of old ... laughing, singing, barely audible through the screams of those
(Turn to Page 21)

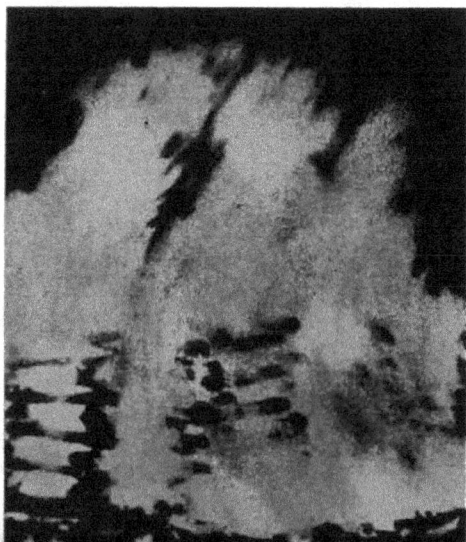

BURNING EMBERS ... of resentment towards the Beatles still blaze in some regions of the country. Latest "flare up" was this massive bonfire in Longview, Texas. More than 7,500 righteous residents were on hand to toss Beatles records, wigs and other souvenirs into the blaze. In general, however, anti-Beatle sentiment was on a marked decrease, and the group departed "the land of the free" amidst the customary cheering, screaming and fainting.

'We Love You — John AND God'

It was a moment many had predicted would never come. Swirling, reaching, screaming ... the crowd was a contradiction — and a happy one.

It was the last hour in the United States for the Beatles. Flashbulbs popped. Beatlemaniacs — an uncountable number of them — craned, stretched and stood on their tip toes to get a glimpse of the foursome as it tunneled through the mass.

Placards, bobbing and twisting, protruded above the raucous gathering. One read, "We love you — John AND God."

The Beatles, surrounded by a reinforced brigade of uniformed policemen, were at last out of the terminal and heading slowly towards their private plane.

They were laughing, waving ... occasionally reaching past their police escort to touch one of their admirers.

"It's them," shouted a 16-year-old girl in near hysteria. "We love you! We love you!" moaned a girl wedged next to her.

Finally they were climbing into their plane. They looked back momentarily, and were gone.

Time Heals Wounds; Stations Lift Ban

Time heals many wounds.

And while the John Lennon controversy may never be completely forgotten, it has at least been softened by recent clarifications and explanations.

So now the Beatles are steadily regaining their stronghold.

Their records are again being played on major Hot 100 format stations around the country and their latest single, "Yellow Submarine" b/w "Eleanor Rigby," is rapidly climbing the charts.

Most of the stations playing Beatles records say public demand forced the action. Most radio station personnel said taking Beatles records off the air would greatly hurt their station's ratings.

One station in the midwest announced it was banning Beatle records — obviously thinking public opinion warranted it — and the ensuing results were nearly disastrous.

The next day, the station was presented with a petition containing 9,500 names. The petition was a threat to ban, not the Beatles, but the station.

The station quickly recognized its position, backed down ... and "Yellow Submarine" was an hourly occurence.

JOHN ... Singing, Not Talking.

Inside the BEAT

Those Soulful Beatles	2-3
Letters to the Editor	4
On the Beat	5
Readers Write More	6
News in Pictures	7
"Sunny" Bobby	8
The Songwriter's Songwriters	9
A Big Bird & A Beatle	10
Sir Douglas and His Quints	11
For Girls Only	16
Tough Young Rascals	17
Psychedelic Music	22-23
And more, more, more, more, more	

The BEAT is published bi-weekly by BEAT Publications, Inc., editorial and advertising offices at 6290 Sunset Blvd., Suite 504, Hollywood, California 90028, U.S. bureaus in Hollywood, San Francisco, New York, Chicago and Nashville, overseas correspondents in London, Liverpool and Manchester, England. Subscription price: U.S. and possessions, $5 per year; Canada and foreign rates, $9 per year. Second class postage prepaid at Los Angeles, California.

BEATLES ... Last hours in U.S.

BEATLES ARCHIVES 1

Whatever Happened To The

Beatlemania – a word which was non-existent until February of 1964. Now, it describes a very real emotional reaction to four talented entertainers.

Rubber Soul – until last year, a still-unconceived album title, which was destined to become a standard phrase used to describe a creation of exceptional excellence in the field of music.

Revolver – a brand new Beatle album, too-infrequently referred to as a second "Rubber Soul," and definitely a musical creation of exceptional excellence.

Beatlemania is no longer the wild, uncontrolled, hysterial phenomenon it was in the early days of 1964. It has simmered down a little now as its greatest exponents – the Beatlemaniacs – have grown up a little.

There is less screaming now and more appreciation; much more observation and attention is in evidence at current Beatle concerts.

But even that is somewhat sad. It is almost as though the enthusiasm – the uncontrolled exuberance – which became associated with Beatlemania from the beginning has died.

Enthusiasm

True, it isn't really the enthusiasm which has died – only the hysteria. And yet, it is the enthusiasm, the interest, the attention – which seems to be suffering from anemia. Beatlemaniacs have become somewhat jaded – just a little bit blase' – and now at times they take the Beatles more or less for granted.

This summer has seen the birth of a great new album from the Fabulous Foursome, and album which involved weeks and weeks of long rehearsal, extensive arrangement, and hours and hours of recording. It is an album of which the Beatles should be justifiably proud, and yet it is receiving only a fraction of the attention and respect due.

In recent months, a number of albums released by other artists and groups have been labeled a "Rubber Soul in its field," indicating some form of high achievement.

But, there have been relatively few cries of a "second Rubber Soul" where the "Revolver" album is concerned – and these are the boys who *started it all!*

Oddly enough, several of the numbers included in the LP are already well on their way toward becoming contemporary standards, but the whole process is occuring with an amazing absence of fanfare and discussion.

Taxman

One of the best and most commercial George Harrison compositions for some time is the first cut on the album, "Taxman." It is also one of the best, most concise satirical comments on the British society and current tax situation (not to mention our own!) to come along from *anyone* for some time.

"Eleanor Rigby" must be destined to become a contemporary classic. Certainly the haunting melody is one of the most beautiful to be found in our current pop music, and the words – the universal description of the countless thousands of "lonely people" who are to be found everywhere – is both accurate and unforgettable. And need we mention the beautiful string arrangement – or is that something to be found in *every* run-of-the-mill pop release?

George has created a new extension of the music form which he introduced in "Rubber Soul" with his sitar arrangement for "Norwegian Wood," extending the Indian influence to his own composition – "Love You To." Well done and musically valid. Also musically unrecognized.

Love Song

"Here, There and Everywhere" is probably the most beautiful – or one of the most beautiful – love songs to be written and recorded in many, many years. It is also one of the least-mentioned, least-played cuts on the album. Fantastic new vocal arrangement from Paul here.

"Yellow Submarine" – the satirical "children's song" that *isn't;* "She Said She Said" – the up-tempo, semi-electronic lament; and "I Want To Tell You," the third Harrison composition on the LP, unusual, newly-melodic, and interesting – all of these receiving very little comment.

Of course, there have been a large number of attempts made at analyzing "Yellow Submarine," but as they are all highly hysterical and wholly inaccurate – they don't really count!

And then of course there is "For No One" – still another contender for the Contemporary Classic Hall of Fame. A fantastically beautiful

BEATLES ARCHIVES 1

Beatle Soul?

and haunting love song, musically sighed as only Paul can.

Finally, "Tomorrow Never Knows" — a weird and polished electronic creation from John Lennon. Also, an unintended prophesy; tomorrow really doesn't ever know — if you don't believe that, just take a look at today.

The Beatles are returning for their third major American tour, but they won't be playing to stadiums sold out well in advance. Is their popularity really dying? Hardly. Fans are simply not interested in the mere "freak value" of the Beatles any more. They are no longer purchasing tickets priced high above their pocketbooks simply so they can catch a glimpse of the Beatles.

For Real

We've all seen them now. We know what they look like, we know they're for real. But this time around — we'd kind of like to hear what they have to say . . . and sing . . . and play.

And that's a pretty big order in a stadium which holds 50 or 60 thousand people. It's great if you want to watch nine faceless, nameless ball-players with only numbers for identification on their backs running about a field for a couple of hours. But, if you would be interested in seeing and *hearing* the performance of four of the most talented and most interesting performers in pop music today . . . it's pretty discouraging.

So, many promoters are somewhat discouraged, because they aren't selling tickets as they thought they would. This may slightly injure the Beatles' image — but it isn't through any direct fault of their own.

Political

Of course, there seem to be a large number of American individuals who are more interested in the Beatles' political views than the music which they are creating, and perhaps this is part of the reason why we are simply hearing about the "souls" of the Beatles rather than their "Rubber Soul."

It is always sad to see the diminishing of healthy, sincere enthusiasm, but it must be. If it were to continue, it would become only a monotone of emotion and be rendered eventually meaningless.

Impact

Perhaps there won't be quite as much screaming at Beatle concerts this year, and perhaps everyone isn't aware of the musical impact and importance of "Revolver" — but it is certain that "Revolver" has fired a shot which will be heard around the globe wherever people really care about the music they are listening to.

And the Beatles won't be soon forgotten either — at least not as long as there are Bibles resting beside the seats in air liners.

. . . THE MANY FACES OF MR. LENNON

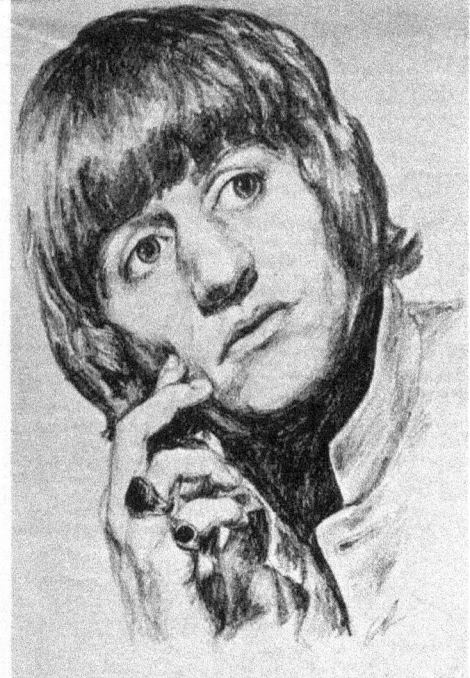
. . . RINGO CAPTURED IN A PENSIVE MOOD

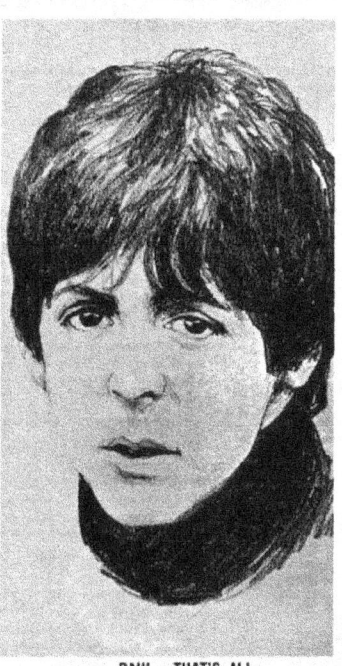
. . . PAUL — THAT'S ALL

. . . THE SMILE THAT FOLLOWS

BEATLES ARCHIVES 1

Letters TO THE EDITOR

Lennon Vs. Christianity

(Ed. NOTE: The BEAT has received hundreds of letters, both pro and con, concerning John Lennon's remarks about Christianity. Unfortunately, we do not have nearly enough space to print all of the letters but we would like to thank each of you for writing. Perhaps, if in the future you concentrate on writing shorter letters, we will be able to print many more each week. Thanks again.)

Shut Mouths

Dear BEAT:
When a group of singers become stars, I feel that they take on the responsibility of when to make a statement of opinion and when to keep their mouths shut! This responsibility seems to have been overlooked in the last four or five months by our beloved (?) Beatles.

What has happened? When they were new to the world of fame they seemed to know their place and stayed in it. When a reporter asked a question on politics or religion they retorted with a cute quip and that was that. Now, it seems they have to give a five minute oration of what *they* think is wrong with the world.

I have been an avid Beatle fan ever since their first tour to America but I believe that these last few months have been the "straw that broke the camel's back."

I think it's about time somebody had a heart to heart talk to them to let them know that everyone does not enjoy hearing four young "men" say things that if given time to cool off or just think over would realize never should have been said.

I realize this will probably never be published but I just had to speak my mind as I know many people have my same opinion.
Sue Abbot

Dear BEAT:
I have read in our local paper that John has said that the Beatles are more popular than Christ. My mother thinks what he's saying is that most people aren't very religious these days—not saying it should go.

I don't think it's fair to condemn a whole group's future just because of what one member said. I thought that the Beatles, Rolling Stones, etc., were known and respected because they had no false fronts and spoke their minds often. The people who are burning their Beatle things will be sorry someday. In the years to come, the Beatles will always be known and respected for their musical and acting talent.

Also, why must people be continually trying to find fault with the Beatles. Can't they praise the group once in a while? They should think of the countless things the Beatles have done to help make the world-happy.

They should be thankful there are four charming, talented guys like the Beatles together in a group.
Pattie Lockwood

Dear BEAT:
I hope you will print the following as an "open letter" to John Lennon. I will attempt to express my feelings for the banned album cover and John's attack on Christianity.

John, I have always respected you for the things you have accomplished and your fabulous career, even before George was my favorite.

When your album came out, I was shocked at the cover. I read in The BEAT how your fans made excuses for it. You have said: "The fans we have now were the real ones we had at the beginning." You implied that if they are true fans they will stick with you through thick and thin.

But your attack on Christianity was where I got off, buddy.
Mr. Lennon, I am ashamed to say that I once liked you. I'm sorry the thought ever entered my head. If you think you're so great, that your fans will always love you, you have another think coming. You, sir, are no better than anyone else. From what source did you get the idea that you were more popular than Jesus?

If my guess is right, you got it out of your warped mind. If you think rock 'n' roll will outlive Christianity, you're nuts.

I can't wait to hear your poor fans' excuses for why you said this. They'll probably say it was for "shock value." You wasted what's left of your brain thinking that one up, if you did it for shock value—you got enough of that with the gory cover.

John, the sad thing about this Christianity bit is that you're not only going to lose your popularity but you're going to lose Paul's, Ringo's and George's. But don't worry too much. You've still got your wife.
Marilyn Iturri

Hurt By John

Dear BEAT:
You may not print this in your newspaper because it probably isn't that important to you—but it is to us.

We all read The BEAT. Also, we all liked the Beatles before all of this happened to them.

All of us have our own opinions about religion, as we know everyone does. But what John Lennon said about them being bigger than Jesus really hurt us.

How can anyone say that he or anyone is bigger than Jesus? Even if he doesn't mean it, he shouldn't have said it because it left a lot of people mad at them and very hurt because of them.
Diane DeCicco
Joe DeCicco
Florence DeCicco
Elizabeth Hunt
Donna Oldham
Becky Oldham

Is Religious

Dear BEAT:
I am tired of people taking potshots at the Beatles. There was nothing wrong with the album cover—we see the same thing in Mad Magazine.

As to the Manila situation, a couple of wisecracks never hurt anyone. Now to John's recent statement about Christianity.

What the papers printed was taken out of context. John *is* religious and was discussing religion privately.

Remember, *anyone* has the right to voice his opinion about anything. I'm still with the Beatles and so are my friends. Any station that bans Beatle records is wrong and is only hurting themselves.
Larry Schweikart
Harry McCoy
David Ruffin

Dear BEAT:
I'm writing about the controversy surrounding John. First, I'd like to express my opinion. Personally, I think John is right, although he could have put it in a less sarcastic way.

The Beatles, among other things such as golf, the beach, the show, etc., are more popular than the church. But it's a shame. And I think John was just stating a fact.
And, besides, if you were a *real* Beatle fan (such as I am), you wouldn't care about their religious beliefs.

Now, just take account of yourself for a minute. How many times a year do you go to church? Every week? Great, I can't think of anything better. But for those of you who go maybe five times a year—listen. How many hours have you spent listening, reading and watching the Beatles? Quite a few, I bet.

Now, truly, how many hours have you thought about church? I'll bet not half as much. Aren't you ashamed? I am. Not because I love the Beatles but because I don't spend the time I should on my religion.

So, you so-called true Beatle fans, stop complaining. John's like that and isn't that the reason we luv 'em?
Jeanne

Dear BEAT:
I think this whole Beatles vs. Christianity controversy has really been blown-up out of proportion. I believe it when John says that he meant that with the world situations as it is, the Beatles do seem to have a more loyal following.

The people who really are angry with John and denounce him firmly in this country are really like hypocrites. They make a big incident of what John said but when it comes to the pressing issues of such things as the rising number of divorces and how God, in whose name this country was founded, seems to be eliminated from everything in the United States, these "Christian" Beatle critics say nothing.

They are emphasizing the wrong issues. This may be because of their inability to cope with anything important or their refusal to face the truth and admit that something may be lacking in their own society. So, they must capitalize on someone else's good name because he is famous and loved by so many.

These people, so fast to ban and criticize, had better take a good look around in their own backyard before peering across the pond to criticize another's lawn.
JoAnn

Dear BEAT:
This is my first letter to your wonderful newspaper. And all I want to say is that "the Beatles STINK!"

After Mr. Lennon said they were more popular than God. Now, I seem to get the message Mr. Barry tried to get across to some of us, but we chopped the poor guy down.

What are the Beatles trying to pull? I don't think Mr. Lennon takes his religion very seriously. And I'm not just writing this letter because I go to church every Sunday but because I respect both the church and rock 'n' roll.

So, if Mr. Lennon thinks I'm going to bow down to him just for a couple of "Yeah, yeah" songs he can go to the London Bridge and jump off.

And I'm getting tired of reading all these letters you get everytime the Beatles get criticized for the things they do.

Their cry-baby fans start backing them up by saying that they are only human, that people don't want to accept them for what they are. Well, I've accepted them up to the ultimate.

So, I'm getting all my Beatle albums and pictures together and am going to have a bonfire of my own.
Ex-Beatles Fan

Want Out

Dear BEAT:
I just had to write this letter after reading the article in the newspaper about the Beatles. It stated that the Beatles said: "We are now more popular than Jesus."

It is quite evident that the Beatles are trying to kill themselves. First, it was their records that weren't up to usual, then that charming record cover, and now this statement about being more popular than Jesus. They're millionaires, they have all they want. They want OUT!

Plenty of kids will probably get mad about this letter saying that only people who aren't "true" Beatle fans will think this way. They'll probably make-up some excuse for the Beatles' behavior. Well, all I can say to them is "forget it, kiddos," because the Beatles don't want you. They've got what they want and now they want out. Good-bye, Beatles.
Naomi Hardin

Dear BEAT:
So, John Lennon thinks he is more popular than Jesus now, does he? If he wants to be crucified I know quite a few people who would do it gladly.

You stated that the Beatles were entitled religious freedom. I agree with this but on the other hand, I think John Lennon had no right to criticize it the way he did. If he doesn't believe in Jesus, okay. He just doesn't have to show everyone that he thinks he's greater.

I have always liked the Beatles as pop artists and I shall always think this but I will never again respect John Lennon as I have in the past.

I feel no one has the right to think less of a person for what he believes in but he doesn't have the right to cut down a great, great number of people just to get his message across.
Brenda McNally

BEATLES ARCHIVES 1

Can't Compare

Dear BEAT:
Now that I've heard the entire story, I'd like to express my opinion. It seems that John was discussing religion and he observed that followers of Christianity are decreasing. That now, in this mixed up world, people actually worship other human beings. He observed that because of this they probably had more followers than Christ and that it was ridiculous.

Well, I agree. I'm not saying it's wrong to love the Beatles—I do, very much. But it *is* wrong to put them above Christ. But really, it's something that can't be compared.

Pam Kelsey

Letters To The Editor
(Continued from Page 4)

Beatles Sick Of Fame?

Dear BEAT:
For the past three or four issues, I have been calmly reading and tolerating people's opinions of the Beatles. Now, I would like to give mine.

To make a long story short, it's about time these so-called Beatle "fans" stopped thinking of themselves and started thinking about the four boys they keep trying to tell me they love so much. The Beatles are four wonderful human beings who have had their taste of fame and glory and are quite sick of it.

Their "fans" have treated them as if they were four dolls who must bow to every girl's command. Now, I ask you, is that right? Their "fans" have no right to command them like slaves.

But, I must say, their fans—their true fans—have been wonderful. They know the Beatles and they love them. What I'm truly sick of are these adults who sit in their ancient caves and just wait for the poor Beatles to do one little thing wrong so they can ban them, insult them, and would you believe it? Even beat them up!

I think these poor adults are too chicken to admit they're growing old and that they just don't fit in this generation. They keep telling us to stop trying to grow up so fast. If you adults want us to keep out of YOUR generation, how about keeping out of OURS!

One last thing. The Beatles are very wonderful people. Why? Because they don't lie to their public. They don't put on an act in front of us, just so we'll like them. Not very many people in show business have enough courage to be themselves in front of their public. The Beatle fans, their true fans, love them for what they are—*not* for what some penny-pinching magazine (BEAT not included) or adult tries to tell us.

We know what the Beatles are, and we love them. You can't change that, so stop trying!

Dale Hoover

Ridiculous Controversy

Dear BEAT:
I would like to thank you very much for printing so many wonderful articles about the Beatles, and I hope you will continue to do so as long as they are still the Beatles.

The Beatles have certainly changed a lot through these last two and one-half years. They have been wonderful changes. But now many of these fans have turned against the singers they once would maybe have even given up their lives for. Why?

Because controversies got started. The incident in Manila. Their appearance on Ed Sullivan. Their false accusations of no longer caring. And many, many more.

But the latest controversy about John's statement of over six months ago, which has lost them more fans than ever, was the most misinterpreted. People didn't (or didn't want to) take time to hear the true story and why he said it.

It is ridiculous the way these people are acting. John has his right to voice his beliefs and I think those anti-Beatle organizations should listen to him, maybe they'll learn something.

These people who turned against them were never true fans, because if they were they would accept them for their goods and also their faults.

These people don't even deserve the Beatles if they begged them back. Now there is more of the Beatles for us fans who still appreciate them.

I plan on staying a Beatle fan until they are gone and I hope that remaining Beatle fans feel the same way.

Pat Bartley

Big Mouth

Dear BEAT:
Those dearly beloved Beatles have really done it now! First came their distasteful LP and now John's big mouth. He, of all people, had the nerve to say: "We're more popular than Jesus now."

Don't get me wrong. Sure, I went out and bought all their albums, not to mention spending a fortune on magazines and books with information on the foursome.

But now you can count me out! I'll just sit and watch their disc zoom to the top and I'll pass up the newest magazines.

I'll also watch them go down the drain. Yes, all you Beatle fans, just wait. You'll be in for a Big Surprise!

E.B.F. (Ex-Beatle fan.)

Yellow Thingy

Dear BEAT:
I subscribe to *The BEAT* and love it the best of all the mags and newspapers in the world. I have but one small complaint. On the front of each *BEAT* there is a little yellow-fiendish-thingy that has my name and address on it, well . . . It just ruins those luscious, gorgeous pictures! Couldn't you put them somewhere else? At the top? On the bottom? In the corner? On the back? But not on the picture, please! I've tried to scrape it off but failed by making a hole in the page when I did so. All I can say is please. Think about it!

Unsigned

We have thought about it. But unfortunately we discovered that postal laws require the address stamp to be placed on the front of all publications going through the mail.

Editor

Mann Gentlemanly?

Dear BEAT:
Hooray for Gene Pitney and Gary Lewis! Boo for Len Barry and Barry Sadler . . . Boo for people who do the same song over and over (Len Barry, Four Tops, Nancy Sinatra Jr., etc.). Hooray for new gear style LP covers (Dylan and Beatles). Boo for the new, dreary Beatle cover—ungear . . . Hooray for *The BEAT* recognizing Gene Pitney's greatness! Boo for Jackie McGinty for bringing national fields into R&R . . . Hooray for "Double Shot (Of My Baby' Love'), "Gloria," "Satisfaction" and all realistic songs.

Hooray for Manfred Mann and all their songs! Why are only some versions of "If You Gotta Go, Go Now" banned? The Liverpool 5's version was played in Florida. Why was "With God On Our Side" banned? I don't know what a flamingo is, except a colorful tropical bird . . . As for "If You Gotta Go, Go Now," I admire it. It is a "gentlemanly," civilized song. I only wish most guys made a similar speech to girls, instead of being so aggressive!

Dorothy Boswell

MOM DEFENDS JOHN

Dear BEAT:
I hope I'm not too late to get my two cents worth into *The BEAT* concerning the current controversy raging over the heads of the Beatles. I'm not a teenager, but rather a mother of five, two of them teenagers already. I was never particularly interested in their choice of music, but after taking them to see the first Beatle movie I was completely captivated by everything about them. Their freshness, their talent, their obvious enjoyment of life and each other, all of it.

If there is anything worse than a teenage Beatlemaniac, it is an old one! We saw the movie many times so as not to miss one gesture or off-camera nonsense that had been overlooked before.

Our home was rocking with every album released and we couldn't get enough news about them.

People have tried to explain and reason out Beatlemania; there's no explaining it really. It is rather like a sickness but one you don't wish to recover from. Unlike popularity fads which come and go, they only served to carve their way deeper into our hearts as their fantastic, fabulous careers progressed. They didn't *force* their way in, we couldn't get enough.

It's been said that many idols have feet of clay and it is always a disheartening let-down when fans are forced to realize this and accept it.

But anyone who has ever professed to be a Beatle fan should hang his head in shame and disgrace if he is turning on them now. How*ever*, people are and what*ever* they do *they* are not to blame. The wild, screaming, insane fans, causing riots and near riots are behaving like people have never behaved before in the history of show business.

They are the ones to carry this blame. While they were loved like gods by millions, John, Paul, George and Ringo are people. They had human feelings and emotions like all of us. No amount of money in the entire world could ever compensate for the lives they have been forced to lead, and by whom?

Those adoring "fans" who ruined it all for them whenever they dared to venture out. It's been said before but what can money do, if you can't go out and see the cities and sights of a never before seen country?

Oh! We were unthinkably rude and indescribably thoughtless when they came to America. True, it came about as result of our "love" for them, but how I wish we had another chance to welcome them again and stand back and feast our eyes but keep our mouths shut.

They would still be the same Beatles they were in the beginning. And really, what has happened? An album cover? Rude remarks? And a religious issue.

I would challenge anyone to live through what they have and not turn surly and say much more than they ever have. We excuse all kinds of things in our artistic people, and if ever there were four geniuses it is the Beatles, maybe Paul and John a little more so because of the writing and composing.

They have *never* hurt anyone, they wouldn't want to. But they *have* had to endure more criticism and bad publicity and if one slip was made off that pedestal—POW!

I wish it was possible to get a letter to them. I'd like them to know how this fan, for one, really feels. I think they do care.

Some of the letters in this week's *BEAT* expressed some good thoughts, the phony fans have now been heard from, and I am glad to be able to count myself among the true ones.

So, true, they haven't stopped to remember what the Beatles have given us. Wonderful moments for over two years, in movies and in music. Has there ever been a thrill to equal what every heart experienced when we heard: "And now, here they are—the Beatles!" Not in my memory, there hasn't.

What have we given them? Money? Ha!

In conclusion, I wish to express the hope that this current trend of putting them down at the slightest provocation will die out. Let up on them. And maybe we can yet salvage those four unbelievable guys who got all this started.

Heartsick with worry they won't forgive us for what has been done to them.

JBL

SOUND IS WHERE IT'S HAPPENING!

Trini Lopez, Chet Atkins, Johnny Rivers, The Beach Boys, The Rolling Stones make it with JBL sound.

JBL is the sound of the scene at the top!

Fender, Jordan, Ampeg, Gretsch, Standel, Guild, Gibson, C. F. Martin, Sunn amplifier systems groove with JBL loudspeakers.

High notes that won't quit, thundering bass at peak volume from JBL F-Series loudspeakers. Write us for free information about use and installation.

James B. Lansing Sound, Inc.
3249 Casitas Avenue
Los Angeles, California 90039

BEATLES ARCHIVES 1

On the BEAT
By Louise Criscione

The Beatles are here and they've succeeded in once again taking the spotlight from everyone and everything else. Despite fears of antagonistic crowds and security leaks, the four Beatles have spent a rather peaceful and harmless three weeks Stateside.

They arrived in Los Angeles two days earlier than originally expected when they touched down on the 24th for a press conference at Capitol Records — the scene of last year's Beatle press conference.

Last Tour?

Other than the religiouze issue (which has already been overplayed to the point of boredom) the only other serious problem facing Beatle fans is "will this be the last Beatle U.S. tour?" With those close to the scene predicting that it will indeed be the last major U.S. tour for John, Paul, George and Ringo.

However, the Beatles remain charmingly unpredictable so I wouldn't worry too much if I were you. If the Beatles want to make another Stateside tour next year, they will. And if they want this to be their last, you can bet your "Revolver" it *will* be their last. Anyway, enjoy them while they're here and fret about next year later.

Shoppers at the posh DeVos on the Sunset Strip were pleasantly surprised last week when they wandered in only to find all of the Mama's and Papa's as well as Mick Jagger and his girlfriend, Chrissie Shrimpton, spending wads on DeVos clothes.

Our *BEAT* photographer was on hand and next issue we'll have loads of proof on the entertainers shopping spree.

... PAUL McCARTNEY

JOHN LENNON made headlines around the world with his widely misinterpreted statements concerning Christianity. Despite the controversy raging around him, however, John is going ahead with plans to appear in his first film effort without the other three Beatles, and will play the part of a soldier in "How I Won The War," scheduled to begin filming in Germany immediately after the Beatles' tour of America.

Beatles ...
(Cont. from Page 1)

who proclaimed them their undying idols.

For about an hour there had never been a Manila ... or a withdrawn album cover ... or a seemingly insignificant quote lifted from context and blown out of proportion.

Critics had eagerly anticipated the Beatles' tour as ample proof that the Britons had fallen from the kingship of rockdom. If they have, then their U.S. tour — and especially their California performances — certainly didn't prove it.

Sandy Koufax and Juan Marcial seldom lure more customers to the erstwhile baseball parks. With tickets selling for $3.50 to $6, the Beatles played before huge crowds.

But it was the crowds' reactions — not their size — that was most convincing. There was no predicted air of uncertainty ... no cautious skepticism.

It was just plain Beatlemania in one of its finest hours.

The Beatles Don't Forget

The Beatles haven't forgotten the people that have helped make them what they are today.

The Beatles aren't doing a Christmas special this year but the television special honoring John and Paul's writing will be shown in England around Christmas time.

Paul says they are doing the show to repay someone who helped them earlier.

"One of the reasons we're doing this show is as a favor to Johnny Hamp, who risked his job by including us on an early TV show when we were unknown," he explained.

John added, during the taping of the show, that there aren't many other performers who really get a lot out of his and Paul's writings.

"There are only about 100 people in the world who really understand what our music is all about," he said, and that 100 includes George and Ringo.

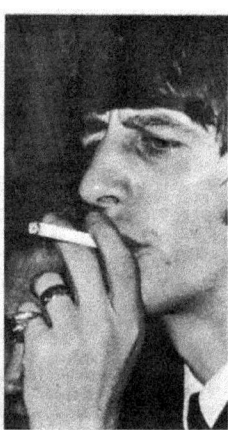
... RINGO STARR

BEATLE SNAPSHOTS

Paul's Father Recalls Brothers Inseparable
By Jamie McCluskey III

'ello, la—'ow yer doin' this week? It's time once again to open up our *BEAT* scrapbook, and this week as we peer inside we find none other than Mr. Paul Beatle staring back at us. Hello Pauly!

Paul's father James McCartney, provides some of our first glimpses of Paul as a child with these poignant snapshots:

"Michael (Paul's brother) and Paul did everything together, especially anything that they were told specifically *not* to do!

"As children, they were inseparable. Wherever one went—so did the other. I remember that amongst their friends they were known as the 'Nurk Twins,' but I never did find out why. I believe that John and Paul used the same name for one of their first playing dates.

"Paul was 18 months older than Michael so naturally, he was the leader. I remember that he always seemed to know exactly what he wanted and usually knew how to get it. He didn't moan or nag in any way, but persuaded us in the nicest possible manner. I think he was a born diplomat!"

Did'ja ever wonder how Paul was able to get up on stage with his three long-haired cohorts, and sing, play guitar, and *still* have time to flirt with *every* girl in the audience all at the same time? Well, it seems that Pauly has *always* been somewhat "ambidexterous!"

"He also had the fascinating ability of being able to do two things at once. In the evenings, he would sit at the table doing his homework and watching television at the same time. How he managed it, I don't know, but the extraordinary thing was, that afterwards, he usually knew more about the program than I did. And he got his homework correct as well!

"He seemed to have the sort of mind that could easily grasp things that used to take a lot of concentration from other boys."

While Paul's father is only too happy to show us these little snaps of Paul — complete with halo over his Beatled head — he also has a few candid shots of Paul being *not* so angelic.

"Although Paul was a typical tearaway, ragamuffin, he was very close to Mike. I always remember one incident when they were caught stealing apples, Paul, Mike and another boy went scrumping from a farm in Speke. They were only 12 and 10 at the time, and they called the place Chinese Farm, although I didn't know why.

"Apparently, they were just about to climb the trees when the farmer appeared. They all ran away, but Paul got stuck and Mike went back to help. The first I knew about it was when the farmer rang me up and told me that my two sons were locked up in his barn.

"I went along to the farm to see him and he was very reasonable about it, so we decided to scare the boys a bit before we let them off. We stood outside the barn door and said things like: 'Do you think they will get a long sentence', or 'Shall we just spank them now and not tell the police?' When we thought they had enough, we opened the barn door to let them out only to find we'd been completely wasting our time.

"The two boys trotted out and greeted me with 'Hello Dad, about time you got here.' I was really amazed that both of them seemed so completely unconcerned by the whole proceedings.

"When I talked to them afterwards, I found that because they didn't actually steal any apples, they considered that they had done nothing wrong and therefore were not worried. I did the usual thing and sent them straight to bed without any supper, although at the time I didn't think it would do the slightest good. I believe that a few years later, they did realize that they had done wrong."

There are many more snapshots of Paul which Mr. McCartney has brought along to share with *The BEAT* scrapbook, but I'm afraid that they are going to have to wait for next week.

See ya then? Ta for now, luvs.

BEATLES ARCHIVES 1

PAUL AND RINGO look like a couple of tourists as they catch their first sight of the California Pacific during their week-long visit here. While Southern Californians were seething with Beatlemania, the Beatles calmly basked in the sunshine at their Benedict Canyon retreat.

On the BEAT
By Louise Criscione

The Beatles have won the lawsuit filed against them by United Press photographer, Joseph Bodnar. The photographer alleged that he was beaten by a guard employed by Globe Protection, Inc. during the Beatles' 1965 concert at the Hollywood Bowl and asked for $10,000 in punitive damages from each of the defendants (which included Capitol Records and Globe Protection as well as the Beatles), plus $1,000 each for compensatory damages.

However, Superior Judge Richard Wells awarded judgment in favor of the Beatles with no decision yet reached regarding Globe and Capitol Records.

The Beatles As Seen Thru The Eyes Of An American

LONDON — While in England last week, we scooted over to the Finsbury Park Theatre in London to see and hear Capitol's fabulous Beatles, the group sitting in the #1 spot on the **Cash Box** best seller list this week.

We were fortunate enough to see the Beatles, but we definitely did not hear them.

From the moment the quartet hits the stage, a wild, screaming frenzy envelops the theatre and doesn't let up for even a second. The atmosphere in the theatre is reminiscent of the Elvis Presley rage of recent years and far stronger than the screams that tore through the Brooklyn Paramount Theatre in the early rock and roll days.

Contrary to general beliefs, the group is not a wild crew selling crazy antics. Other than their hair cuts and tight black outfits, their performance is subdued and features good material, tremendous harmony and an overall look of uniqueness the teenagers can identify with.

The Beatles haircut has also caught on throughout London. A glance down the line of teenagers waiting to get into the theatre gives one an idea of what haircuts here might look like in a few months, now that the group is so big in the U.S.

We heard an interesting story in England about the Beatles effect on, of all things, the Old Vic Company presentation of a Shakespearean play. In a dramatic moment during a recent performance, when the lead actor finished his touching soliloquy with the words "she loves you"—then paused, a member of the audience said in a soft voice "yeah, yeah, yeah" and completely shattered the remainder of the show. "She Loves You" is the Beatles' Swan hit with the "yeah, yeah, yeah" phrase heard throughout the deck.

The Beatles' Plans For '67: Records, TV Specials And . . . ?

By Tony Barrow

Newspaper reporters and magazine editors on both sides of the Atlantic seem to have had a thoroughly enjoyable time over the past couple of months moulding an astonishing variety of make-believe futures for THE BEATLES. If any of their prolific predictions should grow from guesswork into fact it will be little more than fortunate coincidence for the writers concerned.

The truth is that The Beatles themselves haven't mapped out a future for the group. They've never been strong for planning ahead and now that their schedule isn't sewn up with contracted touring timetables, they're free to think about next month when next month comes, next year when 1968 comes.

Beatle Workshop

They've been recording together at the E.M.I. studios near Paul's home in St. John's Wood since the first week of December. By the middle of January they'd completed three tracks. If that doesn't sound too healthy a product from something over 100 hours of studio time it's only fair to remember that they use sessions for much more than just recording. The studio has become their workshop for writing, arranging, rehearsing. They scrap as many as four out of five tapes. They wait while specialist musicians are fetched in to augment their backings.

With breaks when they run out of material and have to start from scratch on new words and tunes, The Beatles will go on recording until the time comes to start work on their third much-delayed motion picture.

They are not expected to make guest-star appearances on any television shows in London or abroad this year BUT they like the idea of making their own TV specials and are hoping to build a complete program around the new songs now being recorded for their first 1967 album.

Remain A Group

For recording, filming and a limited amount of television activity they'll stay together as a group. There's no question of The Beatles splitting up or ceasing to exist. At the same time there's every reason to believe that Ringo will follow John and make his solo screen debut and that the other two would be prepared to do the same thing if ideal scripts come into their hands.

On Friday, January 13 an unsuperstitious JANE ASHER flew out from London Airport at the beginning of a four-and-a-half month American tour in which she'll play Juliet with the Old Vic Company. On the eve of her departure she confirmed that she loved Paul very deeply and that "he feels the same." She denied that there was any possibility of their wedding taking place in America but Jane will have several free weeks during the Old Vic touring season when she could easily return home to London to see her family. And, of course, Paul.

All The Beatles – plus their two road managers – have grown mustaches. Chronoligically speaking, the whisker cultivation project went like this: – GOERGE let a small crop of hairs cover his upper lip before he left for India. PAUL produced a sort of inverted 'U' shape of hair around his mouth in preparation for his France/Spain/Kenya vacation.

RINGO started his mustache and decided to spread it into a beard as long ago as October when he and Maureen visited John and Cyn on the "How I Won The War" movie set in Spain.

GEORGE came home and had a shave.

JOHN'S healthy luxurious of mustache-with-accessories (hair all down each side of his face from ears to the jaw joints, long line across the upper lip and drooping clusters of hair running straight down towards the chin) took effect once the boys started recording in December.

GEORGE had a re-think about the whole thing and re-grew a mustache with beard before Christmas.

MAL EVANS has the most powerful-looking mustache of all – but he's had three months to work on it.

NEIL ASPINALL claims that his mustache will not be truly presentable before Easter although it has been under cultivation since early November.

BRIAN EPSTEIN has neither beard nor mustache.

BEATLES ARCHIVES 1

IN "HELP" JOHN CAME DOWN TO EARTH IN SNOW-CLAD ALPS

Beatles Stage Happening With Monkee, Stones . . .

By Tony Barrow

41 of Britain's most accomplished classical musicians wearing formal evening dress, false noses, assorted king-size sun shades and other good-humoured embellishments.

20 or 30 lean, luverly mini-skirted and trouser-suited birds wandering at random amongst the massive orchestra.

Two dedicated young men with powerful projectors throwing onto the walls a series of curiously colored "oil slides."

DONOVAN and his mate GIPSY DAVE lighting hand-held sparklers. MONKEE MIKE NESMITH meeting recording manager GEORGE MARTIN and each exchanging words of praise about each other's diverse artistries.

MARIANNE FAITHFULL pouring a fresh cup of sparkling champagne for MICK JAGGER when the supply of regular champagne glasses ran out. MANFRED KLAUS VOORMANN and his wife Christine decorating two large balloons with Crazy Foam from a spray pack.

KEITH RICHARD taking movie-making lessons from a professional cameraman. PATTI HARRISON and CYNTHIA LENNON chatting with two (female) cousins of PAUL McCARTNEY.

These were some of the basic ingredients for a Beatles Happening which was held on a February Friday evening at the huge No. 1 studio of E.M.I. Records in St. John's Wood, London.

There were two excellent reasons for the holding of the Happening. The Beatles were using for the first time ever a 41-piece orchestra to add extra instrumental accompaniment to one of their new album tracks. At the same time they were creating the first film sequences which will be used in the 60-minute TV Special they are making to coincide with the international release of the album.

The Beatles are acting as their own TV directors for the project. In the studio were at least seven hand-held movie cameras, two used by professional cameramen while the rest were available for impromptu use by any of the forty assembled guests. Ringo, Mick, Keith and Klaus were amongst the impromptu users.

To increase the fun-atmosphere and the visual glamour of the occasion everyone had been invited to wear the brightest available gear. Indeed it bordered upon Fancy Dress.

Everything was accomplished with remarkable speed, the session lasting from eight until eleven in the evening. Paul perched himself on a tall stool in front of the orchestra and conducted. John and George hurried to and fro making last-minute suggestions. Ringo used reel after reel of 16 mm movie. Ten brilliant arc-lamps played down on everyone from high places, bathing the whole Happening in as many different colors. A balloon burst in the middle of Take 3. Paul's telephone on the conductor's rostrum rang loudly in the middle of Take 4.

At the stroke of eleven the 41 musicians, all good union guys, wrapped up their instruments, stripped off various false noses, bald-scalps and so forth.

"No, I really enjoyed it actually," said a serious-looking but convinced violinist.

"We'll get extra money for the filming, you know," declared a horn player.

"Now we'll do the choir bit," shouted John, rounding up birds and boys and gathering them round a couple of mike booms. Ten arc-lamps followed the crowd.

"I'll count you all in each time," started Paul. "Klaus will give you the notes on the piano. Klaus? You ready?"

The choir bits were put on tape. Beatles and selected guests wandered off to join George Martin in the control room. Play-back time. Each Beatle satisfied. Eleven-thirty.

"Pity you can't edit in the voices now," sighed John.

"Bag Of Nails tonight or Scotch Of St. James?" asked Paul.

"We're going home," said George and he took Patti away.

"Try the Bag first, eh?" decided Ringo.

"Goodnight, gentlemen," from George Martin.

The Bag Of Nails was too crowded and nobody had booked a table. We all finished up in a comparatively deserted Scotch Of St. James.

But everything was anti-climax after that fantastic studio Happening. There's never been a Beatles session like it. There's never been a session like it.

You'll hear the resulting track when The Beatles release their album in the Spring.

BEAT EXCLUSIVE
Beatle's New Single

The BEAT has learned some exclusive news from Tony Barrow which will probably be met with mixed reactions from Beatle fans. The Beatles follow-up to "Nowhere Man" will be "Paperback Writer", sung by Paul with John and George on chorus, backed with "Rain" sung by John with Paul and George supplying the falsetto chorus.

What's bad about that? Not a thing except that you will have to wait practically a whole month before the record is released! Due date is June 6, which means that May will have to roll by without a new Beatle record and "Nowhere Man" has already fallen off most of the charts.

Meanwhile, the Beatles are working on their next album which really should have been released long ago as "Rubber Soul" has been out for months although it still finds itself nestled securely in the nation's top twenty best-selling albums.

The June 6 release date for "Paperback Writer" will be met with approval by most pop groups as it means that they have a whole month to release their new singles. It's gotten to the point now that no one in their right mind will release a new record the same time as the Beatles. Even the Rolling Stones and the Yardbirds have admitted to cooling it with new releases until the Beatles have had time to hit.

The Stones' new one, "Paint It Black," will have no trouble in racing up the charts to number one and will, undoubtedly, be coming down as the Beatles' next single is coming up — therefore, avoiding collision at the top.

BEATLES ARCHIVES 1

Beatles, Swarming All Over Charts, Go Into Carnegie Hall Feb. 12, Capitol To Cut Them On A "Live" LP

NEW YORK—The rafters of Carnegie Hall will be put to perhaps their severest test when The Beatles invade the once all-long hair concert hall for two performances on Wed., Feb. 12. First show is 7:30 pm, second is 10 pm.

Capitol Records will be on hand to cut the sensational English group there for an LP, "The Beatles at Carnegie Hall," to be released in April. Voyle Gilmore, the label's A&R vp, will fly to New York to produce the "live" session.

Meanwhile, Beatles' waxings already on the market continue on their merry sales way. Capitol claims a million-seller for "I Want To Hold Your Hand," which tops the Top 100 chart for the second week, and sales of 250,000 for its LP, "Meet The Beatles," which jumps into the number 9 spot on the LP chart this week in its first appearance.

As the trade well knows, there are other labels marketing Beatles product. Most noteworthy so far is Swan's "She Loves You," which moved from 51 to 11 this week. A Vee Jay waxing, "Please, Please Me," makes the Top 100 this in the number 71 spot.

A measure of the team's impact in the U.S. came from radio station WINS-New York, which last week played both "Hand" and "She Loves You" as its number one sounds.

In the legal arena (see last week's story, "Legalmania Over Beatlemania"), a Vee Jay suit against Capitol and Swan, in New York Supreme Court, has been taken under submission by Judge Saul Streit. Capitol has already received temporary injunctions against the sale Vee Jay's Beatle product, including an LP, "Introducing The Beatles," in New York and Chicago.

Beatles Making A Flick, Release Is Through UA

NEW YORK—The Beatles are going to make a feature film. The English stars will be starred in a film that will be shot in England sometime in March or April. Set for release in the U.S. this summer, it will be distributed by United Artists Pictures. The soundtrack album that will result will probably be in the hands of the flick company's disk affiliate, United Artists Records, although it could not be confirmed by the label when it was reached late last week. Walter Shenson is producing, and Richard Lester will direct from a screenplay by Alun Owen.

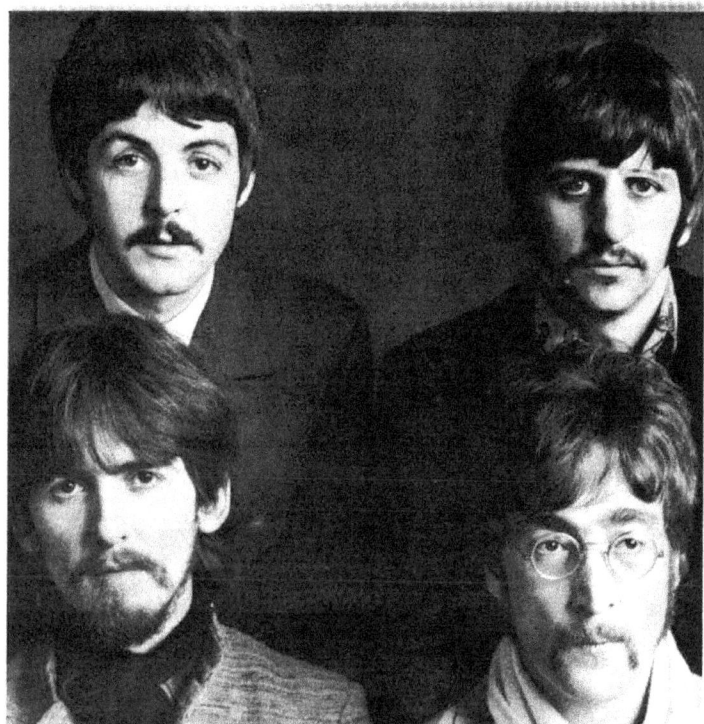

THE NEW LOOK for the Beatles—hair and more hair! Beatles, moustaches and all, will make third movie.

The Beatles Ink New Nine Year Recording Contract

The Beatles' manager, Brian Epstein, has signed a new nine year contract for the Beatles with EMI (Electric & Musical Industries, Ltd.), which is the principal stockholder in Capitol Records).

In announcing the signing of the new contract, Capitol Records President, Alan Livingston, said: "We are, of course, extremely pleased to be able to continue our association with the group that has proved to be the most creative and talented foursome the recording industry has ever known.

"Since they were introduced to America, the Beatles have demonstrated that as performers and composers they have no peer. Their songs, besides earning the 'usual' Gold Records and starting industry-wide trends, have also established phenomenal sales records.

Unequalled

"For instance, 25% of all Gold Records awarded for singles by the RIAA have been earned by the Beatles. And, last year, every fourth Gold Record awarded by the RIAA for million dollar albums went to the Beatles. The overwhelming acceptance of their new single is evidence that this unmatched success will continue throughout 1967 and in years to come."

Capitol had received over one million orders for the new Beatle single, "Penny Lane/Strawberry Fields Forever," before it was ever released and, consequently, have asked the RIAA for certification of the single as a million-seller.

This will be the 22nd Gold Record earned by the Beatles. All previous Beatle million-sellers were qualified for Gold Records before being released, a sales feat no other recording group, American or foreign, has ever equalled. In fact, 22 certified Gold Records are more than any other artist has ever earned in the history of the record industry. Ten of the Beatles' Gold Records are for albums, 12 are for singles.

World's Record

The Beatles' first single, "I Want To Hold Your Hand," released in the U.S. in December, 1963 has, to date, sold over 4.5 million copies and their first album, "Meet The Beatles," is currently approaching the five million sales mark. The Beatles' total world sales figure now stands at 180 million records sold.

The Beatles' new contract came as a complete shock since Paul McCartney had recently admitted that he was "no longer one of the four mop-tops." McCartney went on to add that: "Now we're ready to go our own ways. We'll work together if we miss each other. Then it'll be hobby work. It's good for us to go it alone."

The word out of London was that the Beatles would not renew their contract with Brian Epstein when their present contract runs out. This, however, remains to be seen as there has been no official word on the subject.

Inside the BEAT
LOVIN' SPOONFUL MEDICINE 2
MONKEES MEET BEATLES 5
SWITCHED ON FASHIONS 7

The BEAT is published bi-weekly by BEAT Publications, Inc., editorial and advertising offices at 6290 Sunset Blvd., Suite 504, Hollywood, California 90028. U. S. Bureaus in Hollywood, San Francisco, New York, Chicago and Nashville; overseas correspondents in London, Liverpool and Manchester, England. Sale price 25 cents. Subscription price: U.S. and possessions, $5 per year; Canada and foreign rates, $9 per year. Second class postage prepaid at Los Angeles, California.

PETER AND GORDON IN SEMI-SPLIT

Peter Asher and Gordon Waller announced in London last week that following their current American tour they will no longer be a full-time act.

In a joint statement to the press, Peter and Gordon said: "We shall get together once in a while when we feel like it—it's as simple as that. But basically, after our present U.S. tour, we are going our separate ways."

Peter will concentrate on becoming a record producer and will also spend part of his time managing his bookshop. Gordon will become a solo artist for Columbia and will make his first personal appearance minus Peter in British clubs this spring.

BEATLES ARCHIVES 1

BEATLES FOOL THE PUBLIC
WHO IS SINGING WHAT??

"In My Own Time," a cut from the Bee Gees' new album, has caused a stir of controversy. Although sources close to the Beatles have confirmed the suspicion that John Lennon and Paul McCartney are singing on the track, the Bee Gees have hedgingly denied the rumor.

Maurice Gibbs states, "but that song that we did on the album was written quite a while ago, and we just did it for the album, and I can't think of why people would even think that the Beatles would sing on the album."

Colin adds, "I don't even know the Beatles; and that would be very difficult if they sang on one of our records. I'm sure I'd get to meet them or something. I think people, when a new group starts out, someone has to say something about them, you know, everyone feels the need to start a controversy. And this is what has been started about us. But it's far from true."

The rumor is given impetus because the Bee Gees' manager is Brian Epstein who also manages the Beatles. Then too, the similarity of sound is astonishing. If indeed, it is not John singing, it is a flawless imitation.

However, Colin goes on to insist, "It's an easy rumor to start because we're working with NEMS and Robert Stigwood and Brian Epstein who handle the Beatles, so we're really sort of the same family, but we've never met the Beatles, you know. Unless the Beatles came in after we've finished the tracks and then wiped all the voices off and did them again, you know, this is the only way they could have done it."

Not really the only way, Colin. The Beatles could have come in and recorded a whole new track for the album, ignoring yours completely. It will be interesting to see if time will reveal that the Beatles actually recorded the song, just as time finally revealed that Paul wrote "Woman" under an assumed name, and performed the whisper for Donovan's "Mellow Yellow."

BEATLES ARCHIVES 1

BEAT Scrapbook
George And John Look Ahead

By Jamie McCluskey III

If you have been reading *The BEAT* regularly – as you *undoubtedly* have! – you know that we have been taking weekly peeks into our *BEAT* scrapbook and peering backwards into the Beatles' early lives.

This week, however, we are going to view a few snaps from the present. And presently, we, will be viewing George Harrison and John Lennon of the MBE set. Okay, Ready – Steady – Goooo!!!!

Now we all know how hectic a Beatle's schedule can get, and how hectic the Beatles' schedules have been for the last couple of years. But suddenly George informs us that the fab foursome has found itself with some time on its hands.

"It may seem funny to some people that we Beatles haven't got a single date in our 1966 diary. Not one job of work is fixed! It's about the first time I can remember since we first started that we haven't been able to say 'we've got to play at such-and-such a place on that date.'

Another Film

"Mind you we *know* that in about two months we've got to make another record and we *know* that some time this year there's another film to do. But that's quite a way off."

Gee fellers – if times are really all that hard, we could always use a couple of extra copy boys up here in *The BEAT* offices!

As we turn the page in our *BEAT* scrapbook now, we can see a few snaps of George's home. In fact, if you look real closely – you may even see George telling us all about the things he's *going* to do with his Humble Hearth.

"I'm getting tape recorders – like Johnny and Paul have – fixed up into a sort of home studio. They can over-dub vocal and instrumental tracks so that when they get an idea for a song they can make a demo record by themselves. I want to do the same."

Of course, George is now living in Weybridge, England – which is quite a considerable distance from the familiar old Liverpudlian homestead of yesteryear – but never say that George isn't loyal:

Goes Home

"I go home to Liverpool about once a month now to see relatives and friends. We're still getting things for the house I bought my parents, so that takes up some of the time.

Alright Beatle fans – now that we have seen a few little candid glimpses of George, how 'bout turning the page and joining John-John?

Just for fun, we decided to let Johnny have some words to play around with – being that he's a famous author in his own writ and all! – and in these pictures you will see his very own reactions.

Money: "Nice. Great." *Guitars:* "Guitars are great. Part of life." *Airplanes:* "I don't like them. At first they were a nice adventure. I like flying less the more we do. We can get to most places well enough by road. We've flown so much, something could happen the more we do."

Eppy: "He's great, you know. When people talk about him, they say he's harsh and hard. He's a businessman, so he has to be. He's never a businessman with us, though. We only talk business about twice a year. He sometimes has a go at us, then we have a go back and it's forgotten."

Liverpool: "It's still home. Even though my aunt has moved away and I have to stay with Paul if I go there. If I'm in London, home is Weybridge, but if I say I'm going home, I mean Liverpool. It'd be the same if I was from Paris and lived in Marseilles. Paris would always be home."

Sketching: "I don't sketch. I occasionally draw things but I don't sketch."

Sure John

Okay John, luv – if you say so. But you lost me!!

Anyway – hope you've all enjoyed going through *The BEAT's* scrapbook with me today – I know *I* have. But then, what can you expect from an incurable Beatlemaniac??!!!!

The whole country is in the grip of **The Beatles**! The reaction here to England's hottest stars is quite fantastic right throughout the nation—it's very reminiscent of the early days of Sinatra and Presley when these artists carried enough influence to sway the whole industry right around the world.... It has been years since anything has created a fuss to equal that of The Beatles. The demand for their records is staggering to say the least. Before their current single ("I Want To Hold Your Hand") was released, EMI had sufficient orders on hand to make it an all-time best seller within the first week of release. In addition to this, the other singles, EP's and albums are being sold as though they were gold! One prominent dealer reported to **Cash Box** that the new album by The Beatles was outselling all singles except those by The Beatles! You should see the smile of delight on **Jack Argent**'s face—through Leeds Music he controls the local publishing rights to a great deal of The Beatles material.

"MEET THE BEATLES!"—Capitol T 2047
The Beatles, who are currently riding high on the Top 100 with "I Want To Hold Your Hand," unleash their potent vocal and instrumental talents full-blast on this their premiere U. S. album entry. The swingin' British group turn in outstanding renditions of "This Boy," "All My Loving," "Little Child," and their current chart-rider. Disk should pull loads of loot.

BEATLES ARCHIVES 1

America's Largest Teen NEWSpaper

KRLA *Edition* **BEAT**

Volume 1, Number 48   LOS ANGELES, CALIFORNIA   15 Cents   February 12, 1966

Exclusive: George And Patti – Rumors Now Fact

KRLA BEAT

Los Angeles, California — February 12, 1966

Harrisons In Seclusion After Surprise Wedding

HOTLINE LONDON:
Eyewitness Report On Beatle Wedding

(Editor's Note: This is the first of what will be a weekly report written exclusively for The BEAT by Tony Barrow, a widely-known British journalist who made many friends in America while accompanying the Beatles on tour. As friend and press officer, he was one of the few persons attending George Harrison's wedding.)

By Tony Barrow

LONDON — In the suburban town of Epsom, ten miles south of London in the heart of Surrey's well-known stockbrokers' belt, a third Beatle took his bride.

The occasion had been a closely guarded secret and there was no crowd of fans outside Epsom Registry Office to see the couple arrive. Inside Ashley House were best man Brian Epstein, Beatle Paul McCartney, Mrs. D. Gaymer-Jones (Patti's mother), Mr. and Mrs. George Harrison (George's parents) plus some of Patti's other close relatives including her sister Jenny and brother Colin.

Few people were told about the wedding in advance but George and Patti shared their secret with the Lennons and the Starkeys. Cynthia and John, Maureen and Ringo were told before they left for their vacation in the West Indies. Patti and George received a lengthy telephone call from the West Indies shortly after the ceremony today.

Wedding gifts include a magnificent antique dining table, the present selected for Patti and George by Brian Epstein.

For the wedding ceremony George wore a black Victorian suit. Nobody can remember when they last saw this Beatle wearing a formal suit; he does so only upon the most special of special occasions. Petite and pretty Patti wore a dark red shot-silk dress with a red fox fur coat. I don't know why they call it red fox fur because it looked a sort of ginger color to me.

Patti's very beautiful ring is of white and pink gold. George claims it is about half an inch thick and it certainly looks more bulky than the average wedding ring.

Dave's Cool On Marriage

By Sue Greene

I spoke to the Hullabalooer shortly after the third Beatle marriage, and he gave me a few of his own ideas on the events just past. Said he, "It was all done in secret: nobody knew it was coming. But then, this is the way they have led their lives — in secret. Of course it took us all by surprise, and it was a shock for all of George's fans who love him — but now they can just love him in a different way.

"George is the one who is a little fed up with being a Beatle now — in fact, he always has been. And now he wants to settle down, and invest his money, and raise a family. I think that if any of the Beatles were going to leave the group, he would be the first one to do so.

"I think now it will be only a matter of time until Paul gets married — he has no reason not to now. I think that it will probably happen within a year's time. Between now and the first of next year, I am sure that Paul will probably marry Jane.

"I think that it's time that George and Patti were married — all of the boys are going to marry the girls that they have been going with anyways. And I think that alone should say something for them. They are more mature now, and I'm glad it happened."

Jones, McCartney Hurt

Paul Jones, singing favourite with the Manfred Mann unit, will undertake concert engagements next week with his shoulder in plaster. He's just spent almost a week in the hospital after smashing a collar bone in an automobile accident.

Less severely hurt in a recent road crash was Paul McCartney. The Beatle was visiting his father and step-mother at their Cheshire home, just south of Liverpool.

He was out riding around the Cheshire countryside on one of his two Moped motorized bicycles when the machine skidded on an icy road and threw him to the ground. Paul collected a deep cut to the side of his mouth and five stitches had to be put into the wound.

Now it's healing nicely and Paul feels fine again. The injury is not leaving a scar and Paul says it hasn't turned him against his fave pastime of Moped cycle riding.

News Briefs

Tom Jones, currently touring Australia with Herman's Hermits, will fly direct from down-under to New York for his latest "Ed Sullivan Show" appearance on February 13. His next single in the U.K. is to be "Big Man Cry," out early next month...

Paul Simon — half of your highly successful "Sounds Of Silence" duo — has penned a new number called "Some Day One Day" for the Australian folk unit The Seek-

(Turn to Page 15)

PATTI'S PROFILE

What's the new Mrs. Harrison like?
Patti is a doll. Her vital statistics:
She's 21 years old, has blue eyes and is five feet seven inches tall. Educated in a convent, she comes from a family of six, was born in Somerset in Southwestern England and spent most of her childhood in Kenya, where her father had a farm.

Patti started work as a hairdresser, like Ringo's wife, Maureen, but soon became bored with it and turned to modeling. Her "Dolly Girl" looks made her a favorite among leading fashion photographers and led to her part in "A Hard Day's Night."

They met during the movie and started dating.

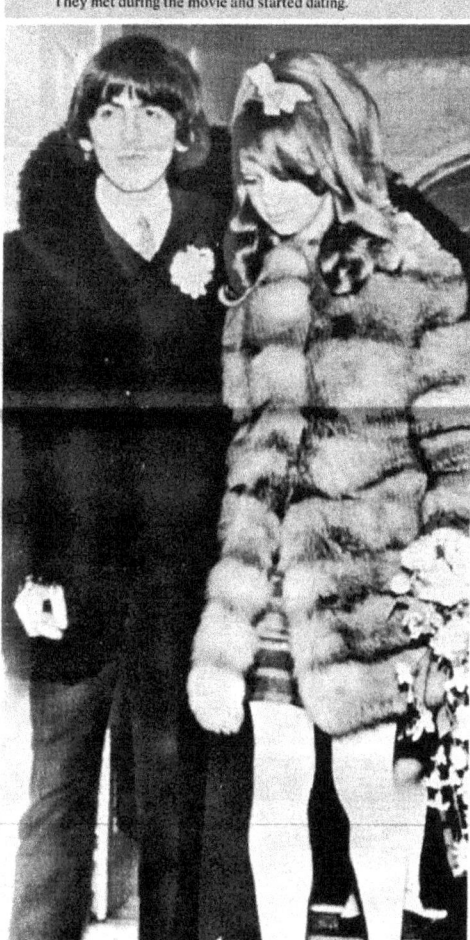

GEORGE AND BRIDE LEAVE REGISTRY OFFICE AFTER WEDDING.

BAT-TLE FATIGUE
Batman Collapses!

Krunch! Bamm! Zot! Crash! Holy Popcorn, the worst has happened!!!

Stop the world, our fearless leader, crime stopper of all times, half of the dynamic duo, BATMAN is ill!

In an exclusive interview with a bat, *The BEAT* has learned that Adam West, also known as Bruce Wayne, better known as Batman, recently worked himself to the point of collapse and was given three days off from his exhaustive schedule to recuperate.

The bat revealed that the entire Batman crew has been working from 6 a.m. until almost midnight every day and even a Batman

(Turn to Page 5)

Another Beatle Gone; Now Paul Is Only Survivor

By Elden Chance

ESHER, ENGLAND — Surrounded by a 14-foot-high wall, England's most famous newlyweds remain in seclusion after a long-rumored surprise marriage that left only one unmarried Beatle.

George Harrison and his bride, baby-faced fashion model Patti Boyd, are staying at George's $56,000 five-bedroom bungalow in Esher, a wealthy residential estate in southern England.

It is only a few miles from Epsom, where George married his girlfriend of the past two years in a seven-minute ceremony on Jan. 21.

"It's the happiest day of my life," said blue-eyed Patti, who met George when she made her one attempt to act — a two-minute appearance in the 1964 Beatles' movie "A Hard Day's Night."

Said George, "Of course I am very happy, but we shall not have a honeymoon yet. We would just be hounded and wouldn't get any privacy."

Only immediate relatives and a few close friends knew about the late-morning wedding in the little blue and white registry office in Epsom. Paul McCartney, now the only bachelor of the group, was the only other Beatle present.

"Both George and Patti decided they wanted the quietest wedding without any fuss," a spokesman for the couple told *The BEAT*.

News of the closely-guarded wedding was announced half an hour after the ceremony, and word quickly flashed to fans around the world that another of the Beatles had taken a wife.

After the ceremony Paul said with a sigh, "Now the rumors can start about me, I suppose."

Actually rumors of Paul's impending marriage to actress Jane Asher started long ago, but nothing has been announced.

Rumors about George and Patti also started in 1964 when they went on vacation together to Ireland and then to the Bahamas. But George denied there were any wedding plans — right up until the day of the marriage.

Inside the BEAT

Paul and Barry In 3
Walker Brother Speaks 4
George and John Look Ahead 5
Mitch Ryder Takes A Ride 7
Marvellettes And Miracles 8
Wild Affair At The BEAT 11
Adventures of Robin Boyd 13
Success Of T-Bones 15
Beat Goes To The Movies 16

BEATLES ARCHIVES 1

America's Largest Teen NEWSpaper

KRLA Edition BEAT

MARCH 12, 1966

Three Faces Of Paul McCartney

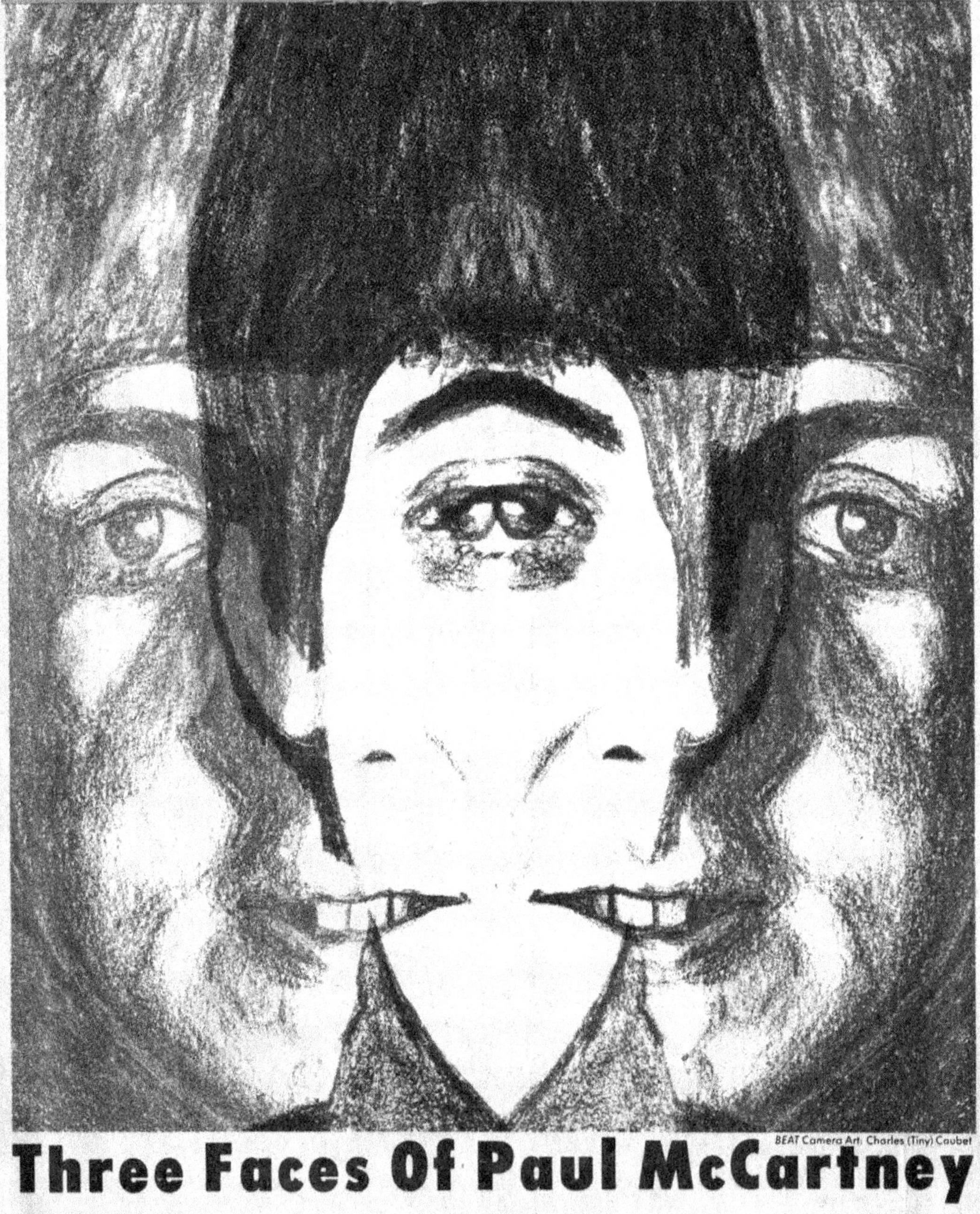

BEAT Camera Art, Charles (Tiny) Caubet

KRLA BEAT

Volume 1, Number 52   March 12, 1966

HOTLINE LONDON
Strangers Sleeping On Ringo's Lawn

By Tony Barrow

Richard and Maureen Starkey—Ringo and Mo to you—seem to be settling in very comfortably at their new and very secluded hideaway home close to the Lennon property at Weybridge in Surrey. They have a nanny to look after baby Zak but she takes two evenings off each week and then Ringo and Mo stay in, firmly avoiding the idea of bringing in baby sitters although a million fans might gladly accept the task!

Ringo spends most of his afternoons at John's place. Maureen enjoys a weekly shopping trip to London's West End.

Beatle People who have been ambitious enough to seek out the Starkey house come away with stories of a strange caravan (that's a trailer to you!) parked in the garden. Each night five or six men sleep in that caravan and what the fans don't know is that these are labourers who are still working on internal re-construction and improvements to the house.

The Starkeys thought all the work would be complete but they fixed their Christmas move-in schedule long before the men were ready to leave. The team of workers live about fifty miles from Weybridge—right over in the county of Kent—so Ringo arranged for them to set up the king-sized caravan in his garden so that they could sleep right there beside the house until the job is complete.

AND THAT'S ONE REASON WHY RINGO CAN BE FOUND AT JOHN'S HOUSE ALMOST EVERY AFTERNOON OF THE WEEK—HE CAN'T STAND THE NON-STOP NOISE OF HAMMERING AND DRILLING AT HIS OWN PLACE!

Incidentally, it doesn't seem like a whole year since Ringo married Maureen does it? In fact the couple celebrated their First Wedding Anniversary on Friday, 11 February!

More Beatle Music

An hour-long television spectacular, "The Music Of Lennon And McCartney," screened in Britain last December and now being made available for showing throughout the world, will represent the U.K. in this year's Golden Rose Of Montreux contest. The annual television festival at Montreux features special programmes entered by numerous TV companies from various countries.

A long list of international stars are featured in "The Music Of Lennon And McCartney." They include Henry Mancini, Esther Phillips, Peter And Gordon, Marianne Faithfull, Peter Sellers, Billy J. Kramer With The Dakotas, Cilla Black, Dick Rivers, The George Martin Orchestra and Antonio Vargas with his Spanish Dancers. John and Paul act as comperes and the show includes fifteen Lennon/McCartney compositions presented in as many different styles. One hundred singers, dancers and musicians are involved in the fast-moving production. The Beatles make two appearances to perform their latest numbers, "We Can Work It Out" and "Day Tripper."

The 1966 Golden Rose festival takes place in Montreux in Switzerland throughout the final week of April.

Keith Produces

Keith Richard has recorded an album of instrumental tracks in which he conducts "The Aranbee Pop Symphony Orchestra!" The ten tracks include "We Can Work It Out," "There's A Place," "I Got You Babe," "In The Midnight Hour" and "Rag Doll."

In the meantime, The Stones have not been short of press publicity to tie in with the U.K. release of "19th Nervous Breakdown" which smashed into our charts at Number Two less than a week after release. Suddenly, after a quiet spell, the fivesome (plus Andrew Loog Oldham) became available for interview and every pop paper in London took advantage of the situation, splashing pix and stories across their pages.

Almost immediately after his solo stint as a panel guest on "The Eamonn Andrews Show" (like your Carson programme), Mick Jagger flew to New York ahead of the group. Before he left he had this to say about "19th Nervous Breakdown:" "It's not supposed to mean anything. No, it's not intended to be a social comment at all. I thought of the title and then started to write around it. It's about this bird who is neurotic."

Andrew has cultivated a very fine and very ginger-coloured moustache which spreads out like a pair of immobile wings beneath his nose. With this he uses thick-rimmed glasses and an enormous tie. Bill Wyman has also taken to wearing a moustache but on their behalf, Mick assures everyone that neither Andy nor Bill were influenced in their decision to grow whiskers by the briefly displayed and hastily shaven beard of Ringo Starr! *(Turn to Page 4)*

...GEORGE, RINGO AND JOHN OFFER PAUL THEIR CONDOLENCES ON HIS BACHELORHOOD.

Now Only Beatle Left
What Will Happen To Paul?

By Louise Criscione

And now there is only one—unmarried Beatle, that is. What will become of Paul McCartney now that he is the sole eligible (?) bachelor? To say the least, Paul is not over-joyed with the situation.

Up until the Beatle world got wind of George and Patti's marriage, Paul was forced to carry the burden of being the "charming" Beatle, the one who soothed over any irritation caused by the other Beatles' (but particularly John's) sharp-tongued remarks.

He was the one who could be counted upon to wink at the girls in the audience with an amazing amount of regularity. He was indeed the charmer.

That alone was enough to keep Paul busy but he had one extra little quality which caused him to work harder than his three companions. When the Beatles first visited Stateside Paul was awarded the title "Most Handsome Beatle." An honor? Well, yes and no. No, because it meant that Paul always had to look sharp.

Never Paul

Ringo could grow a beard, John could forget to shave, George could let his hair grow untidy, but Paul had to look great no matter what. Think back. Have you ever seen Paul's hair too long, his clothes too messy or his beard too noticeable?

So, there was Paul the charming and polite young man and Paul the handsome Beatle. Paul who was funny even when he was being sarcastic and cutting. He probably got tired of smiling. He was the only Beatle who continually wore a smile across his handsome face.

The others got neatly out of the smiling bit. Ringo became known for his usually deadpan expression, George took to not talking much and smiling even less and John—well, John did just as he pleased. Sometimes he laughed the loudest, cracked the funniest jokes and produced the widest grin. Other times he neither laughed, nor smiled. But what ever he did was accepted as easily as a Beatle's autograph. After all, he was John Lennon—the unclassifiable Beatle.

That left only Paul to keep the smile on. Tired, hungry, sick—it didn't matter, he *had* to smile and be friendly. He wasn't allowed to let the Beatle image be covered by even a hint of a shadow.

That Day

It was Paul too who carried the brunt of the Beatle marriage rumors. I don't suppose Beatle fans will ever forget the day they opened their morning papers in February of '64 to be faced with the "news" that Paul and Jane Asher had gotten married.

Beatle fans read the short story with a sinking, sort of everything-is-lost feeling. Was it true? It was by-lined by Walter Winchell and whether it was true or not it had the strength of having been written by a world famous and powerful newspaperman.

It goes without saying that plenty of tears were cried and thousands of Paul McCartney pictures were torn to shreds before Paul ever got around to denying it. And even when he did there were those who doubted his word.

They couldn't help it—they had just become aware of the Beatles and they didn't know much about them, except that they were the most exciting act to hit the pop scene since Elvis Presley had first wiggled his hips and shocked the life out of parents whose teenage daughters seemed to actually *like* this side-burned, guitar-toting character with the unlikely name of Elvis.

Always Present

On the boot heels of that very first Paul-Jane marriage rumor came a score of others. They didn't have nearly the impact of that first one but they were there just the same.

Along about this time the romance of Ringo and Maureen became known so the rumor-mongers took to making up stories about them. And then along came George and Patti and some more rumors. You couldn't say that Paul *wished* the rumors on Ringo and George but then you also couldn't say that he wasn't relieved to have someone else sharing the marriage rumor business with him.

It gave Paul a welcome rest. But one year ago Ringo and Maureen— *(Turn to Page 11)*

Inside the BEAT

Johnny Rivers — Live! 3
Al Martino Greets Success 4
Pop Comic Strip 5
Jackie Lee Ducking 6
Boy Wonder Sings 7
Byrds Interviewed 10-11
Cher 'Shot Down' 12
Girls in Beatles' Lives 13
BEAT Goes To The Movies 15

The BEAT is published weekly by BEAT Publications, Inc., editorial and advertising offices at 6290 Sunset Blvd., Suite 504, Hollywood, California 90028. U.S. bureaus in Hollywood, San Francisco, New York, Chicago and Nashville; overseas correspondents in London, Liverpool and Manchester, England. Sale price 15 cents. Subscription price: U.S. and possessions, $5 per year, Canada and foreign rates, $9 per year. Application to mail at second class postage rates is pending at Los Angeles, California.

BEATLES ARCHIVES 1

The Only Single Beatle

(Continued from Page 1)

reen made the rumors fact leaving George and Paul wide-open to face the rumors alone. And then George went off and got married and once again only Paul was left for the rumor people to carve up.

If you think this rumor business isn't a very real problem you're off your rocker because it most definitely is. Even though Paul was very happy for George and Patti, he commented to the reporters gathered outside the registry that he supposed *he* was now in for an onslaught of newly-made-up marriage stories.

Hounded

Even George felt badly about leaving Paul the only bachelor Beatle: "Actually, I feel sorry for him. He'll be hounded to death now us other three are married."

But surprisingly enough a whole month has passed and not one single rumor has hit the papers. Maybe none will, but don't bank on it. There is always someone around to stir up trouble, always someone who thinks he can sell a few more papers or boost his magazine's circulation by printing a huge spread on Paul and Jane's "marriage."

And, of course, there is Jane herself who continues to insist that she and Paul are getting married while Paul is equally firm in insisting that he has no marriage plans.

Where it will go from here is anybody's guess. Probably even Paul isn't sure. About the only thing in the whole mess is that the Beatles will be around the pop scene for a long, long time to come — whether Paul stays the charming, handsome, bachelor Beatle or not.

Say you saw it in The BEAT

'Revolver' Is Title For New Beatle LP

By Tony Barrow

During their Germany/Far East tour THE BEATLES worked out a final running order for their upcoming U.K. album, due for Parlophone release August 5.

Having settled on a final sequence for the 14 all-new numbers, they held a series of concentrated discussions about a suitable title for the album. More than 50 different ideas were discussed but the unanimous choice favoured Paul's simple yet effective one-word suggestion–"REVOLVER."

GEORGE HARRISON has written three of the 14 numbers and on each of these he is the featured lead vocalist. They are "TAX MAN," "LOVE YOU TO" and "I WANT TO TELL YOU." On the second of these tracks George has created a terrific sitar introduction and on the third Paul plays piano in the background.

RINGO STARR'S vocal solo is "YELLOW SUBMARINE," and I'd say this kiddie-angled ditty is destined to become his most successful track to date. Paul, John and George join him vocally for the catchy chorus lines and there's a series of carefully-placed sound effects at appropriate points throughout the arrangement.

Of the remaining 10 Lennon-McCartney compositions, five have vocal leads handled by John and five feature Paul. The Lennon quintet runs like this: "I'M ONLY SLEEPING," "SHE SAID, SHE SAID," "AND YOUR BIRD CAN SING," "DOCTOR ROBERT," "TOMORROW NEVER KNOWS." That last number was given its title by Ringo and the track includes a host of weirdie sound effects created specially for the occasion by Paul.

Paul's set includes "ELEANOR RIGBY," "HERE, THERE AND EVERYWHERE," "GOOD DAY SUNSHINE," "FOR NO ONE" and "GOT TO GET YOU INTO MY LIFE."

"Eleanor Rigby" is Paul's ballad specialty in the "REVOLVER" program. The precision-built lyrics tell a meaningful story and Paul is backed by strings just as he was for his two biggest previous ballad hits. For me this is one of the album's stand-out performances and the commercial chart potential of "Eleanor Rigby" is limitless.

(Turn to Page 5)

Lennon And McCartney Win Three Composer's Awards

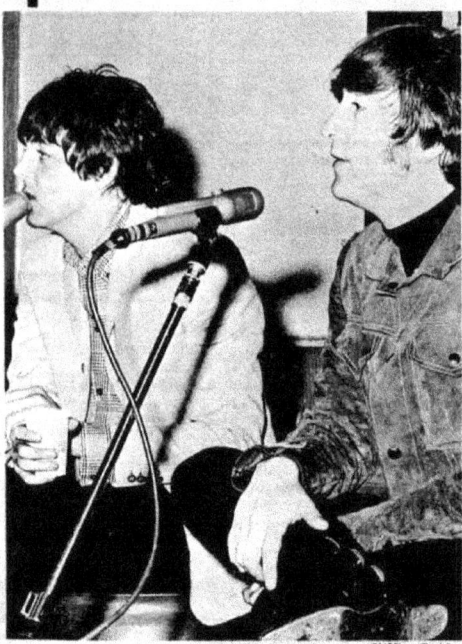

... McCARTNEY AND LENNON — TRIPLE WINNERS!

Winners of the Ivor Novello Awards, presented annually for the outstanding British compositions of the year, have just been announced. As expected, the Beatles walked off with three of the awards. Lennon and McCartney took both the first place and runner-up trophies in the category of Highest Certified Record Sales for a British composition in 1965. In first place was "We Can Work It Out" and coming in second was the Beatles' "Help!"

Lennon and McCartney's third award was won by "Yesterday" as the Oustanding Song of 1965. Runner-up in that category was the Jackie Trent English hit, "Where Are You Now," written by Jackie and Tony Hatch.

Donovan's "Catch The Wind" was voted the Outstanding Folk Song of the Year and the Tom Jones smash, "It's Not Unusual," written by Gordon Mills and Les Reed, was named the Outstanding Beat Song of 1965.

The Seekers' first number one hit, "I'll Never Find Another You," was named the Most Performed Work of The Year. In the Oustanding Novelty Composition category "A Windmill In Old Amsterdam," written by Ted Dicks and Myles Rudge, took the top honors with "Mrs. Brown You've Got A Lovely Daughter" coming in a close second.

Beatle 'Revolver'

(Continued from Page 1)

"Got To Get You Into My Life" is the track we've heard so much about over the past few weeks although it has not been publicly named until now. Here a full-blooded brass sound backs Paul and I'd say those blasting trumpets constitute the nearest approach to the Memphis studio sound ever created on our side of the Atlantic. Forget the nonsense about this brass work being jazz-angled. It is R&B, but certainly not jazz.

I have no information (at the time of writing) about Capitol's plans to issue the "REVOLVER" material in America. Although three of the titles are already in your "Yesterday and Today" collection, eleven others remain un-issued in the U.S. and will obviously form Capitols' next album later this summer.

MY OVER-ALL REACTION TO THE "REVOLVER" MATERIAL . . . Without doubt some younger Beatle People will find at least three or four of these recordings too complicated, too intelligent (musically) and/or too weird. On the other hand there is more than a fair sprinkling of perfectly straightforward performances ranging from Ringo's simple but extraordinarily infectious "Yellow Submarine" to the rocking "Doctor Robert," from the thoughtful "Eleanor Rigby" to the boisterous "Got To Get You Into My Life." On listening to the whole album, it becomes plain that The Beatles didn't waste any of those days and weeks between Easter and their June tour of Germany. Every track has been produced with perfectionist polish – one took over 55 hours of recording time to complete! Nobody is likely to be disappointed by the finished product — and that, after all, is the aim of any recording artist.

"TWIST AND SHOUT" (2:10)
[Mellin, Progressive BMI—Medley, Russell]
"THERE'S A PLACE" (1:58) [Gil BMI—McCartney, Lennon]
THE BEATLES (Tollie 9001)

The group that turned the industry upside down should quickly continue their fantastic ways with this single on Tollie, the new VeeJay label. It's the Isley Bros. smash oldie, "Twist And Shout" (culled from the crew's "Introducing The Beatles" VeeJay LP) that they belt out in exciting fashion. Tune, performed on the recent Ed Sullivan TV'er, is already busting wide open. The captivating less frantic thumper, "There's A Place" (also from the LP), can also zoom way up the charts.

BEATLES ARCHIVES 1

Why Not Popsters As Comic Heroes?

By Tammy Hitchcock

Now that we've been blessed with "Batman" The BEAT sees no reason to discriminate against the rest of our great comic book heroes. After all, that would be un-American in the extreme. Television officials are busily buying up the rights to all our comic strip favorites so be prepared for an onslaught on all stations next season.

Since it is a foregone conclusion that such heroes as Charlie Brown, Snuffy Smith, Wonder Woman and the Human Torch will shortly be coming to life we thought that the very least we could do would be to help the television people cast their up-coming rating-grabbers with our Top 40 performers. A wild idea, right?

So, here is a list of pop artists who we are convinced would make fab comic book heroes. Let us know if you agree, disagree or can come up with some even crazier suggestions.

The BEAT Suggests

Mick Jagger as The Human Torch
Tom Jones as Captain Marvel
Nancy Sinatra as Wonder Woman
Keith Richard as Flash Gordon
Jim McGuinn as The Submariner
Bill Wyman as Spectre
Lou Christy as The Green Lantern
Donovan as Hawkman
Barry McGuire as Captain America
Bob Dylan as The Plastic Man
Roger Miller as Little Abner
P.J. Proby as Superman
Keith Relf as The Spirit
Cilla Black as Little Lulu
Brian Jones as Dennis The Menace
Dino, Desi or Billy as Archie
Leslie Gore as Orphan Annie
David McCallum as Dick Tracy
Jeff Beck as Beetle Bailey
Joan Baez as Brenda Starr
Eric Burdon as Prince Valiant
Paul Revere & The Raiders as Terry & The Pirates
Jackie DeShannon as Blondie
Ringo as Dagwood
Herman as Charlie Brown
Elvis Presley as the Phantom
Paul McCartney as Daddy Warbucks
John Lennon as Snuffy Smith
Sonny as Popeye
Cher as Olive Oil
Simon & Garfunkel as the Katsanjammer Twins
Brian Wilson as Joe Palooka

THE BEATLES: The Girls In Their Lives

By Sue Barry

There is probably no group of people more talked and written about than those four young men collectively known as the Beatles. In fact, if there was one, I am sure these boys would walk away with the award for the largest number of words written on one subject in a short span of three years. Yet, for the millions of words printed about these four there remains a cloud of mystery over one aspect of their lives. This concerns their relations with the opposite sex and, in particular, Cynthia Lennon, Maureen Starkey, Pattie Harrison and Jane Asher.

It is no accident that these girls have been carefully guarded from the spotlight. For there is an unwritten agreement among John, Paul, George and Ringo that their private lives are indeed private and should be kept from the spying eye of the press. One has to admire the boys for this policy. They have protected their girls from the needless and unnecessary hurt that so often arises out of "scoop" stories written by so-called fan magazines.

Yet, one cannot help but wonder about these girls. After all, fans are fans and although they don't wish to pry they do like to know about these all-important femmes in the Beatles' lives. So we of *The BEAT* have decided to give you a little of each girl. We do not mean to pry, nor do we want to spread any falsehoods, but wish to share with you the girls in the lives of the Beatles.

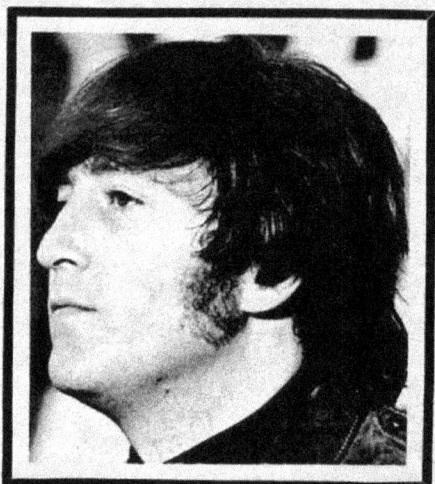

BEAT Photo: Robert W. Young

"My girl was at home in Liverpool. I'd met her one day and we'd suddenly fallen in love. A little while later we were married. I love her." The man speaking was John Lennon once pegged as the "married Beatle." The girl he spoke of is, of course, his wife Cynthia.

Theirs is a story of love and one any girl would delight in telling. In a way it's like a fairytale come true. But perhaps it would be better for you to find out for yourself. Let us go for a moment into the world of John and Cynthia Lennon.

They first met in art school. John was a young man struggling between his love for a guitar and art. Cynthia Powell was a quiet, intelligent girl. They met and as John says, ". . . suddenly fell in love." It must have been evident for a Mr. Ballard who tutored John at art school has this to say: "She was his guiding light, and even though she was the top girl in her class, she always managed to spare time for John. Even in those days they were really made for each other." Yes, they were made for each other and when John finally quit school to devote all his time to his music Cynthia encouraged him. Often she would travel up to thirty miles from her home on Trinity Rd. in Hoylake to hear John and the other boys play. A friend recalls how during breaks John would sit on the edge of the stage quietly talking with her.

But times changed and when they married on August 23, 1962 it was decided that the best thing was not to let out word of their marriage. The Beatles were on the road up and a marriage in the group might have caused them to lose a great amount of popularity. Perhaps this was the hardest time of their marriage—that first year or so when it seemed so important that John's marriage be kept hidden. They lived at John's aunt Mimi's. During their stay, a baby, John Julian, was born on April 8, 1963.

It wasn't too long after this that pictures of Cyn appeared in the papers. The truth was out! And what did John have to say? "I never denied it at all. It's just that nobody asked me." A typical straight forward Beatle answer!

Cynthia remarks: "At first it was horrible. John used to get terrible letters and if I'd been unstable, I would have been terribly upset by them. But afterwards the friendly ones far out-numbered the unpleasant ones."

And so there was one married Beatle. John was careful not to let the press get to his wife, "I haven't deliberately hidden her from the public . . . but I have tried to keep her away from the press. I don't see why they should treat her like a freak just because she married a Beatle."

But what is this woman like? Cynthia had remained the same girl from Liverpool although her tastes run expensive now that she has the money. She is a shy, quiet girl who likes to spend her time at home with her young son. In fact, she recently let her cook go, deciding she would be happier cooking her own meals, taking care of her home. Her love of art still remains and she often finds time to put her brushes to use. Cynthia's flair for fashion is evident to anyone who has seen this lovely blonde, blue-eyed woman. She once said of John, "I understand everything he does. He may surprise many, but he never surprises me."

But perhaps the highest compliment ever paid her was when a friend said of John and Cyn, "I don't think he would have been half so good if they had not met."

(Series To Be Continued)

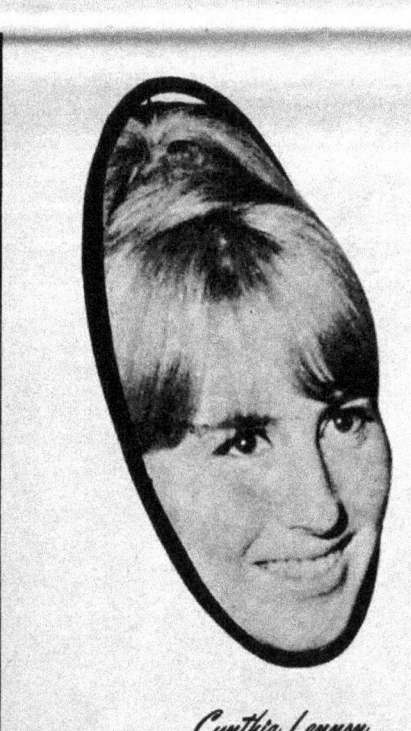

Cynthia Lennon

KRLA BEAT

FREE TRIPS TO LONDON! (See Page 4)

May 12, 1965 — Los Angeles, California — Ten Cents

BEAT SUBSCRIPTIONS AVAILABLE! (See Page 5)

HERE COME THE BEATLES!

Contract Signed -- Preparations Underway

PLANNING THE CONCERT — Promoter Bob Eubanks discusses 1965 Beatle tour with KRLA's Dave Hull and Derek Taylor. With the famed Hollywood Bowl as a backdrop, the three music and public relations experts talk over the unending details required to present THE BEATLES effectively and still provide for everyone's safety and enjoyment. This year's show will feature performances on both August 29th and the 30th.

Fans Eager
Liverpool 4 Here In August

Now it's official! The Beatles will return to Southern California this summer for two concerts at Hollywood Bowl —Aug. 29 and 30. They will be presented by the same sponsors who brought them here last year — KRLA and Bob Eubanks. Ticket applications will be taken by mail only this year. You'll find the information, including a ticket application coupon, on page 7 of this week's KRLA Beat.

Their performances here will climax a North American tour that will take the Beatles from New York to Mexico City.

Bob Eubanks began negotiating with the Beatles for this year's performances immediately after their concert at Hollywood Bowl last year. But so did dozens of other people, including a number of other radio stations who offered them almost unbelievable sums of money for the privilege of sponsoring their Hollywood Bowl concerts.

However, the Beatles were so impressed by KRLA's reputation as the Beatle station in America and by Eubanks' handling of their 1964 performance that they rejected all other offers.

Last year at this time — before he joined KRLA — Derek Taylor was working with the Beatles as their press officer. Below you'll find his interesting account of their first visit to Southern California, which John, Paul, George

—MORE ON PAGE TWO

ENTRY INTO STATES IS SERIOUS PROBLEM FOR BRITISH ACTS

Organized protests are under way, trying to force the U.S. Immigration Department to allow more British recording stars to make personal appearances in this country.

At present the U.S. allows only a few "alien" performers to obtain work permits to perform over here.

The restrictions are particularly frustrating right now, since British artists are completely dominating pop music in America. Recently only two American artists were on the top 10 and the rest were English.

Many critics say the problem was caused by our government "passing the buck" and delegating its powers to the various entertainers unions to judge the performers' merits for work permits here.

Dislike Pop

The unions, often unfamiliar with recent pop music trends and openly showing a strong dislike for this type music, are rejecting many performers on grounds that they are not good enough or not well known.

The situation has gotten so bad that some American TV producers are threatening to tape their shows in England.

And to make matters worse, KRLA Beat sources in London say the British are threatening to retaliate by clamping down on American artists who try to perform in England.

Many in the business feel the present turmoil and hardships could be avoided if the U.S. Immigration Department would bring in one person with some background and knowledge of the music business to handle the work permit applications.

Derek Taylor Reports

So we have the Beatles. It is all over. We have them for KRLA. Bob Eubanks has done it again — against fierce, frightening opposition. I'm naturally delighted and although I knew that Brian Epstein strongly favoured Bob and KRLA as promoters, I couldn't say so for certain until all the signatures were inked. Elsewhere in this issue I've attempted to capture the details of our stay here last year when the Hollywood Bowl erupted in Beatlemania. It has one advantage over all the other various versions of those four frantic days. It's true!

"Go Now," a wonderful disc and a smash in England and over here for the Moody Blues, has not been followed up as well as expected. Their other disc is crawling feebly up the charts in the UK. Maybe it will do better here.

There is, of course, no guarantee that one smash will be followed by another. I can't see the Righteous Bros. making No. 1 with their latest.

Personally — and regretfully — I find it rather dull and shapeless. I think the able Mr. Spector has over produced it. A pity because

—MORE ON PAGE 8

TOP TEN

1. WOOLY BULLY
2. GLORIA — BABY PLEASE DON'T CRY
3. MRS. BROWN
4. WHEN I'M GONE
5. TICKET TO RIDE/YES IT IS
6. JUST ONCE IN MY LIFE
7. OOH BABY BABY
8. THE LAST TIME — PLAY WITH FIRE
9. GAME OF LOVE
10. NOWHERE TO RUN

—TUNDEX ON PAGE 4

The latest listenership ratings are out of sight!

Both Pulse, Inc., and C. E. Hooper show that KRLA has increased its first place rating and is now even farther out front than before — the most popular major radio station in the United States!

The new Pulse report shows that KRLA has more than twice as many listeners as any other radio station in Los Angeles or Orange counties.

This includes all age groups with KRLA leading in both adult and teenage listeners.

All of us at KRLA are deeply gratified by your support. We will continue to do our best to merit it.

BEATLES ARCHIVES 1

The First American Beatle Trip

FROM PAGE ONE
and Ringo regarded as the highlight of their tour.

by Derek Taylor

The Beatles and I have lost count of the rumors, mis-statements and guesses about our stay in Hollywood when they appeared at the Bowl last year.

In fact, we had a very peaceful working vacation. We arrived here in the small hours of the morning at Los Angeles International Airport. We were met notably by Dave Hull — plus Bob Eubanks — who, with KRLA, was promoting the show. We had come many hundreds of miles throught the night on our Electra turbo-jet after an open air concert in Vancouver, British Columbia. Though we were tired, we were sufficiently excited by the prospect of seeing Hollywood properly that we kept alert. And when we arrived at the house in Bel-Air, John and I went for a dawn swim in the pool.

The house in Bel-Air was no disappointment. It was as large and luxurious as any house we ever saw in the movies. With two-level rooms, gigantic beds, mirrors covering whole walls.

Finally Sleep!

After our swim, John and I joined the other Beatles and our touring managers for breakfast. Then we went to bed for a few hours sleep.

The Beatles were up early — early, that is, for them — at about 1 p.m. and we all spent the afternoon by the pool.

In the evening we drove to Bob Eubanks' Cinnamon Cinder in North Hollywood for a wild, unruly news conference attended by hundreds of teenagers and adults — who seemed almost as excited as the younger Beatlemaniacs.

The news conference lasted an hour. The Beatles then shot off for the Hollywood Bowl in their limousine. I stayed behind to comfort a mother and daughter, both of whom were in tears because they had come from Pheonix by bus to present a plaque to Ringo. But because of the crush they hadn't been able to get near him.

The story of the actual concert is legend. As soon as the last echoing notes of "Long Tall Sally" had died in the hills above the Bowl, The Beatles were driven off by Jim Steck, KRLA newsman.

Unusual Night

There were many human interest stories in the Bowl that night. One man had his leg broken by a run-away car tire. An emotional girl threw herself into the Bowl fountain after the concert.

The press and TV cameramen were having a hard time moving among the audience, for police officers had strict instructions to prevent movement and keep order at all costs.

I experienced the greatest difficulty getting in the Bowl at all. I had to empty my pockets to produce four or five forms of identification. My English accent — normally a guarantee of access to any hall where the Beatles were appearing — wasn't enough because the police thought it was phony. Finally, I got in by producing two sets of Beatle autographs.

Back at the house, we spent a quiet hour or so talking and reminiscing. Paul played the piano.

I suppose most people would call it a dull evening, but anyway it was nice to relax.

More Reporters

The following day we spent more hours at the pool and photographs were taken which eventually found their way into publications all over the world. Col. Tom Parker, manager of Elvis Presley, arrived to take Brian Epstein to lunch. The Beatles and I lunched with their road managers Neil Aspinall and Mal Evans.

Col. Parker and Brian returned in good spirits after a nice lunch. They had discussed the problems and delights of managing the hottest show-business acts in the world, and Col. Parker's aides presented us all with gunbelts, magnificent toy pistols, and models of old pioneer covered wagons.

The Beatles then went off to wash, shave and dress themselves in their best suits for the charity garden party held nearby at the home of the mother-in-law of Mr. Alan Livingston, president of Capitol Records.

This was the most glamorous affair — guests paid $25 a head to be there and the profits went to the Hemophilia Foundation. Hundreds of young people were meekly lined up to meet The Beatles, who sat on high stools in a reception area.

Again I had difficulty getting into the grounds. This time Brian Epstein was with me, and we both found the way barred by stone-faced guards.

"I'm Brian Epstein," said Brian gently. And the guard laughed and said, "I'm Errol Flynn." We finally got in because our credentials were vouched by a man called Hal York, who was organizing arrangements inside the gate. This was odd since Hal York had no credentials whatsoever and was, in fact, a notorious —though amiable—gate crasher.

Stars Attend

There were many famous faces at the garden party: Edward G. Robinson and his granddaughter, Mrs. Dean Martin and her beautiful children. Jack Palance was there, along with Lloyd Bridges, Shelly Winters, Eva Marie Saint, Hedda Hopper and her hat; Gary Lewis — this was long before The Playboys — and many others.

It was a wonderful day and everyone was thrilled with The Beatles and their impeccable conduct. They were on their best behaviour that day. They looked well and they had a great time.

There was, of course, no work that night so we had a party at the house. Bobby Darin and Sandra Dee came. So did Paul and Paula and many other of the Hollywood younger set. The party lasted 'til dawn.

At 10 a.m., I was awakened by John Lennon who decided he wanted to go out shopping. So with a cameraman friend of ours, Ron Joy, John, Neil Aspinall and I drove down to Beau Gentry where we all bought light-weight jackets. John picked up a couple of cowboy shirts and arrangements were made for Beau Gentry to send other samples to the house.

The other three Beatles were up by the time we returned and we spent the remainder of the day by the pool.

In the meantime, Jayne Mansfield had expressed a desire to meet The Beatles, and they thought it would be interesting to meet her. So I was asked to telephone her. Miss Mansfield was playing at a nearby theatre and she said she would love to meet The Beatles. I said The Beatles would prefer not to have a cameraman present because it would look like a publicity stunt. They simply wanted Miss Mansfield and her escort to be their guests for cocktails by the pool.

Miss Mansfield thought a photographer would enhance the occasion and a compromise was reached when it was decided we would all meet at the Whisky-a-Go-Go at midnight.

The Whisky-a-Go-Go was asked to provide privacy and security, but, alas, we achieved neither. And when John, George and Ringo met with the glamorous star, there was mass pandemonium, noise and panic, and the meeting ended in complete disorder.

Confused Facts

The story of this has been accurately described in many magazines — with the untrue embellishment that George Harrison threw a beverage over a photographer. What happened was that George tossed a couple of ice cubes in the direction of the camera. I don't blame him.

Earlier that evening, Paul and I had gone to Burt Lancaster's magnificent home at his invitation for a private viewing of "A Shot in the Dark." This was a wonderfully relaxed evening and Paul wisely decided not to go to the Whisky-a-Go-Go.

The following morning, tired but sunburned and pretty fit, we left Los Angeles for the next stage of the tour — for Denver, Colorado.

Though we didn't spot them then, Dave Hull and Jim Steck astutely stowed away on our plane and revealed themselves in Denver. Smart work in the best tradition of news gathering.

Thus, Hollywood 1964. No one can guess what it will be like this year.

But I anticipate that the highways, byways, fields, hedges, and hills for miles around will again be swarming with Beatle-hunting youngsters.

DICK CLARK
CARAVAN of STARS
STARRING
DICK CLARK
MONDAY, MAY 17
TWO PERFORMANCES
5 & 9 P.M.
ONE NITE ONLY!
FEATURING 15 OF THE NATION'S TOP RECORDING ACTS!
DEL SHANNON
The **ZOMBIES**
The **SHANGRI-LAS**
JEWEL AKEN
The **LARKS**
TOMMY ROE
DEE DEE SHARP
MEL CARTER
The **AD LIBS**
The **VELVELETTES**
JIMMY SOUL
MIKE CLIFFORD
The **IKETTES**
The **EXECUTIVES**
DON WAYNE
PRICES . . . $2.50, $3.50, $4.50
TICKETS AT BOX-OFFICE, BY MAIL AND ALL SOUTHLAND AGENCIES

FOR INFORMATION CALL
ANAHEIM (714) 776-7220

FUTURE D.J.'S
Join the Ranks of
DON MARTIN GRADS
YOU WILL FIND THEM ON
EVERY MAJOR STATION
IN
LOS ANGELES
"A Career In A Year"
— Jobs Assured —
DON MARTIN
SCHOOL OF RADIO
& TV
Call or Write for Information
1653 N. CHEROKEE AVE.
HOLLYWOOD

---

23 SKIDOO
Dancing to Live Name Bands
2116 Westwood Blvd., West Los Angeles
Girls 18, Guys 21
23 Skidoo Dancers are now seen on TV's Hollywood A'GoGo Saturday on Channel 9 at 9:00 p.m.
Closed Mondays

BEATLES ARCHIVES 1

THE BEATLES RETURN!

HOLLYWOOD BOWL AUGUST 29 - 30

Radio Station KRLA and Bob Eubanks Proudly Present Two Concerts By The Fabulous Beatles AT HOLLYWOOD BOWL AUG. 29 . 30

Tickets are available by mail **only**. Applications will be filled by date of receipt. No ticket applications accepted before May 8.

1. No more than six tickets to any one person.
2. Tickets are $3, $4, $5, $6 and $7.
3. A self-addressed, stamped envelope must be included with your order.
4. Tickets will be mailed July 15.
5. If tickets are not available at the price you order, you will be sent tickets for the alternate date. If tickets at that price are not available for either date, you will be sent tickets at the next lowest price, along with a refund.

MAIL TO:

HOLLYWOOD BOWL
P.O. BOX 1951
LOS ANGELES, CALIF., 90028

ON OR AFTER MAY 8

TICKET APPLICATION

I have enclosed a check or money order (NO CASH) payable to HOLLYWOOD BOWL, plus a self-addressed, stamped envelope. Please send me the following BEATLE TICKETS:

- ☐ 1 TICKET ☐ $3.00 ☐ AUGUST 29
- ☐ 2 TICKETS ☐ $4.00 ☐ AUGUST 30
- ☐ 3 TICKETS ☐ $5.00
- ☐ 4 TICKETS ☐ $6.00
- ☐ 5 TICKETS ☐ $7.00
- ☐ 6 TICKETS

SEND TO ....
ADDRESS ....
CITY .... STATE .... Zip Code ......
TELEPHONE NO. ....

BEATLES ARCHIVES 1

RUMORS CONTINUE
Paul and Jane

By Sue Barry

There remains today one bachelor Beatle—his name is, of course, Paul McCartney. Two years ago no one would have bet a halfpenny that Paul would be the last single Beatle, for it is around him and Jane Asher that the most often and violent rumors of marriage have persisted. Yet today, after the marriage of George Harrison, Paul finds himself the only unmarried Beatle. But, although Paul does date other girls, it is common knowledge that he prefers the company of Jane Asher to that of any other girl.

Paul first met Jane in 1963. Jane was a young seventeen year old actress who had been asked to do an interview with the Beatles for a radio show.

The story goes that after the official business was completed the boys asked her to a party at a friend's flat.

For many months Paul and Jane kept their meetings secret, but eventually their privacy was shattered when in December of 1963 they were spotted together at the Prince of Wales Theater. From this date on they were completely harrassed by marriage rumors.

Some people claimed to have been at the wedding, seen copies of insurance policies for the two or to have seen the marriage certificate. An example of these fantasies was the case of Noel Harrison. He had been quoted saying that he had been at the wedding. His reply was: "Don't know how these stories got around. All I can say is that it is all a complete load of nonsense." This was even before we Americans had ever heard of the Beatles!

By the time the Beatles invaded "the colonies" in February, 1964, Paul and Jane were seeing quite a bit of each other.

On his return to England, Paul continued dating Jane, this time very much in the eye of the public, saying, "We are not going to dodge the cameras any longer. We are still not married. But if I ever marry Jane, there will be no engagement, just a swift, simple ceremony."

It was not long after this that Walter Winchell reported on March 14 that "Paul McCartney, 21, was secretly married 72 hours ago in London to Jane Asher, 22." This story was followed up a few weeks later by a quote from a letter that read: "For goodness sake, don't breathe this to a soul. Jane and Paul were married in London. I was at the wedding." Paul answered with a quick retort that he was not married.

But even the word of Paul himself would not stop the onslaught of marriage rumors and when Ringo and Maureen and Paul and Jane journeyed to the Virgin Islands in May of 1964, the press still insisted that a marriage between the two had taken place.

It was not until the day of Ringo's marriage that people became satisfied that if a Beatle got married he would let it be known to the world. Only then did the ugly rumors about Paul and Jane calm down a bit.

But what about Paul's girlfriend? What kind of a person is she? What does she hope for?

Jane Asher, a red haired, blue-eyed actress was born in London on April 5, 1946. She is 5-ft. 5-in. tall and weighs 112 pounds, lives with her parents in the Harley Street area of London where Paul often visits with her. Jane's shy manner has a hint of dignity inherited from her wealthy London background.

She and Paul are often seen together at the famous Ad Lib in London's West End when she is not working. For Miss Asher is an accomplished actress and was so long before she met Paul.

About her career Jane says, "My career as an actress is very important and I've got a long way to go before I could think of marriage. Acting is my life. At the moment this comes first." But looking ahead Jane says that her main ambition is: "The same as every other single girl. To eventually get married and have children. Nothing unusual."

To date Jane and Paul are still not married. No one knows when or where Paul will get married, but he says this, "When will I get married? That's simple, when I find someone I want to marry. And when I find her I'll marry her, career's end or not. I like my success, it's been great, but I don't think any Beatle would put it ahead of his personal happiness, do you?"

Expecting Baby

Since she's expecting her first baby, Marianne Faithfull has been relatively inactive on the pop scene. But last week she journeyed to a recording studio to cut "Yesterday"—yes, the same "Yesterday" which Paul McCartney has made into such a fantastic hit here in America.

In England, however, the Beatles have not seen the song released as a single, though it is on their "Help" album. At Marianne's invitation, Paul attended her session which was reported to have had a 100-voice choir backing.

Matt Monroe of "Walk Away" fame has already cut the record and has succeeded in getting it onto the British hit lists so it will be interesting to see if Marianne can catch up and knock Monro's disc right off the charts.

... MARIANNE FAITHFUL

The Beatles have really cut their personal appearances down to the absolute minimum. They have decided to forget their annual Christmas show in London and their "huge" winter tour of Britain has been slashed to only nine dates which will include among others—London, Liverpool and Manchester.

Mama Meets John

Well, Mama Cass finally met John Lennon and as an extra added bonus Paul McCartney showed up too! Guess Cass wasn't disappointed because she said after her meeting with John: "He was charming, courteous and intelligent. Witty, amusing and entertaining."

Cass said the two Beatles sat around and talked for hours and that Paul even played the piano. "They were everything I hoped they would be," finished up Cass.

BEATLE CHANGE ERASES PROFIT

The Beatles have released a conventional album cover entitled "Yesterday and Today" after banning the first cover to the album because it was "misinterpreted." The untimely transfer cost Capitol Records and the Beatles at least $250,000.

More than 750,000 copies of the original album had been distributed across the United States and were poised for release when a backlash of protest from those who received advance copies forced the withdrawal.

Capitol officials made the decision to ban the cover. They quickly sent word to those who had received the advance copies and informed them the cover was being withdrawn.

The 750,000 albums were reclaimed, and then began the mountainous process: by hand, the records had to be taken out of the covers, and by hand again, stuffed into the new covers. Then they were re-shipped to the distributors.

But reclaiming and restuffing the covers was only part of the problems. Streamers that went to dealers, and other printed promotional material all had to be junked and new ones put out.

"It will cost us about $250,000," a record company spokesman said. "That wipes out the profit."

The Beatles had intended the first album cover as pop art. But it was vehemently rejected and some even charged it was cannibalistic. It showed John, George, Paul and Ringo in butchers smocks festooned with chunks of raw meat and the severed parts of a toy doll's body.

The new cover, however, is much more sedate. It shows the Beatles simply standing around a stage trunk.

But even though the album had hard luck in its early going, it is still expected to be a smash in sales. A Capitol spokesman said close to one million copies of the album with the new cover were shipped to distributors on release date. The initial allocation is one of the largest in Capitol's history.

Of the 11 tunes in the LP, none have ever before been released on an album. Five ("Drive My Car," "I'm Only Sleeping," "Dr. Robert," "And Your Bird Can Sing," "If I Needed Someone" have never been released in the U.S. The six other songs were all previously released as singles. They are: "Nowhere Man," "Yesterday," "Act Naturally," "We Can Work It Out," "What Goes On?" and "Day Tripper." All of the songs with the exception of "Act Naturally" (written by John Ressel/Voni Morrison) and "If I Needed Someone" (written by George Harrison) are Lennon-McCartney compositions.

Everything All Set For Beatles Tour

HERE IT IS! The final list of dates and cities that the Beatles will appear this summer:

New York (Aug. 15), Toronto (Aug. 17), Atlanta (Aug. 18), Houston (Aug. 19), Chicago (Aug. 20), Minneapolis (Aug. 21, Portland (Aug. 22) L.A. (Aug. 29 & 30) and San Francisco (Aug. 31).

After completing their tour they will return to Los Angeles for a few days of rest and relaxation.

Our tipsters report that they will be staying at the home of a well-known Hollywood movie star while they vacation here.

Beatles On World TV

LONDON – The Beatles will reach an estimated audience of 500 million in 31 countries in a two-hour special to be aired over world-wide television. The Beatles will be seen live, recording a new tune on June 25. The song was written by John Lennon and Paul McCartney especially for the TV program and will be the next Beatles' single release if the foursome like the results.

The BBC will beam the show, called "Our World," around the United Kingdom. More than 100 U.S. stations have agreed to broadcast it. Three American and one Russian communications satellites will participate in the global telecast.

BEATLES ARCHIVES 1

A Beatle Hunt Revisited

By Martie Henderson

With the August appearance of the fabulous Beatles just around the corner now, the waves of Beatlemania are once again reaching a crest and the familiar excitement of that happy affliction is once again at high tide.

But, it has been over two-and-a-half years since we were first introduced to the British quartet who have revolutionized the entire pop world—and by now, some of us have almost gotten used to the whole aura of Beatlemania.

But, I can remember the first time that I contracted the disease, and I bet that you have many of the same symptoms which I experienced.

Beatle Hunt

It was August of 1964 then, and after months and months of waiting—the Beatles had finally arrived. Hidden away in a private home which they rented during their stay, they were surrounded by police—who in turn, were surrounded by Beatle-hunters.

It was very unusual to see teenagers climbing fences, hiding under bushes, scaling walls, and digging tunnels in order to get at least a glimpse of these four young men they had heard so much about. But it wasn't *half* as unusual as seeing their *parents*—doing the very *same thing!*

Never one to be left behind, I decided to join in the fun and go on a Beatle hunt of my own. So, accompanied by a close friend—who is also a nut!—and armed with only our Beatlemania and a package of chocolate chip cookies, we began our first onslaught.

In order to get to the house, we had to first cross a wide ravine. However—this was no *ordinary* ravine. This one included a marvelous selection of overgrown shrubs, poison ivy, hideous spiders, oversized trees, and just for added effect—a couple of barbed wire fences. But what's a barbed wire fence where a Beatle is concerned, right?

Needless to say, by the time we had crossed through the jungle of mud and drippy shrubbery, we were drenched. And the fact that it was only six o'clock in the morning and the sun was still asleep didn't add to our comfort too much, either. But, onward in the names of John, Paul, George, and Ringo anyway.

When finally we arrived at our very last hurdle, we found ourselves just across the road from the Beatle house, separated only by the road—a few trees and plants—and a *barbed wire fence!*

We quickly exchanged hysterical glances, then forged ahead quickly to attempt to crawl underneath the dangerous obstacle. However, there wasn't really enough room between the fence and the ground—about an inch and a half to be exact—so we began looking about for an alternate route.

As we were doing so, we were joined by a group of about eight other boys and girls—all very noisy, and like us—all very wet.

Together, we decided that we would climb the tree in a nearby corner and avoid the wire fence.

Now, mind you—I have nothing personally against the Tom Sawyer life, or anything—but about the most climbing I had ever done in my life was up and down the two steps in front of my home. So you can probably imagine the joy which was inhabiting my heart as I began to *fake* my way up the side of the tree.

Well—I now have a two inch scar to prove that I once climbed over a barbed wire fence . . . but, on to better things. Once over the fence, we all cotton-tailed it across the narrow road to the side of the house, and hid ourselves beneath the shrubbery—which was still soaking wet, due to the fact that the people inside had been running the sprinklers the night before to ward off "guests" just like us.

Atmosphere???

It was very nice sitting on top of those wet and muddy leaves while the trees above us dripped upon us continuously for about two hours. It gave us sort of a feeling of *atmosphere*. You know, it was sort of foggy that morning, so we could pretend that we were doing all of this valiant suffering across the great foam in Jolly Olde. Oh, the loveliness of our little wet selves as we tried to munch on some equally drenched and soggy chocolate chip cookies.

For about two and one half miserable hours, we watched cars driving up and down that hallowed road. We saw such fave raves as Pat Boone, Pat Boone's children, and a number of young actors, actresses and singers driving by. Along with a rather large number of police patrol cars, also driving by, and as they did so—they spoke through a loud speaker the following immemorable lines: "Everyone *out!* If you do not come out of those bushes within five minutes, you will all go to jail!

It was a toss up. Which was worse? The soggy, foggy, drippy underground retreat in which we were currently ensconced—or a nice, dry, warm, well-lighted jail complete with something warm to eat and drink? Well, the jail didn't include a glimpse of the Fab Foursome, so we continued to drippingly cower in great fear everytime a policeman drove by.

At long last, our waiting was rewarded though—we heard a great roar of engines, and a long procession of cars began to stream past us. One by one they drove by, complete with the police escort, until finally a long black limousine pulled into view.

Beatles

Yes—it really was J, P, G, and Ringo—all four waving and smiling at their many fans gathered by the road side. (The same fans who weren't supposed to be there...). So, being good-natured about the whole thing, we decided to wave back—and grinning as widely as possible—we dangled our hands—still clutching the soggy chocolate chip cookies—furiously about in the air above us.

Paul rewarded us with a smile and a wink—and then, they were gone.

And now it is two and a half years later. The Beatles will be returning very soon, and perhaps there will be other Beatle-hunts, in other places, with other Beatlemaniacs. Because Beatlemania, is indeed, an incurable disease—but probably one of the greatest and most enjoyable afflictions known to the human race.

Beatles' Ski Talent "Eager ad Lazy" Instructor Reports

OBERTAUERN, AUSTRIA — Filming another segment of their second movie, "8 Arms to Hold You," the Beatles have been the center of attention on the ski slopes.

How do they rate as skiers? Observers say John Lennon isn't bad. He's had private lessons and spends most of his time on the slopes.

But George has apparently been having a difficult time. Ski instructors are required to catch or tackle him at the bottom of the hill to keep him from coming to grief.

Franz Lang, who has been teaching skiing fundamentals to the Beatles, put it this way: "Some of them are very eager, but others are rather lazy."

He did not name names.

... GEORGE HARRISON

Another Beatle note: They have received EIGHT Grammy Award nominations! These awards are the recording industry's answer to the motion picture Academy Awards, so you should be proud of your boys. The winners will be announced on April 18, and again the Beat wishes the Beatles good luck.

... OBJECT OF BEATLE HUNT

THE BEATLES were unable to attend our Pop Awards Banquet, as you all know. They were kind enough to send us a telegram explaining that they were on their British tour at that time. But this morning the postman delivered a real surprise to us—actual proof of where the Beatles were on December 8. They were getting off the plane in Sheffield, England. So **The BEAT** forgives them.

BEATLES ARCHIVES 1

PAUL McCARTNEY IS CREDITED with starting a musical revolution. The success of his "Yesterday" has prompted a frantic search through other centuries-old material for similar sounds. Matt Monroe and Marianne Faithfull are the latest to record "Yesterday." Strangely enough, despite its huge success in the U.S., Paul's version of the song has not been released as a single in England—only on album.

Beatles Bag Their Tenth Gold Disc

The phenomenal Beatles have won their tenth Gold Record for singles for "Nowhere Man/What Goes On." At least, Capitol Records has asked the RIAA for a Gold Record certification for the disc.

"Nowhere Man," undisputedly the "A" side of the record, was released on February 15 and according to sales figures it sold nearly 750,000 in the first eight days of sales and topped the one million mark on February 28. Since that time sales on the single have continued to soar with an average of 75,000 records moved each week since March 1. Naturally, the disc's sales are slipping now but it is definitely a million seller anyway.

Just as '64 and '65 were the years of the Beatles it looks as if '66 will be no exception. "Nowhere Man" has been their only single released thus far in the new year and being awarded a gold record for it certainly seems to indicate that the Beatles have not lost their tremendous popularity.

And now that they've announced their summer tour of the U.S., *real* Beatlemania will assuredly start up in full force again — as always.

"WHY (2:54) [Al Gallico-BMI—Sheridan, Crompton]
"CRY FOR A SHADOW" (2:22) [Gema—Harrison, Lennon]
THE BEATLES With TONY SHERIDAN (MGM 13227)

The Beatles with Tony Sheridan clicked with, "My Bonnie," and this second MGM entry, contained in their hit LP should be headed up the same success path. Sheridan takes the vocal lead on this rhythm ballad with the Beatles coming in for some close-harmony chanting and big beat instrumentation. Strictly instrumental on the other end with the crew dishing up a pulsating dance delighter. Another solid coin-puller.

'67—Paul's Turn For Putting Foot In Mouth
By Tony Barrow

It's just about one year since JOHN LENNON involuntarily sparked off worldwide controversy via some seriously considered opinions he expressed about stagnation in the church and the contemporary popularity of Jesus Christ and The Beatles.

This year it is obviously PAUL McCARTNEY'S turn! The 1966 Lennon quote was first printed in a *London Evening Standard* feature written by Maureen Cleave and reproduced in America via *Datebook* magazine. The 1967 McCartney quote was first printed in a *Life* feature written by Thomas Thompson and reproduced in Britain via the *News Of The World*, the largest Sunday newspaper.

In gist, McCartney gave the *Life* interviewer a brief but entirely honest answer to a question about LSD. "After I took it, it opened my eyes," he said "We only use one-tenth of our brain. Just think what we could accomplish if we could only tap that hidden part!" He went on to simplify the complexities of world politics by suggesting that if statesmen took LSD there wouldn't be any more war, poverty or famine.

The irony is that Paul's story broke boldly throughout the U.K. national press on his 25th birthday, Sunday, June 18.

The largest headline of all blasted its way across the front page of *The People*. In words two inches tall *The People* screamed: BEATLE PAUL'S AMAZING CONFESSION – "YES—I TOOK LSD."

The *News Of The World* carried a front page picture with the heading BEATLE PAUL SAYS: I TOOK LSD. Inside the paper devoted one entire page to a verbatim reproduction of the Thomas Thompson article from *Life* together with a couple of Henry Grossman's photographs.

The *Sunday Mirror* filled its front page with news of China's H-bomb explosion and a 20-year-old typist accused of taking cabinet office papers. But the main headline on Page 2 shouted: LSD: MIRROR DOCTOR RAPS BEATLE PAUL. The *Sunday Mirror* doctor wrote: "It is not for Paul McCartney to say LSD is or is not addictive. It is a great pity that someone of this popularity should be associated with drug-taking of this kind. Anyone who takes LSD except under proper medical or psychiatric supervision is asking for terrible trouble."

Of course a bunch of Fleet-street reporters invaded Paul's home in St. John's Wood, North London, to invite application of the original *Life* quote.

Paul told them he thought a lot of rubbish was talked and written about LSD. "I had read a lot of sensational stories – like calling it the 'heaven and hell' drug. But that's nonsense" he told the *Sunday Express*.

"I am not, never have been, and never will be a drug addict. The need today is for people to come to their senses. And my point is that LSD can help them. It is obvious that God isn't in a pill but it explained the mystery of life. It was truly a religious experience. It means I now believe the answer to everything is love" he told *The People*.

Confirming that he had taken several trips ("incredible experiences which brought me closer to God"), Paul emphasized at all stages of his press interviews that he was "not advocating that anyone else should try the drug." The last thing he wanted was for his fans to stampede to LSD.

He said "A lot of people talk about LSD without ever having experienced it. I just wanted to understand this drug. I really sincerely hope that people don't get the wrong idea about me. I do not want kids running to take it when they hear I have."

Personally, I thought a lot of fuss was made over nothing when people made such a big thing over Paul's broken tooth. Well, he's had it capped now but I guess he felt he had to explain about it 'cause he told the whole story. "It was quite a serious accident at the time," says Paul. "It probably sounds daft, having a serious accident on a motorized bicycle but I came off hard and I got kicked about a bit. My head and lip were cut and I broke the tooth."

Paul's Fault

Paul admitted that it was entirely his own fault. Says he hit a stone in the road because, "It was a nice night and I was looking at the moon!" He probably won't be looking at the moon anymore because although he had his tooth fixed he still has a scar on his lip. And the moon just isn't worth it.

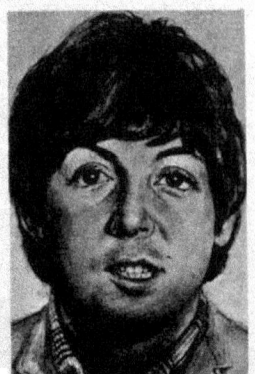

... PAUL McCARTNEY

BEATLES ARCHIVES 1

Another New Book From Beatle

FROM PAGE ONE
scene is pretty wild. John hasn't been doing too much this morning. I presume you got up later than Ringo?
JOHN: Ringo got up about 7:00. I got up at about 9:00, which is late for a film. It's early for me.
DEREK: How do you come to terms with getting up so early when normally you are late risers and late to bed?
JOHN: Well, we just go to bed about 12:00 every night. We go out at 6:00 and pretend it's 11:00 at night, and come in at 12:00, you see.
DEREK: Are you finding it fairly easy to move around in the Bahamas?
JOHN: Oh yeah, it's not bad at all. Just the usual tourists. Aside from that it's not bad.
DEREK: Did you have a big send-off at London Airport?
JOHN: Yes. It was very big because it was a half day for the schools. There were about eight or ten thousand there. It was like the crowd we had when we got back from America. It was very good.
DEREK: That's probably the biggest send-off . . . Well you have had huge crowds going in. Normally you don't get a big crowd to see you out.
JOHN: No, that's right. That's probably the biggest send-off we've had.
DEREK: The Beatlemania level in England, if you'll forgive the phrase, I know you don't like the phrase, is still pretty high. It's very high in America, too.
JOHN: Good.
DEREK: When are you due back in America?
JOHN: I think it's about the autumn or fall, as they call it, I think.
DEREK: There are a few other things I would like to talk to you about, John. Like killing a few rumors. Is it still true that you have only one child?
JOHN: I have the only one child and none on the way.
DEREK: There are an awful lot of rumors about your having been in Hollywood recently, with Cyn, and that wasn't true either?
JOHN: No, I haven't been in America since we were last there.
DEREK: When you leave here where will you be going?
JOHN: To England for two days and then to Austria for a week, and then back to England for the rest of the film.
DEREK: Thank you very much, John. I'l turn you over to Dave now.

DAVE: How are you, John?
JOHN: Fine, Dave, how are you?
DAVE: How's Cynthia?
JOHN: She's great.
DAVE: Good, good. How do you like the weather down here? I understand you're not too happy with it.
JOHN: It's too humid for me. It's not bad . . . it's better than rain, I suppose.
DAVE: The weather's quite different back in England right now. Rather grey, isn't it?
JOHN: I think they're having a bit of snow here and there.
DAVE: What about the movie. How do you feel about it compared to "Hard Day's Night." Is it somewhat the same for you? Are you having less work to do?
JOHN: So far we've had less to do but it's only in the first week. But you know, it's okay.
DAVE: What about your part in "Hard Day's Night." You know a lot of it was spontan-

eous. The part in the bathtub, you recall you talked to me last time . . . are you doing the same here or are you sticking to the script?
JOHN: We're sticking to the script until there's an opportunity of, you know, going away from it. We've done a bit that has nothing to do with the script . . . filmed little bits that the director thought might come in handy for something or other. Whenever a situation arises we do it.
DAVE: Are you thinking of a great deal of things yourself, John?
JOHN: Well, we've hardly done anything on it. It's mainly been people chasing Ringo. So far we haven't done much at all.
DAVE: What about your new book? "A Spaniard in the Works" is the title. It's being published by whom?
JOHN: Simon & Schuster, I presume.
DAVE: They're the ones who published your other one. Is it almost the same as your other one?
JOHN: Well, it's pretty similar, yeah. Better, I think, because it's developed a bit bigger. The drawings are better and it's longer . . . there's more of it.
DAVE: Well that's good. I know it will make your fans happy.

Your other one was a very successful book. Is this one done on short stories again?
JOHN: Yeah, but the stories . . . but there are none that are really short, they're all about four or five pages long.
DAVE: Are these new stories, or are they ones you did a long time ago?
JOHN: They're brand new.
DAVE: The title is "A Spaniard in the Works." Now, you've made a play off the word spanner.
JOHN: Spanner is a wrench in America. When you "put a spanner in the works" you louse everything up. In America you say "put a wrench in the works."
DAVE: Yes, toss a wrench in the works. How do you use the play off words for the title of the book?
JOHN: It's the title of one of the stories about a Spaniard who gets a job in Scotland, that's all. I thought everybody knew the expression. I didn't know they had a different expression in America.
DAVE: Well, we do. Usually we say "don't throw a monkey wrench in the works," or don't throw a monkey wrench in the machine." But now we understand. You use "a spanner" and "a Spaniard"

to play off words. It's very clever.
JOHN: Thank you.
DAVE: What about the sales? The book is published?
JOHN: No, it's not published yet. Won't come out for another month, I don't think. It's finished and everything's done. They're just putting it together in the publishers.
DAVE: Did Paul get a chance to write the front . . . ?
JOHN: There's no introduction on this one. They're thinking of putting the same introduction again exactly. They thought it didn't need one this time or they didn't want one. There were enough pages as it was.

DAVE: What about the people here? Have you had many problems getting around the Bahamas?
JOHN: No, it's not bad at all. There are not many people here.
DAVE: What about your night life. Are you enjoying any night life here?
JOHN: We've been to a couple of places. The club's aren't sort of wild. We wouldn't bother normally with them but they're the only places to go so we have to go to them.
DAVE: You and Paul and George are more or less protectors during the movie. You're trying to keep him from being chased by these different people?
JOHN: He comes in possession of this ring and whoever wears it has to be sacrificed by this big mod that Derek described before, and we're trying to save him and get this ring off his finger. They're other people trying to get it off for various reasons. It's very complicated. Basically what it is is to stop him getting sacrificed.
DAVE: John, there's been a controversy in the States concerning one tune out of your recent "Beatles for Sales" album. The tune was also on the "Beatles '65" album released in the States. Most magazines say that it's Paul doing the tune "Rock 'n Roll Music" and I've continued to say it's you. Will you please straighten this out for us once and for all?
JOHN: It's definitely me. There's only one voice on it and it's me. On the British album, you see, they explain who sings what exactly, and who sings the harmony. They seem to miss it off in the American one, which is silly. It saves all the messing. I heard one on the radio last night who said George was singing and it was me and Paul. There were about eight voices on it and it's all me and Paul. It's mad. They should print it on the album like they do in England and there wouldn't be any messing.
DAVE: On these trips that take you away from your family . . . don't you miss Cynthia and Julian a great deal?
JOHN: Yeah, I miss them like mad. I was going to bring them out here but they'd just be hanging around all the time because that's all there is.
DAVE: You've kept your son out of the press. Has that been your own doing or is it that the press is not really interested in your son?
JOHN: I don't know. They want pictures, I suppose, but I'm . . . you know . . . he's going to have enough problem as it is being my son without getting pictures in when he's a kid. I don't like family pictures anyway.
DAVE: When you go away for any length of time and return, do you find he's de-

—MORE ON PAGE 4

BEATLES ARCHIVES 1

BEATLE RUMORS ENDED!

(Editor's Note: This is the third in a series of Beatle interviews by Dave Hull and Derek Taylor, who talked to John, Paul, George and Ringo at length while they were in the Bahamas filming scenes for their second movie. The recorded interviews were originally broadcast over KRLA. In this interview Derek and Dave are talking with John Lennon while sitting on the beach at Nassau.)

DEREK: John Lennon, in dark glasses, white trousers, blue Plimsolls, black socks, lilac shirt, and multi-colored jacket. Lovely to see you again, John, after about 3 months.
JOHN: Good to see you, Derek, in your grey shirt, blue tie, grey trousers and the tweedy thing.
DEREK: How many songs have you written for the film, John?
JOHN: Altogether we've written fourteen but only seven will be in the film, Derek.
DEREK: Could I have a few titles?
JOHN: Uh, no.
DEREK: Why?
JOHN: Because they don't like giving titles out until they're published. People might write songs with the same title and confuse the market.
DEREK: How many songs were there in "Hard Day's Night," how many originals?
JOHN: I can't remember. They were all originals.
DEREK: What I meant by originals was, how many were created especially for the film?
JOHN: Oh, I don't know how many of them were. Say eight out of ten, if it was ten. But all of these are for the film in this one.
DEREK: Are you taking the same pains to introduce the songs naturally as part of the plot?
JOHN: I think it's very easy in this film. A lot of them are going to be behind-the-scene, like the running in the field in "Hard Day's Night."
DEREK: Sort of background music?
JOHN: Yeah, and a lot of them are going to be just potty. We've done a lot of mad stuff.
DEREK: The script, which I had a look at this morning, looks rather eccentric. The end of the operation, I presume, is to get a different sort of film from "Hard Day's Night."
JOHN: Yeah, and we've done it, haven't we?
DEREK: Well, from the look at the set you have — sitting on the beach in holes in the sand and people in khaki uniforms, red sashes and red turbans . . . some of them carrying guns and some of them carrying shovels. Over by the water's edge Leo McKern, the British actor, is standing looking like a Polynesian high priest. The whole

—MORE ON PAGE 2

Beatlemania Hits Los Angeles Again

The voice at the other end of the trans-Atlantic telephone was brisk but friendly, still retaining a trace of Liverpudlian accent.

"I suppose that takes care of everything. We're looking forward to seeing Los Angeles again. Dodger Stadium should be quite an experience, you know."

"At the rate the ticket orders are pouring in, even Dodger Stadium may not be big enough. There seems to be even more enthusiasm this year."

"Marvelous! Well, give the rest of the fellows at KRLA our regards."

"Thanks. Tell the boys we've never seen Los Angeles so excited. It's going to be a fantastic

Ignited by the recent announcement over KRLA, Los Angeles is again throbbing with an annual summer madness known as Beatlemania.

Ticket orders are pouring in—the deluge began the instant it was announced—for the KRLA Beatle Concert at Dodger Stadium Aug. 28.

To make the concert even more enjoyable, the Beatles are bringing their own special sound system with them to accommodate the large outdoor crowd.

The KRLA disc jockeys will also take part in the program, serving as emcees. It will begin at 8 p.m.

Tickets are priced at $6.00, $5.50, $4.50 and $3.00 and there is a limit of four per order.

Send a certified check or money order, payable to Beatles KRLA along with the coupon below to BEATLES KRLA, Pasadena, Calif.

Be sure to include a stamped, self-addressed envelope and specify the number of tickets desired. See you there.

More Beatle Answers

FROM PAGE TWO
veloped new traits that you weren't aware of before?
JOHN: Oh, yeah, they change all the time at that age. He's only two. Mainly new words he's learned. Quite good fun to see what he's learned.
DAVE: You made a statement that I understand was more a put-on than anything else. I thought at the time it was a John Lennon put-on, but most of the American press are not aware of your talent of kidding and that was when at the marriage of Ringo and Maureen when you and your wife drove up in your Rolls-Royce, and you said that George had driven over on his bicycle. You were putting on the world, weren't you?
JOHN: Yeah. Did that get around? I didn't know it.
DAVE: Yes, it made press all across the nation. Everybody was saying "which was the Beatle who arrived on a bicycle?". But he really didn't, did he?
JOHN: No, it was just a joke. He came with me in the Rolls. I just said it to a friend of ours, Maureen Cleve, on the phone and we thought she'd know. But it was so early in the morning that she probably didn't think. She just wrote it down. I forgot to apologize to her, but it's got around the world.
DAVE: Well it was a surprise to everyone, Ringo's marriage. I know it wasn't a surprise to the Beatles because I knew for some time he's been very much in love with her. How long was it before they really got married did they plan on it . . . actually the marriage date?
JOHN: I haven't a clue. I knew there was something in the air but I went on holiday so I was way out of touch . . . nobody was in touch. And I just got back and they suddenly said the date is in two days' time. I said, right. It was quite a shock to us, too, because we knew he was going to get married but not exactly when.
DAVE: Your last holiday was spent where?
JOHN: St. Moritz, Switzerland, skiing.
DAVE: The fact of the matter is, I saw a picture of you sitting down in the snow . . . you had fallen while skiing. Did you take your wife? And Julian?
JOHN: I didn't take Julian because he's too young to learn to ski. They learn about four. I'll take him about four. I took my wife. It was great.
DAVE: Was it a publicity set-up or did you really fall down?
JOHN: Well I fell down a few times but that actual photograph I couldn't fall over. When they waited for the fall, I kept doing it right, so the skiing instructor told me I had to go downhill and fall over as well. So I did fall over. I did fall over a lot. Obviously everybody does.
DAVE: Are you really a good skier? An average skier? How do you rate yourself?
JOHN: Well, both my wife and I did well because we had a private instructor, you see. The people who were in big classes were doing the same stuff at the end of two or three weeks.

And we were going down from the tops, so I suppose we were above average. It takes a long time if you're in a big class of forty. They can't teach you properly.
DAVE: Well, I don't want to bug you anymore. I know you'd like to relax for a second. Thank you so much, John.
JOHN: Good to see you again, Dave.

```
KRLA BEATLE CONCERT 1966
Dodger Stadium, August 28, 8 P.M.

NAME_____
ADDRESS_____
CITY_____
ZIP CODE_____
PHONE_____
```

TICKET PRICE	NUMBER OF TICKETS
$6	1 2 3 4
$5.50	1 2 3 4
$4.50	1 2 3 4
$3.00	1 2 3 4

BEATLES ARCHIVES 1

Derek Taylor Reports
REFLECTIONS OF ENGLISH WEEKEND IN CALIFORNIA

Well . . . many weeks ago I made an aggressive, unqualified and, at that time, unjustifiable predication about a certain group.

"I'll say no more about it this week. But next week . . . watch out for much boasting.

KRLA did it again with the Beatle album. I was driving home when I heard the unmistakable accents of George Harrison on the car radio. He was singing a song I had never heard before and I presumed it was one of those Dave Hull "Hamburg" scoops — you know . . . one of those early Beatle discs which crop up from time to time.

But no. It was a brand new George Harrison composition — the first since "Don't Bother Me" — and on a brand new album which, to be quite honest, I didn't know Capitol was releasing.

As soon as I arrived home I phoned Dick Biondi, who was beside himself with excitement — who can blame him? — and he said, in the words of Al Jolson, "You ain't heard nothin' yet."

And promptly played a beautiful new Lennon-McCartney creation. Plus "Dizzy Miss Lizzy" and "Bad Boy" — two early rockers featured regularly in the Beatles' Hamburg stage performances.

So. A bonus Beatle album slipped dramatically onto the market two months before the breathlessly-awaited soundtrack from "Help."

It's now quite clear that the Beatles are being influenced by folk music. It's equally obvious — and I personally am glad — that they retain a nostalgic longing for hard Rock 'n' Roll.

Dick Biondi was very generous, I thought, allowing Dave Hull to take over the microphone for the last forty minutes of his show. Dave's Beatle link is now so strong that there's no separating the Liverpool four from the Hullabalooer. He was just about to go to bed when the disc became available and he dragged his levis over his pajama trousers and raced to Pasadena.

It's enthusiasm and personal involvement like this which keep KRLA ahead. Believe me. This is true.

What a "home from home" KRLA was during their English weekend. So many songs from across the Atlantic.

FREE BEATLE PIN-UPS
(Regular 50¢ Each)
TO EVERY CUSTOMER WHO PRESENTS THIS AD AT:
HOLLYWOOD WAX MUSEUM
HOLLYWOOD BLVD. AT HIGHLAND AVE.

Beatles At 200 Million

LONDON – Beatles, John, Paul, Ringo and George combined world sales have now reached 200 million singles, according to a recent announcement by E.M.I. Records. An album is counted as six singles.

The group's latest album, "Sgt. Pepper's Lonely Hearts Club Band," which has been released illegally by some U.S. radio stations, was officially released in America on June 1.

BEATLES RECORD ANOTHER SMASH – NO 'HELP' NEEDED

Despite the panic-stricken titles of their two new songs — "Help" and "I'm Down" — the Beatles have no cause for distress.

Their latest single appears to be just as hot as all the other Beatle million-sellers, with heavy sales reported from the moment it was released. As usual, there was also a tremendous backlog of advance orders.

And with the boys scheduled to arrive shortly for their third American tour and the premiere of their movie, it looks like the U.S. is in for another epidemic of acute Beatlemania.

Aside from the commercial success of their latest single, both sides are also drawing raves from the music world.

"Help" — the title tune from the movie — is a prime example of their unique ability to cut a record which is unmistakably Beatles and yet "different" from their previous sounds.

New Bag

In "Help" (a Lennon-McCartney tune, naturally) the Beatles opened a brand-new bag. They used much stronger vocal backing behind John's solo voice. And it is this two-part vocal which gives "Help" that slightly "different" sound.

The flip, "I'm Down," is also a striking example of their versatility. It's a hard-rocker, as wild if not wilder than anything else they ever recorded. Paul takes the lead on this side, but he manages to disguise his voice so well that even the hard-core Beatle-buffs had a hard time deciding just which Beatle it was.

The McCartney voice which shouts out "I'm Down" sounds not even remotely like the McCartney voice which croons "All My Loving."

Bowl Show For Dylan

The Beatles' exciting performance at the Hollywood Bowl will be followed within a few days by another blockbuster—a Bob Dylan Concert.

"Bob Dylan will be at the Bowl on September 3," Bob Eubanks, producer of both concerts, announced.

While the Beatles are scheduled to leave following their Hollywood Bowl performance on August 29 and 30, Eubanks says he will invite them to stay and see the Dylan concert.

Tickets for the Dylan performance can be obtained at Mutual Ticket Agencies, The Automobile Club of America, Wallich's Music City and the Hollywood Bowl Box Office.

Tickets to the Beatle Concert were completely sold-out when the first day's mail arrived, so you'd better hurry if you don't want to miss this opportunity.

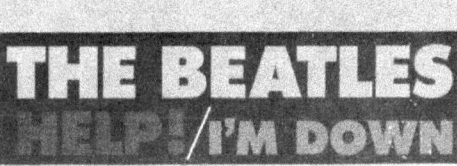

. . . ANOTHER MILLION - SELLER?

BEATLE QUIZ

Here we go again! Five more questions for the KRLA Beatle Quiz.

Those of you who missed the first three weeks of the Beatle Quiz may still catch up by ordering the issues of June 9, June 2 and May 26. You'll find instructions for ordering back issues elsewhere in the BEAT.

The winner, of course, will get to interview the Beatles for the KRLA Beat when they arrive in August. The winner and a friend will also attend a Beatle Concert as guests of the KRLA Deejays.

Additional prizes will be provided for runners-up. In case of a tie there will be additional questions or a drawing to decide the final winner. The contest will cover a ten-week period, with at least five new questions asked each week. KRLA's Derek Taylor, a close friend of the Beatles and their former press officer, will judge the entries for accuracy.

Here we go with five new questions. Join in the fun. Good luck!

Beatle Quiz
KRLA BEAT
Suite 504
6290 Sunset Blvd.
Hollywood, Calif. 90028

CONTEST EDITOR:

Below are my answers to the fourth set of questions in the BEATLE QUIZ CONTEST.

My Name .... Address ....
City .... State .... Zip Code ....
I (☐ am) (☐ am not) presently a subscriber to the KRLA BEAT.

NEW QUESTIONS

16. The Beatles stayed in a house during their last visit to the Hollywood area. On what street was it located? ....
17. What is the largest number of records the Beatles have ever had in the American top-ten at one time? ....
18. On what television program did America get its first look at John, Paul, George and Ringo?
19. Paul McCartney's brother now has his own group. What is the group called and what is Paul's brother's stage name? ....
20. What Hollywood-area club promised the Beatles privacy and then notified the press they would be appearing there? ....

MORE QUESTIONS IN NEXT WEEK'S BEAT

BEATLES ARCHIVES 1

HOW TO MEET THE BEATLES

Faking An Accident Old Trick, But It's One Way To Be Noticed

By Sondra Lowell

You *can* meet the Beatles when they come here, get their autographs, even sit and talk with them. Getting into a Beatle press conference or even a Beatle party isn't nearly as difficult as getting into, for instance, Fort Knox. Of course, you have to be awfully lucky, but sometimes you can help luck along with careful planning. If you really want to meet them, there are all sorts of things you should be doing right now.

One thing you can do is study. Of course, the only way to get an "A" is to end up face to face with a Beatle, and knowing a lot about algebra and history won't do you a bit of good. But reading and rereading all your old movie magazines can be very helpful. It might help to read a few spying manuals, too, and maybe even a couple of books on voodoo or teleportation—that means traveling by mind waves or something.

Anyway, if another girl got to them in a certain way, that might just end up being the way you can meet them. Or somebody else's schemes might give you ideas for your own.

I read one story where a girl was invited to a big party at the Bel-Air hide-out in Southern California last year (and alone!) with the Beatles because Paul shook hands with her at a charity function and liked her. That story probably won't help you at all. Too far-fetched.

The ones about Pat Boone's kids meeting them in Las Vegas or Burt Lancaster's having them over for an evening aren't of much use, either—unless your father is a movie star. Well, maybe your parents are active in some big charity and you can suggest they invite the Beatles to a fund-raising affair.

Or, if your house is large and secluded, you can ask the group to stay with you. But that's pretty impossible too.

Success Story

Not that you shouldn't think up impossible brainstorms. Even if they're absolutely wacky and could never happen, it doesn't hurt to try. Last year five girls from Phoenix dreamed up something that couldn't work in a million years. They started getting ready for the Beatles in February, contacting the mayor of their town and doing a hundred billion other things so that when the Beatles came the girls could present them with the key to the city.

Well, the Beatles never even got to Phoenix so the girls went to Las Vegas, hoping against hope to give them the key there. The Beatles' press agent had been notified, but hadn't told them yes or no.

Then, during the performance, a few minutes before the boys went on, Derek Taylor came out to the girls in the audience and brought them backstage. He'd taken a vote of the Beatles, who agreed to see the girls. You can imagine how they felt! Ringo was lying down at first, but he got up and talked to them, and, along with the other Beatles, answered all their questions.

Each girl shook hands with each Beatle about five times and every girl got autographs of every Beatle on both her white gloves. The girls were especially delighted because they hadn't realized such big stars would be so nice and polite.

See what you can do if you really try? Not a single reporter was allowed inside the dressing room, and yet these teenagers made it. Afterward they got another treat. The Beatles asked where they were sitting and then waved to them from the stage.

Accidental Meeting

Oh, there are hundreds, even thousands of ways to meet the lads. Some girls bumped into them accidentally last year. Some caught up with their limousine in a race down the freeway. As the Beatles scrambled into an elevator in one city, a girl was almost pushed in with them by the crowd.

Paul picked her up and set her down outside the elevator. Granted, it would have been more exciting if he'd put her down *inside* the elevator, but when has he picked you up lately?

In most Beatle-meeting schemes, you're going to have to depend on luck, no matter how good your idea is. So figure out what things might happen that could help you. But don't waste your time waiting for the impossible.

Here are a couple of hints that were learned last year.

1. There's a rule against sticking heads out Beatle windows, and it's hardly ever broken.
2. It's awfully doubtful that you'll find a Beatle in a hotel swimming pool even in the middle of the night or traipsing around outside their hide-out even in disguise. I heard about Ringo combing his hair back and walking through an Atlantic City hotel unrecognized, but it's too hard to believe. Who could mistake a face like that? No, when they go anywhere, it's in freight elevators and limousines and anything else that's sneaky.

Next week I'll tell you how to meet them the way I did, at one of their parties.

figured out. His name, of course, was Charlie Watts, and he was at the time playing with the Alexis Korner band.

Charlie remembers when the Stones first approached him about joining up with them. He says: "So they asked me about kicking in with them. Honestly, I thought they were mad. I mean they were working a lot of dates without getting paid or even worrying about it. And there was me, earning a pretty comfortable living, which obviously was going to nosedive if I got involved with the Stones. It made me laugh to think of them trying to get me in with them too.

"But I got to thinking about it. I liked their spirit and I was getting very involved with rhythm 'n' blues. I figured it would be a bit of an experiment for me and a bit of a challenge, too. So I said okay, yes I'd join. Lots of my friends thought I'd gone stark raving mad."

Six Stones

Finally, the five Stones were together in a group. Actually, there were six Stones because Ian Stewart was still playing with them. They were a long way from that first hit, but their dates were becoming more regular. They played the Flamingo Club
TURN TO PAGE 14

HOTLINE LONDON
Beatle Fourteen

By Tony Barrow

Immediately prior to their Germany/Tokyo/Manila tour THE BEATLES made their first live U.K. television appearance of 1966. On "Top Of The Pops" they did both "Paperback Writer" and "Rain." The last-minute decision for them to appear on the show was made by Brian Epstein after thousands of fan requests had poured into his office, into the U.K. fan club headquarters and into the production suites of just about every major TV company in London!

In Germany the foursome's concert at the Munich Circus Krone was video-taped for subsequent screening as a 45-minute TV spectacular and in Japan Tokyo's NTV channel made a 60-minute Beatle Special out of the boys' Budo Kan Hall concert performance plus newsreel film material.

Kiddie Song

On the day of the "Top Of The Pops" appearance, The Beatles also undertook a late-night recording session at which they completed one of the final tracks for their upcoming U.K. album. Now they have a total of 14 all-new recordings, including the three already available on your side of the Atlantic via Capitol's "Yesterday and Today." GEORGE has penned three new numbers for the set and every one of the others is a LENNON/McCARTNEY composition. Although Ringo has not been involved as a writer, he is certainly featured vocally on one stand-out track which the boys themselves describe as a "special kiddie song."

As previously reported in this column, the eleven new numbers as yet unreleased in America or England are likely to make another U.S. Capitol album later this summer.

RINGO FOLLOWS JOHN: BEATLES TO NEW YORK?

Apparently Ringo Starr would like to follow in John Lennon's footsteps and go the movie route alone. According to the Beatle drummer, their third movie venture has been postponed again and while John, Paul and George seem to have things to occupy them during the long wait, Ringo does not.

"So, it would be very nice if the right film part came along. Brian gets offers for all of us every week, but none of them have suited me as yet.

"I'd rather the four of us filmed together," added Ringo, "but if there is going to be a long wait I'd be happy with something to do in the meantime.

And even if we do go ahead early in the new year I could do something on my own later."

So, Brian Epstein is reportedly on the lookout for a suitable movie role for Ringo.

As you know, the Beatles have announced that they will do no more personal appearances. But there is a gentleman in New York who is doing his upmost to change the Beatles' minds. Sid Bernstein, who promoted the Beatles twice in Shea Stadium in New York, has offered the Beatles $500,000 to return to the United States for two back-to-back appearances at Shea.

The Beatles received $320,000 for their two performances at Shea during 1965 and 1966. In return for his $500,000 offer, Bernstein wants the Beatles' Shea date to be their only performance in the U.S. "so I can get all of the kids from Chicago, Philadelphia, Boston and Washington as well as the New York area." Bernstein lost $680 on the Beatles' 1966 show but declares that "it wasn't really a loss because the experience was so rich."

No word has been forthcoming from the Beatles as to whether they will accept or decline Bernstein's offer.

BEAT Photo: Howard L. Bingham
... RINGO WANTS FILM PART

BEATLES ARCHIVES 1

GEORGE HARRISON doesn't think that America is all that wonderful. "In the U.S.A. people are very hard to get through to, and when you do you find you've got hardly anything in common with them. The living is so fast over there I just can't keep up with it, and Americans who are geared up to it can't understand this," he said after his last visit.

The Four Tops not only received a royal reception from their English fans but from the world of British pop as well when Brian Epstein threw a huge party to honor the American chart-toppers. Guests at the party included John Lennon, George Harrison, Mick Jagger, Keith Richard, Charlie Watts, Eric Burdon and Donovan.

Despite the fact that John Lennon has finished up his movie and returned to England, the four Beatles have yet to get together. George is in London (complete with mustache) but Ringo has journeyed off to Liverpool for a visit and Paul is enjoying himself "somewhere in Europe." However, if all goes as planned, the four Beatles should congregate in London sometime this month to record a single.

"Soul" Nets Gold One For Beatles

By Louise Criscione

A surprise to no one we're sure is the fact that the Beatles have won a gold record for their latest album, "Rubber Soul." What *is* a surprise to many of you is how a gold record is certified. So, with the help of Ron Tepper from Capitol Records we have uncovered the mystery. Would you like to be let in on the secret?

"We'll use "Rubber Soul" as our example of how a gold record is awarded. In the case of "Soul" the album earned a gold record in one day by selling a million dollars worth of albums—not a million albums.

It took the Beatles seven sales days to sell a million albums. Actually the sales figures for the first week totaled 1,192,000 albums sold.

Perhaps you think Capitol counts all those records itself. If you do you're wrong. Before 1958 any record company could award a gold record to whomever they wanted to and there was no one around to dispute the sales.

Legit Winners

But now things have changed. Today the R.I.A.A. does the counting. When a label feels that one of their records has sold the necessary million dollars worth it either writes or wires the R.I.A.A. and then the R.I.A.A. takes an independent accountant out to the respective record company's plant to total the sales.

If the sales are off so much as $100 the gold record will not be certified. The record companies must pay a fee to belong to the R.I.A.A. and they must also foot the bill for the certification of the gold record.

Since the R.I.A.A. has been in existence the number of gold records has been fewer but the number of *legitimate* gold records awarded has gone up. In fact, in the entire year of 1965 only 33 gold records were awarded.

Besides winning a gold one for "Rubber Soul" the Beatles are also set to win another gold record for "We Can Work It Out." What about "Day Tripper?" Wasn't it the flip and didn't it therefore sell just as many copies as "We Can Work It Out?"

Most Requests

Right you are. But in the case of a double-sided hit the gold record is awarded to the side which has the most requests. Okay, but how do you find out which side is the more popular?

They do it very simply. Each record store keeps a chart on which they tabulate the number of requests for records which they receive each week. "Cash Box" and "Billboard" in turn call these stores to find out how the records are doing request-wise.

Having a two-sided hit is a definite disadvantage (funny as that may sound). It means that the requests as well as the air play is split, making it twice as hard to get a record high on the charts.

Except, that is, if you're the Beatles. In which case you earn a gold record in one day and sell a million albums in a week. Pardon me, I mean 1,192,000 albums in a week.

Times are sure hard, aren't they?

THE BEATLES TAKE A BREATHER on Huntington Hartford's Paradise Island during the filming of "Help". Standing behind them is Jerry Pam, a fellow-Britisher who now lives in California and handles publicity for the Beatle films and other enterprises. John seems to fancy the odd hats the boys wear in the movie— he's wearing one of them now.

BEATLES ARCHIVES 1

Formula For Pop Success

By Carol Deck

Ever notice how most of the successful pop groups fall into a pattern? It's almost as though there's a formula for creating a successful group.

Like, for instance, there's the genius — every group (and I'm only talking about the groups that make it — forget those that don't) has at least one genius at it's core (a John Lennon, Eric Burdon or Brian Wilson.) Some groups are lucky and have more than one genius, but it's essential that you have at least one.

Musician

Then too, you've got to have a top rated musician, someone who's mastered at least one instrument to such an extent that he's recognized by his peers as tops for that instrument (a George Harrison or a Jeff Beck.)

It's also essential that you have at least one very good looking member whom fans can point out to their parents as proof that not all rock and roll singers are ugly. You've got to have a Paul McCartney (keep calm kids, I know there's a lot more to Paul than just his looks), a Mark Lindsay or a Davy Jones. Even the Stones, who aren't exactly world reknowned for their beauty, have Keith Richard.

And every group has a quiet member — someone who says absolutely nothing during interviews and generally refuses to express his opinions on the world (Charlie Watts, Chris Dreja and Peter Tork.) These are the ones that worry reporters for we know that usually the less they say the more they think and often have great insights into the world about them but getting it out of them is like pulling teeth. These are also the ones the fans tend to want to mother.

Combinations

Well, those four are the basic essentials for a group, but there's one more that really shouldn't be left out and that is the clown. A successful group usually has one member who is a fun loving, outgoing, extroverted character who generally keeps everyone's spirits up. There's Micky Dolenz, Dennis Wilson, Zollie Yanovsky, Phil Volk. A clown may not be totally necessary, but he sure helps.

And of course you can have any combinations of the above. There's the quiet genius (John Sebastian, Jim McGuinn), the good looking genius (Herb Alpert), and the good looking clown (Herman.) And there are many top rated quiet musicians, for people who dedicate their lives to an instrument tend to be a little on the quiet side with society.

This formula, and variations of it, have proved successful with numerous groups. Look at the Beatles. They're almost a prototype of it. They've got a genius (Lennon), a musician (Harrison), a good looker (McCartney) (I know, I know there's more to Paul than just what meets the eye) and a combination clown and quiet one (Ringo — he's not the extroverted kind of clown, but he has a natural sense of comedy that may put him in the Buster Keaton category some day).

But then there's the Stones. They've got a little bit of everything, as every top group does, but they've also got the mighty mouth — Jagger — who never has played by the rules. Jagger is likely to be, at any point in the game, all or none of these all by himself.

Then There's...

And then there's the Association, who can't be anything but tops just because they have so much of everything. All six of them are capable of genius, they've got a couple of really top musicians and when it comes to clowning, they're all out-right idiots. I suppose if you're looking for great looks, Ted will stand out and when it comes to being the quiet type, theoretically all six are capable, but Brian probably would get the credit in that department.

So you see it really isn't that hard to create a good group. You just find one member in each category, or any combinations thereof, add a lot of luck and you're on your way to your first million seller.

BEATLES have all components for success — Bob Vaughn has UNCLE.

MONKEES have a clown in the form of one Micky Dolenz.

STONES have a non-conformist.

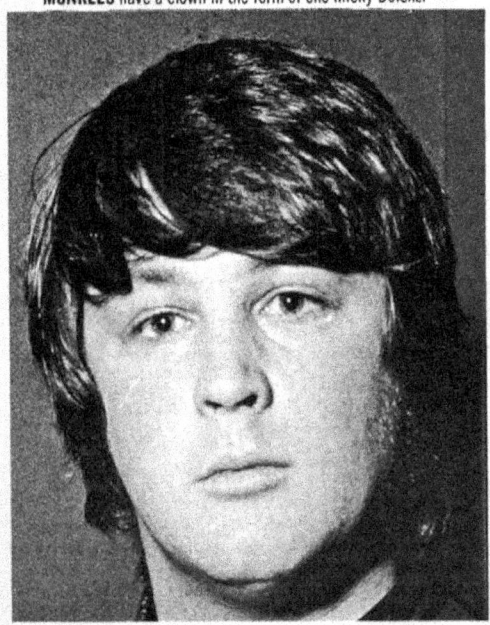

BEACH BOYS have the "genius" of Brian Wilson.

RAIDERS have pony-tailed Mark.

ASSOCIATION number six but wish Elke Summer was lucky seven.

BEATLES ARCHIVES 1

Beatles Writing Songs For Full Length Color Cartoon

By Tony Barrow

The Beatles have written and recorded new songs for inclusion on the soundtrack of a full-length cartoon film which will be shown in cinemas throughout the world as a main feature early next year!

The film, produced in color, has the tentative title "Yellow Submarine." The project is a direct result of the highly enthusiastic reception given to The Beatles' television cartoon series which has yet to be scheduled for showing in the U.K.

King Features of New York, the powerful organization behind the TV cartoons, are handling the production of the full-scale picture. The Beatles handed over to production executives the first recordings of the special new songs at a meeting which took place during one of the group's most recent sessions at the Kingsway Studios in central London.

"Yellow Submarine" will include many existing Beatles' hits plus three entirely fresh compositions designed exclusively for the soundtrack. Two of these are Lennon/McCartney creations; the third will be penned by George Harrison.

Current plans are to delay the commercial release of all three recordings until the cartoon film is seen. At that time the Beatles will bring out a single to coincide with the screening of the picture. To minimize the possiblity of copyright leakage between now and the spring of 1968, a full security clamp has been put down on the titles of the three original songs involved.

For all records up to and including their "Sgt. Pepper" album, the Beatles have used studios belonging to EMI Records in St. John's Wood, North London. Since the end of April they have been moving around several independent recording studios including Olympic at Barnes and Kingsway at Holborn. The first of the three cartoon songs was started at Olympic and completed at Kingsway.

The Beatles are back. Back from their first triumphant visit to America where they dealt a knock-out blow for Britain unparalleled in the annals of political or recording history. The impact that The Beatles have made, first in Britain and Europe, and now in the United States, since they emerged from the cellars of Liverpool just over a year ago is indescribable. They have carried the Liverpool sound from the Mersey to the Hudson and yeah yeahed their way into the hearts and homes of countless millions the world over. The prestige they have brought to the British record industry is an incalculable as the fortune they have taken from it in terms of record sales and music royalties. Their British sales now stand at well over six million and in the United States, where they have left no less than four singles in the Top 100 including the No. 1 and No. 2 and the No. 1 L.P., sales will be even higher. To date they have won four Silver Disks, a Silver E.P.

BRIAN EPSTEIN

two Silver L.P.'s and two Gold Disks plus one Cash Box International Gold Award for their chart topping "I Want To Hold Your Hand" with more to come. The man behind The Beatles and the whole Liverpool operation, 30 year old Manager and Impresario Brian Epstein, accompanied the group on their stateside invasion. This week he, and the entire staff of Nems Enterprises, move into luxurious new offices in the heart of London. From this nerve centre they will master mind the next moves in the Beatles bid to dominate the world. The Beatles two week onslaught on the new world marked the first climax of a steady British campaign to reverse the dominant American post-war trends and influence in popular music. A campaign designed to register internationally with songs, artistes and sounds identifiably British. It has been a collation and concentration of national composing, recording and performing talent which has gradually accumulated sufficient force and potency to achieve its present unprecedented impact.

...JOHNNY MATHIS AND PAUL McCARTNEY grin understandingly as Ringo Starr does his very best to explain a point.

"CAN'T BUY ME LOVE" (2:12)
[Northern Songs Ltd. ASCAP—Lennon, McCartney]
"YOU CAN'T DO THAT" (2:33)
[Northern Songs Ltd. ASCAP—Lennon, McCartney]
THE BEATLES (Capitol 5150)

Here's a Capitol offering that just can't miss. Orders for this brand new Beatles' deck, waxed in England for simultaneous release throughout the world, have already zoomed past the million mark. One half, tabbed "You Can't Buy Me Love," is a driving, beat-filled rocker that sports the foursome's famed 'Liverpool' sound. "You Can't Do That," on the other end, is a pulsating stomp'er bound for chartdom. Watch 'em take off.

BEATLES ARCHIVES 1

A Look Back At Ringo

By Jamie McCluskey III

Time once again to open up our *BEAT* scrapbook and take a look at the childhood memories in picture form, of your Beatle and mine — Ringo Starr.

By now, just about everyone is aware of the fact that Der Ringo had a great deal of illness to contend with during his childhood. As these are not the happiest of memories, there aren't any pictures of those days of Ringo in our book, but there is one which sort of looks back to Ringo's days in school.

Mr. Dawson — who was Ringo's physical training instructor at Dingle Vale Secondary Modern School in Liverpool — provides us with this snapshot:

"He was always wanting to do the same things as the other boys, and I remember one incident which typifies this. It was during the middle of a physical training lesson. All the class was jumping over the vaulting-horse in the center of the gym.

"When it came to Ringo's turn, he was obviously pretty doubtful whether he would get over the obstacle because he had never done it before. He ran up to it, jumped, and just managed to clear it. When he found that he had succeeded and not fallen flat, his face burst into a really broad, satisfied grin."

Ringo's Desk

Mr. Dawson continues his reflections by recounting incidents in the present: "Recently the school put an old desk of Ringo's up for sale. We had thousands of girls queueing up to try and buy it. He has certainly helped to make Dingle Vale School famous."

The next snap in our collection comes to us from Ringo's wonderful Mum — Mrs. Starkey, and she tells us about Ringo's first interest in the fine art of drumming:

"It was in 1957. He was working in Hunt's Sport's Equipment store in Speke at the time, and he started a group, which they called the Ed Clayton Skiffle Group with his only really close friend at that time, Roy Trafford.

"Later on Ringo joined Rory Storm and the Hurricanes. He was playing with the Dark-Town Skiffle group at the time, and met Rory at a 6.5 Special Talent Contest. They got talking and Ringo found that Rory was short of a drummer. He gave Ringo a try, and shortly afterwards, the future Beatle became a permanent member of the group. The Hurricanes had just changed their name at the time. They used to call themselves the Roving Texans, and altered it because they started to play Rock instead of Skiffle."

Nix On Muck

Ringo is a movie star now, and of course he must wear theatrical make-up when he appears on the screen. But he wasn't quite resigned to the whole idea back in "the good old days!" An old friend — Iris Fenton — who also knew George and Paul in the time of the Rory Storm days, provides us with this candid glimpse into Ringo's past:

"The boys were appearing at Butlin's Camp at Pwllheli and it was mutually decided that they

would all look more professional if they wore make-up. Mutually, that is, *except* for Ringo. Ringo flatly refused, saying that he absolutely would *not* "put that muck on my face!"

He was finally forced to smear on at least a thin layer, which he did — somewhat begrudgingly! Iris continues, saying:

"I remember that he was very popular with the girls staying at the camp. They all loved the grey streaks in his hair, even though Ringo hated them.

Starr Time

"Rory thought a lot of Ringo and gave him his own spot in the act calling it 'Ringo Starr Time.' Ringo sang 'Matchbox' and 'Boys.'

"He did not grow his beard until their second session at the camp. I think it was to try and draw attention away from the streaks in his hair."

Iris' mother joins in here to share a snapshot of Ringo's very first swimming lesson with *The BEAT*: "Rory found out that Ringo could not swim a stroke so he decided to try and teach him. It was fine at first, but then they became more ambitious and decided to go underwater swimming which almost caused a tragedy. Rory told me that suddenly a pair of hands appeared from beneath the waves, desperately searching for something to grab onto. Ringo's swimming obviously wasn't good enough for under-water yet. Luckily Rory saw what was happening and pulled him out."

We have lots more pictures in our book of Ringo, but I'm afraid that you're gonna have to wait till next week to see those. See ya then.

RECORD QUIZ

It's happening again. Old songs are coming back! Several of today's chart-busters are past tunes with a new twist. Below, you'll find seven such hits. Some are recent revivals, others may take some remembering. The column on the left lists the names of the songs and their present artists. The column on the right is a jumbled collection of the original artists. See how many you can match!

1. "You've Got To Hide Your Love Away" — Silkie
2. "Over And Over" — Dave Clark Five
3. "Hang On Sloopy" — Ramsey Lewis Trio
4. "Don't Think Twice" — Wonder Who?
5. "Fever" — The McCoys
6. "All Of A Sudden My Heart Sings" — Mel Carter
7. "Where Have All The Flowers Gone" — J. Rivers

a. Paul Anka
b. Little Willie John
c. Kingston Trio
d. Thurston Harris
e. John Lennon
f. The McCoys
g. Peter Paul & Mary

ANSWERS (AND STOP THAT TRYING TO READ THEM UPSIDE DOWN, IT'S BAD FOR YOUR EYES): 1-e, 2-d, 3-f, 4-g, 5-b, 6-a, 7-c.

McCartney —

By Tammy Hitchcock

Labels seem to be essential in the music business. The powers-that-be dictate that an entertainer is not truly successful until he has been labeled. Thus we find one Paul McCartney, "the charming Beatle."

It was often said of McCartney that if he hadn't been an entertainer he probably would have been a politician since he could be relied upon to say the right things at the right time, soothe the ruffled feelings caused by his not-quite-so-tactful cohort, John Lennon, and to smile, smile, smile.

Cunning

There is no question about it — Paul has a cunning way with words. Asked if the Stones are more popular than the Beatles, McCartney lifted a questioning eyebrow: "Are they? I don't think so. I wouldn't like to say who is more popular. The Stones have got their publicity agent and we've got ours. It's up to you who you believe. The Stones are good lads and I don't want people to think that it'll come to us sticking our tongues out at each other like school kids."

Responsibility

At the very beginning when adults were blaming the Beatles for their son's stubborn resistance to the barber's shears, Paul announced that the Beatles didn't have any responsibility whatsoever to their fans. "It would probably be a nicer answer if I said yes we have a responsibility to fans, but I can't be noble for the sake of it."

The Beatles had no sooner land-

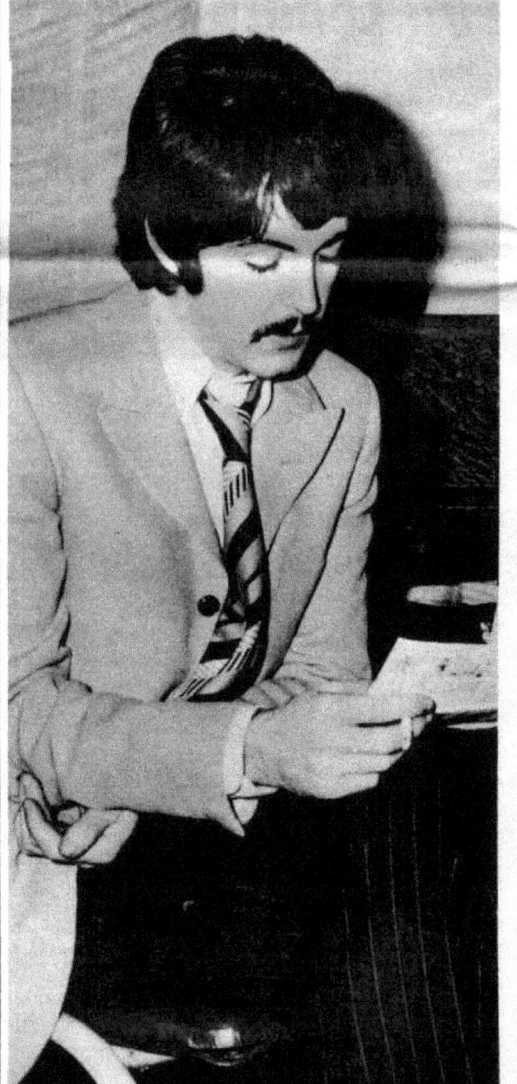

PAUL LOOKS OVER a lead sheet during one of his recording sessions.

BEATLES ARCHIVES 1

Once Through The Charm

ed in America for their first visit than a nationally-syndicated columnist broke the Jane Asher/Paul McCartney romance and the rumors have haunted Paul to this day. Every reporter asked the same question of McCartney: "Are you married or planning to marry Jane Asher?" He smiled and bore the monotonous questioning until finally he was fed up. "I've no plans but everybody keeps saying I have. Maybe they know better. They say I'm married and divorced and have 50 kids – so you might as well say it too."

Charming

McCartney's "charming" label became a drag as time went on and he concentrated more on saying what *he* felt rather than what others wanted him to say. He disliked the protest song movement intensely and said so. "They make me concentrate too much on the lyric – which I don't like.

"I think Barry McGuire's 'Eve Of Destruction' is rubbish. And when I first heard it I thought it was bad. When I saw McGuire in person leaping around in those boots and growling, I just fell about!

"The Manfreds did a protest number on television which was the end. It was so bad they must have written it themselves."

But to say that Paul completely gave up being "the charming Beatle" would be a lie. He was as charming as he'd ever been – only quite a bit more frank and a little more outspoken.

In 1965 the Beatles turned-down an invitation to appear before the Queen at the Royal Variety Show in London and it was Paul who explained the group's decision to the press. "It's not our audience. If we went on and those people didn't like us everyone would say, 'ha, ha, the Beatles failed, they're on the slide'."

His sense of humor he kept intact; his ability to laugh at himself, at the Beatles and at the world, no doubt, saw him through some pretty rough times. Walter Shensen tells one of the funniest stories about McCartney.

"Boorish"

It seems that once Paul approached Shensen with a newspaper review from one of the London papers. "I don't think it's fair," moaned McCartney. "This chap says we're boorish. That's the one thing we're not – we never bore." Shensen explained that "boorish" does not mean "boring" it means "uncouth." "Oh, uncouth," said the relieved Paul. "Well, I think *that's* fair enough!"

The deafening waves of screams which traditionally accompany a Beatle concert received much notice in the press. Reporters demanded to know how the Beatles felt about performing amid the noise.

And it was Paul who answered: "The fans pay their money to come in and if they want to scream then that's their perogative. We don't mind if they scream. Why should we?

"The only thing that counts is that they are having a good time for their money. Anyway, five years ago we were playing without the screams and, friend, it wasn't half as nice. I mean, the bread is important too, you know."

Although it was Lennon who received the attention for making "How I Won The War," it was McCartney who first left the group to try his hand alone. He wrote "Woman" for Peter and Gordon, but asked that a pen name be used rather than his real name. His idea worked – for awhile.

"I knew someone would find out the truth sooner or later," said Paul, "but I'm glad the story didn't leak out until after 'Woman' had become a hit in Britain and America. I hate to read record reviews which say that so-and-so will have a hit just because a Beatle number is involved. It's not fair on the artists concerned.

"Anyway, my idea worked. Incidentally, this is the only song I've published under a pen name. I don't plan to repeat the idea . . . well, not at the moment, anyway!"

Keeps Cool

Paul is well-noted for his cool. It's amazing how he keeps it when people ask some of the most ridiculous questions imaginable. An "image" is manufactured by a press agent and the press itself. It often times has nothing to do with what entertainers are really like. Yet, during the summer of '66 a reporter stood himself up and asked Paul to explain the Beatles' image.

"I don't know," snapped the hard-to-irritate McCartney "Our image is what we read in the papers. You people make up our image. We know what our *real* image. is and it's nothing like 'image'."

McCartney once said: "I'm always pleased when somebody has a hit with one of our songs – it's almost as good as us doing it." Yet, a rather well-informed reporter wanted to know what Paul thought of other artists "stealing" the Beatles' material.

Don't Steal

"They don't steal them," fired back Paul. "No, I know they don't," replied the reporter. "But you just said they did," countered Paul, "and besides, we pinch just as much as the rest of 'em."

The Beatles will never tour America again. The press will never have the opportunity to try their hand at making Beatles squirm. But, undoubtedly, McCartney will continue to look through his charm and allow the world an occasional glimpse of what goes on inside his mind.

McCARTNEY peers over the shoulder of a Byrd.

"BECAUSE IT WAS DARK and I was looking at the moon instead of the road."

BEATLES ARCHIVES 1

HOTLINE LONDON SPECIAL

Behind The Scene With The Beatles

By Tony Barrow

The 'remote control' June 5 appearance of THE BEATLES on CBS Television's "Ed Sullivan Show" was pre-taped in color by Brian Epstein's Subafilms production unit in London on May 19. John, Paul, George and Ringo broke into their current prolonged series of album recording sessions to go in front of the color TV cameras. Location was the EMI recording studios in St. John's Wood, North London, where the boys worked in the massive No. 1 studio for the best part of five hours on the special Sullivan insert.

They arrived for shooting at 9:45 a.m., a ridiculously early start to a Beatleday. By ten they were ready for the first take of "Rain." Two hours later they were ready for a belated breakfast and road-manager Mal Evans brought in four boiled eggs plus a plateful of bread and butter.

At one o'clock they moved onto the second title—"Paperback Writer." For this all four Beatles wore shades—John and Paul used shades with orange tinted glass, George's were green and Ringo's were blue. For this sequence, John and George perched themselves on a grand piano while Paul sat on a stool raised up on a sort of lectern-type rostrum immediately in front of the camera.

Before breaking for lunch the boys taped a special introductory segment of talk to be slotted into the Sullivan Show. In this they said that they'd have loved to make a live-on-the-spot appearance on this particular edition of the Sullivan Show but it just wasn't feasible because of their tight album-making schedule.

The color taping was just one part of a two-day project. Throughout the afternoon of the first day The Beatles stayed in the EMI recording studio to make a series of black and white inserts for screening via various British television shows—the first of these being the BBC "Top Of The Pops" program seen throughout the UK on June 9, the day before the "Paperback Writer"/"Rain" single is issued on our side of the Atlantic.

On the second day the boys traveled out to the West London district of Chiswick where they used the grounds of the impressive Chiswick House as the picturesque open-air setting for further

(Turn to Page 3)

...BUSY FILMING TV INSERTS

Beatle Scope

(Continued From Page 1)

television tapes of the same two songs.

By having these special TV performances pre-taped by the Subafilms unit, The Beatles gave themselves considerable scope so far as background locations are concerned. Much greater scope than they could have been offered in the TV studios where shows like "Top Of The Pops," "Scene At 6:30" and "Thank Your Lucky Stars" are produced. In color or in black and white, the "Paperback Writer" and "Rain" tapes will be made available for TV screenings in more than a dozen different countries all over the world.

After the tremendous reception accorded the Beatles on their American tour, it appears that if all goes well John, Paul, George and Ringo *will* return to the States again next year!

During the filming of "Help," the Beatles as well as their Big Chief, Brian Epstein, let it slip that after this tour their personal appearances would be cut down to the absolute minimum by bypassing next year's U.S. Beatle invasion.

However, now all five of them have apparently changed their minds. Epstein predicts confidently: "They will be back here again next year."

Paul adds: "We love it here and I'm sure we'll be coming again as long as they want us." As long as we want them? He's *got* to be kidding!

Paul Exposed

By Tony Barrow

Here's what I consider to be the best "now-it-can-be-told" pop story of 1966!

Where shall I begin? Well, for a start, let me put it this way—there *is* a fifth Beatle and his name is Bernard Webb. I'd love to send you his photograph but it can't be done. Bernard Webb is a faceless Beatle.

Look closely at the record label on your copy of "Woman," the current chart-climber by Peter and Gordon. You'll see that Webb gets a composer credit and that the song is published through The Beatles' own music company.

In London pop press circles there have been rumors that Webb is connected very directly with The Beatles. Eventually one particularly enterprising journalist did some concentrated investigation at the headquarters of the Performing Rights Society and came up with the mysterious fact that composer royalties for "Woman" were pouring into Northern Songs Limited, the London publishing company which has never handled anything but Beatle compositions!! This raised the question of why Bernard Webb should be handing over all his hard-earned cash to John and Paul.

'Woman' Mystery

Apparently, Bernard Webb was a young university student whose hometown was Leeds, Yorkshire. He had sent in "Woman" to Northern Songs as a possible number for The Beatles to record. The song had been passed on to Peter and Gordon. Apparently Bernard Webb had a current Paris address but had left it and disappeared on some kind of extended skiing trip in the Swiss Alps.

On the face of it, the talented young Bernard might have met up with PAUL McCARTNEY who has just returned to London after vacationing at a secluded ski center hideaway in the Swiss Alps!

Now the secret behind the "Woman" rumors can be told—in one way McCartney and Webb *did*

BEAT Art: Jon Walker

meet for Paul has admitted he is the composer of "Woman!" Bernard Webb was born in the fertile McCartney mind and exists only there and on the label of the Peter and Gordon "Woman" disc!

Behind this deception are perfectly good reasons for cloaking the true identity of Bernard Webb. Paul wanted to put out one of his songs anonymously to see if it could hit the Top Twenty without carrying the usual much-publicized Lennon/McCartney tag. On the other hand Peter and Gordon were anxious to record "Woman" without being accused of riding on a Beatle bandwagon.

I'd say these were two pretty good motives for what turned out to be a totally successful project.

Not Fair

Says Paul: "I knew someone would find out the truth sooner or later, but I'm glad the story didn't leak out until after "Woman" had become a hit in Britain and America. I hate to read record reviews which say that so-and-so will have a hit just because a Beatle number is involved. It's not fair on the artists concerned. Anyway my idea worked. Incidentally, this is the only song I've published under a pen-name. I don't plan to repeat the idea . . . well, not at the moment anyway!"

Who created all the background

(Turn to Page 2)

'Woman' By Paul

(Continued from Page 1)

biographical data for an invisible Bernard Webb? The details were worked out by Paul himself—with helpful suggestions from Dick James who runs the Northern Songs organization.

"Naturally other people in the business wanted to get Bernard Webb" reports Dick. "They recognized 'Woman' as a terrific song and wanted him to write more material for them. For very fair reasons Paul wanted to use another name and I was happy to go along with him on this. Everyone at Northern Songs stuck to the fictitious Webb story until the true story broke and Paul made up his mind that the time had come to tell all!"

Paul is to be congratulated on his elaborate scheme to let "Woman" stand or fall on its own merits. High placings for "Woman" in the charts of so many different countries prove that Paul has made his point. And nobody can claim that Peter and Gordon took their latest winner into the Top Ten on the strength of The Beatles' popularity. Two important points have been proven, nobody has been hurt and the mystery-sheathed secret of an elusive Fifth Beatle has been solved!

Say you read it in The BEAT

BEATLES ARCHIVES 1

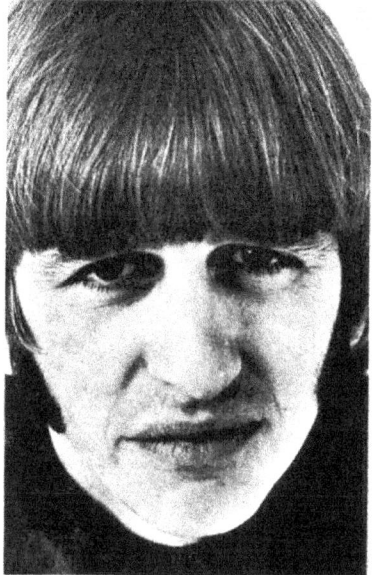

..."HOW COME I ONLY GOT ONE?"

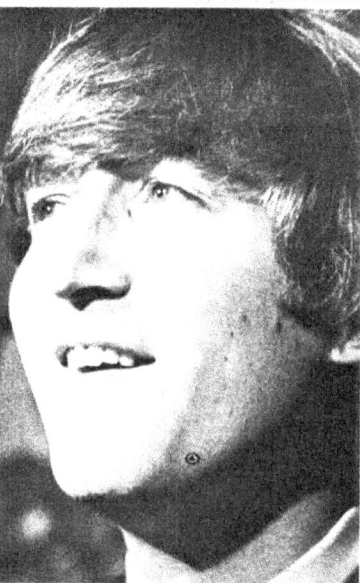

..."'CAUSE THAT'S ALL YOU DESERVED."

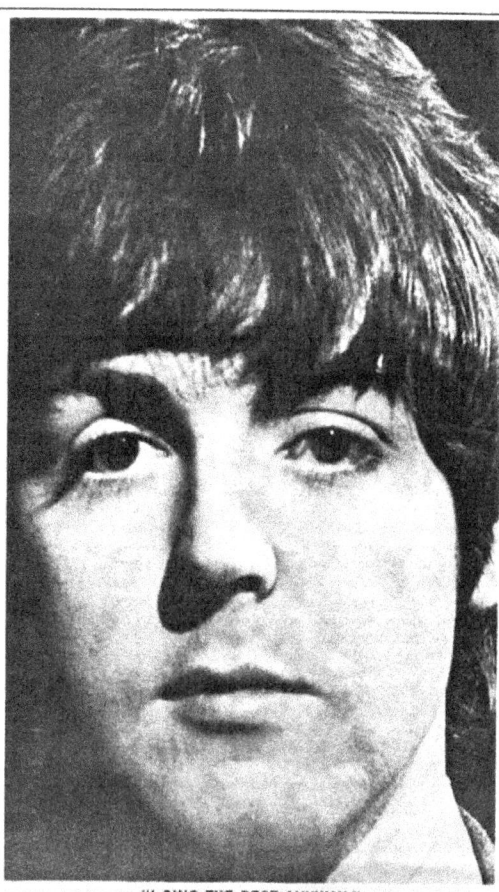

..."I SING THE BEST ANYWAY."

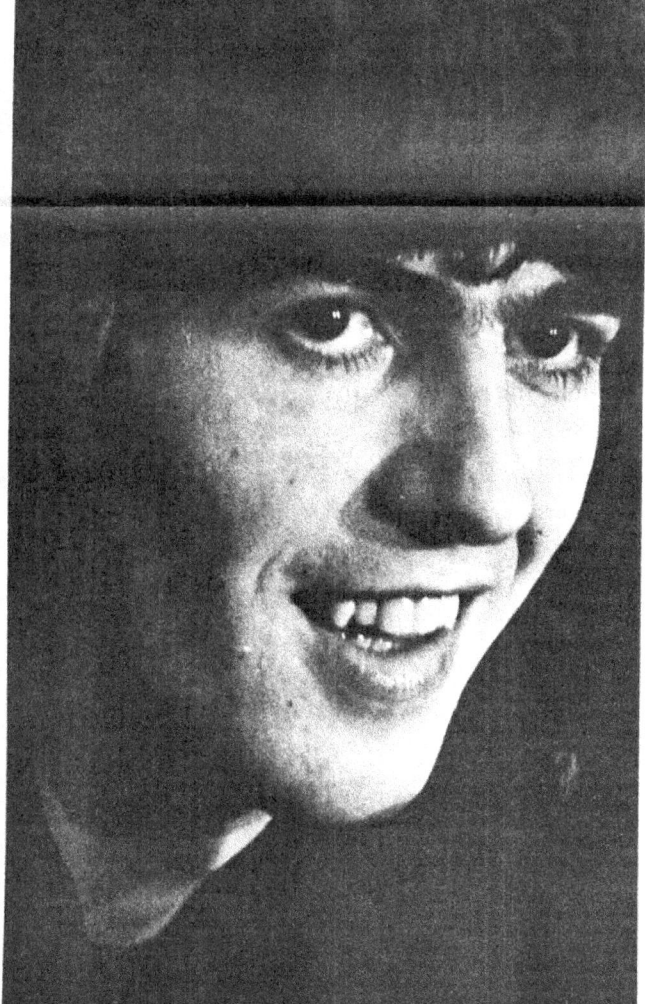

..."YOU MUST BE KIDDING!"

New Beatle Album: 'Yesterday – Today'

Get ready everyone, 'cause here they come again. Talking about the Beatles who are once again about to upset the entire recording industry.

In the last month since the announcement of the release date of the new Beatle single was made, nearly every top group about to release a record of their own went into rush production in order to get their product out before the Beatles' new disc came along and whipped up the charts.

Release Date

It looks as though it's about to begin once again, as the Beatles have tentatively scheduled June 15 as the release date for their brand new album.

Entitled "Yesterday . . . and Today" there will be eleven new tunes on the LP and the new single —"Paperback Writer" b/w "Rain" —will *not* be included.

Many people have protested the choice of Beatle tunes which are included among the American versions of the Beatle albums as well as the number of tunes which are included.

A representative of Capitol records explained to The BEAT that the reason for this is primarily a financial one. In this country, a record company must pay the composer of a song two cents for each song in royalties.

Therefore, on a normal 12-cut record, the composer (if he composed all 12 tunes) would be receiving 24 cents for each album sold. For this reason, if the full 14 to 16 tracks which are on the British LP were included on the American version, it would increase the royalties paid to approximately 32 cents per album.

Extra Tunes

If this were done, the record company, in turn, would be forced to increase the price of the whole album to the general public by at least one dollar. Capitol admits, however, that they are perfectly willing to include the extra tunes if the Beatlemaniacs who are purchasing the albums are equally willing to shell out the extra portions of their allowances.

In the meantime, we can probably expect some rush-releasing of albums from people such as the Association, the Lovin' Spoonful, the Animals, and maybe even Bob Dylan.

There is also a good possibility that this new album by the Fabulous Foursome will be another "Rubber Soul" sort of thing, as reports coming in to The BEAT from across the foam indicate a very extensive use of unusual instruments and instrument combinations as well as some very unusual technical effects.

So, we extend fair warning to all pop performers with an eager eye glued greedily to the nation's charts: Watch out, 'cause the Beatles are coming back!

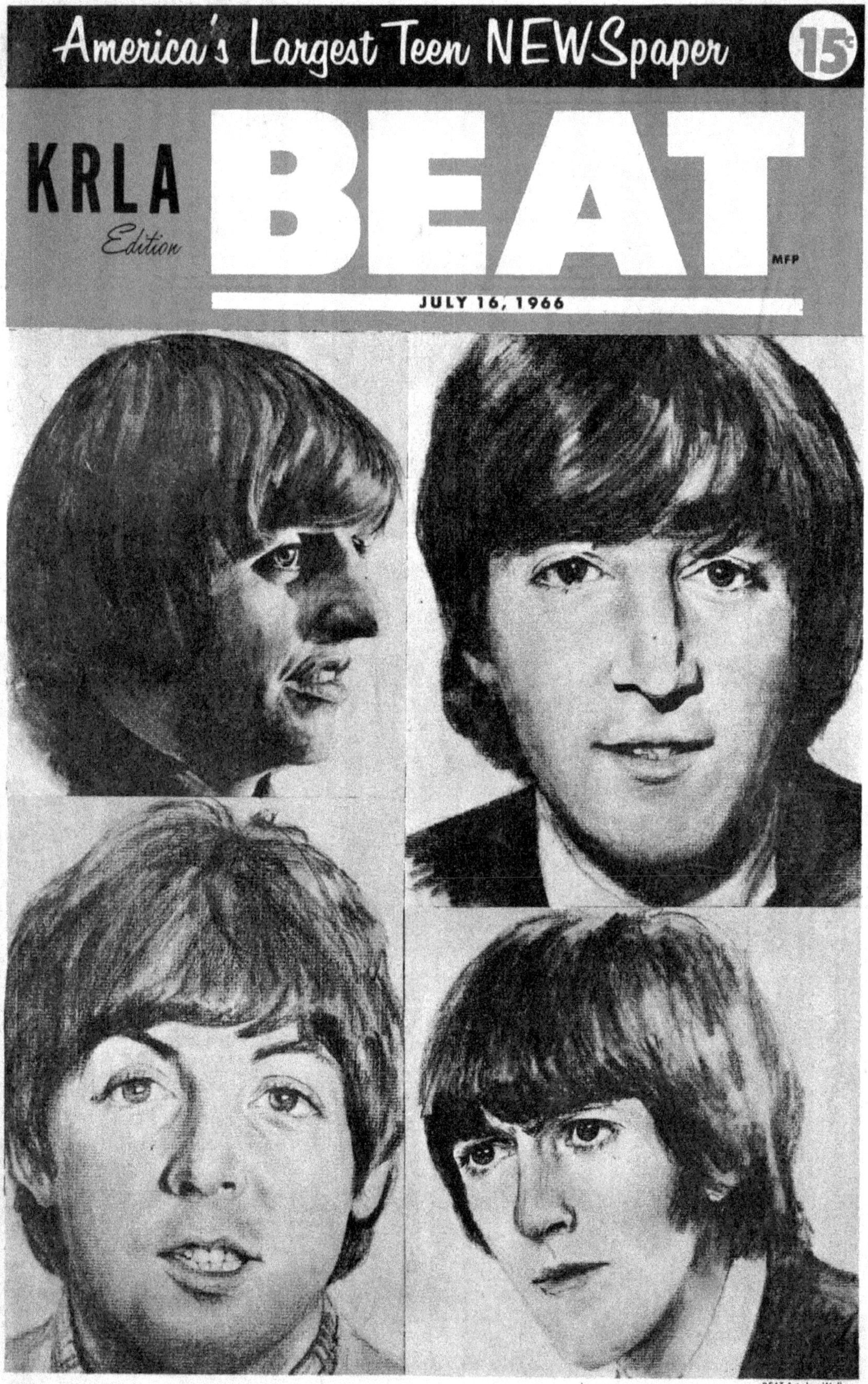

BEATLES ARCHIVES 1

BEATLES ARCHIVES 1

BYRDS Follow Beatles Path To Fame — SEE PAGE 4 —

KRLA BEAT

STONES Say They're Falling In Love — SEE PAGE 12 —

Volume 1, No. 15   Los Angeles, California   Ten Cents   June 16, 1965

BATTLE OF THE BEAT!

DEREK PRESIDES AT NEWS CONFERENCE

Derek Taylor Recalls Early Beatle Appeal

(Editor's note: Last week Derek Taylor began the story of his association with the Beatles. He told of attending a concert in which he first heard and saw the four lads from Liverpool—before they were known to the adult population—and of the tremendous excitement they generated within the audience. This is part two of a three-part series).

I have never been able to isolate their primary appeal, but as Sinatra once said of someone who criticized Judy Garland, "Anyone who doesn't see her talent must have been living under a rock."

We left the theatre with our heads bursting with excitement and enthusiasm. I had convinced the news editor of the London Daily Express that it was worth making a trip to the theatre, and I was expected to turn in about five inches of copy on the concert.

I had also persuaded the picture editor to send along a cameraman just in case there were any scenes.

Nothing Like It

Any scenes! He was an older man than I and he joined us outside the theatre, complaining bitterly about the noise. But he had to confess that in 30 years of journalism he had never known anything like this show.

I asked, "What have you got?" He said, "I've got three lots of pictures. I've got Gerry toweling himself after his act. I've got the screaming fans. And I've got some good pictures of the Beatles in their shirttails, pointing at the camera."

"Marvelous," I said, and the three of us went immediately into a pub.

This is the English journalist's second home where practically all the stories are written — all the best ones, anyway.

In the pub we ordered beer and a packet of potato chips. And the cameraman complained about his ears. I said, "Never mind your ears. What about the Beatles?"

Something Happening

"They ought to get their hair cut," he said, "But they've certainly got something."

I couldn't begin to write because I was still too excited. "Do you realize what's happening?" I asked the cameraman. "This is like nothing we've ever seen."

He said, "It's just as well it doesn't happen every night. I would go out of my mind."

My show-business colleague on the London Daily Herald (one of our rivals) wandered in. He was a middle-aged man of somber countenance with a drooping ginger

—MORE ON PAGE 6

BEATLES vs. STONES

Have the Rolling Stones replaced the Beatles in the hearts of West Coast teens? You'll hear a lot of strong arguments on both sides.

The Stones are red-hot right now with their recordings and drew capacity attendance during their recent concerts in California.

On the other hand, interest is already at a fever pitch for the Beatles concerts scheduled in August, and their new album is causing much excitement.

Recent telephone polls by the BEAT indicate a possible trend away from the Beatles and toward the Stones. But many believe that John, Paul, George and Ringo are in a class by themselves and that any other trend can only be temporary.

What do you think? Write a postcard to the KRLA BEAT or fill out the form below and let us know whether you favor the Beatles or the Rolling Stones.

We'll keep score for the next several weeks. Here's your chance to boost your favorites and prove once and for all which one is tops. Don't let them down.

KRLA BEAT
6290 Sunset Blvd., Suite 504
Hollywood, Calif. 90028
(Check One)
☐ The Beatles are unbeatable!
☐ I vote for the Rolling Stones!

INSIDE THE BEAT
BYRDS, P. J. PROBY
HERMAN, 4 TOPS,
SAM THE SHAM,
THE MIRACLES,
BEATLE QUIZ
PUZZLE PIC

RECENT POLLS SHOW THEM AHEAD

STONES NOW 'IN THE GROOVE'

How It All Began

By ROD ALAN BARKEN

The Rolling Stones are fantastic! They are not only great entertainers, but absolutely the greatest guys in the world.

During the time that I was with The Stones, I asked thousands of questions, and received answers to almost all of them. When The Stones left, I had pages of information.

Here is some of it. More will appear in future issues. (The scene, room in The Ambassador Hotel. There are five Stones sprawled out on two beds, sipping cokes and smoking cigarettes.)

Hello, Rolling Stones!
Mick: Hello.
Keith: Yeah . . .
Bill: Hi, Rod.
Brian: Greetings.
Charlie: Hmmph!
Today, fellows, let's start by going back to the days when it all began. Okay?
Keith: S'pose so.
What was the actual start of The Rolling Stones?
Mick: The day I saw Keith with a Chuck Berry record in his hand. That was the real beginning, when we were still going to school.
Did you form a group?
Keith: No, not then. We just listened to records in those days. The group and all came later.
Mick: Then we met Brian Jones, and he became "Stoned" like the rest of us.
Brian: But we didn't have a name yet.
When did the rest join forces with you?
Mick: After we all decided that we liked the same thing in music. There was Ian playing piano and organ for us, and a friend named Dick Taylor, who used to play bass.
How were those first days, when it was all just beginning?
Charlie: Rough. Nobody understood us.
Mick: They were all caught up on Elvis and Cliff Richards then . . . in 1962 . . . and they gave us trouble about our long hair.
Brian: Bill was the only one with any money to spend in those days, and he used to help us out a bit.
What about the "long hair?"
Mick: It was long . . . you know,

—MORE ON PAGE 12

DEREK TAYLOR AND BRIAN EPSTEIN

MICK JAGGER

BEATLES ARCHIVES 1

A Tender Dylan?

(CONTINUED from PAGE 1)

The album has been delayed for some time now and word had reached *The BEAT* that it was Dylan himself who delayed it.

It had been cut and mastered when he called it back to re-mix some of the numbers on it.

He also changed the title from the original "Blonde on Blond" to "Blonde on Blonde."

There *are* a few things missing on the album, like for instance photo credits and times on the tracks. We can report though, that one side of one record, in the two record set, is one song, titled "Sad Eyed Lady of the Lowland" and it's 11 minutes 23 seconds long.

As for the most important part of the album—the songs—you're in for a surprise if you're expecting more of his far out, highly symbolic babblings that he's becoming known for.

It does contain his latest two singles, "Rainy Day Women #12 and 35," "I Want You," but it also contains some numbers that are probably as close to tender and gentle as Dylan's come in a long time.

One track in particular, "Just Like A Woman," could almost be called a love song—something that we haven't heard from Dylan in quite a while.

Dylan seems to have come back one step closer to the earth in this album. Some of it is down right close to being *real*.

That Hat

One number however, will probably have people talking for quite a while. It's called "Leopard-Skin-Pill-Box Hat," and it's pretty obviously not about a hat. We're rather curious to hear what people are going to get out of this number.

If you listen carefully to the entire album, you'll find some great blues things and, every now and then, a very *human* lyric or two.

For my personal opinion, as a *BEAT* reporter and sometimes Dylan fan, Dylan became a living, breathing, human being for the first time in my mind after I'd listened to this album about 10 times. He was never real to me before, but now I see in my mind a human being rather than just a mind.

We have to assume that all the material on this album is new—written recently—because Dylan doesn't usually regress and pick up material written some time ago.

So we have to assume that this album is Dylan now, as opposed to the Dylan that wrote "Blowing In The Wind," or even the Dylan that wrote, "Like A Rolling Stone."

We haven't seen Dylan for some time and probably won't see him again for a while. The only personal appearances he's made recently were his recent British tour.

Appearances

The only appearance he's even rumored to have scheduled is the Newport Folk Festival in Mass. However, he hasn't appeared at the festival for several years and it seems unlikely he'd go back to it. Dylan rarely goes back to anything once he's left it.

So all we have of Dylan now is this album, but there's enough of it to keep us busy a while.

Beatle fans may note one of the pictures inside shows Dylan holding a framed picture and a pair of pliers that looks very similar to the cover of John Lennon's last book.

True Dylan fans shouldn't be able to keep their eyes or ears off this album for some time.

The BEAT can't offer any explanation for anything Dylan does. We just have to assume that everything he does is deliberate. We *can* recommend that you take this album and give it a lot of concentrated attention.

It's Dylan and it's Dylan now. Maybe he's ahead of his time, or maybe he's outside of time all together. But this latest album is all we have of him as he is today. He won't be the same next time we hear from him.

Behind The Scenes At

Millions of words have already been written about the latest Beatle single, "Paperback Writer," b/w "Rain." Since its release just one month ago, this last single from the Fabulous Foursome has caused more talk and controversy than almost any other Beatle tune to date.

This is, of course, the first more or less electronic effort by the boys and it came as somewhat of a shock to the many Beatlemaniacs around the world. It took some longer than others to catch on to the new styles which the boys set down in this new record, but now everyone seems pretty generally agreed that—like all previous Beatle records—this one is also fantastic.

Instead of criticizing the songs further, then, *The BEAT* is going to take you *behind* the scenes at the actual recording session when the two controversial tunes were created on wax. Come along with us now as we journey to the Number 3 studio at the famous E.M.I. studios in London, and watch a private Beatle recording session.

Scattered all around the studio, you will notice a fantastic assortment of equipment, in the middle of which are the brand new, massive amplifiers the boys are using on this session. Arranged in great disorder around the rest of the room are all manners of pianos, grand pianos, guitars, percussion instruments, amplifiers, and various assorted unnamed pieces scattered about.

Four Beatles

Also situated about the studio are four Beatles. Paul is wearing his customary casual recording outfit, consisting of black trousers, black moccasin-type shoes, a white shirt with fawn-colored stripes, a black sleeveless pullover sweater, and a pair of bright-orange tinted glasses, probably the same specs he was wearing on the now-famous Ed Sullivan show of June 6.

John is clad in green velvet pants, a blue wool vest which he has buttoned up, and black suede boots.

Ringo looks very much like he always looks, in dark trousers and a black turtle neck sweater, but George has distinguished himself on this auspicious occasion with a Mongolian lamb fur coat, black courduroy "Lennon cap" and oblong metal glasses.

Now—the stage is set for an important recording session. Everyone seems tensed and ready to begin—with the possible exception of Ringo, who is calmly seated in one corner of the room behind a large screen where he is engrossed in a game of chess with road manager, Neil Aspinall.

A gentleman present leans over to Paul and asks what he is hoping to do with this record. Paul inquires if he has already heard the lyrics, and the man replies that he has and thinks them to be quite unusual. Paul leans back and explains, "The trouble is that we've done everything we can with four people, so it's always a problem to ring the changes and make it sound different. That's why we have got all these guitars and equipment here."

Elusive Bass Line

Paul then climbed down from the stool he had been perched on, gently placed the red-and-white Rickenbacker guitar he had been playing down, and strode over to the piano. John, George, and George Martin gathered around him in a close huddle and after a few preliminary attempts to find a new bass line, John got up and

..."WHERE'D ALL THE HORSES GO?"

BEATLES ARCHIVES 1

The Beatles' London Recording Session

... BEATLES ARRIVE STATESIDE AUGUST 12.

tried to find the elusive notes on an orange-colored Gretsch guitar, while Paul got up once again and switched this time to a Vox organ.

The original concept for this particular number had been Paul's, and he makes a request for the engineer to play the track (already recorded the night before) back at half speed, so that John and George can add some vocal bits to it.

Once this has been done, they are ready to begin the hardest part of the vocal recording. As the recording light goes on, each Beatle clamps a microphone down upon his head to listen to the track being played back, and then John and George begin to sing, going after some of the very high notes.

Tea Time

But George stops and informs his fellow Beatles that "I don't think I can make it unless I have a cup of tea."

Mal Evans is recruited instantly and dispatched to secure some tea and biscuits. As an extra treat, Mal brings back some toast and strawberry jam which proves to be very popular.

Just as the "tea break" is just about over, Paul receives a sudden spark of inspiration which sends him flying to the nearest piano to tweak out a few notes of "Frere Jacques." He seems to think that it might be very interesting to have this melody line in their new record, and gathers John and George and George Martin around him to try it out.

A few experimental notes are heard from three Beatles, then Paul's head pops up and he asks, "Did you come in at the right place?" But John just grunts, "We can't hear it properly, and anyway I thought that was the end of it." George just glanced at John and explained that it was the *beginning!*

After a few more of these experimental bits are gotten down on tape, they are compared and the "Frere Jacques" idea seems to come up favorites. At this point, Ringo looks up briefly from his chess game to comment that it sounds as though John and Paul are singing through water.

Dum Dum Dee Dum

Those words are definitely *not* music to Paul's ears, so he's off to the organ once more to find a new sound.

Within seconds, Paul has begun creating a sound strongly resembling those made by the Scottish bag pipes. Almost immediately, John leaps across the studio crying, "*You've got it. You've got it!*" and Paul continues playing, adding a few "dum-dum-dee-dumm-dumms" to it. George Martin sticks his head over the piano to inform Paul, "I see what you mean," at which point Paul promptly informs George that he thinks someone else should play it. In other words – *George!*

John and Beatle George go back to the mikes to add some more vocals to the track, and then Paul asks them if they think they are singing right. George Harrison turns around very slowly to Paul, lowering his tinted shades, and looking very much like a rather superior school teacher, replies: To the best of our ability, Paul!"

At last, the tracks are all completed, and all four Beatles seem satisfied with their efforts. It has taken over ten hours of studio time until this tune is finally pronounced "in the can!" but now it is finished and it sounds like a hit to everyone present. Oh yes – they have decided to call it "Paperback Writer." Sounds like a good title for a Beatle record, don't you think?

... "HERE THEY ARE."

BEATLES ARCHIVES 1

Impressive Sight on Beatles Tour

AT FAMED RED ROCK STADIUM IN DENVER

MORE ABOUT: DEREK TAYLOR'S LIFE WITH THE BEATLES

(Continued From Page 1)
mustache.

"What on earth's going on next door?" he said. I told him the Beatles were there.

He repeated the name and asked who they were.

I said, "Get in that cinema and see for yourself."

"You know we never cover pop shows," he said. "The office isn't interested."

"Well, listen," I said, trying to convey some of my own excitement, "You will be covering them the next time they hit Manchester."

Finally he did wander off again to watch the fans outside the theatre. In the months that followed, he and I met many times on the Beatle trail because by the end of the year, the Beatles were the biggest sensation Britain had ever known. But on our later meetings we not only had one cameraman with us, we had two or three and about four reporters per newspaper to cover every single detail and aspect of Beatlemania.

"Let It Run"

Well, anyway, that first night I phoned my office, told them about the show and — though calmer than I was — the night editor decided to give me more space. "If it's as good as you say," he said, "Let it run." This means, "write as much as you like and we'll assess it when we see it."

I was due to cover another act at a nightclub and I was already late, so I went straight on the phone to one of the Daily Express typists who takes down the reporter's story and dictated to him the following report:

"London Daily Express — May 31, 1963.

"Measuring it word by word, let me make a solemn declaration that because of the city of Liverpool, popular music, after years of turmoil and unspeakable rubbish, has become healthy and gay and good again.

"The Liverpool Sound came to Manchester last night and I thought it was magnificent . . .

"The spectacle of these fresh, cheeky, sharp, young entertainers in apposition to the shiny-eyed teenage idolaters is as good as a rejuvenating drug for the jaded adult.

Limitless Energy

"Their stage manner has little polish but limitless energy, and they have in abundance the fundamental rough good humor of their native city.

"It was marvelous, meaningless, impertinent, exhilarating stuff."

No other newspaper carried the story.

My next step was to see the shy, remote, young man who was said to be the genius behind the Beatles. He then had an office in Liverpool, 38 miles from Manchester. And as a Liverpool exile, I was always glad to make the trip back there, whatever the excuse.

Bear in mind that a 38-mile journey in England is quite a distance. England is not yet as blase about mileage as America.

Saw Epstein

So I made an appointment to see Brian Epstein. He was difficult, withdrawn, and not happy to be interviewed.

He kept standing up, straightening his tie, and then sitting down again. He refused for an hour or more to be photographed, but minute by minute the cameraman and I wore him down. And taking a comb from his pocket, he said, "Very well, then. But I do hate personal publicity."

In spite of his coolness, I quite liked the man and I detected in him a desire to be liked — although he went to great pains to conceal this. Below are extracts from the interview published in the London Daily Express on June 20, 1963:

"Flanked by the symbols and symptoms of his success sits Brian Epstein, 28, ex-public schoolboy, ex - drama student, ex - furniture store boss, who suddenly owns the top three places in the nation's disc charts.

Guiding Hand

"Epstein's is the cool, clear brain behind the extraordinary flight to stardom of the Beatles, of Gerry and the Pacemakers, and of Billy J. Kramer and the Dakotas.

"These three vocal and instrumental groups have been signed up by Epstein since October, 1961. All like Epstein are from Liverpool.

"This week Gerry, with "I Like It," Kramer, with "Do You Want to know a Secret?" and the Beatles, with "From Me to You," are 1, 2, 3 in the hit parade.

"Never before have three groups — as distinct from solo performers — topped the charts. And when did any one provincial city ever figure so indestructibly in any branch of entertainment?

Liverpool Sound

"The success of the Liverpool Sound — that curiously tough nasal vital impact of beat and voice — has been a feature of the pop music scene for some months.

"Epstein is not surprised. Not by that, or by anything.

"He is a very calm customer, a bachelor, extremely well spoken, fastidious, neat. Were it not for his buckled shoes and the royal blue initials on his white shirt, he could be in shipping or cotton. Or the bank, with an eye on the managership.

"He dislikes publicity, has a deep sense of personal privacy.

Has An Ear

"Also he has an ear for music. Though he can't read it — like each and every one of the young men in his group — and he cannot play any musical instrument."

So It Went On

Well, in the high summer of 1963 and in the fall, the Beatles stepped from the world of pop music into the history books. Beatlemania erupted and the Liverpool foursome became the chief talking point. As Epstein himself remarks in his book, "A Cellarful of Noise," on the writing of which I was later to collaborate, "It became impossible to have a conversation with anyone on any subject without the name of the Beatles cropping up."

(Continued Next Week)

"ATTRACTION FOR"
SHOWS-DANCES
FAN CLUB:
P.O. Box 12
Stanton, Calif.
Tel. (714) 539-5880

The Only Real Fifth Beatle

Dear Readers,
I wasn't sure whether I wanted to write this or not. Now that I've completed it I still don't know. It is a bit sad and rather reflective. It is also a part of the Beatles' life that is often omitted for those very reasons. But Stu Sutcliffe was a part of the Beatles' life and I don't think that they would want him to be glossed over.

Gil McDougall

One of the things that fans like the Beatles for is the fact that their climb to the top, and indeed their lives, has been far from the proverbial bed of roses. At one time or another they have all been hit with unhappiness or tragedy. The greatest tragedy of all fell upon a young man named Stu Stucliffe. Stu, perhaps more than anyone else, would today have the right to call himself "the fifth Beatle."

John and Stu were both attending the Liverpool Institute of Art when they decided that it was time to get out and make their own way in the world. This was very premature as their income was practically negligable. Despite this they moved to a bed-sitter in down-town Liverpool. For some time they had a ball, throwing party after party. Eventually though, starvation got the better of them and they all decided to go home.

John, Stu, Paul and George continued to play all of the bookings that they could get. After a while they got something of a break when they were booked to back singer Johnny Gentle on a tour of Scotland. Great things were hoped for from the tour but absolutely nothing was to come of it. Drummer Peter Best, who's mother owned the Club Casbah in Liverpool, persuaded her to book the Beatles, and this was some encouragement to them. One of their biggest breaks came when they were booked for the Kaiserkeller and the Star Club in Hamburg. Paul was especially pleased about it, and as they had no drummer he talked Peter Best into going with them.

It was in Hamburg where they began to develop the style that was to take the world by storm. Had you told them this at the time you would have probably gotten a very sour retort. They were earning forty-five dollars a week, and were forced to live in two rooms over a cinema. John, Stu, and George shared one room and Paul, Pete and singer Tony Sheridan shared the other room. Tony Sheridan was later to cut, "My Bonny," with the Beatles.

Their home was furnished by six army cots and a single light bulb. Ventilation of the flat was by a fanlight, and there was no heating at all. The flat, with wall-to-wall wood, was threadbare by any comparison. Washing was a problem also, as there was no running water. Just a wash-basin, a stand and a jug. Their diet of cornflakes, bread, and beer probably made John and Stu wish for the old Liverpool bedsitter days.

Despite the privation that they endured this was really a very lucrative period for the boys for this was where they began to form the Beatle-Style. In those early days they all took turns to vocalize. Stu liked to specialize in the soft slow ballads, and really had the frauleins rolling in the aisle. Not that there was much of an aisle to roll in. The clubs in Germany are invariably crammed as full as possible with tables, leaving only a few feet for dancing.

The Star Club and the Kaiserkeller were no exception to the rule, in fact they might well have been ahead of every other club in that parricular sphere. In the vocalizing Pete Best had a couple of comedy numbers which were very well received. When Paul or John played piano, Stu would take up bass or rhythm guitar. He also played some lead.

With all of the frauleins flocking to where they played, the boys were at no loss for dates. Though by this time John had made up his mind to marry Cynthia, and so he took it pretty easy. Stu, on the other hand, met a fraulien named Astrid Kirschner and they went steady from there on in.

The Beatles would proabably have stayed in Germany much longer, but the German Police discovered that George was only seventeen and John had no work-permit. There was nothing for it but to return to England. Stu, being hooked on Astrid, decided to remain in Germany. He then enrolled at the Hamburg College of Art, but had the boys returned he would have probably rejoined the group immediately. Fate however, was not to have it so.

Eventually the Beatles were able to remove the legal restrictions which prevented them from playing in Germany. So, with a string of engagements at Liverpool's Cavern Club having re-inforced their ego, they once again set off for Deutschland. They were looking forward to seeing Stu, all of their friends and even their rooms over the cinema, crummy as they were. A tear-stained Astrid met the Beatles and told them that Stu was dead. Dead of a brain tumor that neither Astrid or the Beatles had known about. They were all stunned, it was too unbelievable. Lennon said hardly a word, there was nothing he could say. Stu was dead and that was that. But John was close to Stu, having known him longer than the others, and he was completely shattered by the news. He said nothing but it was there on his face for all to see. For the remainder of their time in Germany John often went to see Astrid and after leaving he wrote her several times.

Sutcliffe's personality is perhaps still a part of the Beatles, because out of all the musicians that have played with John, Paul and George, he like Ringo Starr is of the same mould. Stu died a painful death. The fact that he lived will be remembered.

BEATLES ARCHIVES 1

Beatles Go Wild On Charts, Come To U.S.

(Continued from page 7)

With this remarkable sales showing to back them up, The Beatles arrive in the U.S. on Feb. 7 for what will undoubtedly be 17-days of tremendous excitement.

BEATLES' U.S. ITINERARY

The group's American trek, as outlined by Capitol Records last week, starts with its arrival this Friday afternoon (7) at Kennedy International Airport. There will be a party of nine, including the four members of the crew, Paul McCartney, George Harrison, John Lennon, and Ringo Starr; its personal manager, Brian Epstein; Biran Summerville, press rep; and two road managers.

Capitol will officially greet The Beatles and transport them from the airport to The Plaza Hotel here following an arrival press conference.

The group will spend the next day (Sat., Feb. 8) preparing for its guest shot on the Ed Sullivan Show next Sunday (9) (A second Ed Sullivan appearance takes place Feb. 16).

On Monday (10), they will face the press and dejays for an entire day of interviews (by appointment) at The Plaza (Fred Martin, the label's public relations director, will handle press activities).

On Tues. (11), The Beatles move on to Washington, D.C. for their first American concert at The Coliseum.

They return to New York on Wed (12) for two concerts (7 pm and 9:30 pm) at Carnegie Hall, which Capitol will record for an LP release.

On Thurs. (13), the group flies to Miami, Fla., where they will prepare (rehearsal day is Sat., Feb. 15) for their second Sullivan Show appearance on Sun., Feb. 16. Plans are indefinite for Fri., Feb. 14.

On Monday, Feb. 17, they return to New York en route to London. As for the group's Carnegie Hall date, the producer of the engagement, Theatre Three Productions, has reported a sell-out for both performances on Feb. 12. The firm also said it is making attempts to bring The Beatles into New York's more than 15,000 seat sport arena, Madison Square Garden. According to Walter Hyman, head of the firm, Brian Epstein, the group's personal manager, had turned down the offer as of late last Thurs (30). However, Hyman indicated that he would pursue the matter further with Epstein.

Open Letter On Alleged Split Between Beatles

Dear *BEAT*:

I've just finished reading your "Beatles Split?" story, and would like to send along some information that might help clear up this new controversy.

When the Beatles appeared in my city this summer, my father attended the press conference. He taped the entire conference for me, and I wouldn't part with this tape for anything, but I will have a copy made and send it to you if you require proof of what I'm going to tell you.

This is the portion of the conference which applies to the subject at hand, and I repeat it verbatim.

A Possibility

Reporter: "Recently, have you seriously thought of breaking up?"

Paul: "What do you mean by breaking up? We haven't thought that the time has come for us to break up, but we've realized the possibility that breaking up is a natural progression because we can't go on forever like this. We have to think about it and prepare for it in case it did happen, which it should, you know. It's got to sometime."

Reporter: "Then you consider breaking up a natural progression?"

John: "Yes, you never know..."

Paul: "Well, we don't know, but we've got to think about it now, so we're not at a loss if it does happen."

This is exactly what the Beatles said, and I think their comments are proof enough that the recent developments are not evidence of any "sudden decision." They are more evidence of "indecision," and not the "sudden" kind.

If they were already willing to discuss the possibility of breaking up way back in August, they must have been thinking about this for a long time. I feel they're *still* just thinking about it.

Comparing their statements in Washington with what they've said on the breaking up subject since, I feel they're thinking about it *less* seriously than they were three months ago. It just seems more serious now because everyone is printing what they're saying.

I hope I'm making myself clear. If their Washington comments had been printed all over the country at the time they were made, the big Beatle-Break-Up scare would have happened then. And probably with more reason than it's happening now. Since they returned to England, they've said nothing this definite. As a matter of fact, they haven't said much of anything.

I think the whole thing is nothing but another attempt, by adult publications (newspapers, etc.) to keep cashing in on the way the Beatles sell more copies for them. Until the trouble in Manila, nothing was said about the Beatles for a long time. But that controversy, and then John's bit about religion sold a lot of newspapers, and now everyone is just trying to keep the ball rolling.

Unfair?

I don't think this is fair, to the Beatles or to their fans. It's making them apprehensive, like they've got to make up their minds right away, and it's making us terrified that they might make a decision we'll find hard to accept.

The possibility of breaking up does exist in the Beatles' minds, or they wouldn't have mentioned it last summer. And they probably wouldn't have mentioned it or felt quite so strongly about it then if they hadn't been under all the pressures that come with a Beatle tour.

I think it is imperative that all publications (including The *BEAT*) drop the subject. If this doesn't happen, the Beatles might be pressured into doing something they had no intention of doing this early in the game. Surely everyone must realize that their eventual break-up as a group is *inevitable*. Much as we love them, even *we* know they can't go on as they are *forever*. But with all the rumors and hysteria, they might just start thinking, "Well, we're going to have to do it someday, and since the trouble has already started, why not get it over with now?"

Premature Burial

If the Beatles do decide to break up within the very near future, I'll always believe it was a premature burial of the group, caused by this latest controversy. But whenever they break up – this year or ten years from now – I hope everyone realizes that we will still have them as individuals.

Paul and George will undoubtedly remain in the music field, while John may divide his time between music and writing (maybe even acting). And if people don't stop speculating on "what on earth Ringo will do with himself," I'm going to start screaming. He's my favorite, and everyone seems to have forgotten that during the first year or so of Beatlemania, Ringo was considered to be the "most likely to succeed" on his own. There were even a lot of rumors about him receiving multi-million dollar offers to star in comedy films.

There are many things Ringo can do when and if he's minus his Beatle-status. And if all else fails, he can always run for President again. Only this time, maybe we'd be fortunate enough for him to win!

Name Withheld By Request
Washington, D. C.

BEATLES (RINGO, JOHN, PAUL, GEORGE) ON WHAT MAY TURN OUT TO BE LAST U.S. VISIT AS A GROUP.

BEAT Photo: Howard L. Bingham

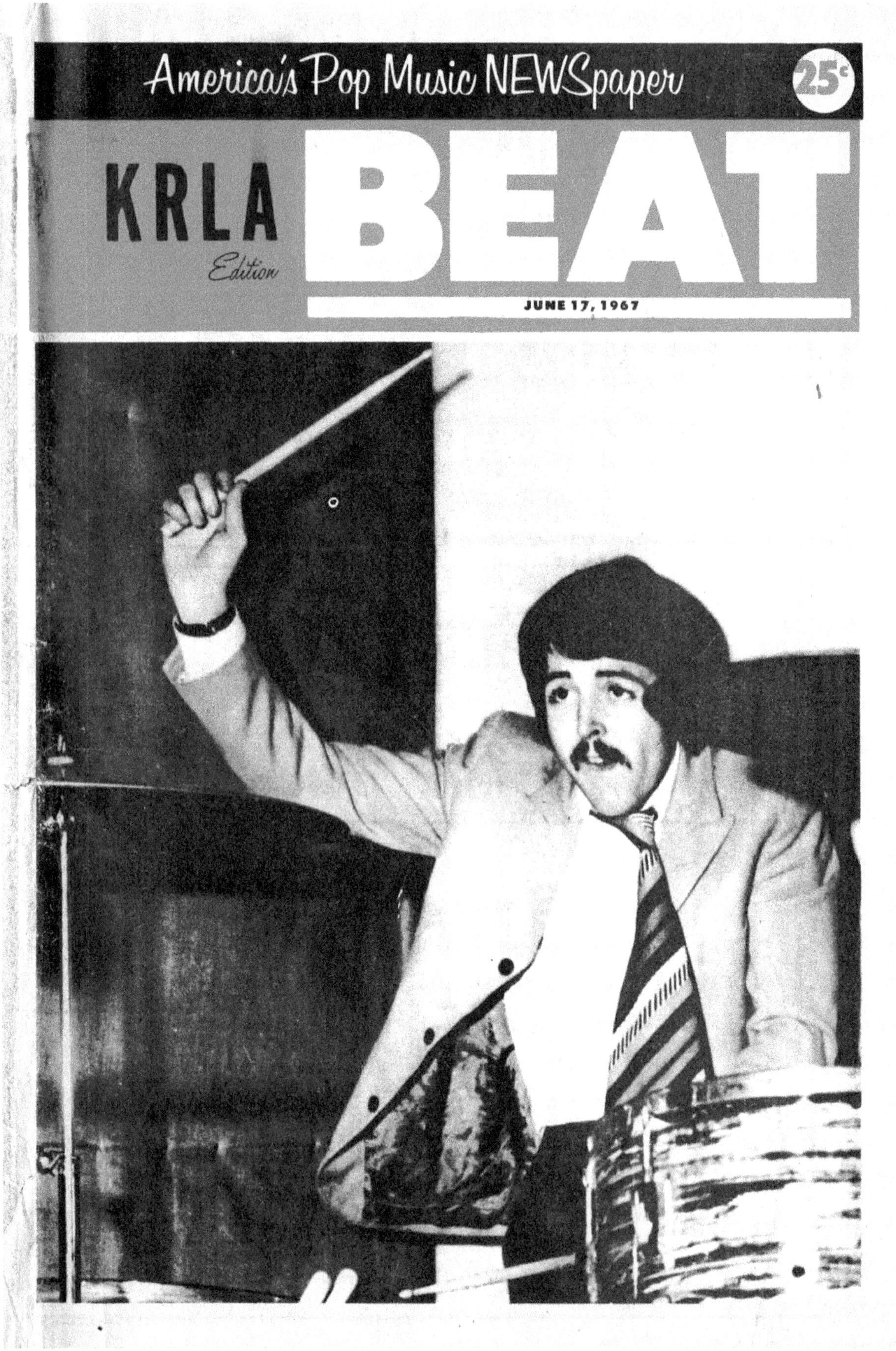

BEATLES ARCHIVES 1

BEATLES ARCHIVES 1

KRLA BEAT

Volume 3, Number 7 — June 17, 1967

FANS FEAR FOR MONKEE'S VOICE

HOLLYWOOD — Millions of Monkee fans have shoved Davy Jones' draft status to the back of their minds and Mike Nesmith's tonsil trouble to the front. Monkee Nesmith entered Cedars of Lebanon Hospital in Los Angeles to undergo a long-postponed tonsillectomy.

Nesmith's personal physician, Dr. Rexford Kenamer, announced that he foresaw a routine recovery period of two weeks but millions of Nesmith's anxious fans are worrying about whether the operation will change Mike's voice.

Said one young fan: "I pray that it won't change Mike's beautiful voice but, you know, sometimes a tonsillectomy will do that and I'll just *die* if Mike sounds even a shade different after this operation!"

During Nesmith's two-week absence, "The Monkees" television show will shoot around him. The recording sessions for their next album have had to be adjusted.

Beatle 'Day' Banned

By Tony Barrow

LONDON — "A Day In The Life," the finest of all the brilliant new "Sgt. Pepper" album compositions, was banned by the British Broadcasting Corporation ten days before the record was released in the U.K.

It is not clear whether or not the B.B.C. followed the example of their American counterparts but the utter folly of the whole thing is that everybody is finding separate yet equally substantial excuses for banishing the ballad from the airwaves.

Apparently your American censors misheard a whole sequence of the lyrics and thought that lines mentioning the town of Blackburn in Lancashire included something about thousands of holes in an arm. So the ban was based upon totally inaccurate information in the first place.

In their announcement the B.B.C. thought that lines about boarding a double-decker bus and going upstairs for a smoke went "a little too far and could encourage a permissive attitude to drug taking." It's difficult to imagine a more unlikely scene than that of a bunch of pot-puffing hippies dreaming away on a London Transport bus, but there you are!

Said deejay Kenny Everett (in whose BBC show the entire "Sgt. Pepper" album was premiered — minus the best item of all): "The B.B.C. have a lot of nice people who just do not know what it is all about."

The most curious fact which emerges from this mass of nonsense is that not one of the self-styled censors on either side of the Atlantic has mentioned the line "I'd love to turn you on" which could be interpreted as a blatant reference to drugs, but has not been. In fact Paul suggests that this refers to turning people on to a better type of pop music.

+++John and Paul have now completed work on the special composition they were invited to write for the worldwide TV show, "Our World" to be screened live via four satellites to a potential audience of 500 million viewers in 31 countries on June 25. The Beatles' contribution to this two million dollar project will take the form of a direct transmission from their recording session at the E.M.I. studios at St. John's Wood in North London. In writing the lyrics, the Beatles have taken into account the fact that the simplest English words should be incorporated in the song so that a maximum of viewers will understand. In addition, they're toying with the possibility of having big boards held up in the studio with some of the words spelt out in different languages. "Our World" will be carried by more than 100 TV stations in America. Nothing will be pre-recorded or pre-filmed but in countries where the time of the "live" transmission is during non-peak TV hours many stations will repeat the entire program hours later.

BEATLES' "Day In The Life" banned ten days before release by BBC because lyrics went "a little too far and could encourage permissive attitude toward drug taking," say the BBC spokesmen.

ROLLING STONES, MICK JAGGER AND KEITH RICHARD, are pictured leaving the Chichester, England courthouse where they pleaded not guilty to charges of possessing narcotics and asked for a trial by jury. The trial date has not yet been set and the two Stones are free on bail. According to the London daily papers, another member of the Stones, Brian Jones, has also been charged with possessing narcotics. The blond-haired Stone was charged separately — he was not at the party thrown by Richards and raided by officers with a search warrant issued under the Dangerous Drugs Act. Jones made his appearance at a West London court and was freed on a reported 250 pound bail. However, he must return to court in early June. Speculation is running quite high as to whether these drug charges will end the successful career of the Stones as a group and whether or not they will be granted U.S. work permits.

BEATLES ARCHIVES 1

The LP Everyone's Been Waiting For Is Here!

Complete with full printed lyrics for every song!

PLUS . . .

Sgt. Pepper paper cut-outs . . .

and inside—a double size, full color foldout . . .

NOW AVAILABLE AT YOUR LOCAL

BEATLES ARCHIVES 1

Lennon's Legend

By Gil McDougall

The perpetuation of Lennon's legend has begun. The legend has begun to spread. It is being spread by the people who know John; by the people who wish they knew him; and by the people who couldn't care less. All are in awe of such an obvious abundance of talent, but it is his attitude to life and the people he meets that confounds critics and friends alike.

When a performer attains stardom he sometimes gets that well-known illness commonly known as being big-headed. John doesn't act this way, and because of this he expects the people that he meets to have regular size heads as well.

To Lennon a rude or snobbish attitude is completely unacceptable, not only in himself but in others as well. Meeting a person with an arrogant fault such as this will provoke insults from John in return.

It has been suggested many times that some promoters, and theatre managers, are actually afraid of John and the other Beatles. Afraid, that is, of the possibility of being humiliated by the boys. It is all part of the myth, but any intelligent person would never allow such thoughts to enter his head. True, John and the others have a bit of a sarcastic way with themselves, but they usually refrain from insulting anyone who hasn't provoked it.

Softy?

Aggressive, intelligent, belligerent, witty, intolerant (with idiots) and irreverent as he is, there is the possibility that Lennon is a lot softer than he likes to let on. He might even be the most vunerable Beatle of all.

Since the loss of his mother Lennon had developed a tough

Of course Lennon's legend is not completely inaccessible. Since achieving his present standing he has developed, perhaps faster than he would have normally, into a mature human being who is capable of great understanding. He has also developed musically at a fantastic rate.

Lennon simply refuses to put on any airs, and acts the same way in public as he does in private. Perhaps this kind of honesty is a little too much for some. After all, though many people surely need it, few of them actually enjoy being told "Where it's at."

Annoying

Lennon often annoys people but he never fails to impress them. A British reporter described his opinion of John: "His face has the fear-neither-God-nor-man-quality of a Renaissance painter's aristocrat." Brian Epstein maintains that John has "a controlled aggression that demands respect." To all of this Lennon would almost certainly say "they must be soft or something."

Interviewers are often shaken, and sometimes amazed by the total impression that they get of John. Like most of us he is a mass of contradictions, but unlike the majority, his talents are very bright indeed.

One of Lennon's greatest qualities is his ability to make friends. Like the time that the Beatles met Elvis Presley during their 1965 tour of the United States. John immediately broke the ice as he said in his best Peter Sellers accent: "Zis is ze way it should be. Ze small homely gathering with ze few friends and a little music." Elvis grinned and Lennon was immediately in.

John and the Beatles don't forget old friends either. They have often gone out of their way to do shows etc., when they are asked by someone who has helped them in their climb to the top.

John and Paul compose at a pretty fantastic rate, and their compositions are recorded by singers and stars from almost all spheres of popular music. While appreciating the compliment John is not always happy about some of the versions of their songs. According to John: "The reason that so many people use our numbers and add nothing to them is that they do not understand the music. Consequently they make a mess of the music."

Lennon himself enjoys running over their first compositions and trying to find some sort of progression in their music. John revealed: "Sometimes, when I am at home, I sit down and put all of our albums on the phonograph. I hardly ever manage to hear them all. I get to the stage where I'm beginning to realize that we have progressed musically and then somebody will start knocking on the door. I feel like an idiot sitting there listening to my own music."

"Coming Home"

John doesn't exactly need the money, but he is doing very nicely as a writer at this particular moment. More important, is the fact that both of his books were received very well critically. Much of his work was compared to that of author James Joyce, who in his day was something of a celebrity. At first Lennon was surprised by the comparison, but he picked up Joyce's "Finnigans Wake," and after reading it reported that "it was like coming home."

It is impossible to say that Lennon is the literary Beatle, or the married Beatle because John simply does not fit into a neat slot like that. John and the other Beatles are different things to different people. The important thing is, however, that Lennon knows exactly what he is and exactly what he wants out of life. He simply wants to enjoy it. And the best of British luck, mate!

"MY BONNIE (MY BONNIE LIES OVER THE OCEAN)" (2:06) [P.D.]
"THE SAINTS (WHEN THE SAINTS GO MARCHING IN)" (3:14) [P.D.]
THE BEATLES With TONY SHERIDAN (MGM 13213)

This sizzling, MGM rock refitting of "My Bonnie Lies Over The Ocean," could turn to gold simply because it bears the name the Beatles, who are currently resting in the #1 slot (among others) with "I Want To Hold Your Hand" on Capitol. Featured singer is Tony Sheridan, who's not a member of the group. Flipside, also with Sheridan spotlighted, has the fellas zipping through a romping up-dating of another oldie.

REJECT MOVIE SCRIPT
Beatles Quiet

By Louise Criscione

The Beatles have a new single out. Another number one I'm sure. But what have they been up to since they tore across the U.S. last August? They've kept pretty quiet, haven't they?

Of course, they did cause quite an uproar when they appeared before the Queen to receive their MBE's. And they also evoked a murmur of controversy when they refused to appear in the Royal Variety Show several weeks ago.

But besides the record, the MBEs and the Royal Show the Beatles have kept well out of the public's eye. They were originally scheduled to begin their third movie, "A Talent For Loving," immediately upon their return from America.

However, the film was postponed for several reasons. The official explanation given was that the weather in Spain (where "Talent" was to be filmed) was highly unreliable during that time of year.

Beatles Unhappy

But conflicting reports leaked out of London. The weather was not the real reason at all. The Beatles were, and apparently still are, a bit dissatisfied with the script as it stands.

If you've read the book, you'll know why. The plot just isn't enough to base a successful Beatle movie on. With a little rewriting, though, it is fairly certain that the Beatles will go ahead and film "A Talent For Loving" as their third movie venture.

The Beatles didn't shed any tears over the postponement. It meant some unexpected free time
(Turn to Page 16)

Two Pooped

NEW YORK — Citations for valor above and beyond the call of duty should be made to Fred Martin, Capitol's director of public relations and Brown Meggs, the label's director of eastern operations, who arranged for the Beatles' whirlwind invasion of Gotham and Miami. The executives displayed herculean stamina and strength throughout the group's occupation of the city. In the top pic a finally exhausted Fred Martin (left) is shown with John Lennon (incognito). In the bottom photo Brown Meggs (right) begins to show signs of fatigue while Ringo Starr, unmoved by the turmoil around him, calmly signs an autograph for a fan

BEATLES ARCHIVES 1

KRLA BEAT

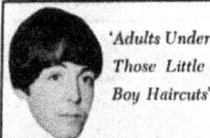

'Adults Under Those Little Boy Haircuts'

Ruined Six New Suits In Filming Scene

March 17, 1965 — Los Angeles, California — Ten Cents

BEATLE MOVIE A BLAST!

Derek Taylor's Report

The Beatles are fine. They feel fine, they look fine, act brilliantly, sing better than ever. On and off-set they have the air of assured young men who have it made. They may not ever claim to be the greatest act showbiz has ever known, but they certainly look it and certainly are. I hadn't seen seen them for three months and of course, they hadn't changed too much. But the feature which struck me most was that they looked more mature. They have more assurance than ever; they are no longer boys.

As Peter Evans, Britain's most important entertainment columnist wrote in the London Daily Express: "They are man-talking adults beneath those little-boy haircuts."

Evans came away from meeting them in the Bahamas, soured. He wrote a biting attack on their off-stage attitude to the press and described them as "rude and arro-

Turn to Page 2

VISITORS TO MOVIE LOCATION TELL OF BEATLEMANIA ANTICS

By Dave Hull

If I wasn't a complete raving, total Beatlemaniac before, then I certainly am now!

What an experience! After spending four days with them in the Bahamas while they filmed portions of the second movie, I feel as wrung out as a piece of laundry.

There is so much to tell I'm sure neither Derek Taylor nor I will be able to do much more than scratch the surface during this edition of the Beat. But we'll continue it from week to week until you have the whole story . . . the whole *book* is more like it, because anyone could write a book after spending a few days with those guys.

They are so full of life and mischief that they're perpetual motion machines. They really wear a person down — even the old Hullabalooer himself.

Different Atmosphere

My previous associations with the Beatles had mostly been in situations where there were crowds all about or near-impossible schedules to meet so that we were unable to really sit down and talk for more than a few minutes at a time.

But this trip was completely different. Although they are working about 12 hours a day on the movie, there is a much more relaxed and casual atmosphere.

After inviting Derek and me to visit them, they were great hosts. Completely friendly, relaxed and outgoing.

To our surprise, Derek and I found that anyone going to the Bahamas where they're shooting the film is allowed to see the Beatles. This includes visiting them on the set!

Friendly to Visitors

Tourists were constantly snapping pictures of them, and the Beatles actually seemed quite happy about it. They even took the time and trouble

—Turn to Page 4

Here they are! The Beatles in the Bahamas on location for their new film. You will see this picture later in other publications, but this week it is a world-wide exclusive for the KRLA Beat . . . a gift from the Beatles to KRLA's Derek Taylor and Dave Hull. Other exclusive pictures of the Fab Four on page 3.

KRLA TOP TEN

1. STOP IN THE NAME OF LOVE
2. EIGHT DAYS A WEEK/I DON'T WANT TO SPOIL THE PARTY
3. MY GIRL
4. THIS DIAMOND RING
5. THE BOY FROM N. Y. CITY
6. RED ROSES FOR A BLUE LADY
7. HURT SO BAD
8. DOWNTOWN
9. FERRY ACROSS THE MERSEY
10. GO NOW

(Complete Listing Page 4)

BEATLES ARCHIVES 1

More About
DAVE HULL
(From Page 1)

to speak to a lot of the visitors. I'll pass along a few of the experiences that occurred while we were there.

At one point, Ringo, who plays a very unusual role — is painted by a savage. That particular scene had to be shot six times, and each time an expensive suit was ruined.

The script called for a giant idol to rise out of the sea on cue. For some reason, the thing fell over, breaking off two of the arms. With boats, a blimp and helicopter required to set it right again, the arms were finally welded back on at a tremendous cost.

Sea Monster

While Malcolm Evans, the Beatles' road manager, was filming a bit as a channel swimmer, a huge sting ray came in close to shore — evidently to see what was going on (You find Beatlemaniacs in every form).

The director quickly ordered Malcolm and the Beatles out of the water. A diver was sent out to scare it off. I didn't envy the diver a bit, because that thing was about 20 feet in diameter and was so huge that everyone on shore could see him out there.

Good Times

We had some great times with John, Paul, George and Ringo and other members of the company. We asked them every question we could think of and got replies to almost all of them. Derek is covering some of those points in his report in the Beat this week . . . and together we'll take up some of the questions and answers, item by item, next week.

Right now I have to sit back and catch my breath while trying to recuperate from an acute attack of Beatlemania.

Paul McCartney: 'If You'll Shut Up About It I Will'

By Tony Barrow

On the evening of Monday June 19, thirty six hours after the British press had reported and examined Paul McCartney's statement regarding LSD (originally contained in a lengthy interview given by the Beatle to Thomas Thompson for Life magazine), Independent Television News sent a reporter to Paul's home to film a follow-up interview on the subject. This was broadcast throughout the UK via the commercial TV network at nine o'clock the same evening.

The following is a direct verbatim transcript of the TV conversation:

REPORTER: Paul, how often have you taken LSD?

PAUL: Er, four times.

REPORTER: And where did you get it from?

PAUL: Well, you know, I mean, if I was to say where I got it from, you know, it's illegal and everything, it's silly to say that so I'd rather not say it.

REPORTER: Don't you believe that this was a matter which you should have kept private?

PAUL: Well, the thing is, you know, that I was asked a question by a newspaper and the decision was whether to tell a lie or to tell the truth, you know. I decided to tell him the truth but I really didn't want to say anything because if I'd had my way I wouldn't have told anyone because I'm not trying to spread the word about this but the man from the newspaper is the man from the mass medium. I'll keep it a personal thing if he does too, you know, if he keeps it quiet. But he wanted to spread it so it's his responsibility for spreading it. Not mine.

REPORTER: But you're a public figure and you said it in the first place. You must have known that it would make the newspapers.

PAUL: Yes, but to say it, you know, is only to tell the truth. I'm telling the truth. I don't know what everyone is so angry about.

REPORTER: Well, do you think you have now encouraged your fans to take drugs?

PAUL: I don't think it will make any difference, you know. I don't think my fans are going to take drugs just because I did. But the thing is that's not the point anyway. I was asked whether I had or not and from then on the whole bit about how far it's going to go and how many people it's going to encourage is up to the newspapers and up to you, you know, on television. I mean you're spreading this now at this moment. This is going into all the homes in Britain and I'd rather it didn't, you know. But you're asking me the question and if you want me to be honest I'll be honest.

REPORTER: But as a public figure, surely you've got a responsibility to not say any . . .

PAUL: No, it's you've got the responsibility. You've got the responsibility not to spread this now.

You know I'm quite prepared to keep it as a very personal thing if you will too. If you'll shut up about it I will!

A few hours before the ITN newscast Paul repeated his desire to emphasize the point that the last thing he wanted was to encourage or even condone the taking of LSD amongst Beatles' fans or anyone else. He said he did not under any circumstances wish to advocate the use of the drug for anyone else and he hoped people would understand this.

. . . AND WORLD REACTION

The new Beatle controversy concerning LSD is affecting an astonishing number of people. The BEAT sought to obtain a concensus of opinion from people involved in the pop scene directly and indirectly.

A police officer in Los Angeles was appalled at what he called "the irresponsibility of the statement. McCartney should realize his influence on his fans and act accordingly." He went on to express his hope that teens who were undecided about the drug would not now go against their better judgment and experiment with LSD simply "because a Beatle took it."

Teachers seemed equally dismayed over the statement. Christine Frees, a Social Studies teacher at a local high school, said she spent a good deal of her time discussing Paul's statement with her classes. She said although she felt the remarks could have some very detrimental effects on teens, she was relieved to hear that her students did not feel influenced by McCartney's statement.

Without Thinking

The fans themselves seem to be divided between those who think that Paul was just being honest and those who think that he acted without thinking. Susan Lefer, a 17-year-old from Chicago, expressed regret that "her favorite Beatle was endangering his health by taking LSD."

The London Daily News tended to agree with Susan when they stated, "Perhaps millionaire McCartney ought to see a psychiatrist who will explain just why LSD is regarded as a dangerous drug. Perhaps he ought to see a psychiatrist anyway."

Unauthorized Possession

"Perhaps Mr. McCartney ought also to consult a lawyer who will tell him it is an offense to be in unauthorized possession of LSD."

However, not all of the comments were antagonistic. Many people felt that Paul was entitled to his opinion and that personal honesty should not have to be sacrificed to public opinion.

Whichever you feel, it is certain that the controversy surrounding both LSD and Paul McCartney's statement concerning its use will not be quieted for a long time.

"And If I'm Elected, I Promise . . ."

BEATLES ARCHIVES 1

BEATLE PHOTOS BY CURT GUNTHER

Behind The Scenes With Beatles... Exclusive Photos

A Hard Day's Night Enroute to Nassau

"Looking for Somebody, Stranger?"

Showdown at the OK Corral

"Please, Ringo, Keep Me In Mind, Anyway"

BEATLES ARCHIVES 1

America's Largest Teen NEWSpaper

KRLA BEAT
Edition

Volume 1, Number 40   LOS ANGELES, CALIFORNIA   15 Cents   December 18, 1965

BEATLES ARCHIVES 1

THE BEATLES GO TO A PARTY

DID THE EXCLUSIVE PARTY BACKFIRE?

When Alan Livingston, president of Capitol Records, tossed a Hollywood party in honor of The Beatles during their recent stay in California, all stops were pulled to make the event—hosted by Livingston at his Hollywood Hills home—as snooty and glamour-laden as they come in Tinseltown.

Creme de la creme was the guest list: Vince Edwards and wife Kathy Kersh (they're back together again and Mrs. Edwards is expecting), Dean Martin, Jack Benny, Bill Cosby, Polly Bergen, Hayley Mills, Suzanne Pleshette, Groucho Marx, Jimmy Stewart, Rock Hudson, and Gene Barry, to mention a mere few. Press was barred and Beatle fans were kept at a distance by courteous but firm police.

From all indications the planned event had earmarks of one whale of an evening in a town that's had more than its share of gay parties.

But something must have backfired.

Only three Beatles attended. George Harrison, in fact, was discovered by BEAT reporters at the Columbia Records Hollywood studios, an interested spectator at a recording session by the Byrds. John Lennon was observed leaving in evident boredom (see photo) before 9:30 p.m. Around 9:45, Ringo Starr and Paul McCartney followed John back to their secluded mansion on Benedict Canyon Road—or elsewhere, perhaps, to livelier happenings?

What happened? We probably shall never know. But we *can* conjecture that the boys weren't any too happy to see fans shivering outside the Livingston house in the night chill while they had to endure the boredom inside.

With the press barred, how then did The BEAT obtain these exclusive photos? Easy. BEAT photographer Chuck Boyd, intrepid and resourceful, merely disguised himself as a punch bowl. He returned empty, of course, but certainly not empty-handed.

Police guard Alan Livingston home in Hollywood, where party was held.

Elated fans and amused policeman await arrival of the boys.

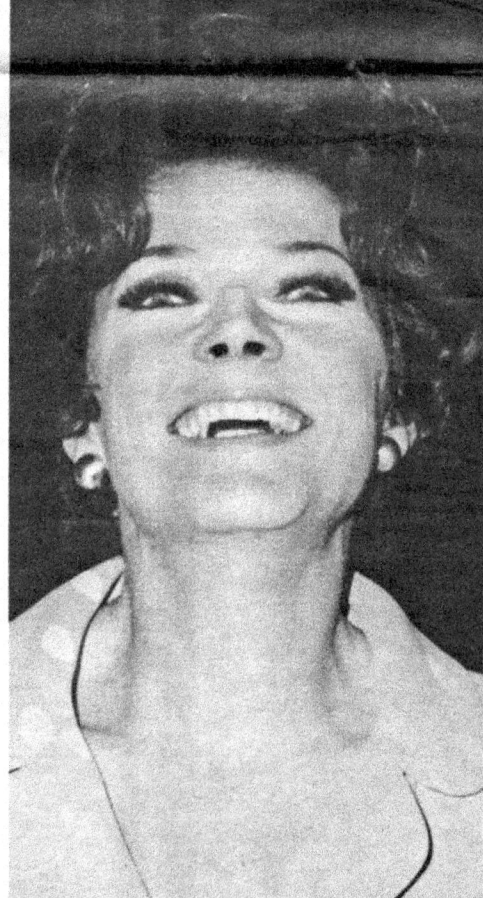

Glamorous singer-actress Polly Bergen arrives at the party

BEATLES ARCHIVES 1

Bored, John Lennon leaves alone — and before 9:30 p.m., too.

In car, hard on John's heels, a dejected Ringo and blasé Paul take off too.

..AND THE BEAT TAGS ALONG!

Departing stars (l. to r.) await their cars: Mr. and Mrs. Vince Edwards (she's Kathy Kersh), Dean Martin (chewing on toothpick), and comedian Bill Cosby.

BEATLES ARCHIVES 1

Beatles Now Talent Scouts

In addition to singing, writing, acting and playing musical instruments, the Beatles are also pretty fair talent scouts!

Thanks to the four, Brian Epstein's star stable now has another boarder — a three man group dubbed Paddy, Klaus and Gibson.

This is a case of knowing each other "way back when . . ." The two groups were friends during the days when the Beatles packed Liverpool's Cavern Club.

After the Beatles' meteoric rise, the two groups sort of lost contact with one another. Recently they met again when Paddy, Klaus and Gibson were appearing at the Pickwick Club in London.

The four Beatles decided right then and there that Epstein should welcome Paddy, Klaus and Gibson into his NEMS camp. And being a wise and shrewd businessman, Epstein seized upon their suggestion.

Of course, everyone is very pleased with the signing, especially Paddy, Klaus and Gibson!

Be on the lookout for these boys — with Epstein's protective wing about them they're bound to go.

THE BEATLES HIDEAWAY (shown here in this exclusive **BEAT** photo by Chuck Boyd) during their vacation-cum-work in Southern California is quiet once more now that the Fab Four have departed our scene. High above Hollywood the rented aerie was under police protection at all times during the Beatles' stay (note guard in photo).

Queen Sends For Fab Four

Millions of people (particularly girl-type people) would do anything to meet the Beatles. Teens, adults, tots, grandmothers and aunts would gladly travel half-way around the globe just to catch a glimpse of the fab four.

However, there IS one lady in this world who is making the Beatles come to her. She is the Queen of England and on either October 21 or October 26, John, Paul, George and Ringo will journey to Buckingham Palace to meet Her Majesty.

Investiture

The occasion is to be the investiture of the MBE awards which the Beatles won some time ago. The announcement of the Beatles' honor caused quite a bit of controversy when several of the previous MBE recipients threatened to return their medals because they felt that such a high honor to the four long-haired Beatles was unbearable and intolerable!

These people even went so far as to demand the Beatles refuse to accept the MBE's. But, of course, you *know* that the Beatles are not about to do anything as crazy as refusing their Queen!

BEATLES PITCH IN, HELP SILKIE FIND HIT SOUND

They have talent, an unusual name, a mastermind manager and the personal help of John Lennon, Paul McCartney and George Harrison.

With all that—the Silkie just couldn't lose. And they didn't either.

Of course, as it most always is, the Silkie's road to record success was long and rather bumpy. They attended Hull University and there in the summer of 1963 three of the Silkie—Silvie, Mike and Ivor—began the first of what was to be many long hours of practice. In October of the same year, the last member of the group, Kev, joined their arduous rehearsals.

Friday, The 13th

But it was not until Friday, August 13, 1965 that the group's big break finally rolled their way. It was on this traditionally unlucky day that three of the Beatles showed up at the Silkie's recording session to oversee the birth of the Silkie's version of the Beatle song, "You've Got To Hide Your Love Away."

Kev Silkie tells us about that historical day: "It all began as a routining session really. We'd no intention of making a record at the time. After working out a basic arrangement with Paul, we asked John to come and help us prepare the number for recording.

"He happened to bring George with him. At first, we were not getting it at all. Too many people making suggestions at once. Then Paul started to play rhythm guitar. It's what you now hear at the start of our record. John shouted: 'That's good—let's use that.' So we all joined in and the instrumental backing was worked out," Kev continued.

Something Extra

"Then we found one of the recording studios was empty and decided to hear what the whole thing sounded like on tape. When we heard our playback, George decided it needed something extra and added the tapping on the back of the guitar.

"Finally we put on the vocal, with George playing tambourine. Four takes and we finished the record as you hear it," Kev explained.

And as we hear it—it sounds pretty good! A hit for the Silkie, the Beatles and, of course, yet another feather in the overloaded cap of the groups' manager, Brian Epstein.

BEATLES ARCHIVES 1

HELP – CLOSEUPS OF BEATLES

By The BEAT Staff

Everyone knows by now what this picture is all about, and millions of teenagers (and postteens) will go and see it just because it's there, and because the amazing Beatles are in it.

So we will not dwell on the story, except to say that some nasty fellows chase Ringo and his pals all over the world, trying to swipe a ring he's wearing.

At the time we saw "HELP!" the Beatles were actually living in Los Angeles, up in exclusive Benedict Canyon. There was some commotion at the rear of the theater, and rumor has it that one of the Liverpool lads snuck in to watch a part of it.

Hundreds Swarming

Police were up in the Canyon guarding the house, hundreds of boys and girls were swarming all over the hills around the house, sometimes getting in trouble, and all the time the Beatles quietly idylled away their few days off.

The long-haired imports from England continued to be the center of the world of show business, as they have been for the past two years.

Some of the girls kept up their vigil for 50 hours at a time.

The Beatles have become such super-stars that it is hard to imagine them as real people. We all get to feeling as though they are fluffs of talcum powder that we just read about all the time.

But they are real, and they seemed to have enjoyed their California vacation, and they

... Ringo

also seemed to enjoy making their second feature film.

Spark Is Gone

It will not live up to the promise of "Hard Day's Night," which surprised everyone by being so good. And even though the same production team also made HELP! the little spark is gone. But don't get us wrong: HELP! is an enjoyable picture, with lots of action and some amazing photography.

It's kind of like "Mondo Cane," only with Beatles. The camera stops here, then there, pops up, down, back, and around first focusing on Ringo's nose, then a musical instrument, then catching the vapor condensing from John's breath as he sings.

It's very much like writing poetry with a 35mm movie camera. Great artistry is shown in the filming of the various sequences, no matter how poorly their supporting cast may have acted the scenes. The Boys themselves hop-scotch through the whole movie with vitality — and with the detachment of the millionaires they are.

The story has at least three good belly laughs and a dozen or more chuckles, and any number of smiles. Interspersed by frowns when you cannot understand what they said or didn't catch the meaning of a fast-flying witticism.

In Full Color

But never mind. It's the BEATLES — right there in full color on the screen! When could you ever see them so clearly, or so intimately?

And who, in the name of the British Empire, can ever forget the famous Paul McCartney Nude Scene? It put Gina Lollobrigida to shame, at least as far as the girls are concerned.

This is the one great value of the picture — *we get to look at the Beatles*, while they cannot look back. We can examine this phenomenon of our age, this quartet that has stormed the gates of mankind and won completely, without ever firing a shot.

The Beatles have conquered the world.

What else is left for them, *except* making expensive home movies?

BEAT STAFFERS (l. to r.) Louise Criscione, Nikki Eden Wine and Susan Frisch clutch passes to "HELP!" as they patiently wait in line to see it again—and again and again!

WAITING FOR 'HELP' — "WE LOVE YOU, BEATLES"

BEATLES ARCHIVES 1

Inside Ringo's Nose

By Gil McDougall

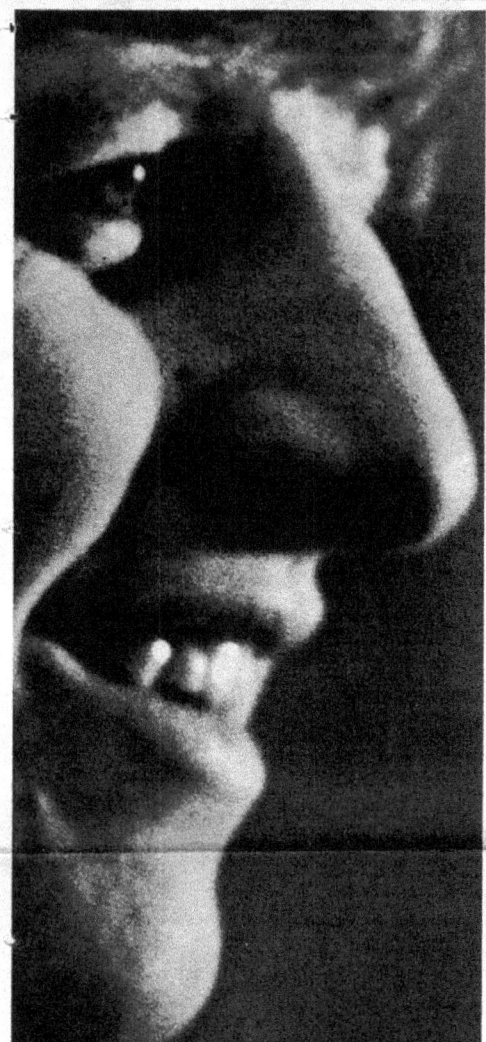

It is clearly one of man's finest super-structures. It is clearly the biggest talking point since the Russians invented Elvis Presley. It is, to coin a phrase of a much wiser man than I, clearly eighteen per cent of his entire body. It is Ringo's nose.

Before all of you Beatle fans take up your pens to let loose a literary onslaught on this writer, let me state quite plainly that I am the world's most fanatical Beatle supporter. I am not knocking Ringo's nose, but merely making observations on it, or rather of it.

Actually the Beatles themselves are right in front when it comes to Ringo nose knocking. They carried on quite a discussion about it in "A Hard Day's Night," and on another occasion when Ringo was asked why he carried so many rings on his fingers he replied, "Because I can't get them all through my nose."

When one considers the many and varied talents that all four Beatles have, it is easy to understand why Beatlemania has been with us so long. But it is also worth a moment of your consideration to ponder as to how the Beatlemania ball first began to roll.

Nose Credit

The place, of course, was England and the causes of the beginning of Beatlemania are numberless, but a large chunk of the credit should be given to Ringo's nose. The Beatles had had a record on the British charts for some time when suddenly the British Press, who love a good story, discovered Ringo's nose. Immediately the Beatles and the nose became the objects of the nation's, and finally the world's, curiosity. The flash bulbs were going so fast that Ringo looked like Blackpool Tower at the height of the season. By October of 1963 you couldn't pick up a paper without staring the Beatles straight in the nose. Marlene Dietrich played on the same bill with them and she said: "It was a joy to be with them. I adore these Beatles." And John said: "It was a joy to be with her. I adore Marlene." in a shrill voice.

Ringo's nose was not the only thing that was subjected to a very close scrutiny. His hair also came under attack. At a British Embassy reception a young man attempted to grab Ringo's hair and received instead a sharp prod in the ribs. The fellow afterwards claimed that he had been attacked. Actually hair is probably the answer to Ringo's problem, if he wants to consider it as a problem.

Beard Goes

Everybody noticed that in "A Hard Day's Night," Ringo looked great with a beard and his hair swept back. When he joined the group John Lennon told him in a phone call, "You can keep your sideburns but the beard has to go." Also his hair had to be combed down in Beatle fashion. If his nose really did start the ball rolling then I guess that it was all for the best. Ringo, I suspect, still prefers the beard. When he, John, Cynthia and Maureen departed London for a vacation this January he was sporting a beard.

Before Ringo joined the Beatles nobody wanted to photograph Ringo's nose very much at all. Working as drummer with the Rory Storm Rock 'n' Roll group Ringo was almost as popular with the girls as he is now. Mrs. Vi Caldwell, who is Rory Storm's mum and a good friend of all the Beatles, had this to say of Ringo: "People are always pointing out his big nose nowadays, but you didn't notice it so much then because he had his hair swept back. It's only since it's been combed forward that his nose has stood out. Paul, John, George and Ringo spent many nights with Rory at his mother's house, drinking tea and talking well into the morning. Mrs. Caldwell remembers Ringo as: "A bit quiet sometimes and could be depressing. But then when John and Paul get started it's a bit hard for anyone to get a word in. Ringo looked a bit small, but he was always my favorite. One day he bought a car, but before he could drive it he had to put a cushion on the driver's seat."

The replacement of Peter Best by Ringo Starr was an unpopular move in just about every possible way. The fans were annoyed and showed it with threats and even violence.

Best Out

Paul and George talked John around to their point of view and then the three of them went to Brian and demanded Best out and Starr in. Despite all this opposition to Ringo he very quickly became as popular as the rest of the Beatles, and Brian Epstein was later to describe him as: "Very uncomplicated and a very good drummer. He is one of the most lovable men in beat music."

It has been said that Ringo Starr is the classic example of how to succeed without really trying. It has also been said that no man ever deserved success more. He doesn't have the drive of Lennon or the charm of McCartney, but he does have a dry wit and a warm friendliness that is guaranteed to defrost solid ice. In his childhood Ringo had more than one illness but he was helped through this period with "the best mum and dad that anyone could wish for." Ringo has expressed his appreciation many times over to his mother and step-father. It took some talking but he finally persuaded them to move into a luxurious home in Liverpool that he had bought for them.

Who Cares?

Still in his mid-twenties the little man from Dingle is a millionaire and about as successful as any man could wish to be. Maybe it was Ringo's nose that started the Beatlemania ball rolling, but who cares! It is his own personality and his value as a performer that keeps him where he is—right on top.

Well, that's it. The two of us, and a couple of million other readers, have been "Inside Ringo's Nose." I doubt if he felt a thing.

Bits And Pieces Of The Beatles

GEORGE HARRISON'S discotheque is not going as well as expected. Actually if there was one thing that the BIG L scene didn't need it was another discotheque. Pretty soon the clubs and the pubs will outnumber the people. Even so, with his name you'd have thought . . . Oh well, maybe if he books the ROLLING STONES!

This writer does try to avoid such epic columnist comments as: RINGO STARR uses pink toothpaste, or JOHN LENNON wears socks, etc., etc. I haven't even revealed that PAUL McCARTNEY likes to sleep in the nude. After all, if I were sued how could I prove something like that. Despite this I would like all America to know that PAUL answered a BBC query on his sleeping attire with: "I wear red, blue and yellow stripes. GEORGE comes round every night and paints them on me." It's an old LENNON retort, but the BBC type just didn't dig the humor.

To build a Go-Cart track in your backyard you've got to have plenty of enthusiasm for that sport. You also have to have as much money as RINGO STARR. I can just see RINGO in about ten years telling young ZAK . . . come on son, I'll race you to the bank . . . and if they wanted to make an obstacle course they could put sacks of two-bob bits at various points along the track.

After observing PAUL McCARTNEY'S father I had to agree with everybody else, he really is a great bloke. It isn't hard to see where PAUL picked up his well-mannered charm. Mr. McCARTNEY senior was a professional musician himself once. If he had met BRIAN EPSTEIN'S father twenty years ago, who knows what might have happened!

No matter how small a comment the BEATLES might make, it is always blown up into something approaching an oration. If one of them happened to mention a partiality for fried onions, many of the fan magazines would build this up into a two or three page story. This really irritates LENNON. When in the Bahamas JOHN said: "People keep asking you who you like and then when you tell them what records you buy, that's it." JOHN went on to say that he had only to casually mention DYLAN once during an interview and in all probability it would be written up as a "big DYLAN thing."

Talking about fan magazines, one of them stated in its February 1966 edition that when the BEATLES played at Hamburg's Star Club, "It was so cold they often had to wear overcoats while performing." I'm afraid that I will have to see photographic proof before I believe that one. A lot of water has flushed through the radiator since 1945. Today the Germans are one of the most prosperous nations on earth, and can well afford heating in their clubs.

It is not true that the BEATLES now own most of BIG L. It's not true at this particular time, but at the rate that they are investing their money in real estate, GEORGE may yet become the Lord Mayor of London. HARRISON especially is concerned with ensuring his financial future. When you think of the many stars who ended up broke, GEORGE'S wisdom certainly shines through.

It is unlikely the BEATLES will ever live permanently any place outside England. It is possible that they may set up "secondary" homes perhaps in Spain. PAUL & JANE already spend plenty of time in Portugal. JOHN is building a home on the Costa Brava coast. LENNON also wants his children to be educated in England. RINGO wants this also but he has said that Spain is a good place to bring up children. GEORGE HARRISON has said very little on the subject, but he does have a sister living in the U.S. Even so it is unlikely that GEORGE will ever call any place outside the U.K. his home.

PETER BEST may not win his libel suit against the BEATLES, but he will surely become the world's best-known loser.

Sam Returning

Those Wooly Bully men, Sam the Sham and the Pharaohs, have just completed trying out their new image on their first European tour.

The group started the tour in West Germany, where their record sales have been fantastic. They then went onto Vienna, Paris and Amsterdam before flying off to London for several television appearances.

The group, who have just shaved off their beards, let their hair grow and changed stage costumes, had one of the top selling records in the world in 1965 with "Wooly Bully."

BEATLES ARCHIVES 1

Yeah, Well Beatles
A Touch of Traffic—A Bit Of Cold

By Tammy Hitchcock

Since George went off and got married (on our deadline day yet—which was most inconsiderate of him really) I thought I should, in all decency, put the Beatles on our "Yeah, Well Hot Seat."

'Course, I'm not too happy with George at the moment. Not because he married Patti. I think that's great! I mean, if he couldn't have *me* he might as well take *her*. What I am upset about is that he got married on *Friday*. I've already explained that Friday is our deadline day but unless you've worked on a paper I don't suppose you really understand what that means.

In this particular case it meant that we had the paper all finished (well, *almost* finished) and George had to go and get married. It tore up the whole office, and I kid you not!

In order to capture the two fab pictures of George and Patti we had to travel all the way downtown to the offices of UPI and AP. Which wouldn't have been too bad except that it was Friday afternoon during the rush hour.

Which isn't funny—honest! Usually the boss and I would have gone over in her Stingray but we didn't have enough time to get lost so "Dear Susan" and I had to go alone.

I drove and Susan ran—literally. You know how hard it is to find a parking space downtown during *any* hour but this Friday everyone outdid themselves. So, I dropped Susan off on the corner in a *No Stopping Zone* and while she jumped out I explained to the policeman how my car just happened to have stopped cold right there at that particular spot.

I don't think he really believed me, but since all the traffic behind me was stopped and everyone was honking he didn't give me a ticket.

Yeah, well that was great but it meant that I had to drive around the block and pick Susan back up. Which was one big mistake. Driving around the block, I mean.

You see, it took approximately one half hour to get around that darn block. When I finally made it I was on the wrong side of the street and that same policeman was eyeing me suspiciously so I decided to make the tour again and pick Susan up on the right side.

The Shivers

Yeah, well it was a little better the second time around (they always say it is, you know). It only took me *fifteen* minutes. That meant that poor Susan had been standing on the corner for a total of 45 minutes—shivering and deciding that I had surely forgotten her but still clutching the precious pictures of George and Patti.

I looked at the policeman, he looked at me—and Susan started walking the *other* way! You see, she wasn't wearing her glasses. She had seen a Mustang pull up but she wasn't sure that it was me and she didn't want to get into a stranger's car. So, she just kept walking.

Yeah, well along about this time the policeman wasn't just *looking*, he was coming over. I figured I'd had it and the next phone call I made would be from jail. I screamed frantically at Susan to for heaven's sakes get in the car and she squinted at the car unable to see for sure if it was me, all traffic came to a halt but all horns were in perfect working order and the policeman was *almost to the car*.

Would you believe total, absolute panic? I'm not exactly sure what happened next but somewhere in the space of a minute, Susan put her ESP into practice, decided it was me after all, hopped into the car just as the policeman reached my window.

Logical Lie

We both explained how George had gotten married and how it had just *ruined* everything and that's why we were holding up five miles of traffic and parked in a No Stopping Zone. Which was really very logical.

Yeah, well that did it. I don't know if it was the sight of a slightly blue "Dear Susan" or the sight of a crazy Tammy (and a woman driver to boot) which did it but something told that policeman not to mess with us. So, he just ordered us to "Get that vehicle moving—at once!"

Anyway, we made it back to the office all in one piece and without making a stop at the local jailhouse. And as a bonus we had two pictures of George and Patti which had come directly from England via Telstar, though I must admit they were almost frozen too.

Yeah, well that doesn't have a heck of a lot to do with the Beatles, does it? And I did start out by saying that I was going to put John, Paul, George and Ringo on the "Hot Seat," didn't I? Would you believe that I tell lies?

You wouldn't? Then I guess I'm forced into talking about the Beatles. The thing I like best about the Liverpool Four is their wild sense of humor. It's gear, fab, groovy and all that other.

Press Agent

You remember the time the Beatles held their New York press conference and someone asked John how he would account for the Beatles' success. "We have a press agent," John replied strictly deadpan.

And then there was the time the Beatles were on their way to the British Embassy in Washington to meet Sir David Ormsby Gore. George turned to their press agent and asked, "Who is this Ormsby Gore anyway?"

"Ormsby Gore," answered the agent. "Don't be soft," snapped George, "I know that but is his name Ormsby or Gore?"

"It's Sir David Ormsby Gore."

"Is he a Lord?" inquired Goerge.

"No, he's a Knight."

"Was he gored when he was knighted?" George asked.

Yeah, well I don't think the press agent ever answered George. And to tell you the truth, I don't know if he was knighted in the gorge or if he was gored when he was knighted.

I think the funniest Beatle quote I ever heard was when George and John were vacationing in Tahiti. They chartered a boat and became regular sea dogs.

Dirty Big Fish

Only John forgot to wear his glasses, so this one day he was peering over the boat's railing when he shouted to George: "Hurry, George, I see a dirty big fish and he's wearing sun glasses."

Being a good friend, George dutifully rushed over and looked down at the water. "John, me lad," George said seriously, "that ugly fish is *you*."

Yeah, well it was too. John can't see much without his glasses (he suffers from "Dear Susan's affliction) and that "dirty big fish" was indeed John's own reflection.

Yeah, well that's the Beatles for you! I wonder how we ever managed to live without 'em.

A Road Tour For Joe Tex

Joe Tex, who first hit the charts with "You've Got to Hang on to What You've Got," is a very busy man nowadays.

He's in the midst of five solid months of one night stands that started in Denver in January and will end in Hollywood.

That's hangin' on to what you've got, Tex.

BEATLES ARCHIVES 1

CHANGED THEIR MINDS

50-Million Frenchmen Not Wrong—Beatles Prove It!

Vive la France!

If you're wondering what that burst of enthusiasm is all about, here's what.

Several BEATS ago, we published an article lamenting the fact that although John, Paul, George and Ringo were hitting the international charts with every new release, they had yet to crack the almost impregnable record market in France.

We went on to chide this country-sans-Beatlemania by saying their lack of interest perhaps proved that fifty million Frenchmen could be wrong after all.

Well, if this was the case, they've changed back to being right. The Beatles have now scored not one but two Left Bank blockbusters. "Yesterday" holds down the number 7 slot on the French charts, with "Help" following on its heels at number 8.

International Charts

Elsewhere in the world, the roar of Beatlemania continues. Last week, "Help" was 3 in Argentina, 6 in Australia, 5 in Belgium, 3 in Holland, 5 in Malaysia, 2 in Norway and 10 in South Africa.

Other Beatle discs on the international charts at the moment are "Yesterday (1 in Hong Kong) and "The Night Before" (2 in Hong Kong and 6 in Malaysia).

As fifty million Frenchmen are putting it (and it's about time), Vive le Beatles!

THEY'LL BE IN HOLLYWOOD in August, and response to ticket availability has been overwhelming. A full-page advertisement, both in THE BEAT, and in the May 8th edition of the Los Angeles Times, brought deluge of applications to the Hollywood Bowl. Management at Bowl is pleased with the KRLA promotion and the amazing response. Perhaps the most exciting news is that THE BEATLES will take a 10-day vacation in Los Angeles in September.

THE BEATLES RETURN!
HOLLYWOOD BOWL AUGUST 29 - 30

Radio Station KRLA and Bob Eubanks Proudly Present Two Concerts By The Fabulous Beatles AT HOLLYWOOD BOWL AUG. 29 . 30

Tickets are available by mail **only**. Applications will be filled by date of receipt.

1. No more than six tickets to any one person.
2. Tickets are $3, $4, $5, $6 and $7.
3. A self-addressed, stamped envelope must be included with your order.
4. Tickets will be mailed July 15.
5. If tickets are not available at the price you order, you will be sent tickets for the alternate date. If tickets at that price are not available for either date, you will be sent tickets at the next lowest price, along with a refund.

MAIL TO:

HOLLYWOOD BOWL
P.O. BOX 1951
LOS ANGELES, CALIF., 90028

TICKET APPLICATION

I have enclosed a check or money order (NO CASH) payable to HOLLYWOOD BOWL, plus a self-addressed, stamped envelope. Please send me the following BEATLE TICKETS:

- ☐ 1 TICKET   ☐ $3.00   ☐ AUGUST 29
- ☐ 2 TICKETS   ☐ $4.00   ☐ AUGUST 30
- ☐ 3 TICKETS   ☐ $5.00
- ☐ 4 TICKETS   ☐ $6.00
- ☐ 5 TICKETS   ☐ $7.00
- ☐ 6 TICKETS

SEND TO ....
ADDRESS ....
TELEPHONE NO. ....
CITY .... STATE .... Zip Code ......

BEATLES ARCHIVES 1

America's Largest Teen NEWSpaper 15¢

KRLA BEAT
Edition

APRIL 2, 1966

BEAT Art: Jan Walker

Pop Lennon Vs. Lennon Pop

KRLA BEAT

Volume 2, Number 3 — April 2, 1966

HOTLINE LONDON
Beatles For U.S.
Tony Barrow

By Tony Barrow

Although definite dates remain unannounced pending progress on the search for a suitable movie script, BRIAN EPSTEIN has released initial information about his 1966 plans for THE BEATLES. They'll be back in America for sure this summer. Brian has been asked to consider the idea of the group undertaking two concerts at New York's mighty Shea Stadium but he has rejected the double date and is thinking in terms of just one performance at the venue.

Before coming to America, The Beatles will undertake short tours in Germany and Japan. It is unlikely that the third movie will move into production before late summer or early autumn but at the end of the year The Beatles will certainly go out on another tour of Britain.

Their most recent U.K. concert tour took place just before Christmas when John, Paul, George and Ringo played 18 concerts in eighty key centres up and down the country.

Keith Relf Married

Keith Relf, lead singer with THE YARDBIRDS, was secretly married on the morning of Thursday, February 24 at Paddington Registry Office in central London. His bride is former riding instructress April Liversidge, 19, who came to England from Kenya in 1964. Keith and April met for the first time the following Christmas when ardent Beatle fan April went to see "The Beatles' Christmas Show" at London's Finsbury Park Astoria. The Yardbirds were amongst the show's supporting acts.

Poor old HERMAN had a hunk of hard luck when he flew into Manchester at the end of his trans-global concert tour. The customs people seized the Gold Disc he'd collected for million-dollar album sales in the U.S. They'll return the award to him when they figure out how much customs duty Herman has to pay. Meantime Herman had to write out

(Turn to Page 4)

Riot At Byrd's Concert

CHICAGO — The Byrds refused to take flight as 300 screaming female fans stormed the stage of the Civic Opera House in one of the wildest rock shows which this city has yet to witness.

The Byrds continued performing and absolutely refused to vacate the stage even when House employees rushed from the wings and attempted to unplug the group's electric guitars.

In the end it took a total of 30 policemen to quell the screaming audience as the Byrds calmly sang "Mr. Tambourine Man." Ushers were pushed aside like cardboard boxes as about 20 of the girls managed to make it on stage to their heroes.

One girl in the audience received a bruised back and two other members of the Byrd audience were arrested — the first for disorderly conduct and the second for simple assault.

The police lieutenant stated that he made the second arrest after being kicked twice in the leg.

The audience was primarily female and many wore buttons proclaiming, "I'm bold," which had to be the understatement of the century!

Questioned after the concert most declared that they had been pleased with the show but apparently the police had other ideas and so stopped it when it was about half over.

In the meantime, Gene Clark is in Los Angeles getting over his nervous strain. Byrd's manager states that Gene will return to the group within the next five or six weeks but a nasty rumor buzzing around the business is that Clark is out for good.

The BEAT is currently checking this rumor and we will, of course, let you know as soon as we find out for sure but as of right now it is *only* a rumor.

Inside the BEAT

On The Beat	2
Beach Boys Visit Animals	3
Adventures of Robin Boyd	4
The Genius of Ray Charles	5
Noted In the United Kingdom	6
Fashionable Turtles	10-11
Yardbirds Speak Out	13
The London Scene	14
Cash On the Right	15

The BEAT is published weekly by BEAT Publications, Inc., editorial and advertising offices at 6290 Sunset Blvd., Suite 504, Hollywood, California 90028. U. S. bureaus in Hollywood, San Francisco, New York, Chicago and Nashville, overseas correspondents in London, Liverpool and Manchester, England. Sale price 15 cents. Subscription price, U.S. and possessions, $3 per year, Canada and foreign rates, $5 per year. Second class postage prepaid at Los Angeles, California.

...PAUL REVERE & THE RAIDERS (l. to r. Drake Levin, Phil Volk, Mark Lindsay and Mike Smith. In the chair, Paul Revere) getting their kicks, or getting ready to give Paul his!!

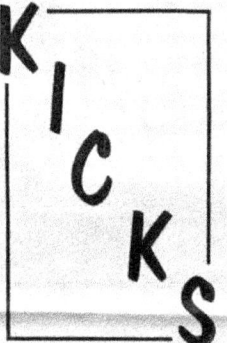

Did you ever wonder how a pop group gets their kicks? Well, Paul Revere and the Raiders recently got their "Kicks" by visiting Santo Domingo.

It's always surprising to me that at least one member of a top group can be easily reached by a simple phone call. And that's all it took to get Mike Smith of the Raiders on the line. Once on the phone Mike eagerly began telling me all about the group's trip to entertain U.S. troops.

"Santo Domingo was a mystery to us," began Mike. "We started out in Los Angeles, then on to Albuquerque, Dallas, San Antonio and to New York to do 'Hullabaloo.'

"Then we went to Florida to an Air Force base where they loaded us onto a C-130, which is really a flying box car. We sat on the paratrooper seats and it was sure a change of pace for us.

"Anyway, we landed at night and all the lights on the runway were off," continued Mike, "because there had been a flare-up in Santo Domingo where the U.S. Army had shot some rebels. So, we had guards all around with guns and they snuck us from the base to the Americana Hotel. You know, that's where all the tourists were pinned down with rebels shooting at them during the revolt.

"The first thing we got was a briefing by Sgt. Pratt about what to do and what not to do. We were one mile from the rebel zone and we weren't supposed to drink any of the water. We could take showers and go swimming but they brought us up purified water to drink.

Tanks And Guns

"We were on the ninth floor of the hotel and we could look out and see the U.S. Army base and across the street was the Commander of the Dominican army with tanks in the back and pointed guns.

"They really seem to hate Americans down there and there are signs all around saying, 'Yankee Go Home.'

"But Drake and I went into the rebel zone carrying cameras. The only way to save yourself is to have a camera because they love to have their pictures taken! We went to a cock fight which was interesting but we could only stay for one because the crowd got worked up. So, we had to leave but we did get some pictures of all that.

"We did USO shows for the troops down there — two shows a day for four days. One day we had off though, because Paul drank the water anyway and got dissentry but I guess we shouldn't go into that!

"We didn't have any girls with us, as Bob Hope always does, so we had to work extra hard during the shows. Most of the service men were young and they really have a poor time down there. You see, the U.S. has seized the land — everything. Therefore, every Santo Domingan hates all Americans. So, the soldiers are very restricted. They don't have any entertainment, only a few USO clubs.

"We had been doing volunteer work for the Job Corps and we had some friends in the White House so when they were putting this tour to Santo Domingo together they asked us to go.

(Turn to Page 6)

John's Father Wants To Knock Off Beatles

By Gil McDougall

When John Lennon was five years old, he and his mother were deserted by his father Freddie Lennon. John has been pretty bitter about this for most of his life. His notable cynicism may be partly rooted in this early shock. Perhaps Lennon's biggest shock since, regarding his father, was to discover that Lennon had embarked on a singing career.

From when he was five 'till he was famous, John didn't hear from his dad, so when Freddie did try to get in touch with his famous son, John was skeptical of his father's reasons. Eventually however, Brian Epstein took the initiative and arranged a meeting between father and son. According to Freddie the conversation was a bit strained. He later stated: "Neither of us knew what to say, but we had a bit of a natter." John's father was also mystified as to John's accent. He said: "I couldn't understand where John had got his Liverpool accent. The last time that I saw him he had a very proper English accent."

This session in Epstein's office was some time ago, and since this occasion the two have not met. John remains very touchy on the subject. During the 1965 Beatle tour he answered a reporter's "how's your father?" with: "Pregnant for all I know, how's yours? My private life is my own concern."

Now that Freddie Lennon has started on his own recording career the fan following of the Beatles is very critical because they think that Freddie is trying to cash in on his son's success. Lennon's pop answers these comments with: "They think that it's just a stunt. I expect to get knocked. I've always enjoyed folk and country and western music. I would like to be judged on my own records."

Despite the fury of Lennon's followers, and the jibes of the press, Lennon senior is very enthusiastic about his new disc career. This is understandable as his last job was washing dishes. He states that he is just waiting for a chance to "knock the Beatles off the top of the hit parade."

Somehow I can't help feeling that he has got quite a long wait.

KRLA BEAT

Volume 3, Number 18   December 2, 1967

Facts Behind Rumored Beatle/Stone Merger

Here are the real facts behind all the merger stories you've been hearing in the past couple of weeks regarding possible joint ventures involving the Beatles and the Rolling Stones.

At the outset, let me emphasize that nothing has been settled, nothing has been signed, nothing has been agreed. The simple truth is that Mick Jagger has had a few wholly informal chats with his close friend, Paul McCartney. In the course of conversation both parties realized that they had a common aim—to acquire and operate a private recording studio. From this, and from nothing more, grew a frantic storm of speculation suggesting that everything was much further advanced, that the two groups would be setting up a joint talent center for record production and the launching of new names.

'Leaked' News

The rumors were given substance via the new Saturday television show, "Good Evening," hosted by Jonathan ("Everyone's Gone To The Moon") King. King claimed to have unearthed evidence that McCartney/Jagger discussions were about to be resolved and a Beatles/Stones merger was all-but-finished. The London-based Sunday newspapers picked up his "leaked" story and gave it front page headlines.

As this issue of The BEAT goes to press, the subject is still open for further discussion between the Beatles and the Rolling Stones. It is true that Mick and Paul are equally capable of handling record production for other artists. It is true that the construction of a recording studio, financed and furnished by the two groups, makes economical and practical sense. At present each group spends a great deal of money renting studios in or around London to make their records. Then they sell the finished product under longterm contract to rival record companies.

Interesting Theory

The theory of a joint corporation is an interesting one so long as we appreciate that this project would be an additional activity in no way replacing nor making obsolete the various professional, music and business relationships which already surround each group.

Obviously, a production unit backed by such important people would be influential. On the other hand, we cannot expect to see any merger bringing together the Stones and the Beatles on one nine-man record since existing longterm recording contracts would prohibit this.

—Tony Barrow

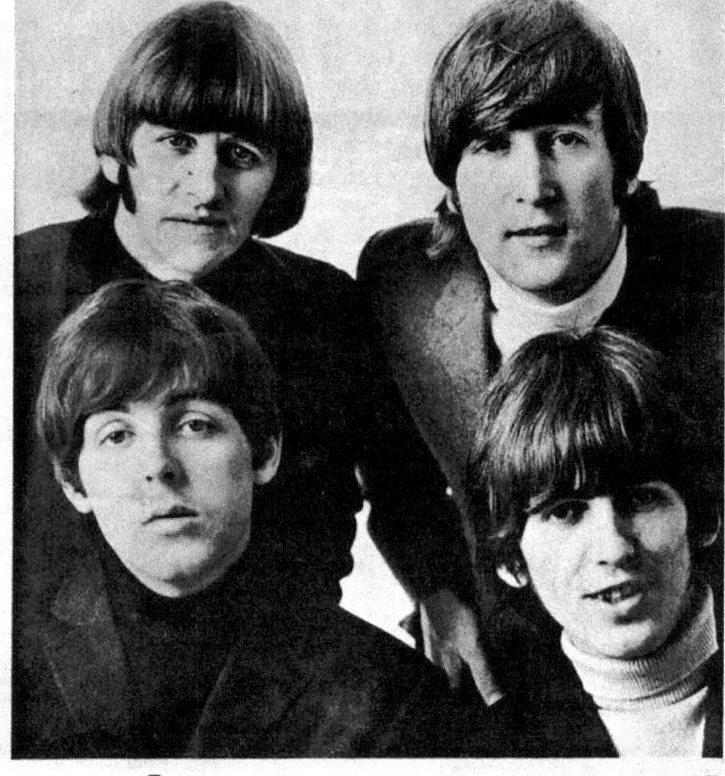

Beatle L.P. Cover Banned

The Beatles have turned out the most nauseating album cover ever seen in the U.S. The jacket is in color and shows the four Beatles in butcher outfits with chopped up raw meat (the meat of what we don't know) lying all over them. If this isn't bad enough, on top of the meat and the Beatles are decapitated baby dolls.

At the very last minute (after 800,000 of these covers had been distributed across the country) someone had brains enough to ban the album cover and demand that no one attempt to sell the album while it is still reposing in that cover.

But the damage is already done. Enough people have already seen the cover and they're all asking the same question—why? Why would a group who will obviously sell a million copies of the album no matter what they put on it stoop to posing and giving their blessing to such a ridiculous attempt at humor, or shock, or whatever it was meant to evoke?

Because it was the Beatles who did it and because no one is supposed to knock them, the comments and opinions which we received from those who had seen the cover will be anonymous. However, we will tell you that they were all given by people in someway connected with the entertainment business.

Not even one person who saw the banned album cover liked it. No one found it even slightly amusing. In short, they all felt it was the most sickening spectacle they'd ever seen. Many agreed that it must have been done for pure shock value. And this poses a question—why do the Beatles feel they must resort to shock to sell an album? Are they afraid that despite all their previous million selling LP's, if they don't put something shocking on the cover of this one, it won't sell?

Others felt that the whole thing came out of John Lennon's head. "If you've read his books," said one of our anonymous souls, "you know Lennon came up with the idea for the cover. Only he could think of something as morbid as that."

Gary Lewis was one performer who did agree to let The BEAT use his name along with his opinion of the cover. "I don't get it. Why? What does it mean? I hate that. They did it just so people would say, 'I hate that.' Harrison looks like he's chopping up another one back there."

Telling Us?

Some were of the opinion that the Beatles were trying to tell us something. "I think they're trying to tell us that this is the beginning of the end," said one. And another added, "You know, we've been getting this strange mail concerning the Beatles. The letters have been pouring in and all have been asking the same questions – 'what is happening to the Beatles? 'Why are they becoming so weird?' Personally, I think the Beatles are now so far from their public that they don't even know what their public wants any more.

Actually, ever since the Beatles first were introduced to America, people have been predicting their downfall. But those wise in the ways of the entertainment business have stuck to the same thought throughout the Beatle reign—"No one can kill the Beatles, except the Beatles themselves." And perhaps they're doing it now.

For months and months the Beatles have been doing nothing—at least, nothing that can be seen. They've been looking for a third movie script. And after almost a year of looking, they say they still can't find one. We're all for the Beatles turning out a fantastic movie but there's no way they would have been diligently looking for an entire year and still not be able to find one. There has to be a hang-up somewhere.

Follow-Up

Then, too, the Beatles have been busy recording a follow-up album to "Rubber Soul." Well, "Rubber Soul" has been on the LP charts for 26 weeks. For someone as popular as the Beatles that's a long time to wait between albums. Because, you see, this new album of theirs (the one with the banned cover) contains only three songs which you haven't heard before—"I'm Only Sleeping," "Dr. Robert" and "And Your Bird Can Sing." It also contains "Drive My Car" which you've heard but which has never been released on an album here in the U.S.

We'd be very interested in hearing your comments on the banned cover. Do you think it was done for shock value, that they were trying to tell us something, or that it means nothing?

Beatles Skip Queen's Show

By Louise Criscione

The Beatles have finally done it—said no to royalty!

The four were invited to appear before the Queen and Duke of Edinburgh at the Royal Variety Show but after discussing it with Brian Epstein the Beatles turned thumbs down on the show with Paul declaring it "not our audience."

Paul went on to say that the Beatles will do something for charity (which is where the proceeds from the show go): "We're making our contribution with a show of our own soon."

The Beatles have appeared on the Royal Variety Show before and at that time they were only too pleased and honored to accept. So, why the big change of heart now?

Apparently, the Beatles are a bit afraid and uncertain of their present popularity status in England. Now, don't you all start writing nasty letters to The BEAT telling us how absolutely horrible we are for saying that just perhaps the Beatles' British popularity is on the decline. Read on and see what Paul had to say and then make up your own mind.

"If we went on and those people didn't like us everyone would say 'ha ha, the Beatles failed, they're on the slide."

Those were Pauls' exact words when announcing to the press the Beatles' decision not to accept the Royal invitation.

When the Beatles made public their decision the Dave Clark Five were quickly chosen to take place. The DC5 probably didn't enjoy being second choice but for such an honor (and it really is an honor) they just as quickly hid their pride and accepted.

So, the Royal Variety Show will go on without the Beatles but with an assured packed house anyway. After all, the Queen will be there.

BEATLES ARCHIVES 1

...THE BEATLES

BEAT Photo: Robert Young

Yeah, Well Beatles...
Chance Of A Lifetime

By Tammy Hitchcock

This week we really scored and managed to cram all four of the Beatles onto the Yeah, Well Hot Seat.

You know, everytime one of the Beatles has a birthday the post office must be notified so that they can assign extra men to the Beatle beat.

Yeah, well I have that same problem. Everytime I get a letter they have to put an extra man on my beat. Not because I get so many letters but because I get so *few* they've taken *my* mailman away!

The Young Paul

Paul's father was recently reminiscing about his son's childhood. One thing about the young Paul which particularly stands out in his mind was Paul's amazing ability to do two things at the same time and do them both well.

Yeah, well Paul has certainly progressed a lot. Now he can do *three* things at once. He can sing, play the guitar and still manage to keep both eyes glued to those girls!

Of course, everyone knows that the Summit Meeting took place between Elvis and the Beatles when the Beatles visited L.A. last August. They all sat around and talked and played guitars and all that. Yeah, well I'm hurt. How come you guys didn't invite me?

The Boss and I

Actually, they *did* invite me. Well, the boss and I that is. I blush everytime I think of it. Are you ready for this? All of the Beatles were waiting for us in their living room. It was like a chance of a lifetime and the boss and I blew it! We got *lost* on the way over!

You should have seen us. We were two hours late when we finally found the right street. So the boss really let her Stingray go and by the time we reached the Beatles' place we had the police sirens chasing us, the Beatle fans chasing us — and J. P. G. & R were *gone!* They had left without us. Yeah, well.

When a reporter asked John if the Beatles were primarily entertainers or musicians, Lennon quipped: "We're money makers first — then we're entertainers."

Yeah, well I'll say you're money makers and MBE'ers too. Some people just have to hog it all!

Blow Their Cool

Lots of performers really blow their cool when a fan comes up to them in a restaurant and asks them for their autograph right when they've got their mouth full of spaghetti. But not George.

"I sign the autograph and thank them profusely for coming over and offer them a piece of my chop."

Yeah, well then I just want to know one thing, George, how come you offered me your napkin?

A reporter asked Ringo if he thought there would be another world war soon and he grinned: "I hope not. Not just after we've got our money through the taxes."

Yeah, well with all the money you guys have it probably takes two years to get it through the taxes! You had better spend it fast before the Queen gets it. And if you have any trouble figuring out just how to spend it — there's always me!

Tams Are Tops In Headwear

What's at the top of the list of today's above-the-eyebrow fashions? Tams are what am (if you'll pardon the most ungrammatical sentence in the history of the continental United States.)

Ringo may or may not have prompted the teen world's sudden fascination for tam-type head-gear by wearing same in the recording-on-the-moor scene from "Help." But whatever started the rush to the knit-wit section of your favorite department store, it is definitely on.

At this stage of the game, plaids seem to be taking a front seat to the solid color variety. One of the most popular tams is the blue-and-green "Black Watch," imported from England and decorated with a crested sable pin.

Do-it-yourself knit-wits will be happy to hear that tams are the world's easiest items to knit (with the possible exception of Barbie Doll blankets.)

All you need is yarn, needles, patience, a few choice locks snipped from your grandfather's favorite shaving brush, and you'll soon be shantering about in your very own tam creation.

BIOS

Beatles

Phenomenologists will have a ball in 1964 and beyond with Beatlemania, a generally harmless form of madness which deluged Great Britain last year. The group has established themselves as Britain's most popular recording group via an impressive series of chart-topping Silver Disc hits.

To kick off the foursome in the U.S. Capitol launched a tremendous promotion campaign which has resulted in their present number one deck, "I Want To Hold Your Hand." But it seems that the American teens like their English cousins can't get enough of the Beatles as evidenced by the fact that two old masters of the group are also currently scoring: Swan's "She Loves You" (#11) and Vee Jay's "Please Please Me" (#73).

The Beatles' (George Harrison, John Lennon, Paul McCartney and Ringo Starr) popularity reached a pinnacle in Britain when, in Nov., at the request of the Royal family, they headlined the annual command performance at the Prince of Wales theatre. In Feb. the boys are coming to the States for three Ed Sullivan CBS-TV shots and some Carnegie Hall appearances.

BEATLES ARCHIVES 1

Beatles in Nassau

ANXIOUS MOMENT IN NASSAU as two BEATLES watch Ringo flounder in surf during filming sequence with stone idol. Photo snapped by SANDY FRAZER of Palos Verdes Estates — whose exciting vacation with the BEATLES will be seen next week!

LET'S TALK WITH PAUL

(Editor's Note: This is the fourth in a series of Beatle interviews by Dave Hull and Derek Taylor, who talked to John, Paul, George and Ringo at length while they were in the Bahamas filming scenes for their second movie. The recorded interviews were originally broadcast over KRLA.
In this interview Derek and Dave are talking with Paul McCartney while sitting on the beach at Nassau.)

DEREK: Paul McCartney just came down on the sands. He probably looks the smartest of the three this morning. He's got on grey trousers, light blue jacket, blue checked shirt, deep tan film makeup, and I think his feet are bare. Good morning, anyway, Paul.
PAUL: 'Morning, Derek.
DEREK: How have you been?
PAUL: Well, you know, Derek, what it's like . . . fine, dandy, everything's going great. You knew I'd say that, didn't you?
DEREK: Well, you see, I just sort of let you walk through the opening, because I don't need to tell you what to say, and never did. Or did I.
PAUL: No. Of course you didn't, no.
DEREK: How many people are in this film who were in the last film besides you, Paul, besides the Beatles?
PAUL: Victor Spinetti was in the last one — he was the TV producer — and this time he's one of the baddies. Dick Lester and Walter Shenson, really, I think that's all. The actors are all different except for Victor Spinetti.
DEREK: I don't know whether the plot has ever been published so I don't want to go into tremendous detail because it would spoil things, but could you just give me a brief run-down what it's all about?
PAUL: Yeah, it roughly people trying to get hold of Ringo's ring for some reason or other, so that he can be sacrificed or something. It's very funny. And they keep trying to get ahold of him and get the ring and we keep trying to rescue him, etc., etc., and it goes on. It fills ninety minutes worth of screen time.
DEREK: There are a lot of new songs. I think in "Hard Day's

Night" there were six or seven brand new ones. How many in this one?
PAUL: There'll be about the same — six or seven new ones. In actual fact I don't think we'll stick in old ones like we did in "Hard Day's Night." I think it's better if we got completely new songs.
DEREK: You mean you wouldn't use any old ones as background music?
PAUL: I don't think so. We might as well . . . We've recorded eleven new songs.
DEREK: Those are actually already on tape are they?
PAUL: Yes, and they could all be done for the film. What Dick Lester is going to do is pick the best seven—the seven he likes best—or that fit best in the film. And if we do need any background music we'll put the others in.
DEREK: George Martin, presumably, is cooperating completely on the score and the background and that sort of thing, is he?
PAUL: Nobody's got round to the score yet because we've only just done the numbers and he'd have to write the score around the numbers. Anyway we've only just started filming so there's no particular panic for that.
DEREK: No. I think when I last saw you when I left you in December, there were no songs at all. Is that right?
PAUL: Right.
DEREK: You must have worked pretty hard since then.
PAUL: No, not really. We just sort of did a couple a week. I know I wrote a couple on holiday and John wrote a couple on holiday too. And we did a lot together. So when we go back we have quite a bit ready. We have about fourteen songs in all to record. We've done about eleven of them. There are still one or two that we haven't done actually. Might do those when we get back to England.
DEREK: It's widely known now that a lot of the songs which bear both your names were, in fact, written by one or the other on your own, and then arranged jointly later. Of the songs in the film, are several of them single records or have you written them alone or are they joint endeavors this time?
PAUL: Well, there are a couple of single efforts and couple of joint. What we normally do,
—MORE ON PAGE 2

RINGO STARR

John and George are about to have a new neighbor—one Mr. Ringo Starr M.B.E. will shortly be moving into a $60,000 house which he has just purchased in Weybridge, Surrey.

The house currently has seven bedrooms, but Ringo is having two of them enlarged because he feels that five bedrooms, a nursery suite, two staff bedrooms, and a staff living room will be a sufficient number of rooms to comfortably house his entourage!

If you are the adventurous type who is thinking of making a thorough search of Surrey in the hopes of locating Ringo's new home, I'll give you a king-size tip. The house is surrounded by trees and stands on its own spacious grounds. There, that ought to help you searchers a little bit.

Of course, you know by now that Herman and his Hermits have completed a small role in the movie "When The Boys Meet The Girls," and that this September they are set to begin filming their first starring role in "There's No Place Like Space." But just exactly what kind of films are these, and is Herman possibly planning on reverting back to acting rather than singing?

BEATLES ARCHIVES 1

More Beatle Answers

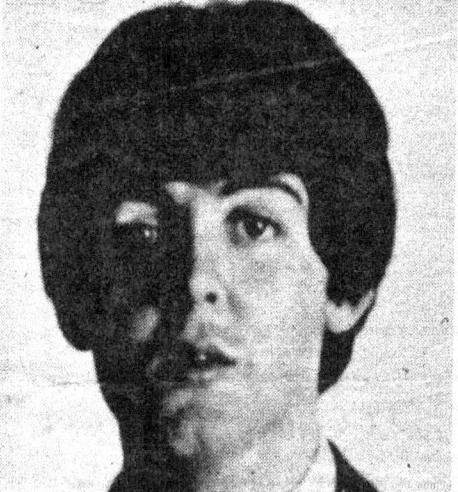

FROM PAGE ONE

though, even if I go away and write a song ... normally the reason I write it on my own or John writes it on his own is 'cause it's daft to sit around waiting for the other one to come up and finish the song. If you happen to be off on your own you might as well finish it off yourself, cause we don't have words and music, as you well know. So what normally does happen is that if I get stuck on the middle of a song, I'll give in, knowing that when I see John he'll finish it off for me. And it'll be a fifty-fifty thing. That's what happens with a lot of them. That's what happened even with a lot of the single efforts. I just sort of forget about the middle eight until I see John, and then say "I need a middle eight for this one," and he says, "Right, okay." And it works.

DEREK: I think "I Saw Her Standing There" was written almost entirely by you, but John put in one word which sort of made it right.

PAUL: Yeah, that's it. What happened was, he took out one word which would have made it very wrong. The first two lines ... I did it going home in a car one night, so I wasn't really thinking too much about it. The first two lines, originally, were "she was just seventeen and she'd never been a beauty queen," which just sounded like it rhymed to me.

DEREK: How'd you happen to write a line like this?

PAUL: You try writing a song going along in a car and, I don't know, you sort of think of things like that. Anyway, when I saw it the next day and played it through to John, I realized it was a useless line. So we sat down and tried to think of another line which rhymed with "seventeen" and meant something. We eventually got "you know what I mean," which means nothing ... completely nothing at all.

DEREK: On the other hand it's not an embarrassing line like 'beauty queen" would have been.

PAUL: No, but on the other hand it could have been a deep and sort of involved line —"you know what I mean," you know, seventeen-year-old girls ... you know ... great ... you know what I mean. You see. It's just a Liverpool expression, as it were, Derek.

DEREK: That's what I thought, a Liverpool expression. A lot of your songs could actually be conversation pieces in Liverpool — "She Loves You," "I Saw Her Yesterday," and that sort of thing.

PAUL: Yeah. Actually, there was some fellow in England who was thinking of doing that, speaking our songs just to use them. Called John Junkin. Do you know him? He was in our last film, played "Shake," the road manager.

DEREK: Yes.

PAUL: He wanted to do a record of something like "She Loves You ... Yeah ... Yeh?" etc.

DEREK: Probably work, I think.

PAUL: It might do, yeah.

DEREK: But it seems to me it might be the only thing left to do now ... an exploitation of Beatle material. I would like to say that during the time I was with the Beatles I never ever saw any professional jealousy. Paul came along with a song that became the "A" side, and John had one which he thought might have been the "A." There was never any sort of nonsense or back-biting or

jealousy. Paul, for instance, came up with "She's A Woman" and thought it was an "A" and other people did, and then John came up with "I Feel Fine" so Paul's "She's A Woman' went on the back. Did you mind?

PAUL: I didn't mind at all. In fact, I wouldn't have liked it to have been an "A." As it happened afterwards, it was quite well received. A lot of people just thought I was singing too high. They thought I'd picked the wrong key.

DEREK: Probably less commercial anyway.

PAUL: Yes, might have been, I don't know. You get those people who come up and say, "Why did you sing it that high, you should have done it in a lower key," because it sounded like I was screeching it. But, ladies and gentlemen, that was on purpose, honest. It wasn't a mistake, honest.

DEREK: Maureen Cleve, who is a London journalist, had a very good line in a piece on this disc when she wrote, "How can a dirty great voice like that come out of such a face?" I think it's often surprising that with a face like yours ... sort of angelic face ... the face of a delinquent choir boy, someone once said ... that you have actually got many voices. One of them you might call a "colored voice." That was your "colored voice" in "She's A Woman," wasn't it?

PAUL: No, it was my green voice.

DEREK: What would you call your anti-lovely voice?

PAUL: I don't know ... soppy, I suppose.

DEREK: Away from song-writing since you're now actors ...

PAUL: Me James Cagney one, isn't it?

DEREK: Yeah, he's playing a James Cagney face, which isn't recording too well on tape. Could you give us a James Cagney line?

PAUL: No, I'm afraid not.

DEREK: Would you do us a quick imitation of any of your friends?

PAUL: Any of my friends? I couldn't, really, I'm not very good on these imitations.

DEREK: You don't like being prompted to do it.

PAUL: You're right.

DEREK: I see Bob Freeman over there.

PAUL: He's done the cover for our latest album in England. I don't think it was in America, was it?

DEREK: No, it wasn't, but the disc is on sale in America.

PAUL: But they changed the cover.

DEREK: They did. But the English disc has another name, "Beatles For Sale," and has a bonus of two numbers over and above the American album.

PAUL: That's it, you see, better value. Buy Britain, folks, buy Britain!

DEREK: When you come back to America, you know you're going to Hollywood again ...

PAUL: Yes, see you there.

DEREK: Well, I'll see you there if not before. Thank you very much, indeed, Paul, and it's nice to see you again.

PAUL: Okay, Derek, see you.

DAVE: Hi, Paul.

PAUL: Hi, Dave.

DAVE: The last time you were in Hollywood you appeared to be a little put out with me because of the addresses I gave out.

PAUL: I was, yes.

DAVE: Are you still put out with me?

PAUL: Well for that, yes.

DAVE: You still think I'm a rotten guy, do you?

PAUL: No, I just didn't like the idea of your giving everybody's addresses out just because if you're trying to keep quiet ever — not that I particularly am — but if I was trying to keep quiet and you were giving the addresses out it would be a big drag, you know.

DAVE: Really the addresses I gave were your folks' addresses, as you know, and not your hotel.

PAUL: That doesn't matter at all, I don't mind. It's just that I know a lot of people who have sort of been cursing you because it's caused them a lot of inconvenience. It's okay, and it's good news for you to give our addresses out, I agree. I would probably do the same thing if I were in the same position. But if you were in my position and other people's position, you'd probably think the same of me giving out addresses as I thought then. Actually it doesn't worry me too much. I don't hate you or anything because of it. In fact, we're quite good friends.

DAVE: What about your getting around the islands here. Have you been other places besides Nassau? Have you been jumping around the island?

PAUL: Well, we've been out here on Paradise Island and to Nassau and a little bit around the island on location with the film. We've been out to nightclubs in the town. It's pretty quiet here, you know. Nobody seems to bother you. There doesn't seem to be an awful lot of people actually on the island. It's a quiet place. So we're having it pretty easy.

DAVE: The people who do bother you, are they mostly Europeans or Americans?

PAUL: Mostly Americans, really. I think mainly because the main lot of the tourists here are American. The natives here don't bother much. They just sort of go out and ... "Ho-ho, the Beatles." And they have big grins on their faces. That's good enough for them. But the people ask you for autographs I think mainly are Americans or Americans living here or American tourists.

DAVE: Do you have many problems getting around when you're on vacation?

PAUL: It depends on where you go. Last time I went to Tunisia and had no problems at all. It's so quiet here, really. As I was telling Derek before about the phones. They're so cut off in Tunisia it's ridiculous. I mean a man from a newspaper came around when we were in Tunisia and spoke to me and everything, and it didn't get back to England. It was ridiculous.

DAVE: You mean nothing of the material got out?

PAUL: No, because all the lines were so bad. I couldn't speak to anyone in England. It was a fluke if you managed to get a good line to England.

DAVE: Isn't it a pleasure, though, if you're on vacation? You get away ...

PAUL: Yeah, right, it was this time. I enjoyed it. Went away for two weeks, lazed around, went to the little soukhs, which are like market places the Tunisian's have. In fact, this very pair of sandals was bought for one dinar. It's about fifteen shillings in English — I think about two dollars.

DAVE: When you go on vacation do you turn into a tourist like most tourists do?

PAUL: Yes, mainly. Like Tunisia I did. Sometimes you don't. You go to somewhere where it's not so quiet, then you don't really get a chance to go out and turn into a tourist. I was completely tourist with a movie camera and snapshots.

DAVE: When you are returning to Hollywood — of course the itinerary hasn't been planned yet, meticulously — but I understand you're going to do a couple of shows in Hollywood, then you're going to San Francisco, then you're returning to Hollywood for a couple of days' vacation. Is that true?

PAUL: I think that's true. I'm not really sure about the itinerary myself yet, but that sounds like it.

DAVE: Were you interested in seeing Hollywood? Remember last time you didn't get a chance to see much. You were locked in the house and really didn't ...

PAUL: Well that was good

—MORE ON PAGE 3

PEN PALS

Clare Davies and Janice Alford
4 Updale Close
Potters Bar
Middlesex, England

BEATLES ARCHIVES 1

Beatles' Yogi In U.S. To Spread The Word

LOS ANGELES—Indian Mystic Maharishi Mehesh Yogi was in Los Angeles for the second time in as many years to deliver talks on the benefits of meditation and to organize academies for the teaching of transcendental meditation.

This year was very different for the Indian visitor. Whereas last year his press conference was held in a private home with all reporters kindly asked to remove their shoes, this year's conference was held at the very proper Los Angeles Press Club before a dozen reporters and various cameramen.

Beatle Interest

The main reason for the gained notoriety is the interest the Beatles have shown in the Maharishi's philosophy.

"The Beatles came backstage after one of my lectures," he explained, "and they said to me, 'even from an early age we have been seeking a highly spiritual experience. We tried drugs but that didn't work.'

"You have come to the right place," I said.

"They are such practical and intelligent young boys, it did not take more than two days for them to discover that transcendental meditation is the answer.

"'We'll do anything you say,' they told me."

It was by the Marahishi's suggestion that the Beatles decided to open an academy for his International Meditation Society in London. They also plan to get together for two or three months in India this October to pursue this way of life.

Questions

During the two days in Wales the Beatles were asked a good many questions by the Maharishi.

"One of them took a badge out of his pocket. I asked, 'What is this?'. He said it was a Ban the Bomb badge. He said there was an organization that wanted to put an end to bombs.

"I told him, 'Be careful, you have a great responsibility, don't go into the abstract idealisms. If you want to ban the bomb you must show a bigger bomb.'

"Then they said the government is awful. I told them, 'As young men, be careful. Whatever party is elected must be supported'."

The Marahishi has yet to hear any of the Beatles music, but he believes that he will eventually, maybe when they join him in India.

The Beatles are not the only pop singers and performers to show an interest in his philosophy. The Rolling Stones, Donovan, some of the Doors and television actor Efrem Zimbalist Jr. have also sought out his counsel.

MAHARISHI: "Don't go into abstract idealism."

BEATLES RUN FOR 'HELP'

HERE COME THE BEATLES, racing through deep snow in Austria in a scene from their new movie, "HELP," which is already drawing an enthusiastic response in England and will open in the U.S. shortly. The running practice will come in handy during their forthcoming American tour, when they will again have to evade hordes of fans. For more exciting photos from the Beatles' new movie, just turn the page.

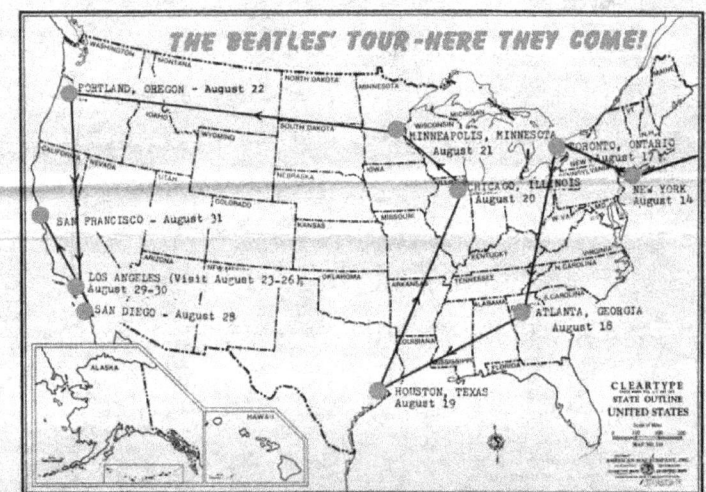

BEATLES ARCHIVES 1

THE BEATLES

"HELP!"

Guess where the Beatles are now? Bermuda!! Austria!! And what are they doing there?

Why are the high priests of the terrible Goddess of Kaili interested in the Beatles?
Why is Ringo being pursued to the ends of the earth by a gang of Eastern thugs?
What do they want of him—they aren't fans.
Two leading scientists hope to rule the world.
Paul is threatened by a beetle.
An Eastern beauty saves the boys' lives time and time again.
A channel swimmer ends up in an Alpine lake and Buckingham Palace has a busy day.

When Scotland Yard arrives in the sunny Bahamas after unsuccessful maneuvers on Salisbury Plain they find four Ringos but only one George, one Paul and one John.
When the power crazy scientists arrive in the Alps the boys miraculously escape their deadly weapons.
Will John live to sleep in his pit again?
Will Paul ever get back to his electric organ?
Will George be re-united with his ticker-tape machine?
And Ringo—will he ever play the drums again?

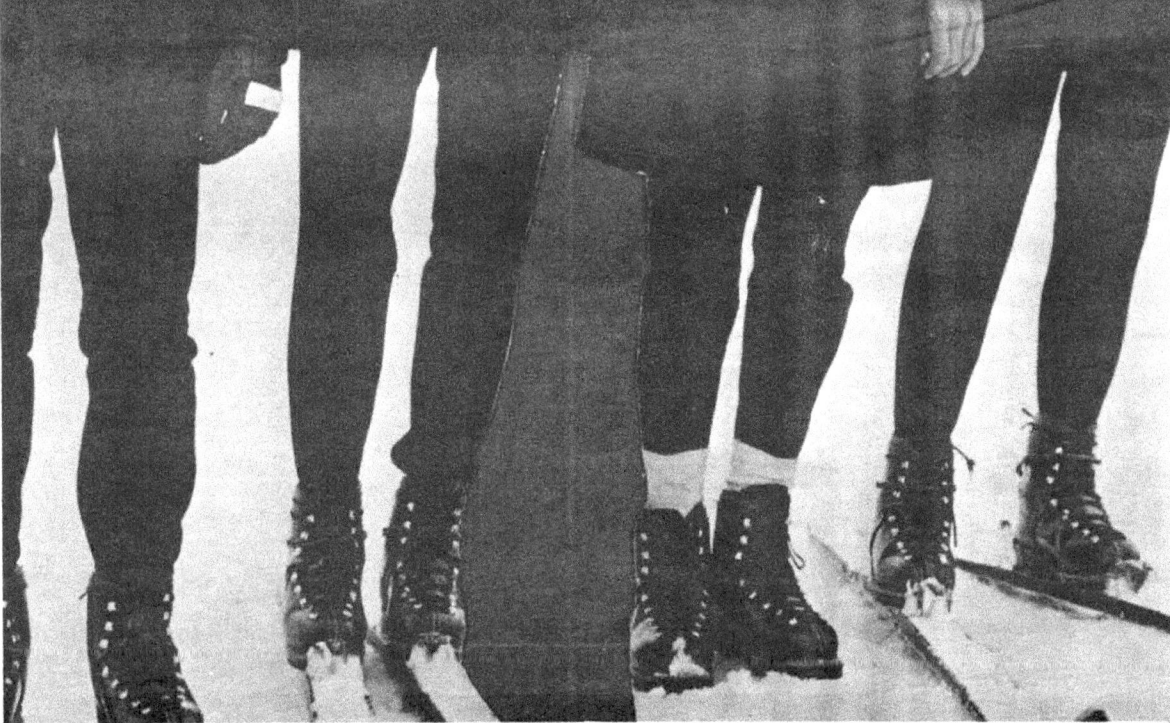

BEATLES ARCHIVES 1

These are a few of the scenes from the year's most anxiously-awaited movie. In coming weeks the BEAT will present further previews of the fabulous Beatles' movie, which has been a world-wide sensation and is due to open in the U.S. shortly.

Many of these scenes also appear on the Beatles' new album, "HELP", which is taken from the sound track of the movie. The album is already a top-seller in both the U.S. and England, and the title song (issued as a single) is one of the most popular the Beatles have ever recorded. It reached the top spot in England 48 hours after its release.

As America prepares for the premiere of "HELP" and the arrival of John, Paul, George and Ringo themselves this month, it's evident we are in for another powerful siege of Beatlemania

"SHOCKING" SCENE WITH POOR RINGO

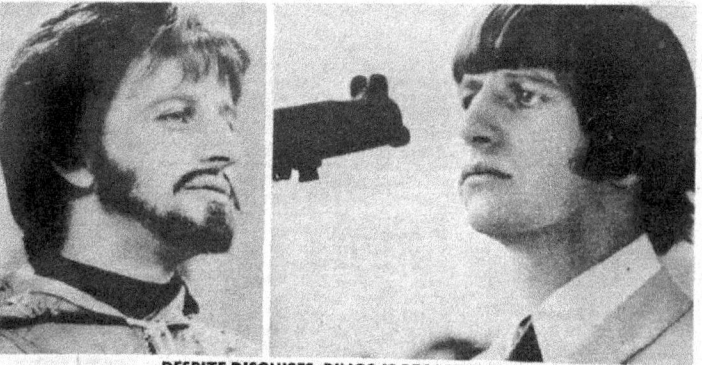

DESPITE DISGUISES, RINGO IS RECAPTURED

UNITED AGAIN, BOYS JOIN A PARADE

BEATLES ARCHIVES 1

Ringo: 'John's Personality Made Us'

By Gil McDougall

Whenever I sit down to write about Ringo Starr I suddenly have an immense feeling of happiness. The same kind of feeling that one would get when meeting Ringo for the first, or the one hundreth time. The little man from Dingle has been described by many, as the Beatle who is the swingingest in private. But in private, or in public, Ringo exhibits a tremendous feeling of good will to all men.

During his life Ringo has perhaps been cursed with a fair amount of illness and misfortune, but parallel to this is the luck and good fortune that he has experienced in his professional career. The Beatles together are a fantastic show business combination, but had they never joined together in one group, who know's what their fortunes might have been. Brian Epstein puts it this way: "Ringo was the catalyst for the others. He suddenly completed the jigsaw."

Ringo's Luck

In a way it was pure luck that Ringo ever joined the Beatles. But for his friendship with Paul and George he might still be playing the drums at Bulins holiday camp in Skegness. Of course, he would be playing them just as well, and probably having as big a ball as he is today, but the Beatles and the world just wouldn't be the same without Richie.

The Beatles are lucky in that they are all friends. As John has said: "Members of a group like this are usually not friends. I mean that they are friends but they don't necessarily hang around together on their days off. Sometimes a couple of them might go off and be friends, but usually they get enough of each other while they're working."

Though the Beatles popularity shows no sign of dying down, at one time or another they have all voiced the opinion that it must sooner or later. Ringo and John have both said: "We don't want it to go on forever you know."

One day the Beatles may dissolve their partnership and concentrate on quieter things. After all, it is a bit wearing to tour the world all the time. It is doubtful that they will ever stop recording as a group, but there is a possibility of each Beatle doing single records.

Comedy Role

If John and Paul decide to take some time out and try to write that musical that they have been discussing for some time, George might go solo and Ringo might decide to try a film comedy on his own. As a comedian he certainly has the potential.

Having been born in Dingle, which is one of the toughest parts of Liverpool, Ringo was more than ready for any obstacles that life might present. His series of illness' more than primed him for the hard aspects of life. Ringo was five years old when he was sent to St. Silas school. He started out well, but soon was stricken with appendicitis. Unfortunately, complications set in and for some time Ringo was expected to die. He didn't, of course, but nevertheless he had to spend some four years in that hospital. Anyone who has ever been in the hospital just a couple of weeks will know how very long that four years must have seemed to Mr. Starkey.

Ringo doesn't confine his activities to drumming and singing however. He would very much like to write some country music. He has actually done this. Together with John and Paul he helped to write "What Goes On," which appeared on the flipside of the Beatle hit, "Nowhere Man."

Ringo has said: "It was John's personality that made us." Though there is plenty of truth in this, it is not the entire story. They all participated, and Ringo no less than the rest. To George's next-door-boyness; to Paul's charming ways; and to John's irreverence, Ringo added the quaintness of the little man. The Beatles are superstars, but they are not super-humans. That is why we find it so easy to identify ourselves with them.

More To Come

Before the Beatles became famous, Brian Epstein made this claim: "They will be bigger than Presley." They may well turn out to be even bigger than Sinatra – and that's really going some. Despite all that they have achieved, despite all of the records that they continue to break, I can not help but feel that the Beatles haven't even begun to show the actual extent of their talents yet.

Ringo is a very fortunate man indeed. Not only is he a fantastic success, but he also has a wonderful wife and some of the most respected friends in the world. He also lives in a very pretty part of England. He lives in the country and yet is only minutes from the second biggest city in the world.

It has been suggested that the Beatles actually changed the face of London. This may be stretching it a bit, but they have had a tremendous effect on the city and its inhabitants. They have changed the lives of many people.

Ringo and the other Beatles get a big kick out of hobnobbing with other groups. At the premiere of "A Hard Days Night," Mick Jagger and Keith Richard turned up unexpectedly and Ringo and John demanded that they be invited in. At the 1965 Beatle concert in New York the Rolling Stones again turned up, and were greeted with great enthusiasm by the Beatles. As the Stones approached John was heard to exclaim: "It's the famous Rolling Stones!"

Ringo enjoys his fame, but he gets annoyed when he is singled out from the other Beatles for any particular honor. After all they are a team, and anything that they do, they do together. During the Beatles first tour he was very embarrassed by the "Ringo for President" campaign. It was only a joke, of course, but he still did not enjoy becoming the sole Beatle in the spotlight.

Whatever is to become of Ringo, the fact remains that he has already secured most of the things that man struggles to gain throughout his life. He has made an excellent marriage; he has achieved fame and fortune; and he has obtained the friendship of half the population of the earth. That isn't too bad for a little man from Dingle.

...THERE, YOU SEE, RINGO REALLY DOES ANSWER HIS FAN MAIL!!!

BEATLES ARCHIVES 1

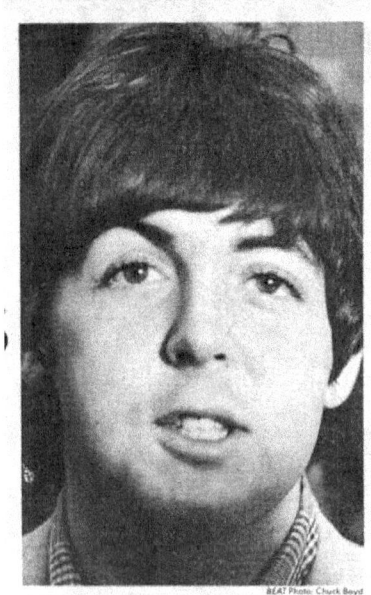

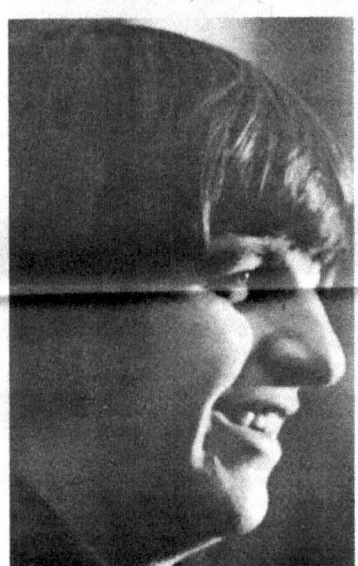
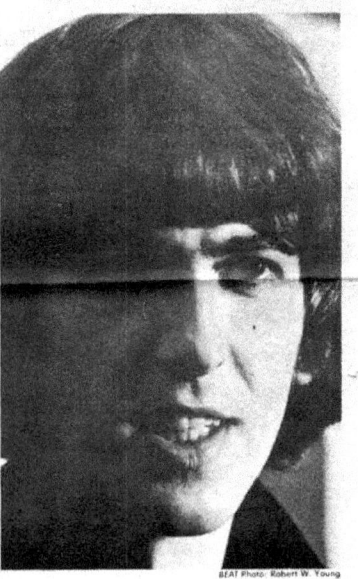

Beatles' Film Another Solo?

The Beatles have been making a lot of solo appearances lately, and if things go as scheduled the four Britons may not even be viewed as a group in their forthcoming film.

Tentative plans reveal John, Paul, George and Ringo will all make appearances in the film, but probably never at the same time. Filming is scheduled to begin in January.

One of the Beatles will have the leading role and will portray a character with a split personality. He will imagine he is four different people – himself plus the other three Beatles.

The lead Beatle has not yet been selected. The film will also have a leading lady, who will be in separate scenes with all four Beatles.

The idea of solo shots was submitted by scriptwriter Owen Holder and approved by Brian Epstein. Four different story lines have been written around the basic plot and one is expected to be approved very soon.

London sources are speculating that due to the film's unusual story line fewer songs will be used than in either "Help" or "A Hard Day's Night." But John and Paul are expected to write a full score of incidental music.

Beatle John Lennon has redeemed himself, in the eyes of his business partners anyway. Northern Songs Co., a Beatle-owned music publishing firm which took a sharp drop on the stock market when Lennon made his infamous remarks about Christianity, will pay shareholders a big 40 per cent this year.

The company announced that current profits this year total $1.7 million.

THAT ELUSIVE MOVIE SCRIPT
Beatles Still Looking

By Louise Criscione

As of today the Beatles are still in hot water over their next movie. They have a bit of a problem as you know – they're minus a script!

All four of the Beatles, and especially Paul, seem to know exactly what they *don't* want. They don't want "A Talent For Loving" because they'd look like four long-haired Roy Rogers singing to their horses.

If they can possibly avoid it they don't want another script like "Help." Although Paul declared that he liked "Help" and enjoyed watching it he did not feel that he and his buddies were necessary characters in the story. He considered them merely incidental to the plot and not a real part of it.

They don't want to do another "Hard Day's Night." Not because they didn't like the movie – they did very much. But after all, it was a sort of documentary type film and how many of those can you make? Especially if you are creative, and the Beatles are.

They don't want to pull an Elvis. They don't want to rush a movie out in three weeks and they don't want to make a movie which is merely a vehicle for music. That would be too much like a pop film – all songs and no plot.

Write Their Own?

Okay, then why don't the Beatles write their own movie – they've done everything else. Well, as a matter of fact, they have attempted to write a script. But they just couldn't complete it to their satisfaction.

Paul reveals that he and John tried to write one but ran into all kinds of snags along the way. The plot revolved around a man named Pilchard, who was really supposed to be Jesus Christ.

However, there were all sorts of holes in the story and so to fill them up John and Paul continued to add more characters. And by the time they had finished the story they had about a hundred characters involved in the plot! So they chucked it.

The Beatles are all a little tired of playing the good guys. They figure that a piece of good goes a long way. They wanta be bad guys for a change. You don't think the four Beatles could be bad guys? Well, then stretch your imagination! Of course, they'd probably be *good* bad guys.

Another problem facing the *(Turn to Page 7)*

HARRISON FINDS HELP IN HOUSE

By Tony Barrow

George Harrison's contribution to the soundtrack of the Beatles' self-directed hour-long television show "Magical Mystery Tour" is a new song which he wrote while he was in California at the beginning of August!

Entitled "Blue Jay Way" the composition relates directly to the location of the hideaway home George rented for himself and his friends during their eight-day visit.

Here's how the song came about. With Pattie, road manager Neil Aspinall and the Beatles' close friend Magic Alex, George arrived at Blue Jay Way on the afternoon of Tuesday, August 1. The long polar just flight from London had left most of the party ready for some rest. But George decided to stay up for a while and Neil joined him. They telephoned a good friend of theirs inviting him to come over for the evening. Detailed instructions for reaching Blue Jay Way had to be relayed over the telephone. It was this call which proved to be George's inspiration for the new song. He sat down behind a mini-organ and went to work while they waited for their friend to arrive.

Hypnotic Song

"Blue Jay Way" is a slow number with an almost hypnotic atmosphere about it. On the whole it is less complex and more commercial than George's "Sgt. Pepper" piece "Within You, Without You."

Incidentally it was in America, almost four months earlier, that Paul started work on the television show's title song "Magic Mystery Tour." Within days of his return home (after being with Jane Asher in Denver for her 21st birthday party) the Beatles recorded the first track for "Magical Mystery Tour." Since then the general construction of that number has been modified and addi-

(Continued on Page 7)

BEATLES ARCHIVES 1

America's Largest Teen NEWSpaper — 25¢

KRLA Edition BEAT

OCTOBER 22, 1966

BEAT Photo: Howard L. Bingham

GEORGE HARRISON, SITAR IN INDIA
SEE PAGE 1

ELVIS PRESLEY SHOWS HIMSELF
SEE PAGE 3

HERMAN HURT
SEE PAGE 1

BEATLES ARCHIVES 1

The Beatles—'66 Style

By Eden

Beatles . . . 1966. Another year, another summer, another American tour. Fifteen cities more are stricken with Beatlemania, and thousands have a relapse.

Beatles . . . 1966. Again the screaming headlines, glaring out into the streets from printed newspapers. Again the spoilers who must try to drag the Beatles down into their own mud-gutter level, and the jealous who seek to destroy all that which they can't own.

Beatles . . . 1966. Still hundreds of thousands are loyal to the Four. Still screaming mobs of happy teens, and quieter mobs of enthusiastic "adults."

Beatles . . . 1966. Four young men returning to our shores to revisit the lands they conquered, the hearts they won, three years ago. But they are four changed young men—four *mature* young men, who have assumed the heavy mantle of fame, and now have learned to wear it well . . . and learned to wear it with *class!*

JOHN . . .

Older now, even more mature. A young man who *knows* where he's been, is *well-aware* of "where he's at," and is in *complete control* of where he's going. He's wearing a new hair-cut this year; he's had his famous golden-brown Beatle locks trimmed and they are a little shorter now than last time we saw him—very much reminiscent of the first time we were introduced.

He seems quite content now, very much at ease. His handsome face is in repose as he calmly answers questions cast at him, and he seems far more lucid, much more communicative than he has been for a while.

There are no signs of strain or over-tiredness; he seems to be at peace with himself for the first time in a year or so.

PAUL . . .

He, too, has been the object of some "growing pains" since we saw him last, and the results are pure success! The famous "cherubic look" of his is not so much in evidence this year, his face has become more manly, and he's not as likely to be mistaken for the mischievous little boy he has been reputed to be.

His words are still inimitably "Beatle," yet his answers are tinged with a little more sophisticated sarcasm this year. And still he remains the essence of courtesy when approached politely with a logical, intelligent question. He will trade his own sincerity of word and action for equal amounts of sincerity on the part of others. That's fair enough.

GEORGE . . .

More confident of his own abilities, more certain of just what those abilities are, now. He, too, looks much better this summer than we have ever seen him before. His hair has also been trimmed, and is kept quite neatly combed—not straggling about his face and neck as it was during our last meeting.

He seems somehow to have matured beyond his 22 years in the 12 months since we have seen him—and he wears his new maturity well.

Remarks around us filter back to our own quite sensitive ears, and we overhear less-interested people saying: 'I didn't know he was so intelligent!' Yes—he is. *We* knew it all along, but it's nice to see him using it so much more to his own advantage now.

RINGO . . .

The "little man from Dingle." The lovable little Beatle who seems to forever remain the same. He's a timeless personality in his own right, a very unique, one-of-a-kind sort of human being.

There has been little change in his large, sad blue eyes—save perhaps the blue-tinted spectacles with which he occasionally covers them now.

His reddish-brown hair still shines and falls softly about his famous face, and more than ever now he looks so like a cuddly little puppy dog, or a little boy who has lost his way home from school.

But this year, it is quite evident that Ringo is no longer lost—from anything. He seems to have found his niche in the life he calls his own — and, happily — he seems quite contented with his lot.

CONFERENCE . . .

Once again a tiny room is filled to brimming with the curious, the prying, the adoring, the cynics; the lightbulbs flashing, blinding, everywhere; the tape recorders whirring, recording every Beatle-sound; the TV cameras filming smiles, and gestures of the Four in front; the fans who only watch in awe.

It's a hot room, a room too-full of people. Crowded over with reporters, pens-in-hand, a question at them ready. A room which somehow seems to be a vault to shelter us from the screaming reality of true Beatlemania just outside the guarded door. A room which temporarily will hold the non-reality of the curious who have come to see the freaks perform—and a room which eventually will see the curious become the caged and watched.

Four Beatles are within these walls—four Beatles who have grown immensely—both personally and professionally—in the last three years.

Four Beatles who have changed —for the better—confronted now by the pushing mass of humanity which hasn't changed enough.

CONCERT . . .

Relief! The things that they have been saying for months are absolutely *untrue!* The Beatles have in *no way* lost their golden, Midas touch. They are still the most phenomenal, exciting act on earth.

They have so much of what must be described as "class"— from their brand new outfits – hued a cross between *Lincoln* and *"Robin Hood"* green! – to the little bits of humor they share onstage.

There has been no let-up in the intensity of excitement—only an increase in the appreciation of their talents. The screams and applause are just as loud and long now—but they're mostly found at the end of songs, in appreciative *response* to the Beatles.

BEATLES . . . 1966. Still the most exciting, exceptional and influential foursome in the world of music. Still the largest, inexplicable phenomena of our times. Still the center of Happiness Production which they continually distribute 'round the world.

BEATLES . . . 1966 — Still John, Paul, George and Ringo!

BEATLES . . . 1966. Still the most exciting, exceptional and influential foursome in the world of music. Still the largest, inexplicable phenomena of our times. Still the center of Happiness Production which they continually distribute 'round the world.

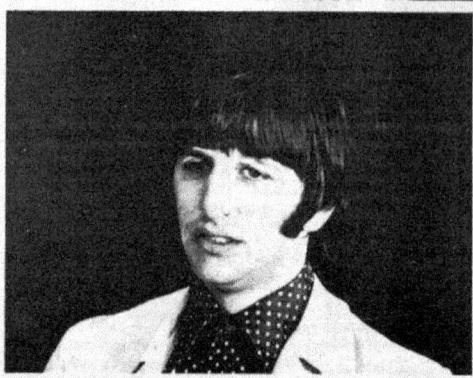

BEATLES ARCHIVES 1

Page 12 — THE BEAT — October 22, 1966

Top 40 Requests

1. NINETY SIX TEARS .... ? And The Mysterians
2. I WANT TO BE FREE .... The Monkees
3. DANDY .... Hermans' Hermits
4. WALK AWAY RENEE .... The Left Banke
5. CHERISH .... The Association
6. HAVE YOU SEEN YOUR MOTHER STANDING IN THE SHADOWS .... Rolling Stones
7. PSYCHOTIC REACTION .... Count Five
8. NEXT TIME YOU SEE ME .... The Robbs
9. CHERRY, CHERRY .... Neil Diamond
10. I'M YOUR PUPPET .... James and Bobby Purify
11. FORTUNE TELLER .... Rolling Stones
12. TALK, TALK .... Music Machine
13. REACH OUT .... The 4 Tops
14. THE GREAT AIRLINE STRIKE .... Paul Revere & The Raiders
15. THE LAST TRAIN TO CLARKSVILLE .... The Monkees
16. BUS STOP .... The Hollies
17. OUT OF TIME .... Chris Farlowe
18. GOD ONLY KNOWS .... The Beachboys
19. IF I WERE A CARPENTER .... Bobby Darin
20. YOU CAN'T HURRY LOVE .... The Supremes
21. YELLOW SUBMARINE/ELEANOR RIGBY .... The Beatles
22. WHAT BECOMES OF THE BROKEN HEARTED .... Jimmy Ruffin
23. BLACK IS BLACK .... Los Bravos
24. SEE SEE RIDER .... Eric Burdon
25. SEE YOU IN SEPTEMBER .... The Happenings
26. I GOT YOU UNDER MY SKIN .... The 4 Seasons
27. WORKING IN THE COAL MINE .... Lee Dorsey
28. POOR SIDE OF TOWN .... Johnny Rivers
29. THE JOKER WENT WILD .... Brian Hyland
30. OPEN THE DOOR TO YOUR HEART .... Darrell Banks
31. MR. DIEINGLY SAD .... The Critters
32. FLAMINGO .... Herb Alpert
33. TURN DOWN DAY .... The Cyrkle
34. BEAUTY IS ONLY SKIN DEEP .... The Temptations
35. LITTLE MAN .... Sonny & Cher
36. ALL I SEE IS YOU .... Dusty Springfield
37. SUNNY .... Bobby Hebb
38. THERE WILL NEVER BE ANOTHER YOU .... Chris Montez
39. SUNSHINE SUPERMAN .... Donovan
40. JUST LIKE A WOMAN .... Bob Dylan

Inside KRLA
By Eden

Leave it to KRLA to come up with the greatest contests ever, right? Right!! And they've really gone and out-done themselves this time, too.

Not only do we have the fantastic football game contest, in which you can win up to $10,000 dollars running, but now there is a brand new contest which offers you the *car of your choice.*

The new contest began Saturday, October 1, and will continue through the end of the month. And easier than this they don't come— or *go!* All you have to do is get yourself together, move on out of your habitation, and lay an eyeball or two on every single new '67 car.

That's right—look at *all* the models of *all* cars and then decide which one you want. When you've made your choice, record it for the ages on a 4c post card, along with your name and address, and dispatch it post haste to "'67 KRLA," right here in Sunny Pasadena, Calif.

Then if you are the lucky winner-type in this great contest, you will find the car of your choice, *whatever* it is—from a Rambler to a Cadillac—delivered to your very own front door.

Would you believe driven onto your *driveway?*

Dropping by KRLA to say hello lately have been Len Berry, the Robbs—great new group from "Action," and the Turtles—who have one of the most-requested new tunes on the KRLA Request List with their new smash, "Can I Get To Know You Better?"

By the way, have you listened to the new Pat Moore show yet? He's really a great addition to the midnight hours, so if you're one of those all-night freaks, forget about the candle-burning jazz and listen in on the Moore show instead. It gives you *Moore* of what you stayed *awake for!!!*

NOW!

THE LEGENDARY
MUDDY WATERS
AND HIS ORIGINAL CHICAGO BLUES BAND

AND INTRODUCING...

ELEKTRA RECORDING ARTIST
TIM BUCKLEY

AT DOUG WESTON'S
Troubadour
9083 SANTA MONICA BLVD.
L.A. NEAR DOHENY
RESERVATIONS CR 6-6168

Win $10,000 In KRLA'S Sweepstakes

You can win $10,000 every week in the KRLA $10,000 Football Sweepstake!

To win all you have to do is correctly guess the exact scores of the five games designated by the station. The games will be a combination of high school games, college and professional games.

The designated games will be announced each Monday, and repeated Tuesday and Wednesday on KRLA.

You can enter as often as you wish but entries must be on post card only.

Entries must be postmarked by midnight Wednesday and received at KRLA by noon Friday.

$10,000 will be offered each week throughout the football season and all you have to do to win it is guess the five scores exactly.

Stay tuned to KRLA for the designated games and you may win yourself a fortune.

Christmas Cheer Starts HERE

KRLA BEAT Gift Subscription — $3 a year
Each Additional Gift Subscription — only $1 a year

(We send you BEAT gift cards to mail to your friends—First issue will be sent in time for Christmas)

My name is _____
Address _____
City _____ State _____ Zip _____

☐ Send BEAT for Xmas (names listed below)
☐ I also want a BEAT subscription.
Total enclosed $_____ for _____ subscriptions.
I enclose ☐ cash ☐ check ☐ money order.

Mail to:
KRLA BEAT #504
6290 Sunset Blvd.
Hollywood, Calif. 90028

Name _____
Address _____
City _____ State _____ Zip _____

Mail to:
KRLA BEAT #504
6290 Sunset Blvd.
Hollywood, Calif. 90028

Name _____
Address _____
City _____ State _____ Zip _____

Mail to:
KRLA BEAT #504
6290 Sunset Blvd.
Hollywood, Calif. 90028

Name _____
Address _____
City _____ State _____ Zip _____

Mail to:
KRLA BEAT #504
6290 Sunset Blvd.
Hollywood, Calif. 90028

Name _____
Address _____
City _____ State _____ Zip _____

October 22, 1966 — THE BEAT — Page 13

Robbs Visit KRLA

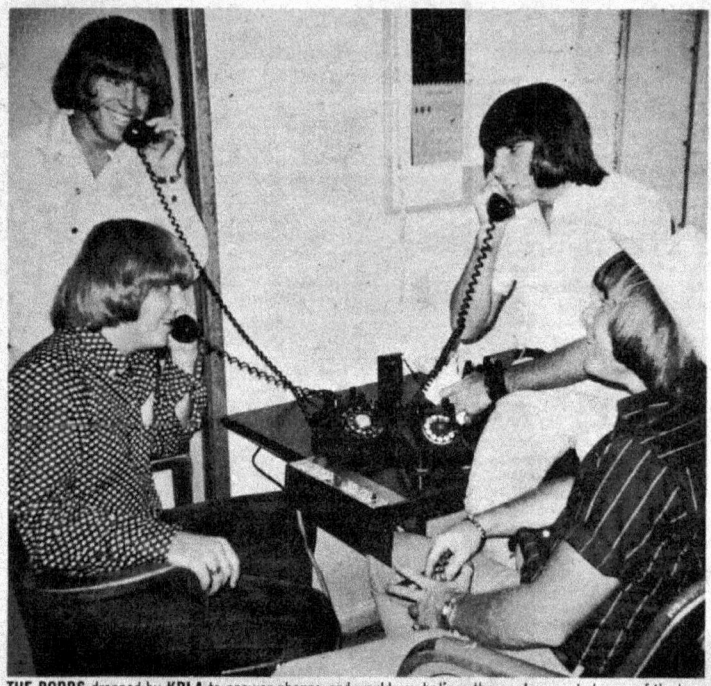

THE ROBBS dropped by KRLA to answer phones and would you believe the most requested song of the hour was their new one, "Next Time You See Me?" That's Joey Robb standing and Craig, Bruce and Dee, (l. - r.)

JOEY AND BRUCE sign autographs for a group of over a hundred fans who turned out to meet the guys when they arrived at KRLA's studios.

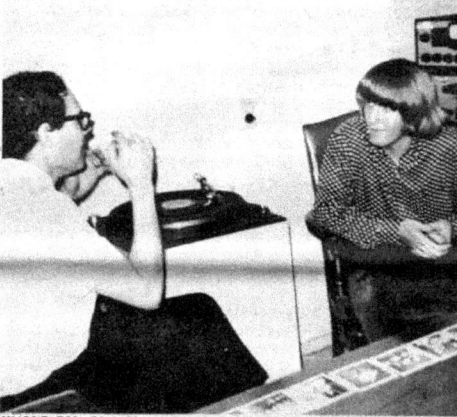

UNCLE DM, Dick Moreland, dropped into the phone answering room while the boys were there and he and Craig Robb layed an ear on, would you believe The Monkees' first album? How about the Robbs new single? How about the Robbs' first album, which isn't even finished yet?

Say you read it in The BEAT

THE DEEP SIX introducing their new Liberty album, "The Deep Six," at the Ice House in Glendale, Oct. 11 - 16.

the ICE HOUSE Glendale
234 SO. BRAND
Reservations 245-5043

WARREN BEATTY
SUSANNAH YORK

From London to the Riviera, a hair-raising tale of gallant love and truly desperate adventure!

KALEIDOSCOPE

the switched-on thriller !!!

A GERSHWIN-KASTNER PRODUCTION CLIVE REVILL · ERIC PORTER
Written by ROBERT & JANE HOWARD CARRINGTON · Produced by ELLIOTT KASTNER · Directed by JACK SMIGHT
TECHNICOLOR® FROM WARNER BROS.

NOW PLAYING! CALL THEATRE FOR SHOW TIMES
EXCLUSIVE ENGAGEMENT
WARNER HOLLYWOOD THEATRE
6433 HOLLYWOOD BLVD at WILCOX · HO. 6-5211

THE SONS OF ADAM
LAST APPEARANCE IN L.A. BEFORE TOUR

BIDO LITO'S
OPEN 10 P.M. NIGHTLY EXCEPT SUNDAY
HO 5-5235

18 & OVER

1608 COSMO ST. (NEAR SELMA) IN HOLLYWOOD — COVER CHARGE

THE NEW CLUB TROPICANA
247 E. MANCHESTER, L.A.
For Reservations — 758-7615
TEENAGERS WELCOME

NOW APPEARING
THE GENIUS OF
CHET BAKER
- also -
THE INCOMPARABLE
RAY BRYANT TRIO

BEATLES ARCHIVES 1

THE BEAT — October 22, 1966 — Page 14

MICK JAGGER
'That's Tough, Mom'

By Rochelle Reed

Keith Richard and Mick Jagger relaxed in the London hotel suite which their manager Andrew Loog Oldham was using as a temporary office and tossed off a few comments about the Stone scene as they see it.

First on their list was the well-publicized picture of the guys, taken on a New York street in early morning, with them posing in their version of wartime U.S. mothers.

A Giggle

"The photograph was just a laugh," Keith confessed, "there's no deeper interpretation to be placed on it than that. A photographer in New York took the picture as a giggle. We intend to bring it out in the U.S. as a cover for the single and on the flipside a photo of all of us dressed normally."

Sure enough, the pop picture does adorn the single jacket of "Have You Seen Your Mother, Baby, Standing In The Shadows?"

"We adopted the names of 'Molly' (Richards) and 'Sarah' (Jagger) for fun. I think Bill must get the 'king of queens' award for his portrayal of the bird in the bathchair (wheelchair to us) in the uniform. I mean just look at her. I mean, that's the one who pressed the button, isn't it?"

What Keith didn't tell us was the rest of the girlish names adopted as a gag by the five. Others are Flossie Jones, Penelope Wyman, and Millicent Watts!

The Stones have received a great deal of adverse comment about the shot from American mothers, but the guys don't seem overly perturbed. In fact, Mick and Keith showed a "that's tough" attitude about the whole thing.

But the Stones wanted to talk about music, not themselves, so they launched into a discussion of "Have You Seen Your Mother, Baby, Standing In The Shadows?"

"We tried trombones, saxes, nearly all permutations of brass before arriving at the trumpets," Keith explained when talking about the instruments backing their recording. "Everything but the trumpets dragged. If you have a question about the lyric," he added, "you must ask Mick — that's his department."

Mick, now pinpointed as the definite lyric writer on Stone records, looked up and nodded. "I get the ideas for the words by sitting down and following a train of thought — one thing just leads to another. This is simply about a boy and his bird. Some songs I write are just for a laugh. Others are extensions of ideas. This is a mixture of both.

"You must listen to it (Have You Seen Your Mother?) and place your own interpretation on the lyric. There is no attempt to present a controversial 'Mother' theme. 'Mother' is a word that is cropping up in a lot of numbers," he continued.

Then the two began to roll off remarks about their many best-selling discs, and how they do it all the time.

"We don't ask ourselves what is most commercial," Keith explained, "We simply say 'We like this best.' What we have liked over the past few years has proved to be what the young people like, so this is how to choose a single. This is probably the way that Mozart wrote. He wrote for himself. So do we. And it is a happy coincidence that what we like should also be what our public likes."

And what would happen if the guys liked something that no one else liked, say for instance, "Have You Seen Your Mother, Baby, Standing In The Shadow?"

"I'm not going to burst into tears if this doesn't go to number one," Mick said, "at least it is the best we could do and I am satisfied that we have given our best."

Then the two Stones broke their ban on themselves and hung out a few sentences on Brian Jones and his injured hand.

Insured Hands

"Brian was telling me that shortly before he broke the tendons in his hand someone had asked him if he had insured his hands," Keith said. "And just after that he broke his hand while climbing. Strange, isn't it?"

"He could play slowly with the hand while we were doing the Ed Sullivan Show," Keith continued. "I think he'll manage the tour all right."

Speaking of their tour, Mick decided to comment about the Walker-Troggs tour which was going on the road the same time as the Stones' show.

"I hope they have full houses," he said, "I hope we have full houses. I hope everyone has full houses," he finished generously.

But Keith was off on his own chain of thought.

"The Troggs are interesting," he said thoughtfully. "They are developing simplicity. We are trying to progress, but in a different direction — forward!"

Naughty Molly Richard!

Four Tops On The Four Tops

By Carol Deck

When four handsome young men from Detroit put out a record that immediately grabs everyone's attention, people soon want to know everything there is to know about those four guys.

Well, the Four Tops released "Reach Out I'll Be There," which is following "Ain't Too Proud to Beg" and "You Can't Hurry Love," other current Motown smashes up the charts, with the usual mighty Motown speed.

And people have been asking "What are the Tops really like?"

The BEAT went straight to the people who know the Tops better than anyone else in the world and asked that very question — we went to the Tops themselves.

That is, we went to three fourths of the Four Tops. At the time we talked with the three exciting young performers, their lead singer Levi Stubbs Jr. was in bed quite ill.

The other three — Renaldo Benson, Lawrence Payton and Abdul Fakir — however, were in great spirits as they sat sprawled about Motown's West Coast office intermittenly answering phone calls from Detroit.

People often comment on the Tops names, particularly Abdul Fakir. Asked where his name came from, Abdul quips, "I got it from my father," but then seriously says, "it's East Indian."

If their real names confuse you, try keeping up with their nick names. Abdul is called Duke by the rest of the group and Renaldo is Obie.

The three came bursting into the office apologizing profusely for missing the interview which had been set up the day before. Motown acts rarely miss any appointment and these three knew that.

So we asked, "what are the Tops really like?" And they told us.

Lawrence describes Renaldo: "He's a great guy with a fantastic sense of humor. He smiles a lot, particularly when he speaks. On stage he's our little sunsport, besides that he's a nut."

Renaldo then offers his explanation for everything — "I had a very good education in starvation."

Renaldo describes Abdul: "He's cool, smart, understanding, patient very warm. Duke's very musical and creative. He's just a great guy."

Abdul on Lawrence: "He's cool, easy going. He doesn't bother no one and no one bothers him. Musically, I'd say he's a genius. He's behind all the Tops' success. He's a really swinging cat."

Renaldo backs up Abdul's praises of Lawrence: "He's a very warm person. Musically I think he's a genius too. He's also a great sports lover — any sport at all. And he's very dedicated, musically and otherwise.

Levi wasn't there, but he needed no defense. The other three had nothing but praise for their stricken leader.

"He's got one of the great voices of today," said Abdul. "He's a real lover of his fans and would do anything to make and keep his fans happy. Like right now, he should be in the hospital but he hasn't missed a show."

"He's a killer," added Lawrence, "one of the best singers I know. He's very sincere and goes out of his way to talk to his fans.

"Like the last time we played Philly. There were some wounded men brought out of a hospital to see our show and Levi braved 100,000 people to go back and to meet and talk to those guys. We all did but it was Levi's idea."

... THE FOUR TOPS REACHING OUT FOR NUMBER ONE?

If You Were A Monkee...

...YOU'D WRESTLE WITH HORSES.

...AUDITION TALENTED (?) NEWCOMERS,

...SING TO EMPTY COUCHES

...AND INSURE GOOD RELATIONS WITH THE SERVICE.

BEATLES ARCHIVES 1

BEATLES ARCHIVES 1

Two Thousand Guard Beatles

Beatlemania struck the shores of Japan last week and caught the population off-guard. The Phenomenal Foursome made their debut performance in Japan before a capacity crowd of 10,000 teenagers — predominantly female, and predominantly hysterical.

The concert was held at the Martial Arts Hall, which is right outside of the Emperor's Palace in Tokyo. The Tokyo police assigned a record number of 1,700 policemen to protect both the quartet and the fans inside and around the hall.

The fire department in Tokyo ordered an additional 500 men, plus a number of ambulances and first-aid stations for the hectic occasion.

Japanese authorities said it was the first time that such heavy security precautions had been necessitated for an entertainment event of this sort. Fortunately, there were no serious injuries or incidents to mar the hysterical — but happy — event.

In the meantime, Beatle Paul McCartney and long-time girlfriend Jane Asher traveled to a remote area of Scotland to inspect a 183-acre dairy farm which he hopes to purchase.

The couple roamed about the property for some time, and then were invited to join farmer John Brown and wife Janet at a meal of bacon and eggs.

According to a spokesman for the Beatles, Paul has hopes of purchasing the farm and would like to move in before the end of the year.

A reliable source informs us that, "To farm has been a lifelong ambition of his and he'd like to go where he can get away from it all."

Inside the BEAT

Letters To The Beat 2
Animals Join Herman 4-5
Jaggered By Mick 7
Davis A Traitor? 10
Keith Relf Speaks 11
A Well-Tanned DC 5 13

The BEAT is published weekly by BEAT Publications, Inc., editorial and advertising offices at 6290 Sunset Blvd., Suite 504, Hollywood, California 90028. U.S. bureaus in Hollywood, San Francisco, New York, Chicago and Nashville; overseas correspondents in London, Liverpool and Manchester, England. Sale price, 15 cents. Subscription price U.S. and possessions, $5 per year; Canada and foreign rates, $9 per year. Second class postage prepaid at Los Angeles, California.

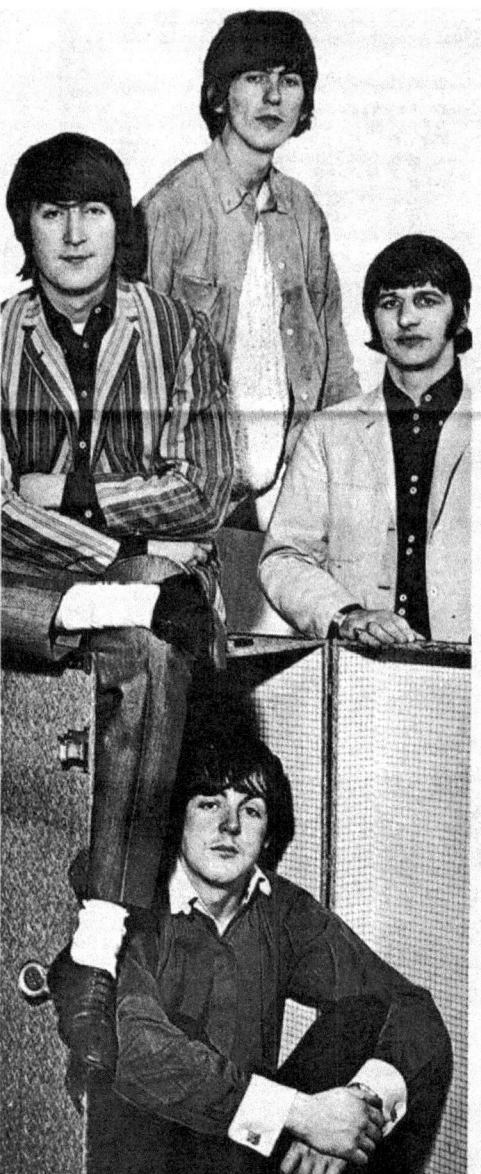

...BEATLES' NEW ALBUM COVER

The Beatles' Movie Script

(Continued From Page 2)

Beatles is simply that there are *four* of them. What difference does that make, you say? It makes a big difference. It means that whatever script they finally decide upon must have *four* equally important roles. Because the Beatles insist on sharing equally.

It also means that before they make that final decision all four of them must agree on it. If only one of the Beatles is against the proposed movie — it's off.

Paul states this emphatically when he says that they must have "complete" agreement among themselves before they will even begin a movie.

So, there you have it. The Beatles know what they *don't* want for their next film and they know what they *do* want. But they can't find it. Want to help?

At this point with only three months left before they are scheduled to begin filming they are open to any suggestions. Piles of scripts are being read everyday in the hopes of uncovering the one they want. If you are a budding script writer or know of someone who is, by all means submit the scripts to the Beatles.

You never know, you may be lucky this time.

Hair Cut For John

Alas, John Lennon's locks must go. Part of them, at least.

Lennon, preparing for the first solo film role for any of the Beatles, will have to undergo a hair trimming before appearing in "How I Won The War."

The hair cut, however, isn't expected to be a severe one.

"We have to do something about John's hair before every film," explained Dick Lester, who worked on both Beatle films and who will direct this one.

"But it will only be a trim."

John will play the part of Private Gripweed, a soldier in an imaginary British regiment during the second world war.

The movie, taken from the novel of the same name by Patrick Ryan,

is expected to be premiered next summer.

"We may ask John and Paul to help with the sound track music later," said Lester. "But that depends on how the film shooting turns out."

BEAT EXCLUSIVE

Will This Be Beatle Movie Number Three?

A NOTE FROM SHIRLEY POSTON: Did you, by any chance, page hysterically through The BEAT, searching for your beloved "For Gawd's Sake"—whoops—"For Girls Only," only to discover that it was gone?

Seriously (oh **sure***), there's a good reason why my weekly ravings don't appear in this issue. And you're about to read that reason. Which happens to be an entire Beatle movie, sent to me by one of both of my many readers.*

After reading it 42,000 times, I decided it was just too good to keep to myself, so I wheedled the boss into printing it in The BEAT.

She agreed on one condition. Since the "movie" was so long, someone was going to have to donate some of their space so it could appear.

However, it's worth giving up my chance to blither about George (ache) for one week. I think you'll think so too **(hah?)** *when you read the masterpiece dreamed up by Linda Souza of Oakland, Calif.*

I suppose Linda will kill me for blabbing that after she completes a "film" (each one takes several months and she's done several), she also dreams up a premiere and an Academy Awards ceremony where her stars win Oscars.

But Linda sure deserves one of those Oscars! Like pass the popcorn and see for yourselves as The BEAT presents . . .

THE RIGHT GUARD(IAN)
OR
ONE BOBBY GIVES YOU 24 HOURS PROTECTION

The movie begins in an English park where Paul is strumming his guitar and singing as his partner in crime, a young girl named Jill, is dancing with members of the crowd. The camera occasionally zooms in for a close up and stop action of Jill cleverly lifting a ring off her dancing partner's finger, or taking a wallet from his pocket. During these stop action periods, the credits are superimposed over the scene.

One of the fellows Jill dances with is Napoleon Solo. Jill easily relieves him of his tie clip, but fails to recognize his identity.

Missing Badge

As the song comes to a close, Jill accepts one more partner—a charming policeman named Ringo. When the song ends, Paul and Jill make a quick bow then casually stroll away. Ringo, too, begins to depart, but after taking two steps, he notices that his badge is missing.

Before the bobby can utter a sound, Paul begins shouting orders to him. Acting like an officer of the law, Paul waves the stolen badge about, and gruffly commands Ringo to stand against the wall.

The stunned Ringo complies, and Paul frisks him, pocketing anything of value. After Paul briefly but soundly reprimands the befuddled bobby for various offenses, he and Jill depart. Ringo stands thinking for a moment, then faces the camera and delivers his conclusion: "I've been bamboozled."

The hoodwinked bobby again gives chase, this time blowing his whistle as he runs. The fleeing couple turns a corner only to find three more bobbies waiting there.

The duo is captured and taken to the local police station where Jill is ordered to hand over the stolen items. She does, with one exception, concealing the spared loot in her long hair. Paul and Jill are then locked in a cell already occupied by one other person. A cunning rogue named John.

The camera has followed Ringo back to the station where a visiting commissioner is telling the officers that one of them is to be given a special and dangerous 24-hour assignment. Facing the lineup of bobbies, the commissioner asks for all volunteers to take one step forward.

All the men except Ringo take two steps backward, leaving Ringo standing alone. The commissioner profusely thanks Ringo for volunteering, but it's a puzzled Ringo who shakes the commissioner's hand.

Meanwhile, back in the cell, Jill and Paul are arguing over who is to blame for their incarceration. As the argument grows more heated, Jill tells Paul she is much more clever than he as she has managed to save part of the loot.

As she hands the tie clip to Paul, Constable Ringo enters, followed by George, who has come to bail out John. However, he decided to bail out Jill instead! Jill, not one to let opportunity knock in vain, accepts George's offer.

"Jill-Ted"

Both John and Paul are outraged. As the trio leaves, John sinks back to his bunk and mumbles: "I believe we've been Jill-ted, mate."

Paul, in anger, slams the tie clip against the cement wall. A small explosion occurs, and the wall crumbles. Paul and John are startled, but they hurriedly make their escape, followed by Ringo.

Not too far away, Ringo encounters the escapees in a dark alley. But as he approaches them, the bumbling bobby knocks over a stack of crates which tumble on John. John lies on the ground, motionless. Ringo is horrified. Paul goes to John, takes his arm and puts the wrist to his (Paul) ear. He gives it a thump and again places the wrist to his ear as if he were listening to a watch.

"He's dead," Paul gasps as the shocked Ringo's eyes grow wider. "Of course you know what this means," Paul continues. "Murder of this sort can send a bumbling bobby like you to prison for a long time. And, as a witness to this foul crime, I am going to see that you get everything that's coming to you!"

Paul goes on terrifying Ringo and finally persuades him to flee the scene, leaving Paul to dispose of the body. Ringo reluctantly leaves, vowing someday he will put Paul behind bars for this treacherous act of blackmail. When the defeated policeman departs, John dusts himself off and he and Paul start out in search of George and Jill.

The camera finds George and Jill leisurely having dinner in a dimly lit, romantic Italian restaurant. Four musicians stroll over to their table and serenade them with a soft ballad. The musicians bear a remarkable resemblance to the Beatles, but look very Italian in their mustaches.

As George continues to woo the sticky-fingered miss, she interrupts to explain that she must go back and rescue Paul. George is not very understanding or keen on the idea, but pursues Jill as she leaves for the police station.

While snooping about the station, George and Jill eavesdrop on a conversation between Ringo and the commissioner, who are discussing the special assignment.

A great treasure is coming to the United Kingdom. In every country where it has been displayed, it has been stolen at least twice. Scotland Yard, however, is determined not to lose the treasure to plunderers, and has devised a plan to thwart the villians.

One man is to take charge of the priceless article. Where he hides it will be known only to him, and his identity is to be kept a secret.

Then, from a brown paper bag, the commissioner removes an exquisite, jewel-laden tiara. Twenty-four hours from now it is to be presented to the Queen and then taken to the Tower Of London to be displayed with the other royal jewels. Until that time, the tiara will be left in Ringo's charge.

George and Jill can hardly believe their ears. How easy it will be to follow Ringo and snatch the tiara! But as they prepare to do just that, Ringo recognizes them and has them questioned for over an hour. When they're finally released, Ringo has left the station and George and Jill must search the streets for him.

Bickering

However, John and Paul find George and Jill before the latter two find Ringo. On the street corner where they meet, the four immediately plunge into an argument. As the bickering continues, a newsstand keeper calls in two bobbies to restore order.

They recognize Paul and John and another chase is on.

John ducks into a house, seats himself at an empty place at the table, and begins to make "small talk" with the others seated there. Paul enters a pub by the front door, while Jill and George stuff themselves into the dark side-doorway of the same building.

The policemen carry on down the street, passing them by.

John finishes his cuppa, then bids a jibberish adieu to his astonished "hosts." Paul opens the door George and Jill are leaning against. George, appearing not to be the least bit surprised, fingers Paul's navy blue tie with white dots.

"The seagulls must be flying lower this year," he says. Paul is not amused. John joins the group complaining that "it's getting so no one is safe on the streets after dark."

The four venture into a pub, but when their drinks are finished, they've no money for the bill. Paul suggests a song and picks up his guitar (which he's been carrying all this time.) Jill then dances with the surly bartender, picks his pocket, and pays the tab. When they leave the pub, George and Paul escort Jill home. John goes off in another direction.

John whistles as he walks down the road. Noticing what appears to be a convention of cats, John invites himself to be guest speaker. At the conclusion of his "speech," there is applause from two hands. John turns around to take a bow and thoroughly surprises his audience of one. Namely, Ringo.

"Thought you were dead," says Ringo.

"I am," says John.

"Then watcha doin' here?"

"I'm yer guardian angel," replies John, quite seriously.

"Oh yeah? Where's yar halo and wings, then?" challenges Ringo.

"I'm a nonconformist."

"'Specially when it comes to obeyin' the law. Yer under arrest!"

Just then, George approaches. "Evening, guv'nor. Luvly night."

"Not for yer mate 'ere," Ringo growls.

In a loud "whisper," John tells Ringo, "he can't see or hear me because I've been deaded."

George, picking up the hint, asks "Who are you referrin' to, sir?"

"To that ruddy bloke standin' behind me." Ringo turns to face John, but he's hidden behind a mail box. "He's gimme the slip," sighs Ringo.

"Yeah, I believe *you've* slipped one, too," mutters George. "night, sir."

Invisible

Ringo watches George leave. John comes out and taps Ringo on the back.

"And where were you off to?" questions Ringo.

"I had to make meself invisible, so George couldn't see me."

"Rubbish, you were probably 'iding somewhere."

"Hold on, mate. If you don't believe me, I'll have to do something drastic to prove I am what I am. (On those last five words, John executes a bit of the sailor's hornpipe, a la Popeye.) "I shall expose your secret."

"What secret?"

The information George had passed on to John, John now passes on to Ringo. "How did you find out?" gasps Ringo.

"E.S.P. (Extra Salty Peanuts)," cracks John.

"Are ya trying to tell me you can read me mind?"

"Well, I hate to brag, but we angels can do a few odd things."

"I'm beginnin' to believe that angel stuff, but I'm still not quite sure you're what you seem."

"Okay, I'll prove it," swaggers John. "I'll tell you where the tiara is hidden."

"If you can do that, I'll believe you." (Ringo is confident John can't.)

John takes out some paper and a pencil. "Write down the hidin' place here and I'll tell you what you've written down."

Ringo writes. "Why do I have to write it down? Why don't you just read me mind?"

"It's kind of a check—I read your mind, then we check the paper to see if I'm right. Now put the paper here."

Ringo places the piece of folded paper on top of the mailbox.

"Now think of what you've just written." Ringo thinks. "Think harder, the message isn't clear." Ringo thinks harder. *"Harder!"* Ringo closes his eyes, making an agonizing face, and thinks harder.

John, meanwhile, reads the note and quickly puts it back before Ringo opens his eyes. "Now, I'll tell you the hiding place and you check the note. The tiara is in the palace, under the throne, right?"

Ringo is amazed, not to mention duped. "Then you - you must be . . ."

"Said I was, didn't I? Say now, what time ya got?"

"'Alf past eleven," Ringo notes.

"Blimey! I'm due at a union meeting at twelve!"

"*Union* meeting?"

"Yeah, could you loan me a pound for dues?"

Ringo gives John a disgusted look and a pound for dues, and with that, John is off down the street.

"You Know"

Ringo calls after him. "Hey, what about me problem of protectin' the . . . the (he looks around, then softly adds) *you* know. Aren't you gonna help me?"

"I'll bring it up at the meeting."

"But it's a secret!"

"Okay, so I won't bring it up at the meeting."

As John turns the corner, Ringo mutters "typical."

The next day, George, John, Paul and Jill meet in the park to discuss plans for stealing the tiara. They decide that the best way to enter the palace is as guards and Paul suggests a costume shop where they would find such costumes.

They journey to the shop, find exactly what they need, but are several shillings short of the rental fee. However, John spots an organ-grinder's costume and asks to borrow the organ for half a mo'. Outside the shop, he grinds out a tune with George acting as monkey. An amused crowd gathers, tossing coins into George's tin cup. By the conclusion of the song, enough money is collected to pay for the uniforms.

Near the Palace, the four knaves don their costumes, then march to meet the real guards. Upon meeting them, John tricks them into believing they are being relieved early. In a matter of minutes, the imposters enter the Palace, snatch the tiara, and return to their assumed post. The real relief guards arrive, and ceremoniously change places with the charlatans, who make a hasty departure.

A few hours before a certain ceremony is to begin, Ringo and the commissioner enter the throne room and find the tiara gone. The commissioner is furious. Poor Ringo is to be drummed out of the corps and placed under arrest. Fortunately, Ringo gets away and wanders about the streets, a wanted man in search of his guardian angel.

In his search, he pokes his head into a church as four choir boys, closely resembling the Beatles, begin to sing. He enjoys the music for a brief moment, then continues

(Turn to Page 14)

BEATLES ARCHIVES 1

Beatle Movie Number Three

(Continued From Page 6)

his pursuit—the music continues also.

This time it's members of a Salvation Army Band (also resembling the Beatles (who are playing. Ringo watches and listens for a few seconds, then to the accompaniment of the music, strolls to the zoo where he observes four monkeys (guess who?)

After leaving the park, Ringo turns a sharp corner and bumps (literally) into John, George, Paul and Jill. Paul drops the sack he was carrying and the tiara rolls out. A short silence follows, after which Ringo thanks John for his aid in capturing the crooks. Then George picks up the loot and runs down the street. Jill and Paul take off after him, and John and Ringo trail behind.

From an aerial view, the audience sees the first three enter a shop through the front door and exit at the rear on a bicycle built for three. Then John and Ringo enter and exit on a bicycle built for two.

The first part of the chase is viewed from the air. Above the background music, Ringo's police whistle is heard. Bobbies on bicycles (two by two, of course) give chase and through the countryside. The parade of bicycles grows and grows, as more officers join in.

There are close-ups of various puzzled spectators as they view George (wearing the tiara) at the front, Jill in the middle and Paul at the rear of their bike, being shadowed by John and Ringo on their bike, followed by fifty bobbies on twenty-five bikes.

But the race ends when George's vehicle skids and falls after narrowly missing a collision with an Astin Martin. Then Ringo's bike falls over, also spilling its passengers. The rest of the bikes pile up, too.

The driver of the car graciously aids Jill to her feet as the bobbies nab her companions. Jill fails to recognize the driver (James Bond, alias Sean Connery), and the driver fails to recognize his cuff-links have been swiped.

The movie comes to a close in the police station. The commissioner congratulates Ringo on his capturing the elusive marauders, and safely delivering the tiara to the Queen. (Ringo has failed to inform the authorities of his escapades with John.)

Back in the jail, Jill has a cell of her own and John, Paul and George occupy one opposite her. The fearless foursome are in the midst of saying goodbye when Jill tells Paul she has a little going away gift for him.

She produces the cuff links and holds one in each hand. Paul is quite pleased (can't say the same for George.) She tosses one cuff link to Paul, but he misses and the link strikes the wall, exploding with a pink poof.

Jill then tosses the other link against her cell wall with the same results.

The boys give her a round of applause—to which she makes a modest bow. Then the group blows a kiss to the remaining walls and ed man in search of this guardian.

Finis? It's About Time!

BEATLE QUIZ

Here we go again! Five more questions for the KRLA Beatle Quiz.

Those of you who missed the first four weeks of the Beatle Quiz may still catch up by ordering the issues of June 16, June 9, June 2 and May 26. You'll find instructions for ordering issues elsewhere in the BEAT.

The winner, of course, will get to interview the Beatles for the KRLA Beat when they arrive in August. The winner and a friend will also attend a Beatle Concert as guests of the KRLA Deejays.

Additional prizes will be provided for runners-up. In case of a tie there will be additional questions or a drawing to decide the final winner. The contest will cover a ten-week period, with at least five new questions asked each week. KRLA's Derek Taylor, a close friend of the Beatles and their former press officer, will judge the entries for accuracy.

Beatle Quiz
KRLA BEAT
Suite 504
6290 Sunset Blvd.
Hollywood, Calif. 90028

CONTEST EDITOR:

Below are my answers to the fourth set of questions in the BEATLE QUIZ CONTEST.

My Name .... Address ....
City .... State .... Zip Code ....
I (☐ am) (☐ am not) presently a subscriber to the KRLA BEAT.

NEW QUESTIONS

21. How many hats was John Lennon wearing during his bubble bath scene in "Hard Day's Night?" ....
22. Who has taken Derek Taylor's place as Beatle Press Agent? ....
23. According to their hair dresser, which Beatle's hair is the softest? ....
24. The Beatles had a name for the pointed-toe shoes they wore in the old days. What was it? ....
25. When the Beatles first landed in New York, their arrival was picketed by a group of local union members. What was the purpose of the picket and what union participated?

Harrison Visits India

Beatle George Harrison and his wife Patti are currently in India, where George is learning to play the sitar.

George and Patti are reportedly registered at a Bombay hotel under the names of "Mr. and Mrs. Sam Wells."

George has not announced when they expect to return to Britain, but has indicated that it may be some time before the two go back. He holds "open" air tickets from Bombay to the U.K.

George's well-known interest in the Indian instrument caused a flood of sitar music in rock and roll, both in Beatle material and numbers by other groups.

John Lennon, on location for the shooting of "How I Won The War," will not return to London until the filming is completed in early November.

The whereabouts of Ringo Starr and Paul McCartney are assumed to be in London. Ringo said earlier that he wanted to spend more time with his wife Maureen and son, Zak.

...LEARNING SITAR IN INDIA

BEATLES EXPAND U.S. TOUR

By Dave Hull

Hi, Hullabalooers!

Everybody else takes a summer vacation, but I take mine in the winter. So, now that summer is here I'm resuming my weekly column in the BEAT.

I'll start with a few hot items that are absolute exclusives at the time I'm writing this.

The Beatles are adding at least three appearances to their August concert schedule. They will schedule one performance in San Diego and another in Salt Lake City between Aug. 22 and Aug. 29.

In addition, they will schedule a second performance at the Cow Palace in San Francisco. At the moment, not even the radio stations and newspapers in these cities are aware of this. It will give them quite a story.

No Changes Here

I'm happy to report that this does not change the Beatles schedule for Los Angeles. In addition to their two concerts at Hollywood Bowl on Aug. 28 and Aug. 29, they will still be spending from seven to ten days on vacation here.

Here's a flash for Beatle fans who have not been able to obtain tickets for their local concerts. If you don't mind travelling, you can still obtain tickets for their Portland, Oregon, concert. For some reason—even though they are sold out everywhere else 10,000 tickets are still available for the Aug. 22 performance in Portland.

Many people have asked other questions about the Beatles. I'll start answering them next week. In the meantime, if you have any questions about the Beatles or other entertainers, write me at KRLA.

See ya next week.

Beatles, Stones Joining Voices?

LONDON—Have the two top British rock groups teamed up for a single release? The question is being asked here as the new Rolling Stones recording, "We Love You," hits the record racks. The cut features the Stones and some unidentified "friends," and these friends sound suspiciously like the Beatles.

Whether John, Paul, George and Ringo did or did not back up the Stones, Jagger and Co. are going more and more into the Beatle groove, not only sounding like them but using a similar lyric theme—love.

BEATLES ARCHIVES 1

John Lennon had a rather profound statement to make about the Beatles' recent American tour: "The weather's too hot and someone's pinched three of my shirts." George promptly blamed Ringo for John's misfortune but Ringo deadpanned: "Don't look at me! I've got nothing to do with the weather!"

Some more Beatle news — the four boys will cut a new record in November for pre-Christmas release and then, of course, around the Christmas holidays they will begin another one of their fabulous Christmas shows. There was some talk of close-circuiting the show so that people in other parts of England (and possibly the U.S.) could also view the Beatles' show but nothing further has been said so I guess we lose!

Dig Khaki Ties

Have you noticed that all of the Beatles have suddenly taken to wearing khaki army ties? Well, there is a very good explanation for this. While they were filming "Help" on Salisbury Plain, Paul happened to mention to an army colonel how much he liked the tie the Colonel was wearing and sure enough the next day the Colonel showed up loaded down with ties for all of the Beatles!

Mick Jagger revealed to a London newspaperman: "When there are thousands of people out there rioting — I don't mind telling you I get pretty scared."

... JOHN LENNON

Beatles Take Mystic Train

(Continued from Page 5)
cries as he poked his head from a window and yelled "Jump, Cyn, jump!" were all too late. Cyn burst into tears and the press and TV cameramen went to work again with a great whirling and much clicking.

Too Beautiful

The grooviest train took nearly five hours to reach Bangor. By that time radio and press news had told the Welsh population what as happening.

"It is all too beautiful" murmured His Holiness accepting a bunch of carnations from a Bangor inhabitant.

"Its all intriguing but I don't know a lot about it," replied Mick Jagger when a Welsh reporter demanded to know the Stone's motives.

"One of the most illuminating and exciting experiences I have had," Paul summed up when cross-examined about the transcendental meditation thing.

So, the Beatles and their closest friends stayed on in Bangor, turning on to the words of their robed and bearded guru Yogi ("Holiness is just a quality of life") during his final days in Britain prior to retirement to "a life of utter silence in Kashmir."

And the brought-down, left-behind Mrs. Lennon? Well, she was driven to Bangor by Neil in his pale blue Jag and Jane Asher joined her for the trip at the last moment so everything was fine and the tension was over.

'MY LIFE WITH THE BEATLES'
Beatlemania Grips England

(Editor's Note: This is the third and concluding installment of Derek Taylor's life with the Beatles, first as a newspaperman covering their exciting rise to world fame and later as their press officer.)

The Beatles returned to Manchester in November of that year at the height of Beatlemania and again I was on the scene. Here are some extracts of that report:

"Beatlemania, in its sobbing, throbbing extremities, gripped Manchester last night.

"It captivated the teenagers of the city and far beyond. It drew 5,000 of them inside the Apollo Cinema to share the thumping ecstasy of their electronic excitement.

"It tore half the city's police force — men and women — from normal duties. It totally mobilized the first-aid resources of South Lancashin — men and women, even earnest children.

"At noon in a curiously apprehensive atmosphere, in places far from the Apollo, plans were rehearsed. St. John's paraded their staff with first aid kits. So did the Red Cross.

Bedlam

"The police were given their final orders. A mobile headquarters — last used in a murder hunt last month — was set up outside the cinema. . . .

"Many girls fainted. Thirty were gently carried out, protesting in their hysteria, forlorn and wretched in an unrequited love for four lads who might have lived next door.

"The stalls were like a nightmare March Fair. No one could remain seated. Clutching at each other, hurling jelly babies at the stage, beating their brows, the youth of Britian's second city surrendered themselves totally.

"It is, quite simply, the ultimate phenomenon of show business."

National Heroes

They were extremely cooperative, envy friendly, and the press was very much in favor of all four of them. There was no question at that time of attempting to knock them. Everyone was in love with all that the Beatles stood for — their gaiety, their honesty, and their enormous commercial value.

Every newspaper by then was boosting its circulation by the size and quality of its coverage of Beatle events. Special editions were published for towns where the Beatles were appearing. The Beatles had become very familiar with the press, with the needs of journalists, and also with some of our strange methods.

Big Honor

I had met them earlier than their second Manchester appearance — two months earlier, in fact, when they played at a dance in Southport, a seaside town some miles north of Liverpool. It had just been announced that the Beatles would appear before the Queen Mother at the Royal Variety Show in London. All the show business journalists were dispatched to Southport to meet the Beatles to get quotes from them on their response to this most important honor.

By instinct every press man assigned to the job met in a pub.

We knew it was not going to be easy to get backstage, so we decided to play it gently and politely until we were forced to switch tactics.

No Admittance

The police were as gracious as ever and kept us outside until we could find one of the Beatles' party to grant us access.

Finally we got into the Beatles' dressing room, grabbed a few quick quotes before they were due to stage.

But most of us felt we hadn't enough to write a decent story so we returned to the dressing room. This time the door was held firm against us. Neil Aspinall, the Beatles' road manager, said, "I'm sorry, the Beatles leave almost immediately and there's no time."

There was a smaller, older man there and we persuaded him to let us in. He, it seems, was the company manager.

We again hammered on the door and Neil reappeared and said, "I'm awfully sorry but we can't give any more interviews."

I pointed to the company manager and said, "He said we can."

Neil muttered, "He has nothing to do with it," and closed the door. I told the company manager, "Neil Aspinall says your word doesn't count," starting a beautiful row between Neil and the company manager.

Because of the diversion caused by the row, we all burst into the Beatles' dressing room and secured our further interviews.

They really were remarkably patient.

But when I met Neil and the Beatles at that second Manchester concert, they pointed at me and said, "Hey . . . you're the one who kicked the door in in Southport." They have good memories.

Join Beatles

Well, to cut a long story short, I became more and more friendly with them. And when the Daily Express decided to pay a Beatle as a weekly columnist, I asked for George Harrison. Brian Epstein and I negotiated a fee of $300 a week (we had offered $90 but the shrewd Epstein wasn't having that!) and I was assigned to help George to write it.

I traveled to Europe with them and in March of last year, Brian Epstein asked me to help him with his book. While we were completing the taping of interviews for the book, Brian finally invited me to join him as his personal assistant and press and promotions officer for the Beatles.

This was what I had been after for six months, and after a short discussion on salary — in which, I might add, Epstein emerged victorious — I left the Daily Express and journalism for a hot-seat at the center of the biggest show business storm of all time.

Lasted Nine Months

Nine months later it was all over. Brian Epstein and I — though we remain friendly and share considerable mutual respect — cannot get on together as employer and employee.

I still believe the Beatles to be the best thing in show business and marvelous companions.

Epstein I will always admire very much. They are a magnificent fivesome and let nobody tell you that there is any fifth Beatle other than Brian Epstein.

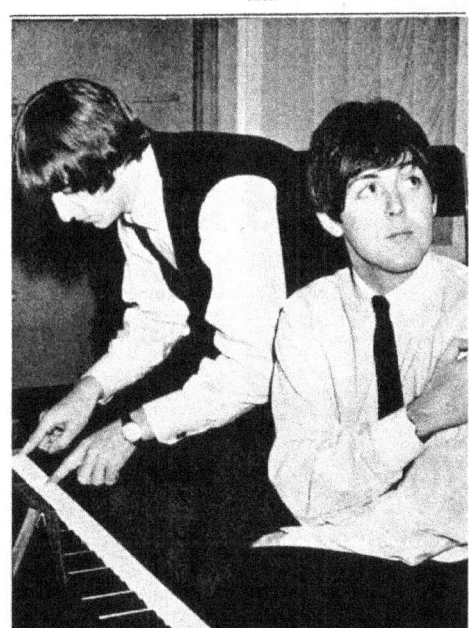
PAUL and RINGO

BEATLES ARCHIVES 1

Beatles Running; Running; Running

By Jamie McCluskey III

Running, running—at a dizzying pace; *running* are the Beatles, faster than the speed of light.

Running to their many concerts, *running from* their screaming fans. *Running* 'round the world in waxen circles of chart-topping records, and *running* circles 'round the world!

Until now, the Beatles had always run together: a relay team of four. But lately there have been some changes in the running line-up, and some of the boys have been venturing forth on solo trots all their own.

Beatle Paul contemplates his tears in mournful solitude.

M. Starkey, MBE, has decided to be himself and in a rare solo performance by The Nose, Ringo bravely sets forth to "Act Naturally."

Of course, it is left to Mr. Lennon—John-John by name—to be the sneaky one, as he deviously demands that "You've Got to Hide Your Love Away."

Yes, it is true that the Beatles are doing more and more individually in the records which they are producing now. However, they have said from the very first that the act was "a whole, and each one of us takes one quarter of the whole."

Among the many countless reasons behind their phenomenal success lies the fact that each Beatle is a very talented individual in his own right. We are all well-acquainted with the works of the talented team of songwriters—Lennon and McCartney—and the genius of John Lennon as author in *"his own write"* is far from secret. In the music industry itself, Ringo Starr has a fine reputation as being one of the best natural drummers in his field, and George Harrison is adding to his own excellent reputation as a great guitarist by writing songs of his own for the group.

But concern has been voiced because John and Paul have gone into record production for one or two other groups outside of their own, and over the now widely-known solo writing and performing efforts of Paul on his beautiful new record, "Yesterday."

The truth is that all four of the boys have always worked on little projects of their own, independent of other members of the group. But just as they have said of themselves, there are four unique individuals in this group and each member is an important entity in himself even before he has joined with the other three to form the perfect foursome.

Yes, the Beatles are *running*—only running far ahead of everyone else on the track. And Paul? Well, he's just leading the pack!!

...**PAUL LEADS PACK**
BEAT Photo: Chuck Boyd

IN THE BACKGROUND HERE, manager Epstein was at the forefront of the Beatles startling success.

Epstein Death Shocks India-Bound Beatles

LONDON — Although the official inquest into the death of Beatle manager Brian Epstein has been postponed, authorities are certain that no foul play was involved in the unexpected passing of the 32-year-old financial genius.

A routine autopsy failed to reveal the cause of death, so the inquest was adjourned to Sept. 8 to allow time for laboratory tests.

Epstein was found in the bedroom of his Belgravia town house with several bottles of pills reportedly at his side. Police said he had been taking the pills for "various ailments, and a friend later disclosed that Epstein had been unwell for some months.

The laboratory tests were ordered to determine if a lethal mixture of the pills and any liquor Epstein had consumed the night before at a party might have killed him.

The Beatles were in Bangor, Wales, on a meditation retreat with Indian mystic Maharishi Mahesh Yogi when they heard about the death of their manager.

"It's a great shock," said Paul McCartney when he was told the news.

The Maharishi broke the news to the Beatles after newsmen brought word to the retreat.

Later in the week the Beatles announced that they would be spending at least two months in India where they would "learn how to meditate better."

Meanwhile reports began circulating that the copyrights to the Beatles' music might be sold to pay an estimated $14 to $16.8 million taxes on Epstein's estate. The eldest son of a furniture store owner, Epstein left an estimated $19.8 million fortune, and according to British tax law, 80 per cent of it must be confiscated by the government.

Rumors were that the copyrights would be sold to an American concern. A year ago, an American consortium offered $9.8 for Epstein's Nems Enterprises, but he rejected the offer.

John And Paul To Be Hosts Of TV Special

Big things are happening in London Town these days for two of our favorite Mop Tops.

John Lennon and Paul McCartney will do their own hosting honors for a fifty-minute spectacular which will be produced by Granada television this fall.

To Pay Tribute

The special program will pay tribute to the talented team of composers and to their international success in the field of song-writing.

It is doubtful at this time that the two remaining Beatles will appear with messrs. Lennon and McCartney unless they have a new record released at that time.

The program will feature musical selections composed by John and Paul and the performing artists may include Peter and Gordon, Cilla Black, Billy J. Kramer and the Dakotas, the Fourmost, and the Silkie.

Clips Of Yanks

There is hope at the moment that the show will also include film clips of some American artists, possibly including Ella Fitzgerald.

It is not known at this writing whether or not the program will be aired in America, although several other Beatle specials probably will be seen here throughout the next few months.

BEATLES ARCHIVES 1

BEATLES, STONE TRAIL HIS HOLINESS

KRLA *Edition* **BEAT** 25¢

SEPTEMBER 23, 1967

BEATLES ARCHIVES 1

Beatles In Air Fright

The Beatles are very nervous about flying, The BEAT has learned from several sources who spent a great deal of time with the foursome during their U.S. tour.

Their fright stems from the fact that the plane in which they toured America last year crashed and burned only four months after the group had used it.

This year, the plane in which the Beatle tour was flying threw sparks over Seattle.

The drummer for the Remains, who has a phobia about flying anyway, became nearly hysterical and had to leave the plane. Two members of the Ronettes decided to leave also.

The Beatles remained aboard, however, and continued their flight, but were reported "a little jumpy."

... STILL IN THE DRIVERS SEAT

BEATLES TOP STONES IN 'BATTLE OF BEAT'

By Dave Hull

Okay! Kings-X! Cool it! We surrender!

We've got mail piled up to the ceiling here in the BEAT offices and the phones are ringing off the wall. KRLA's "Battle of the BEAT" poll is now officially over and here is the result:

THE BEATLES WON!

Beatle fans throughout California jumped up in arms during the final week of balloting. Beatle votes came pouring in like an avalanche and they wound up with a 2-1 lead over the Rolling Stones.

If you remember, the Stones had taken a lead during the first two weeks of the write-in poll. But John, Paul, George and Ringo caught them during the third week, and after the fourth week the Beatles wound up with 65.8 per cent of the total vote.

So, don't underestimate the Beatles. Or their fans.

But the final results are no reflection on the Rolling Stones. They're still burning up the record charts with "Satisfaction"—their greatest hit yet—and the Beatles do not have a current hit.

Surprise?

The outcome of the popularity poll will come as a surprise to many people. The Beatles have been drawing extremely poor crowds in some European cities. Even here in California they're running into some problems at the box office.

Their two performances at Hollywood Bowl were instant sell-outs, but they have had trouble selling tickets for the San Diego concert, sponsored by the House of Sight and Sound. This in spite of the fact it has been heavily promoted by other radio stations in Los Angeles and other cities who claim to be sponsoring the concert.

But the excitement of the Beatles receiving the cherished Order of the British Empire and the criticism which followed in many quarters must have aroused the Southern California Beatlemaniacs. I think that had a lot to do with the flood of mail we received during the final week of the BEAT poll.

More Beatlemania

And when the Beatles release their next record I think it will be as big a smash as any of their previous hits. I think the combined impact of releasing their new movie plus the approach of their U.S. concert tour will start another mass wave of Beatlemania.

Getting back to the popularity contest, I think it also proved that most Californians like both groups. Many found it hard to choose between them because they have completely different styles and both are tremendously talented.

But that's the case in any popularity contest. It's like putting Elizabeth Taylor and Deborah Kerr in the same category and choosing between them for an Academy Award. That's not easy, either.

Many people, in fact, voted for BOTH the Beatles and the Rolling Stones.

I was one of them.

Beatles Map Busy Summer

From now until September the Beatles will be one busy group. As a matter of fact, they are already pretty busy — but the hardest part is still to come.

The Beatles began their summer season and also a continental tour on June 20 when they appeared in Paris to an overflowing and over-enthusiastic crowd. The Paris fans got out of hand, stormed the stage, and literally tore up the auditorium! The Beatles, however, escaped uninjured.

The Beatles then moved on to Lyons, Milan, Genoa, Rome, Nice, Madrid, and Barcelona. The standout city in this package had to be Rome because a very strange incident occurred in the Eternal City. At least, it was unusual for the Beatles. When they arrived at the Roman airport, 150 policemen were there to insure the group's safety from the massive following which inevitably greets the Beatle's airport arrival.

But the Roman massive following consisted of nine fans, all of whom were English! Must have quite a let-down for the Liverpool four.

But then again, maybe they should have expected it because the day before in Genoa only 3,000 turned out to see the Beatles when the stadium could have held 20,000!

Early in July, the Beatles will go to Buckingham Palace to meet the Queen and have their M.B.E. awards presented to them. What higher honor than for an Englishman to meet his Queen.

The rest of July will be filled with radio and television dates, and on August 1 the Beatles will

appear on "Blackpool Night Out", a British television show.

And then the Beatles' second American tour begins. In case you haven't memorized the dates yet, here they are. August 14 — Ed Sullivan Show; 15 — Shea Stadium; 16th — "Rain Date" in case Shea Stadium show is rained out; 17th — Toronto; 18th — Atlanta; 19th — Houston; 20th — Chicago; 21 — Minneapolis 22nd — Portland; 23rd to 26th — stay in Los Angeles; 28th — San Diego; 29th and 20th — Hollywood Bowl; 31st — San Francisco; September 1 — return to London.

Although plans for the autumn are not definite yet, look for the Beatles to undertake a British tour and then start work on their third film.

—Louise Criscione.

Beatles Reveal Secret Desire

If you were one of the BEATLES, and you could do anything or have anything in the world, what would you like most of all on your next trip to the United States?

A spokesman for the BEATLES revealed that the first thing, the most important thing, the one BIG thing they want to do . . . is visit Disneyland!

It's not as easy as it sounds. Such a famous person as the former premier of Russia, Nikita Krushchev, was unable to attend because of security problems—and the same situation may face the BEATLES.

Getting to the Anaheim amusement park may be one thing, but what about the thousands of kids who will storm the place when the word spreads? One idea has been to have them get a quick look by helicopter, but so far no definite plans, or even approval, has been announced by Disney officials.

BEATLES ARCHIVES 1

BEATLES John, George and Paul with His Holiness Marharishi Mahesh Yogi.

UPI Photos

MICK AND MARIANNE board the "Love" train for Bangor.

PATTI HARRISON and sister, Jenny, try to pull Cyn aboard.

LEFT BEHIND, Cynthia Lennon wipes tears from her eyes.

Beatles And A Stone To Wales With Mystic

By Tony Barrow

Any good groupie and, indeed, any teenybopper of average intellect would assure you that one of the least likely places top pop people are to be found is a busy city rail terminal at holiday time. But there's always the exception to the general rule

The date was Friday, August 25, the beginning of Britain's August Bank Holiday Weekend.

The time was just after three o'clock in the afternoon.

The place was London's crowded Euston rail terminal with thousands of vacationing families bustling about with their baggage and their infant children.

Suddenly, without warning, there were Beatles and a Rolling Stone right there in the midst of the holiday crowds. Suddenly the 3:05 p.m. London to North Wales Express became the grooviest Bank Holiday train to pull out of Euston Station that day, this year or this decade!

Meditation Lecture

But I'd better start at the beginning. The previous day, Thursday, Aug. 24, a 56-year-old Himalayan mystic named Maharishi Mahesh Yogi (alias His Holiness The Master) gave a two-hour evening "transcendental meditation" lecture at the London Hilton Hotel. A few hours before the lecture was due to begin George Harrison decided he'd like to buy a couple of tickets—a dollar each—to hear the saintly, tiny, white-whiskered old man of the East preach his doctrine. Eventually Paul and John went along too and all seemed thoroughly impressed by the theories expounded by the leader of the Kashmir cult.

After joining 1500 other believers and intrigued spectators for the lengthy lecture, the three Beatles had a special audience with The Master who sat cross-legged before them in a fine white cloak and brightly colored beads with a little bunch of red roses and carnations clutched in his dark brown hands. He told the Beatles many things. "If you go into your garden and sit down to meditate," Maharishi Mahesh Yogi explained to Paul, "you must not keep your eyes closed all of the time or you will miss the great beauty of your garden."

Invitation to Wales

Before they left the Maharishi invited John, Paul and George to be guests at University College, Bangor, North Wales for the next four or five days. Over the August Bank Holiday Weekend the mystic was to give a further series of meditation lectures and the Beatles would be welcome to attend.

At first it didn't seem likely that they would. For one thing the Beattles had a recording session scheduled.

Twelve hours later, at noon on Friday, John and George determined to postpone all other activities and accompany His Holiness to the North Wales coastal town of Bangor, a 300-mile train ride from London. They contacted Paul who was equally enthusiastic. Ringo decided to delay his journey to Bangor in order to bring Maureen and the week-old baby Jason out of the hospital on Saturday morning. But at the very last moment he switched his plans, after talking to Maureen, and left from Euston station with the rest.

Just before three o'clock, Mick Jagger and Marianne Faithfull arrived at Euston, an unexpected addition to the colorful party of disciples. Everything had been fixed in such a rush that nobody had reserved seats for the train. Mick and Marianne hadn't even bought tickets for the trip.

Paul Arrives

Next to arrive was Paul, riding in Neil Aspinall's elegant pale blue Jaguar. But there was no sign of the others and the train was due to pull out. So Paul, Mick and Marianne got onto the train — along with their silver-haired master and one or two of his Eastern followers.

At seven minutes after three John's beautiful Rolls Royce drew in beside Euston's departure entrance. Out piled George and Patti plus Patti's young sister, Jenny, John and Cynthia and Ringo. Grasping multi-colored Greek bags and a small assortment of musical instruments shrouded in flower-painted cloth covers, the six walked and then ran through the crowds, past the ticket barrier and onto Platform 13. As they drew alongside the first part of the train, everyone realized that there was no time to look for any particular section. It was a matter of leaping aboard blindly. As they do this the train began to move.

A cop thought he'd be helpful by closing the door on the last of the party. But, by coincidence rather than design, he prevented Cynthia Lennon getting on. Poor Cyn was left all alone on the platform as the train disappeared from the station. John's frantic

(Continued on Page 9)

BEATLES ARCHIVES 1

BEATLE HISTORY PART II
BENEATH ALL THEIR HAIR!

By Jacoba Atlas

The fans knew it all along—the amazing talent that lay under that long hair—and the fans were just waiting to be taken along to the best in pop music which the Beatles would offer them.

There were no giant steps really, no valleys cut without bridges for the fans to cross. George didn't suddenly produce the complete Indian Sound, but exposed his audience to it gradually—first with "Norwegian Wood," and later with "Love You Too" and "I Want to Tell You." John and Paul didn't abandon melody for the mathematics of electronic music, but instead interspersed melody with electronics producing "Strawberry Fields Forever," "She Said, She Said," and of course, "Tomorrow Never Knows."

Paul himself stated, "we can make a bridge, you see, between us and Indian music or us and electronic music, and therefore we can take people with /us . . . There is no sense in not taking people with you."

New Maturity

Their lyrics revealed new maturity as in the worn-out love affair depicted in "For No One." "She wakes up, she makes up, she takes her time and doesn't feel she has to hurry, she no longer needs you." Or in the ironic tale of "Eleanor Rigby" "wearing the face that she keeps in a jar by the door—who it is for?"—who indeed.

Love songs were in profusion in *Revolver*; the joyous "Good Day Sunshine," with its honky-tonk piano, the hopeful "Got To Get You Into My Life" and the amazingly beautiful, if sentimental, "Here, There and Everywhere."

But *Revolver* did not just reveal new maturity in the themes of love, but also in such social themes as alienation. If "Taxman" was a special case of social satire, one would certainly be hard pressed to find a person who does not relate to George's feelings of inadequacy expressed in "I Want to Tell You" which deals with the 20th century problem of the inability of people to communicate. The new classic "Tomorrow Never Knows" urged everyone to turn off their minds and float down stream and to intricate electronic sounds thousands did just that.

Separate Careers

This new maturity in songs obviously reflected a growing personal maturity. The world had watched, as it seldom gets the chance, the public education of four young men going from precocious adolescence to intelligent adulthood. All but Paul married, and their tastes ran the gamit from the French playwright Alfred Jarry—a particular favorite of Paul's—to the study of the ancient tribe of the Celts by John.

They branched out into separate endeavors: John to acting, Paul to scoring a film and making his own home movies, George to India to pursue more fully his interest in the Eastern culture, and Ringo to devoting more of his time to his all-important family.

A rather long period without group production led to speculation that the Beatles were breaking-up. From London came disquieting reports and Paul stated that he was "no longer one of the mop-tops." But with their latest album, *St. Pepper's Lonely Hearts Club Band* their future together again seems solidified.

St. Pepper is the progression of *Revolver* following John's desire to make every album better than the last one. Using the theme of a performance, we are given twelve unique songs each with a special and different theme.

Intricate Electronics

Electronics plays a far greater part than ever before, and a full orchestra is used on one number. The Indian influence is carried over to such a non-Harrison song as "Lovely Rita."

From the loneliness of "Eleanor Rigby" we have the haunting declaration "She's Leaving Home" using a similar background as "Rigby" plus some fine and unusual counter-point singing by the Beatles.

"Fixing A Hole" denotes the worth of being alone with one's thoughts—the pleasures of a wandering mind, shades of "Tomorrow Never Knows." "Within You, Without You" expresses similar sentiments as in *Revolver's* "Love You Too."

Cynical Humor

One of the major differences in the types of songs recorded is the lack of love songs on the *St. Pepper* album. For "Got To Get You Into My Life" we have the satirical "Lovely Rita" and for "Here, There and Everywhere" we are given the cynically humorous "When I'm Sixty-Four;" but no real ballads are included.

However, perhaps the most important song on *St. Pepper* both due to its extreme length, almost five minutes, and in the eyes of the BBC who banned the song, is 'A Day In The Life;' a strange tale of a dream employing a forty-one piece orchestra plus electronics. John sings the lead with Paul adding the controversial bridge.

There can be no doubt now that the Beatles have emerged from just being 'bloody phenomena' to brilliant composers and important artists. The fairy-tale image of the clever one, the sweet one, the quiet one, and the sad one have almost completely disappeared, as well they should. The Beatles have much more to give the fans now then just loveable objects at which to scream; and their audience has appreciated that fact. The Beatles are reflectors of an age—as all true artists are—singing of the conflicts and emotions that involve all of us today.

The fairy-tale has ended and with luck we shall all live happily ever after listening for many years to come to four individuals.

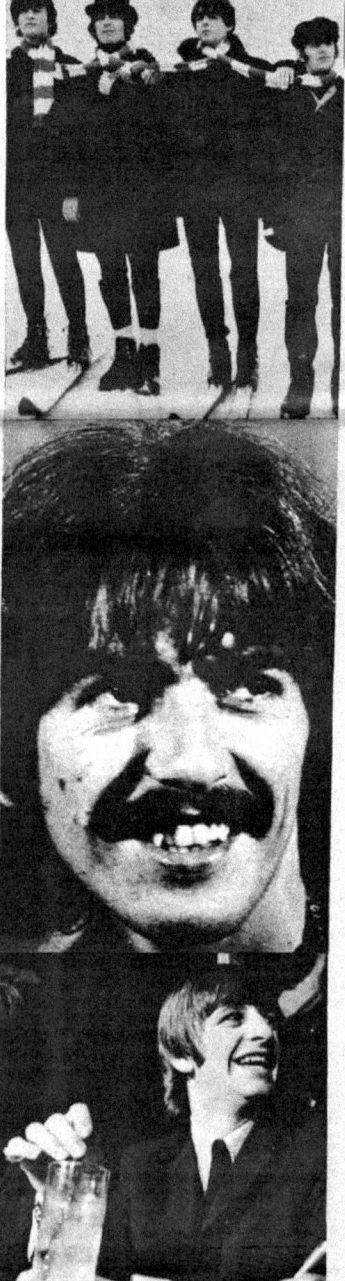

WEDDING BELLS FOR UNMARRIED BEATLES?

...PATTIE BOYD

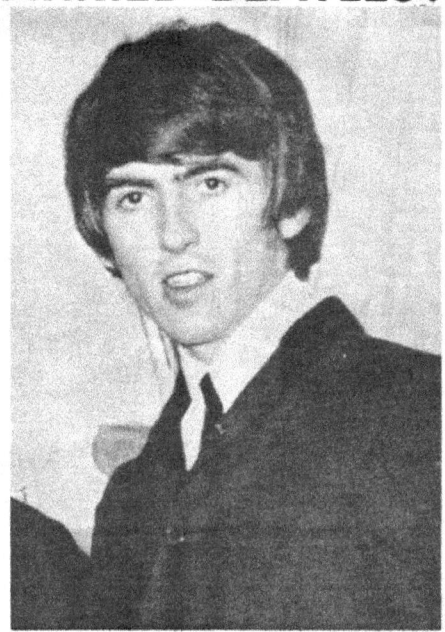

...GEORGE HARRISON

Beatle marriage rumors continue to grow and Beatles continue to fight these rumors by promising that when they DO get married, they will announce it themselves.

There are now only two unmarried Beatles left, and up until two weeks ago both denied that they were even considering marriage.

Paul is still holding to his story. Just recently, Jane Asher appeared on a British television show where she stated: "Paul and I are not married, engaged, or thinking about getting married. I'm just his girlfriend."

However, George Harrison admitted to a reporter in Paris two weeks ago that he and model Patti Boyd, "have definite plans to marry, but where and when is another question. We're not in a mad rush to do anything."

"We have time on our side, and can wait for the right day and the right moment to come along."

"There is no doubt that I will marry Patti. I'm the youngest in the group and Patti's career means a lot."

It's a welcome change to see a pop star (and such a popular one too) admit that he has a girlfriend and that they are thinking of marriage. Much too often such things are hidden from the fans. Why? Do they really think fans won't accept the fact that pop stars are human, that they fall in love, that they get married?

Apparently, George feels his fans deserve honesty from him.

It's nice to see that somebody credits fans with having some intelligence and maturity, isn't it?

FOLK MOVEMENT BOOM WON'T ROLL OVER ROCK

Will folk music replace rock in the U.S.?

A quick glance at the national charts will reassure you that rock is still very much king, but there ARE a few folk songs creeping in among the amplified guitars and throbbing drums.

The Seekers, folk singers from Austrialia, have made it back into the charts with their latest, "A World Of Our Own".

Donovan is still trying to "Catch The Wind" and Marianne Faithful is singing about a "Little Bird".

Although the Byrds cannot be classified merely as folk singers, their national chart-topper, "Mr. Tambourine Man", is a Bob Dylan composition and Bob Dylan cannot be classified as anything but a folk singer.

Still another Dylan composition, "All I Really Want To Do", is riding the charts in both the Byrds' version and Cher's rendition.

In the category of best selling albums, such names as Peter, Paul and Mary, the Kingston Trio, the New Christy Minstrels, Ian and Sylvia, Marianne Faithful, and of course, Bob Dylan, keep popping up.

So while folk does not seem to have replaced rock, it certainly has found a place for itself.

KRLA BEAT

The KRLA BEAT is published weekly by Prestige Publishing Company; editorial and advertising offices at 6290 Sunset Boulevard, Suite 504, Hollywood, California 90028.

Single copy price, 15 cents.

Subscription price: U.S. and possessions, $3 per year or $5 for two years. Outside U.S., $9 per year.

Back issues of the KRLA BEAT are still available, for a limited time. If you've missed an issue of particular interest to you, send 15 cents for each copy wanted, along with a self-addressed stamped envelope to:

KRLA BEAT
Suite 504
6290 Sunset Blvd.
Hollywood, California 90028

ISSUES AVAILABLE
4/14 — INTERVIEW WITH JOHN LENNON
4/21 — INTERVIEW WITH PAUL McCARTNEY
4/28 — CHIMP EXCITES TEEN FAIR
5/5 — HERMANIA SPREADS
5/12 — HERE COMES THE BEATLES
5/19 — VISIT WITH BEATLES
5/26 — FAB NEW BEATLE QUIZ
6/2 — L.A. ROCKS AS STONES ROLL
6/16 — BATTLE OF THE BEAT
6/23 — P. J. — HERO OR HEEL
6/30 — PROBY FIRED
1/7 — SONNY & CHER vs. THE BYRDS

?Beatle Quiz?

Okay Class, come to order. It's KRLA Beatle Quiz Time and we have five more questions for the most educational and rewarding contest in Beatleland.

You Beatle Students who missed the first seven weeks of the Beatle Quiz can still catch up by ordering the July 7, June 30, June 23, June 16, June 9, June 2, and May 26 issues of the KRLA BEAT.

The winner of the quiz will be rewarded with a personal interview with the Beatles for the BEAT when the group arrives in August and along with a friend will be invited to attend the Beatle Concert as guests of the KRLA deejays.

Additional prizes will be provided for runner-ups and in case of a tie there will be additional questions or a drawing to decide the final winner. The contest will continue for two more weeks, with at least five new questions asked each week. Beatle Expert Derek Taylor, a close friend of the Beatles and their former press officer, will judge the entries for accuracy.

Beatle Quiz
KRLA BEAT
Suite 504
6290 Sunset Blvd.
Hollywood, Calif. 90028

CONTEST EDITOR:

Below are my answers to the fourth set of questions in the BEATLE QUIZ CONTEST.

My Name .... Address ....
City .... State .... Zip Code ....

I (☐ am) (☐ am not) presently a subscriber to the KRLA BEAT.

NEW QUESTIONS

1. The Beatles were once sculptured in 1800 pounds of butter. In what country was this artistic masterpiece displayed?..............................

2. John Lennon spent most of his early life in the care of his aunt. What is her name?
....

3. Which Beatle washes his hair most often? ....

4. John Lennon once appeared with a group and was billed as "Barking John Lennon." What was the name of the group?..............................

5. Who Is Anne Collingham and what is her connection with the Beatles?..............................

BEATLES ARCHIVES 1

Another Exclusive Beatle Photo

ANOTHER OF THE EXCLUSIVE BEATLES photos to appear in the BEAT. The camera caught the pair in an unguarded moment inside the private dressing rooms set up for the group while they worked long hours on their island adventure story.

Scrambled Features Winners

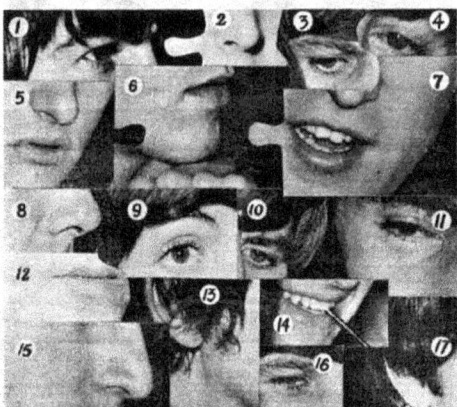

THE BEATLES SCRAMBLE CONTEST PICTURE that brought in so many entires and deluged the offices of the KRLA BEAT. How many did you identify correctly? The actual answers are: 1—George. 2—Paul. 3—Ringo. 4—John. 5—Ringo. 6—George. 7—John. 8—George. 9—Paul. 10—Ringo. 11—John. 12—Paul. 13—George. 14—Ringo. 15—John. 16—Ringo. 17—Paul. Derek Taylor got them all the first time.

Out of hundreds of entries received, there were a number of correct answers, but an El Monte girl got in the earliest post marked entry. We'll have more BEATLE CONTESTS in upcoming issues.

The winner is Valeri Hernandez, of 4566 Esto Avenue in El Monte. Valeri is a freshman at Arroyo High School and says she really digs THE BEATLES because they're "something different" and "out of the ordinary." After she saw them on television, 14 year old Valeri knew THE BEATLES were for her!

KRLA BEAT

Published each week for Radio Station KRLA, Pasadena, California.

EDITOR .... NORM WOODRUFF
REPORTER .... JIM HAMBLIN
PHOTOGRAPHY ..... JERRY LONG
PRINTING .... HENDRIX HOUSE
ARTIST .... STEVE BELLEW

Your comments are invited. Address letters to KRLA BEAT, 6290 Sunset Blvd., Suite 504, Hollywood, California. 90028.

Beatle Quotes

It's Not Quiet In Studio As Beatles Make New Disc

While the Beatles filmed in the Bahamas, George Martin, (the Beatles recording manager), sat back in London listening to tapes of the last recording session.

It was at this session that the FAB FOUR recorded all the songs that will be used in the still un-named movie which will be released this summer, for all the KRLA - BEATLEMANIACS to enjoy.

During a lull at the recording session Paul was fooling around with an electric piano while George and Ringo danced to a playback of another soon-to-be Beatle hit.

Still Mooches

John Lennon sits in a corner, in his own little world. John is the mastermind of the Beatles.

Although a millionaire, John carries little money, and is always scrounging cigarettes. He still uses matches instead of a flashy lighter.

Taking advantage of the lull in the session, John gave his thoughts to the KRLA BEAT, about the Beatles, recording stars, and film stars.

Lennon Talking

"We'll be pop stars as long as we continue making records, and that will be quite awhile. We regard filming," John says, "as a bit of a giggle, too. We're film stars, and pop stars, we hope."

The KRLA BEAT got this quote of John, when asked about rumors that the end of the line has been reached, and the Beatles will disband soon:

"Why are these things even considered? They suppose that just because we've done well, we might as well pack it in. We'll never pack it in completely, because we've made so much money, and we're still making it."

Rubbish Talk

"People talk a load of rubbish about us. We have no plans to break up. We may be interested in more than filming and making records, but the Beatles will always be the Beatles."

John goes on to reveal some of the plans for the future.

"I'm going to do some A&R work. I want to be an independent record producer. I'd like to find someone as good as Tom Jones and record them. Probably, Paul and me will work together."

Friendship

There is an indestructible bond of warm friendship between Paul and 24 year old John Lennon.

John goes on, "Until now, there's never been time for other work, but there might be now.

I was going to have a recording studio built at my house. But I gave up the idea. It couldn't work. Good lord, I can't even work a bloody tape recorder, so I can't see myself doing the big equipment bit.

"I'm getting this shed built," John says, "at the back of the house. I'll discover people, then hire a studio to record them.

"This won't be for some time yet, so I don't want hundreds of people imagining that I'm walking around with a big cigar and open to offers.

What Type?

What variety of talent would John like to discover?

"I've been thinking about this. I'd like to discover someone with the looks of Bardot, and the voice of Dionne Warwick."

Do you like Dionne?

"Her voice is OK. I'm not exactly crazy about her, but that's the sort of combination I'm thinking of. A big symbol. A girl who looks great, and sings wild. She's got to be somewhere. There's never been someone like this as I can remember.

"The sort of girl I'd be interested in would be someone with such a voice that the fellas look up to see what she looks like and then when they see her . . ."

Companys Taken

Does this interest in a single star mean groups are fading?

John says, "This year the record companies will not be signing up all the lousy groups like they did last year. There was a time when the companies would sign up anybody who made a noise like four men with guitars. They were taken and deserved to be taken. They signed up rubbish, and when they didn't get hits they starting running. Can't blame them, but they should have been more sensible."

Does John still get a kick out of recording?

"Yeah," he says, "more now than before. When we started, I didn't know much about it. What to do and what to expect at the end. But, now that we know a bit more, it's much more interesting."

More About

DEREK TAYLOR
FROM PAGE ONE

Beau Brummel's disc Laugh Laugh was causing some excitement over there.

"They sound very British," she said. "And very good." Virginia was wild about another American artist — Roger Miller. "Absolutely fabulous," she shouted over the 8,000 miles of Post Office cable. "When is he coming over here?"

The answer is "soon," both for Roger and the Brummels. Each has yet to dent the British charts. But when the personal contacts are made with fans over there, expect an entirely different story.

The Beatles left the Bahamas a few days ago. Their tropical segment of the film is complete and everyone is very happy. You can still hear them on KRLA. Stay tuned. See you soon.

BEATLES ARCHIVES 1

Another Exclusive Beatle Photo

Like a postman who goes for a walk on his day off, THE BEATLES relax for a few moments by strumming their guitars. The kookie hat is a gift from an admirer who finally got to see them for a few seconds.

PAUL McCARTNEY:
'I'M NO LONGER ONE OF FOUR MOP-TOPS'

(Editor's Note: As we were going to press, The BEAT received a telegram from London announcing that the Beatles have just signed a new nine year contract with EMI and Brian Epstein. However, there was no mention of whether they signed as a group or as individuals.)

Who is getting the run-around? First come the Beatle rumors, next come the official confirmation or denial and just as soon as that's printed one of the Beatles starts talking. Result? One fat circle.

First came the rumor that the Beatles would tour no more, then at press conferences all across the U.S. last summer the Beatles professed to know nothing of any such decision. Still later came the official decree that, indeed, the Beatles would make no more personal appearances but they would go ahead and make a third movie as well as record a new single and a new album.

The new single is, of course, now released and the album is currently being cut. And Paul McCartney has announced that the Beatles will only work together again "if we miss each other."

Paul went on to add that: "I no longer believe in the image. I'm no longer one of the four mop-tops."

The reason for the split is financial — only in reverse. Most groups break up because they haven't made it. The Beatles are breaking up because they've made it too much and any further group effort will only go into taxes.

"We've all of us grown up in a way that hasn't turned into a manly way," admitted Paul. "It's a childish way. That's why we make mistakes. We've not grown up within the machine. We've been able to live very independent lives. Now we're ready to go our own ways. We'll work together if we miss each other. Then it'll be hobby work. It's good for us to go it alone."

Since the Beatles departed the United States, they've worked together only in the recording studio. John, of course, made a movie; George went to India to learn sitar and Ringo put out the word that he's interested in doing a movie. Paul has been on safari in Africa and has put together a movie he shot in France. "It's all part of breaking up the Beatles," revealed Paul.

And all that leaves their proposed third movie where? In the hobby room?

Paul's Penny And Lennon's Strawberry — From The Inside

By Tony Barrow

It's been six months since The Beatles brought out a single. Now as ultimate evidence for all those split-up rumour-builders here comes the group's first new record for '67! There are no 'A' and 'B' sides so far as John, Paul, George and Ringo are concerned. Just two contrasting titles — "PENNY LANE" and "STRAWBERRY FIELDS FOREVER" — which are linked with The Beatles' Liverpool past.

So you want to know the secret of PENNY LANE for a start. Maybe you imagined that Penny must be some fondly-remembered bird from Paul's teeny-boppin' days. Yes, they'd believe that in Iowa — but not in Liverpool. Any Merseysider could tell you about Penny Lane. It's a well-known suburban street to the south side of Liverpool's city centre. It's the meeting point of five different streets — and five thousand different residents who live in that thickly populated neighbourhood. On a Saturday morning at Penny Lane you might easily spot Paul's poppy-selling nurse standing on the traffic island near the corner. Or his bloke with a picture of the Queen tucked away in a waistcoat pocket.

"PENNY LANE," sung by Paul and John contains (for the most part) Paul's own ideas. It is a happy-go-beat number with a busy street-scene atmosphere in the arrangement and the sort of simple, infectious tune you remember after a single spin of the record.

STRAWBERRY FIELDS? Yes, they really do exist but you couldn't grow strawberries there in a decade of Beatle Birthdays! John did most of the composing work on this — so he's the one who solos on the record. He roughed out the first basic lyrics last October when he was filming "How I Won The War" in Almeria, Spain. Liverpool street maps don't mark out Strawberry Fields. That's the name given to a dull-green expanse of grass and a bit of a pond located just down the street from John's original home in Menlove Avenue, Woolton, Liverpool 25.

"STRAWBERRY FIELDS FOREVER," playing for just five seconds more than four minutes, is the longest track ever recorded by The Beatles. As far as John's vocal technique is concerned you might describe it as a further extension of the style he created for "Tomorrow Never Knows." After something like 3-1/2 minutes — the final segment building into a fantastic barrage of percussion during which George and Paul play bongos and tympani, Mal Evans plays tambourine and John thumps out the beat on the back of a wooden chair — the sound fades away to nothing and you think the action's over.

This'll fool a few deejays — suddenly everything starts happening again and the instrumental storm builds back to another crescendo.

"STRAWBERRY FIELDS FOREVER" was the first item The Beatles worked on when they went into the E.M.I. Recording Studios at the beginning of December. It took the best part of two weeks to complete. Two completed tapes were destroyed because the group agreed that the tempo was wrong. When they started work on the third version they took it a little faster and everything worked out right.

HOTLINE LONDON SPECIAL
Two New Beatle Albums Due Here This Summer

By Tony Barrow

Almost certainly American Beatle People will have the chance of hearing TWO new albums by John, Paul, George and Ringo this summer! Capitol Records plan to issue the first of these within the next few weeks and the second should follow around the time of the '66 U.S. concert tour.

The first album has the program title "Yesterday and Today" and it will include three tracks made during The Beatles' lengthy series of current sessions in London. The three are "And Your Bird Can Sing" (subtitled "You Don't Get Me"), "Dr. Robert" and "I'm Only Sleeping."

"Dr. Robert" was made just two days after the boys completed "Paperback Writer" and "Rain." It was recorded at sessions which took place over the Easter holiday weekend and most of the finishing touches were put to the composition on the studio floor.

"I'm Only Sleeping" took time to perfect. John had in mind a particular sound to create a lazy instrumental backing. At two different sessions all the boys agreed that the sound they were getting was far too wide-awake for the feel of the song. At a third-time-lucky work-out they managed to get the effect they'd been waiting for. That was on Friday, May 6.

Other titles included in the "Yesterday And Today" Selection range from Ringo's "What Goes On" and "Act Naturally" to George's "If I Needed Someone." Also in the album are "We Can Work It Out," "Day Tripper," "Nowhere Man," "Drive My Car" and Paul's solo ballad "Yesterday."

The scheduled Capitol release date for this album means that Beatle people on your side of the Atlantic will hear three brand-new titles at least four to six weeks ahead of their U.K. counterparts. Over here in Britain, Parlophone records do not plan to issue a new album by the Beatles before the beginning of August.

BEATLES ARCHIVES 1

Barrow Dispels Beatle Rumors

As Seen By A Beat Reporter After A Long Luvley Chat With Tony Barrow

On August 12, 1966, four Beatles arrived in these United States.

It was their fourth visit, but it felt more like their first. They hadn't known what to expect then, and they didn't know now.

The apprehension they felt was understandable. They had heard about the storm of controversy which had broken in our country, but they couldn't appraise the situation until they could see it for themselves.

So, they came and they saw.

At high noon on August 30, they boarded a plane at Los Angeles International Airport and went home smiling. For, once again, they had conquered.

Conquered really isn't the right term, though. This word is synonomous with winning, and it wasn't a question of that. It was more one of finding out how much they'd lost of what they'd already won years ago.

The reply came on fourteen different stages in fourteen different cities. From those platforms, the Beatles saw the same sea of faces and heard the same roar of welcome, and they knew they had lost absolutely nothing.

That answered their big question. Two days after the foursome had flown back to London, Tony Barrow, the Beatles' Senior Press Officer and The BEAT's London Correspondent, did his best to answer mine.

Tony had remained in Hollywood to attend to some of the countless post-tour details, among them this interview. When I met him that evening, at the comfortably-quiet restaurant in his hotel, I suppose he figured I was going to ask the question he has surely heard a thousand times these past few weeks, and he was right.

Coming Back?

After the usual pleasantries, my first words were: "Are they coming back next year?"

He didn't say yes, but he didn't say no (which was fortunate because I was prepared to plunge my pencil into my heart if he had.) What he did say was this: "Nothing is ever set twelve months in advance, but I see no reason why they won't be back."

He went on to say that two offers have already been made to book the Beatles in 1967 (one from Shea Stadium, the other from somewhere he didn't mention), but that there were no commitments as yet.

I then told him about the rumors which had prompted my question. I'd heard the Beatles were tired of touring, tired of performing, and anxious to devote their time to recording and making movies.

"Everyone is tired at the end of a tour," he said. "There's no fun in being jostled about and packing up every hour and riding around in florist's delivery trucks. But afterwards you look back and think of all the thousands of people who got to see you and it seems different then."

(A slight interruption – The Beatles solved a part of the packing-up problem by bringing along just two sets of on-stage costumes. In some cities they wore the forest green outfits we saw in Los Angeles and San Francisco; in others they wore gray-and-pink-striped suits. But they brought along fourteen different sets of matched shirts, and I imagine they had great fun hauling those around, not to mention the clothes they brought to wear off-stage.

Beatle Movie

The Beatles do plan to devote a lot of time to movies and recording. John's film began shooting the Saturday after he returned home, and the next Beatle movie ought to get underway just after the first of the year.

Tony had this to say recordwise: "Recording is a basic, long-term thing with the Beatles, and also the most rewarding and creative. I don't know that the writing of songs takes them longer than it used to, but they're progressing lyrically, they're more profound; they've passed through the I-love-you-and-you-love-me-stage. They do spend far more time working out how to present a song. They've passed through the three-guitars and-a-drum stage, too."

The following is a "transcript" of the remainder of our question and answer session. Hopefully, I have Tony's answers word for word. If not, I offer him my humblest apologies in advance. I also promise to learn how to read my own writing one of these days.

Q: At the Hollywood press conference, Paul said that the 'sound effects' in "Tomorrow Never Knows" were created by a series of tape loops. Would you explain what these are?"

A: "Tape loops are short pieces of recording tape joined back to back. For this particular record, they used tapes they'd been recording at home on their own equipment. Paul is the most prolific at this sort of thing.

Q: Why did the Beatles decide to appear at stadiums instead of places like the Hollywood Bowl?

A: Los Angeles is a good example of why. You either repeat the Bowl and disappoint the people who can't get in, or you look for somewhere larger. The Beatles played to more people at one performance in Dodger Stadium than they did with two shows last year at the Bowl.

Bomb Concerts

Q: I understand there weren't many complete sell-outs. Did they have any concerts they considered to be bombs?

A: "No – empty seats are nothing to go by. It's all in the way it's reported. You might see a headline that says *10,000 empty seats at Beatle concert,* but read on and you'll find there were 40,000 seats that weren't empty. Tickets weren't even printed for some seats, you know. The stages had to be put somewhere and it wouldn't have been fair to sell tickets in seating areas behind the stage. But, this kind of reporting isn't necessarily an attempt to knock the Beatles. It's just a turnabout so they'll have something new to say. How many ways can you say *Beatles a smash success?*

Q: Was this year's tour as financially successful as 1965's?

A: "It grossed more, and umpteen thousands more saw the Beatles."

Q: I read somewhere that only 12,000 attended the Candlestick Park concert in San Francisco. Could this be true?

A: "It must have been a misprint. I don't have the exact attendance figures, but I'd say there were at *least* twice as many."

Editors Note: Tony's guess was close. There were, in fact, over 25,000 at Candlestick Park.

Fire On Plane

Q: Was there a fire on the plane during the tour?

A: "Not *on* the plane, but as we were about to take off from Seattle, one of the engines backfired and flames did shoot out – we were in a DC6, I believe, and were used to electraplanes where this never happens."

A: Did the incident cause any commotion?

Q: "Two people did get off the plane to find other transportation. One of the Ronettes and the Re-

... TONY BARROW – Beatle press agent and columnist for The BEAT.

mains' drummer."

Q: Speaking of Seattle, what was *that* all about?

A: "We still don't know, and it hardly seems worth further investigation. Four or five days prior to our arrival there, a newsman telephoned me from Seattle – I don't know whether he was from a radio or TV station or from a newspaper, but he was in the news media – and quoted portions of the Paul-Jane rumor to me. Not the whole story, but the basic thing. I said it was absolutely not true. The story broke *after* an official denial had been made.

Q: Is it true that the bridal suite was reserved and a wedding cake actually ordered?

A: "Yes, the arrangements were made by a mysterious Mr. Bartholomew."

Q: Did a lot of people believe the rumor?

Where's Paul?

A: We left Seattle right after the concert, but even then everyone wasn't convinced. A local disc jockey who came back on the plane with us got on board, looked around and said 'Well, there you are . . . ' When asked what he meant, he said *'Where's Paul?'* At this point, Paul emerged from the john.

Q: This incident is mild compared to what happened at the outset of the tour. Do you think the uproar over John's comments ruined the tour for the Beatles?

A: "No. Once John was able to be here and explain himself, the majority of sane, sober people of average intelligence realized that John had made the kind of remark we might all make. That the church itself might make and then say let's *do* something about this. It wasn't an insult, it was a statement. According to an A.P. reporter, even the Vatican has taken it in the way it was intended."

Q: Were there any signs of anti-Beatle reactions across the country?

A: "Not in any way. Five 'klansmen' did show up in their gear in Washington D.C., but they went home in about fifteen minutes – it was dinnertime. They didn't seem to be anti-Beatle. I didn't hear this myself, but I understand second-hand that what they were shouting was 'Don't go in there, there are niggers.'"

Q: Good God – I mean, back to the subject of rumors for a moment. What was all this about the Beatles perhaps not leaving until September 9?

A: "I have no idea how this rumor started or why that particular date. Just yesterday, a reporter refused to believe they had left at all. He challenged me with 'Well, how come *you're* still here?' I asked 'How come *you* are?' 'I live here,' he said. And I said 'For the next couple of days, so do I – do you mind?'"

Brian Overdue

Q: Something else I've been curious about. The papers made it sound like Brian Epstein had to rushed to America solely for the purpose of defending John. Isn't it true that Brian was due to arrive in this country, for other reasons, the week previous to that – before the uproar had even started?

A: "Brian was due in New York the week before, but had to cancel his plans because of illness."

Q: Then he didn't come to *(Turn to Page 23)*

Japanese Editor Tired Of Beatles

One of the members of the press who followed the Beatles on their American tour was Rumiko Hoshika, editor in chief of the Japanese monthly, "Music Life."

Rumiko, who stood quietly next to the bandstand during the Los Angeles concert, said her whole tour was "wonderful" but added that she, for one, was almost "tired of talking to the Beatles."

Sound impossible? Not really, since Rumiko has followed the foursome both here and in London. "It's so noisy and crowded everywhere," said Rumiko, laughing to show she really enjoyed the whole ordeal.

But even with every imaginable pass in her possession, it took Tony Barrow, the Beatles senior press officer, to get Rumiko's photographers on the field on Dodger Stadium. The stadium guards had the photographers detained in the dugout until just a few minutes before the Beatles rushed on stage.

Earlier in the tour, Rumiko asked George Harrison to write a note to her readers. George, as a joke, addressed the note to readers of "Music Laugh," rather than "Music Life." Rumiko, who confessed she has "big troubles" with English, didn't say whether she noticed it or not.

Are the Beatles still as popular in Japan as they were before the ill-fated Manila appearance. "Oh yes!" said editor in chief Rumiko.

BEATLES ARCHIVES 1

Beatles Having A Love Affair

"... we pinch just as much as the rest of 'em." —Paul

"... we really don't need them anyway." —George

"... how do you know their legs are ugly?" —Ringo

"... she's great. I'm going to see her tonight." —John

By Louise Criscione

I rather think the Beatles are currently enjoying a two-sided love affair with California. Even when the "Jesus-Lennon" controversy was enjoying its peak and the Beatles were re-considering touring the U.S., George hastened to add that they were still looking forward to their California stop-off.

It's difficult to know why, exactly. It could be the weather—but I doubt it. After all, they could just as easily spend their free days in Miami. Yet, they continue to schedule their time off in California. I tend to think its' the relaxed atmosphere. And the "in" people who populate California. The Mama's and Papa's, Joan Baez, David Crosby. Find the Beatles and you find them.

Cancelled

When the Beatles finally did land in the U.S. this time and John had officially apologized for his "more popular than Jesus" comment, most of the press conferences originally scheduled were cancelled. And it's no small wonder.

They say, what price glory? And indeed the top price paid by the Beatles is having to deal with the press. There is the trade press, which technically is not too bad since they supposedly know what's going on. However, there is, unfortunately, the rest of the press. And "ignorant" is hardly the word.

They know there are four Beatles, they know they came from Liverpool and they know they are named John, Paul, George and Ringo. But more often than not, they still can't seem to fit the name with the face. Therefore, Paul becomes John, John becomes George and George becomes Paul. Only Ringo remains Ringo.

Still Kicks

I imagine the Beatles still get something of a kick out of being addressed as someone else. It's the trite questioning which must really irritate them.

Take for instance the press conference held at Capitol Records in Hollywood. You can bet the brilliance of the whole ordeal did not escape the Beatles.

Of course, the first question asked concerned the "comment controversy" and it was quite obvious to everyone that John was sick and tired of explaining. He gave a sigh, made a face and said simply: "I've explained it 800 times and I think it should be clear."

That, naturally, was not enough to suit the reporter. "Well, you made an apology before," persisted the reporter, "can't you say it again?" "No," replied John, "I can't because I can't remember what I said. Look, I could have used television or anything else. I used the Beatles because that's what I know the best."

I got the distinct impression that the reporter was still not satisfied but was forced to surrender only because the microphone had left his hand.

A Solo John

What made John decide to make "How I Won The War" minus the other Beatles? A relieved sort of smile spread across John's face—something which said "don't tell me someone is going to ask a *new* question; something which doesn't concern my quote, our money, or if this is to be the last tour."

"Well, you see, this man simply asked me if I'd like to make this movie," answered John, "and I said 'yes.' That's how it happened." And with both hands up, he added: "Really!" And the plot? "I don't know much about it. It's about the last World War," continued John. Would the other Beatles venture off into solo movies? "I've no idea. It just sort of came to me that quick," he finished up.

One reporter, who said he was hoping to stir up another controversy, asked the Beatles if they thought perhaps American girls didn't wear mini skirts because their legs were ugly. Ringo shot him down simply and expertly with: "If they don't wear mini skirts, how do you know their legs are ugly?"

How, indeed? Controversy down the drain, the frustrated reporter took to his seat. Actually, the only half-way controversial question was: "It was reported in the July 3 edition of the New York Times that one of you, it didn't say which one, told Maureen Cleave that 'show business is nothing but an extension of the Jewish religion.' Would you like to comment on that?"

Eyes pivoted on the platform holding the Beatles and rather reluctantly John admitted: "I said that one as well. No comment."

"I'm Sorry"

Again the pressure was focused on John, as he was asked if he was really sorry he had made that "Jesus" comment. Definitely tired now, John said: "I am, yes. Even though I didn't mean it that way, I'm sorry I ever opened my mouth."

Another reporter shot up and demanded to know how much money the Beatles make and if they're having trouble with American taxes. "We don't know about that," stated Paul. "We don't do the money side of it. We pay tax and things," he continued, "but we don't know how much. We'd be nervous wrecks by now if we did."

No doubt, the Beatles have learned their lesson. Say just one negative word and it explodes in your face all over the world. So,

George found out when he made his famous "We're going to rest up before going to America to get beaten up again" remark.

Certainly he was asked about it at every ingle Beatle press conference and this one didn't want to be an exception. "I said that when we arrived back from Manila. We really weren't beaten up. We really just got shoved around a bit. Jouseled."

Don't Need Them

Is it a more enthusiastic fan or actually hostile individuals who attempt to mob them? "I think it's definitely enthusiastic fans," continued George. "The fan thing—I think they proved it themselves. We found out that the ones who can't make up their minds we really don't need anyway."

A truly profound and certainly devastatingly interesting question was next asked Ringo. "Do you carry around pictures of your son?" "No," shot back Ringo, "I don't carry around photographs of anyone."

A reporter did succeed in putting sort of a dubious feather in his cap when he managed to rather irritate the usually calm Paul by asking him to explain the Beatles' image as it stands today in the wake of the current crop of controversies. "I don't know," snapped McCartney, "our image is what we

(Turn to Page 23)

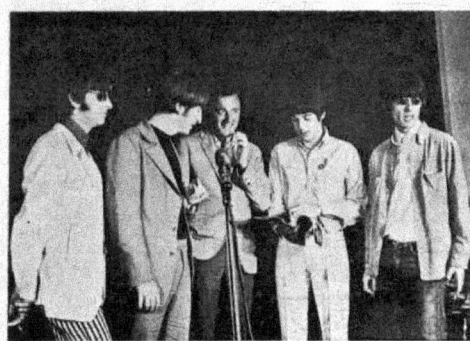

ROBERT VAUGHN whispers a few of his spy secrets to the Beatles.

YOLANDA HERNANDEZ, Stephanie Pinter, Debbie Pinter giving the Beatles initialed steak branding irons.

Baez And A Byrd

By Rochelle Reed

"This just stuns me!" said awed Byrd David Crosby, a Beatle mate. He was standing on the field of Dodger Stadium, gazing up at the stands and shaking his head in disbelief. The Los Angeles ballpark was jampacked that night, and from where David and I stood, it looked like the sky was raining people.

I couldn't have agreed with David more. I was stunned by the Beatles and the audience and by actually standing on the field right next to the bandstand. Guards, posted at every door, stairway, elevator and hall, had challenged anyone who attempted to get access to the dugouts, dressing rooms or field. Clever fans were using every excuse imaginable to get to the Beatles, but not one succeeded.

Bobby Helped

I almost hadn't made it. Once I'd gotten past the entire contingent of security officials upstairs, I was stopped at the dressing room door by another guard who must have ascertained that I looked too excited to be a member of the press. But about that time Bobby Hebb appeared, having heard of my plight, and convinced the guard that though I was a fan, I was also a reporter. And I was IN!

Bobby, "Sunny" as always, led me into the men's dressing room, stopping at the door to make sure everyone was clothed. It wasn't the Beatles' dressing room (they had their own) but the one for the rest of the acts.

I met the Cyrkle, who were sprawled on the floor playing silent songs with drumsticks or their hands. They were a very quiet group, not talking to each other a great deal. Tom, however, kept making comments about a woman being in the mens' dressing room. While he was pulling his suit out of a large case, he kept yelling "EEEEKKKK!!"

Bobby said the Remains were in the dugout, just about to go on, and that Howard and Chuck, BEAT photographers were there too. He pointed the way and then said he'd lead me instead.

"It's just great, the tour and everything," Bobby said, "and I go on pretty soon." He was excited but if he was nervous, he didn't show it.

I reached the dugout just in time to see the Remains run on stage and launch into their first number. Meanwhile, the road manager for the Ronettes said the girls were in their dressing room and why didn't I go back and say "hi."

I ventured back through the underground tunnel to the dressing room where the Ronettes, the only female act in the show were getting ready for their performance.

Or should I say, trying to. Estelle was sitting on a chair, combing her long black hair. "I went swimming today and my hair is a problem. That's one bad thing about swimming – your hair," she went on. Then, "Who are you?"

I identified myself and she continued chatting about the tour – "It's just been fabulous – and the weather and the Beatles' house.

"It's a beautiful mansion – we had dinner there last night with the rest of the acts," she said. Another Ronette lay on the couch alseep with cotton pads covering her sunburned eyelids. I lowered my voice but Estelle continued at full volume as she combed her long hair.

Promises

With promises of a full length interview later, I headed back to the dugout, where I sat down to watch the show while waiting for an escort across the field and up to the bandstand.

Bobby went onstage, his blue silk outfit almost glowing in the semi-darkness. A BEAT photographer and I were ushered across the field and into the second dugout, where we were greeted by Tony Barrow, the Beatles' senior press officer and BEAT columnist.

"The Beatles are in their dressing room," he said, gesturing behind him, but added that no one and that meant NO ONE could get to them. Meanwhile I glanced around to see who else was waiting there to see the British stars. I had ridden down to the field level in an elevator with character actor Don Knotts, and there in the dugout, pacing back and forth, was Batman Adam West, without his Batcape and clad in a grey suit with a yellow shirt.

2 Inches Tall

Then I walked out onto the field. From the bandstand, the stadium looked immense and I felt all of two inches tall. It was a fantastic sight and I rather wanted to stop and just stare with my mouth hanging open in awe.

During the time that I had been in both dugouts, I noticed a very slender girl with an olive complexion and barely shoulder length hair. Her short hair threw me off, however, and I kept saying to myself, "It just couldn't be."

But it was. Now that I was standing on the field, the slender girl in the houndstooth pants-suit walked up and said, "Hi!" How are you? Isn't this just great?"

"Oh yes," I answered, thinking to myself, "my gosh! it is!" About that time, someone said, "You know Joan Baez, don't you?"

I almost couldn't believe it. "You cut your hair!" I exclaimed, "I didn't recognize you." She nodded and with a wide sweep of her arm said, "Just look!"

By this time the Ronettes were on stage, looking very delicate in shiny gold dresses. We all knew it was time for the Beatles.

BEAT photographers were

Watch The Beatles

stationed strategically—one at the entrance from the dressing room and the other at the stairs to the stage. Luckily, the Beatles were acquainted with our photographers and always greeted them with smiles, waves and friendly comments.

George ran out first, then stopped. He continued on in a slow walk, carrying his guitar in front of him like a Bible. George and Joan Baez are good friends, and George sought out Joan as he walked and waved and smiled, and since I was standing with her, he waved my way too. Then came John, Paul and Ringo. They waved to everyone—the stands and the dugouts and the press people near the stage, even those of us without cameras.

The Beatles stopped to say a few words to the man who was to drive them out of the stadium and then ran on stage. They were dressed in tailored green suits and slim trousers. They wore black boots with their famous Cuban heels, except George, who wore brown suede boots without heels. Their shirts, which apparently looked blue polka-dotted from the stands, were actually cream colored and covered with large blue daisies with green leaves and stems.

'It's Great'

The roar of the crowd was deafening but I heard every word of every Beatle song. I was surprised to look around and see members of the press, who weren't madly shooting pictures, bouncing up and down with every beat. Joan Baez was dancing and kept saying "It's just great, just great!"

The Beatles waved while they played and John stamped his foot for a *BEAT* photographer, while Ringo smiled broadly for another.

Throughout the show, the Beatles traded comments with the people standing around the stage. Stars, press, anyone who could get a pass, crowded at the foot of the stage to watch the Beatles, who seemed to be standing on a pedestal rather than a bandstand.

Suddenly our single-minded devotion was shattered when fans at the far end of the stadium broke through police lines and attempted to rush across the field to the stage. The Beatles, who had just finished a song, stopped and stood very still. A chill went through the people standing around the stage. The Beatles hesitated a moment more, letting the screams sink in. John nodded, Paul shrugged his shoulders and they launched into "Baby's In Black." George, playing all the time, kept asking Joan Baez, "What's happening?"

A Useless Try

It was useless to try and explain. Besides, when the Beatles began playing, it calmed the nerves of almost everyone, most of whom weren't used to the idea that the Beatles could actually be in danger.

Thoughts began to turn to how the Beatles would get out of the ballpark. The press had learned that inside the tent labeled "dressing room" were actually two automobiles in which the Beatles would make their getaway. Everyone was anxious to see just precisely how this would work out.

Soon the Beatles launched into their last song. Paul looked down to where I was standing, yelled "Whooppee!!," rolled his eyes and continued belting out "Long Tall Sally." John stamped his foot and George waved. Ringo just beamed from ear to ear.

No sooner had they hit their last note then they bowed low and ran for it. Under the edge of the canvas, I could see Beatle boots and George's brown shoes. Then they disappeared and a gold Lincoln Continental, followed by a grey Ford filled with officials, roared out of the tent and towards the far gate. John and Ringo triumphantly waved white towels out of the back windows.

But just after they've gone through the blue gate at the far end of the field, the Beatles' car was engulfed by fans. I had wandered over there expecting to see the cars driving down the hill. Instead, I saw fans streaming down over a second wire fence and swarming onto the Continental. All I could see were the tail lights.

The police began pulling over-excited girls from the car while a second set of officers closed the outside wire gates. This left the car between the two sets of gates. The car began to back up and I stood there almost frozen as a few girls, who seemed to have lost all reason completely, kept throwing themselves against the car.

The Beatles were frightened for those few moments. As the car backed up to where I was standing, I could see that John was biting his cuff while Ringo, who had moments before been waving his white towel, had a corner of it in his mouth and was biting down hard.

John's Side

I was standing on John's side of the car, less than two feet from him. Apparently recognizing that I was press he waved in recognition and then widened his eyes and motioned as if to ask, "Is everything all right?"

I waved a victory sign to him and the rest of the Beatles saw and smiled. The car peeled back through the fence, made a half turn and sped back to the dugout, where the Beatles ran to their dressing room.

They left not long afterwards in an armored truck after an attempted getaway in an ambulance failed.

They spent the night in their Hollywood hillside home and flew to San Francisco the next day. The day after, they left the U.S. for England, where John Lennon will make a movie and the other Beatles will relax.

The remainder of us will be busy speculating as to whether or not they'll be back next year.

BEATLES ARCHIVES 1

Beatles' Love Affair

(Continued from Page 7)
read in the papers. You people make up our image. We know what our *real* image is and it's nothing like our 'image'."

Back to John again and "did you meet Cass of the Mama's and Papa's?" "Yes," replied John with that fantastically teasing grin of his, "and she's great. I'm going to see her tonight."

Along about this time, a female reporter stood up and asked John if it was true he was going to make a movie without the other Beatles. And it was then that my opinion of John flew up a neat one hundred notches. Because rather than inform her that question had already been asked and answered a mere five minutes ago, he simply said, "yes."

Security?

Positively one of the more brilliant questions was concerning whether or not the Beatles really needed the tight security which seems to follow them everywhere. "What do you think?" thundered John. Silence soared all around the room until the man admitted he didn't think the Beatles could make it without security. Nodding, John answered: "We *wouldn't* make it. We couldn't make it."

"Sometimes we could," argued Paul. "But today we couldn't have made it," he continued in reference to the fans who stood outside Capitol and rushed the armored truck when it came into view.

Someone else wanted to know if the Beatles would draw an equal share of John's salary for "How I Won The War.". "No," replied John, "we only share when we use the name 'Beatles.' If the name 'Beatles' is on a record then we all share but they don't make anything on my books."

Finally, the inevitable question of whether the Beatles would be back next year was asked. It's asked every year, and every year the Beatles give approximately the same answer. This time John did the honors: "We have no idea. We'll probably be back."

Then, of course, someone insisted on asking Paul the same question they've been asking ever since Walter Winchell made the premature announcement that Paul and Jane Asher were in fact married.

And, so once again, Paul answered: "I'll probably get married but I've no plans now."

Shot Down

During the rest of the press conference, the Beatles informed the world that the final script for their third movie had not yet been finished but when it is, and if they still like it, they will begin filming in January, that Lennon-McCartney write most of their songs and that "it's an amicable arrangement" and finally Paul shot down a reporter for saying that other artists have stolen Beatle material.

"They don't *steal* them," stated Paul. "No, I know they don't," replied the reporter. "But you just said they did," answered Paul, "and, besides, we pinch just as much as the rest of 'em."

Another question of magnitude — who are John's favorite groups? "There are so many," said the Chief, "The Mama's & Papa's, the Spoonful, the Byrds, the Beach Boys."

Following the official press conference, the Beatles were presented with their 20th Gold Record by Capitol Records President, Alan Livingston, for their "Revolver" album.

Mr. Livingston made the announcement and then the huge curtains behind the Beatles parted, revealing a gigantic blow-up of the "Revolver" cover and four shining Gold Records.

The Beatles were notably as surprised as the rest of us when the records were presented and it was made known that with this 20th Gold Record they had received more Goldies than any other artist in the history of the recording industry.

Ringo aptly summed up the group's feelings by saying: "It's such a lovely surprise."

Three lucky girls who head up the Dallas Beatles' Fan Club were next on the agenda. They presented the four Beatles with initialed steak-branding irons. About meeting the Beatles, Yolanda, Stephanie and Debbie chorused that "it was fantastic!" The Beatles themselves seemed to think it was rather fantastic too, as they busily set about branding each other with the steak irons!

On a whole, the Beatle press conference '66 style was very similar to the '64 and '65 editions. Probably a drag in the extreme for John, Paul, George and Ringo as the majority of reporters continue to ask the same monotonous questions as regularly as they collect their pay checks each week.

Humor—Tolerance

For their part, the Beatles handled the press as they would a small child — with humor, tolerance and an occasional straight answer where it was deserved.

And now they're back in England. Their third Stateside tour a success. Despite the bannings and burnings, they scored again. It *is* true that the wild, hysterical, follow-the-crowd Beatlemania which was born in '64 and ripe in '65 is a little tarnished in '66. There were fewer sell-outs but as George put it "we don't really need them anyway."

However, even with the not-so-true fans gone the Beatles are still very much in the driver's seat, still the owners of the Pop Throne. Still the heads of their special world.

Will they be back again? Despite all the trade talk that they will not, I think we'll see them next year. Not in a major tour but rather in a few key cities. It's only a hunch, naturally, as no one knows what next year will bring. But I expect it to bring the Beatles back to California. After all, they wouldn't want to kill a love affair, would they?

BEFORE...AND AFTER

Ringo Starr broke millions of hearts last week when he added a fifth ring — a gold wedding band. He married Maureen Cox, a hairdresser whom he began dating three years ago, at the same time that he joined an unknown group of long-haired singers called The Beatles. As you can tell from the picture on the right, he was delighted to give up his bachelorhood.

Tony Barrow Kills The Beatle Rumors

(Continued from Page 6)
America for the reason stated in the papers, which I thought made the situation sound even more serious.

A: "He was concerned, of course, and did want to see what was going on, but you can look at his time of arrival one of two ways — five days late or three days early."

Q: One last subject. Was there a press conference in every city?

A: "The Beatles saw the press in each of the fourteen cities they visited. In some cities, we were able to hold full-scale press conferences. In others, we were able to see only area newsmen due to time or space problems, etc."

Q: How did the press conferences go this year, and which did you consider the best of the lot?

New York Best

A: "Some were better than others — New York was the best. But an interesting thing happened around the country. Many newspapers used to just assign *a* reporter, but this year they sent along people with a more mature outlook. A number of drama and music critics attended. They seem to be accepting the Beatles on a more mature level. The Beatles themselves are far more mature. In experience, age, and intellectually as well."

Q: Weren't there two press conferences in New York?

A: "One was the regular conference, and the other was a junior press conference. It was held at the Beatles' request — they wanted to hear the fans' questions for a change — and they thoroughly enjoyed it. The 'reporters' were picked at random from the New York chapter of the official Beatles' fan club and listeners of WMCA."

Q: Did they scream during the press conference?

A: "They were a bit rowdy at first, but they settled down and it was a good conference. The idea worked, and it will definitely be repeated."

Q: Do you think it bothers the Beatles when they're asked at a press conference, what their music is trying to say? Creative people are often very sensitive about having their work questioned, even if they don't show it.

A: "The Beatles accept questions as they come. At a standard press conference, you get the standard range of writers. There are people like ourselves, who know all about pop music because it's our business. There are others who know very little about it, but are still some of the best journalists in the country. The Beatles take this into consideration, and don't let it bother them."

Plane To Catch

At this point, I noticed that Tony was looking rather nervously at his watch. He was leaving for London that same evening, and had a plane to catch, and when he

John and Paul Sell Stock Fast

LONDON — If you'd like to make a million dollars in a hurry, two young men have discovered the way. All you do is sell 1,250,000 shares of stock at a dollar each.

Of course, it helps if your name is John Lennon or Paul McCartney.

Last Thursday the two Beatle businessmen did just that, offering stock in their music publishing company for $1.09 each.

The public grabbed up the stock — Paul and John picked up another million bucks — and the whole thing took only 60 seconds!

BEATLES IN NEW PACT

Dousing rumors of a Beatles' break-up, Alan W. Livingston, President, Capitol records, announces that a new, nine-year contract has been signed with the foursome at EMI House in London.

The Beatles are breaking records with their new record "Strawberry Fields Forever"/"Penny Lane." Three days after the group's latest single was released, Capitol had shipped one million-plus disks to dealers.

This figure chalks up a record number of any one single ever pressed and shipped in three days under the label. Guess what the previous high mark record was for a three-day period? "I Want to Hold Your Hand," the Beatles first Capitol single held the record at 750,000 and went on to sell more than 4.5 million disks.

Capitol asked the RIAA for gold record certification of the single on its release date. "Strawberry" will be the 22nd for the British quartet since their 1963 American debut. The 22 certified gold records are more than any other artist(s) have ever won in the history of the record industry.

BEATLES ARCHIVES 1

America's Largest Teen NEWSpaper

KRLA Edition BEAT

Volume 1, Number 41   LOS ANGELES, CALIFORNIA   15 Cents   December 25, 1965

Dear Santa,

Please try to make room on your sleigh for some very special gifts which we would like to send to some very special stars. You'll find our list on pages 3 and 4.

Thanks, Santa
The BEAT

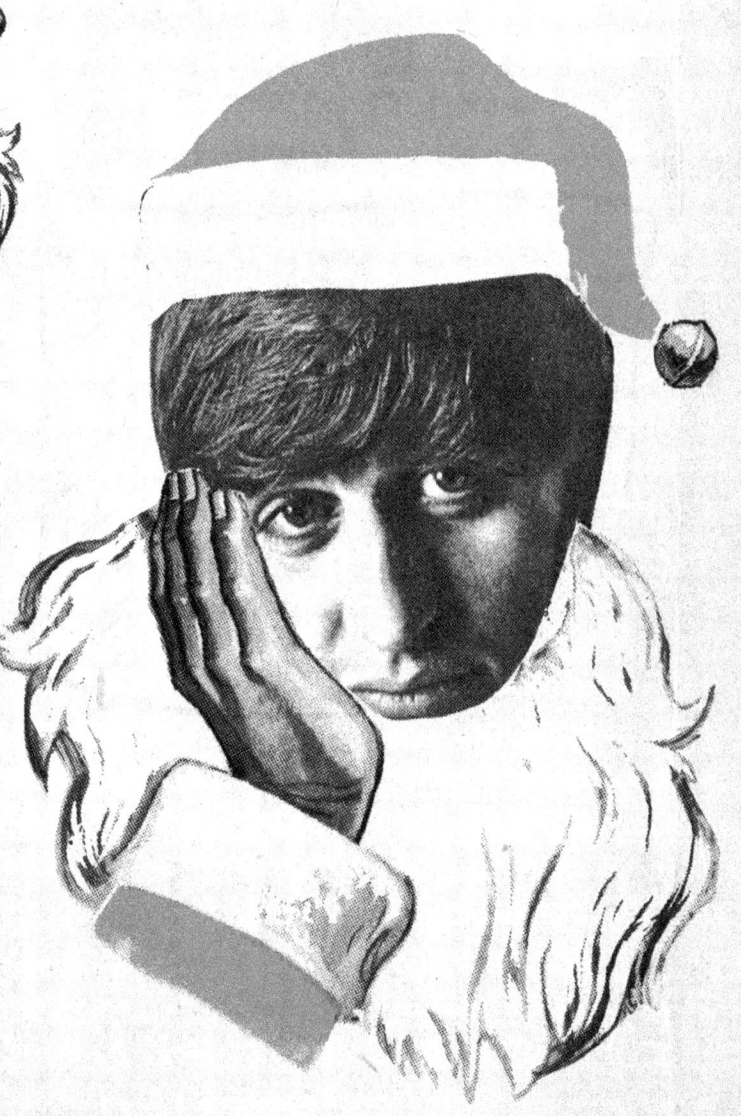

BEATLES ARCHIVES 1

KRLA BEAT

In This Issue:
ROLLING STONES
RIGHTEOUS BROS.
BEAU BRUMMELS

RINGO Before & After

February 25, 1965 — Los Angeles, California — Ten Cents

BEATLE-BALL AT KRLA!

Hull, Taylor To Visit Beatles During Filming

KRLA explodes another Beatle bombshell!

And all of you have a chance to get in on the excitement.

Dave Hull, the world's biggest Beatle booster, and Derek Taylor, the Beatles' press agent and liaison man before coming to KRLA, are flying to Nassau for a series of exclusive interviews with John, Paul, George and Ringo as they film their latest movie.

Fun For You

Here's where you come in. Through Dave and Derek, you can ask the questions! Just jot them down on a postcard and mail them to BEATLE QUESTIONS, KRLA, PASADENA. But hurry — there isn't much time left.

Here are some that have already been submitted:

What does Ringo think of married life? What does Maureen think of John, George and Paul? What's it like to be married to a Beatle? What do the other Beatles think of her? What is their reaction to Ringo's marriage? Do they think it will hurt the Beatles' popularity? Does Maureen want Ringo to stay with the group?

Lots of Questions

What special activities do they plan during their next visit to Los Angeles? How long will they be here? With John and Ringo married, are Paul and George thinking about giving up their bachelor life? What is the truth about the latest report that Paul may be altar-bound? Who is the man trying to break up the Beatles, and for what purpose?

Keep your ears glued to KRLA for the FIRST and ONLY answers to such questions — by the Beatles themselves.

Derek Taylor and An Unidentified Friend

Beatles' August Tour To Include L.A. Show

We can't give you any official word yet, but negotiations are almost completed to bring the Beatles back to Los Angeles for another live concert spectacular.

Word of a final agreement is expected to be announced any day now . . . and KRLA and the Beat will be first to announce it, naturally!

They are expected to do two concerts this time, so that a lot of people who missed out on their first performance will have a chance to see them in person.

The boys have expressed a preference for Los Angeles, and they have reserved two open dates on the schedule for their American tour this summer — Aug. 29 and 30.

Revealing his plans for the Beatles for the rest of 1965, Brian Epstein indicates they will make the third of their three-picture commitment for United Artists this year.

The Beatles are starting their second film this week. They have flown to the Bahamas for location shooting which will take almost three weeks. Then they fly to Austria to film there for about ten days before returning to London to complete the picture.

They will begin their European tour in July with a major concert in Paris, likely to be combined with a TV show over the Eurovision link from the French capital. Other concerts will follow in Barcelona, Madrid, Milan and another Italian city to be named later.

Then comes the big trip American fans are anxiously awaiting. They will leave London for the U.S. on Aug. 13, and the following day tape a spot for the Ed Sullivan show.

The four Liverpool lads have selected nine cities for concerts, including Los Angeles. Others are expected to be Atlanta, San Francisco, Toronto, Minneapolis, Houston, Chicago, Detroit and Mexico City.

They are to begin their U.S. tour Aug. 15 in New York and will probably conclude it with the two shows here.

DEREK TAYLOR, BEATLE ASSOCIATE NOW EXCLUSIVE KRLA REPORTER

KRLA has again made Beatle history!

It's not only the talk of the Beatle world, but the sensation of the radio world.

KRLA has employed the man who helped make the Beatles the most popular entertainers in the history of the world, Derek Taylor — press agent, liaison man, confidant and companion to the Beatles during and after their climb to the pinnacle of stardom — has moved to Los Angeles and will report exclusively for KRLA.

While Derek was with the Beatles, every piece of official news on the group was released by him. In the past he has been quoted and interviewed by everyone — including KRLA — who wanted to know anything about them. Aside from the Beatles themselves, he is the world's greatest authority on them.

And now he will report such news directly and exclusively to KRLA.

He will also provide KRLA listeners with exclusive reports on other British entertainers and has arranged to get us even more exclusive records from England before they are released to other stations in the U.S. You can easily see why

— Turn to Page 4

KRLA TUNEDEX

1. MY GIRL .... The Temptations
2. DOWNTOWN .... Petula Clark
3. YOU'VE LOST THAT LOVIN' FEELIN' .... Righteous Brothers
4. LAND OF 1000 DANCES .... Cannibal & Headhunters
5. THE JOLLY GREEN GIANT .... The Kingsmen
6. THIS DIAMOND RING .... Gary Lewis & Playboys
7. LAUGH, LAUGH .... The Beau Brummels
8. FERRY ACROSS THE MERSEY .... Gerry & The Pacemakers
9. THE NAME GAME .... Shirley Ellis
10. THE BOY FROM NEW YORK CITY .... The Ad Libs
11. TELL HER NO/LEAVE ME ME .... The Zombies
12. KING OF THE ROAD .... Roger Miller
13. 8 DAYS A WEEK/DON'T WANT TO SPOIL PARTY .... The Beatles
14. NEW YORK'S A LONELY TOWN .... The Tradewinds
15. LAND OF 1000 DANCES .... The Midnighters
16. CAN'T YOU HEAR MY HEARTBEAT .... Herman's Hermits
17. ALL DAY AND ALL OF THE NIGHT .... The Kinks
18. TWINE TIME .... Alvin Cash & Crawlers
19. PAPER TIGER .... Sue Thompson
20. KEEP SEARCHIN' .... Del Shannon
21. I GO TO PIECES .... Peter & Gordon
22. HOLD ON TO WHAT YOU GOT .... Joe Tex
23. LOVE POTION NUMBER NINE .... The Searchers
24. GOLDFINGER .... Shirley Bassey
25. THE BIRDS AND THE BEES .... Jewel Akens
26. HE WAS REALLY SAYIN' SOMETHING .... The Valvelettes
27. THE IN CROWD .... Dobie Gray
28. HURT SO BAD .... Little Anthony
29. FOR LOVIN' ME .... Peter, Paul & Mary
30. LEMON TREE .... Trini Lopez

CLIMBERS

1. FANNIE MAE .... Righteous Brothers
2. BORN TO BE TOGETHER .... The Ronettes
3. LITTLE THINGS .... Bobby Goldsboro
4. YEH YEH .... Georgie Fame
5. ASK THE LONELY .... The Four Tops
6. WHAT HAVE THEY DONE TO THE RAIN .... The Searchers
7. I'VE GOT A TIGER BY THE TAIL .... Buck Owens
8. IF I LOVED YOU .... Chad & Jeremy
9. COME HOME .... Dave Clark Five
10. GO NOW .... The Moody Blues

ALBUMS

1. BEATLES '65 .... The Beatles
2. WHERE DID OUR LOVE GO .... The Supremes
3. BEACH BOYS IN CONCERT .... The Beach Boys
4. GOLDFINGER .... Soundtrack
5. ROUSTABOUT .... Elvis Presley
6. COAST TO COAST .... Dave Clark Five
7. 12 x 5 .... Rolling Stones
8. VINTONS' GREATEST HITS .... Bobby Vinton
9. YOU'VE LOST THAT LOVIN' FEELIN' .... Righteous Brothers
10. YESTERDAY'S GONE .... Chad & Jeremy

STIRS LOTS OF TALK

KRLA DJs On New Shows

The big story everyone is talking about is the "big switch" at KRLA.

It brought a promotion for Hullabalooer Dave Hull, and it brought KRLA one of the best and best-known disc jockeys in the entire world — the one and only Dick Biondi.

At the request of thousands of his fans the scuzzy one stepped into the afternoon "traffic" slot from 3-6 p.m. Daffy Dick is messing up people's minds in Dave's old period of nine-to-midnight.

While Dave had the greatest time of his life during his nightly parties on KRLA, he likes to "mix" with his listeners in public appearances and of course he wasn't able to do that with a night-time show.

But look out for him now!

The old Hullaballoer may turn up unexpectedly at your next gathering. If he does, please treat him gently, for he isn't used to being out of his cage.

Everyone is asking for information about Dick Biondi. Like . . . is he for real? Is he really human? Is he dangerous? (We're still not sure about the answer to the second question, but the answer to the other two

— Turn to Page 4

BEATLES ARCHIVES 1

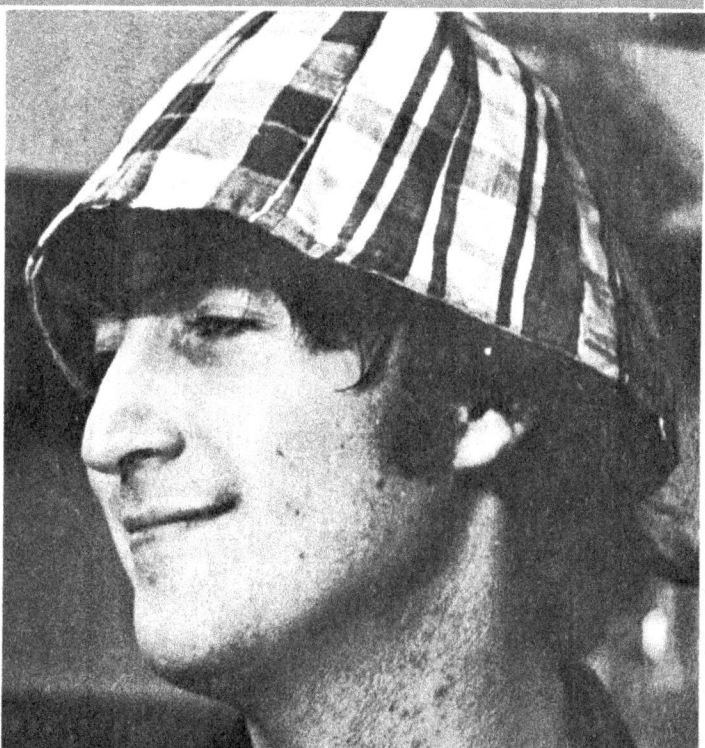
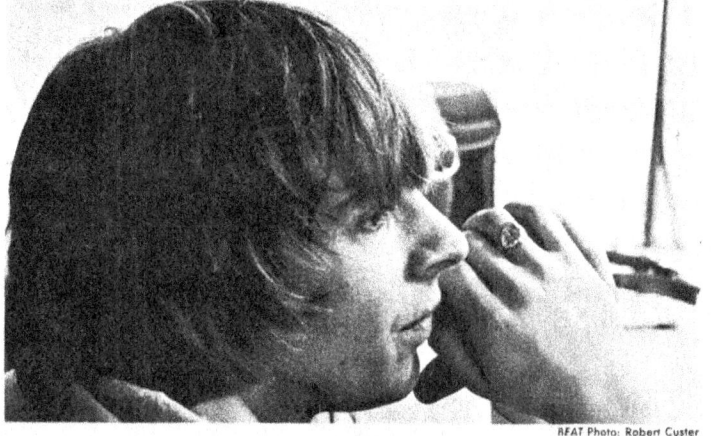

America's Largest Teen NEWSpaper

KRLA Edition BEAT

JUNE 25, 1966

How Individually Important Are They?

BEATLES ARCHIVES 1

What The Beatles Say About Their Movies

By Jamie McCluskey III

Nearly everyone in the wide and wonderful world of pop music is anxiously awaiting the next Beatle movie, now long over-due. At this writing, the boys have still to find an acceptable script, however, they are still searching. Hopefully, they will be able to begin filming — if a script is found — sometime this fall.

In the meantime, we are all going to have to content ourselves with watching re-runs of "A Hard Day's Night," and "Help" about 357 times or so.

And speaking of those two fab films now of the past, did you ever wonder what the Beatles themselves had to say about their work in "Help"? Well, we did, and if you're interested we'll share their answers to some of our prying questions with you.

Ringo: "Help? I thought I'd probably need it when we were shooting on location in the Bahamas. I had to jump into the sea from a boat in one scene and I was a bit scared about it.

"I mean, I don't mind splashing about in a pool, swimming from side to side in about five feet — but leaping into the ocean, that's a different matter!

"I'd like to end up in films, though I always hate myself on the screen and I don't particularly like my voice. But I'd like to be able to get enough confidence to be a good actor — and to be asked to do films because I'm an actor and not just because of being a Beatle."

Paul: "What I liked most about the film is the way the songs were photographed. There's much more variety than there was in the songs from out first film.

"I don't really know what our performances were like — I don't think we improved very much as actors — but I can tell you that the color photography was fabulous.

George: "I enjoyed making this much more than 'A Hard Day's Night.' We had great actors with us and we were always having a laugh. In fact, from the day we got on the plane to go to the Bahamas we were always laughing.

"And in Austria it was even more hilarious. I don't know why but people always seemed to be rushing up to us and babbling away in strange languages. We just felt about.

"One of the funniest things that happened was the crazy relay race we had round the huge lawn when we were filming at Cliveden. We decided to challenge the film crew and about six teams lined up. And I might tell you that the Beatles team won!!

John: "This time it was mostly visual humor — there wasn't so much of us making smart remarks. I think there is a lot of scope for us in films which hasn't been exploited.

"I mean, it took us three or four records before we really got our sound. I suppose it will be the same with films. When we've made three or four we'll probably hit the right formula. But I wouldn't like to concentrate on films. I still prefer playing to a live audience to anything else."

Now, then — if we can only find the right script for the third Beatle flick.

... JOHN, RINGO AND GEORGE searching for a suitable script?

Tokyo Prepares Itself For A Beatle Invasion

The Beatles' forthcoming visit to Tokyo is drawing such enthusiastic support from Japanese students that local authorities are beginning to worry. More than 200,000 applicants have registered for tickets and only 30,000 will be admitted to each one of the three performances beginning June 30.

A lottery was set up to decide which of the lucky applicants would be permitted to buy tickets. Seats are ranging from 1,500 to 2,100 yen ($4.17 to $5.84), but newspaper entertainment reporters expect the tickets to bring exhorbitant prices from speculators.

The concerts will be held at the 10,000 seat Budokan Hall, a templelike building where the Olympic judo competition and other important sport events have been held.

But while police have, at least for the present, solved the touchy problem of attendance, they are still concerned with the security of the Beatles.

The huge turnout of well-wishers expected to greet the Britons is still a problem. One suggestion is that the Japan Air Lines plane, which arrives June 30, be diverted to one of the United States Air Force bases near Tokyo, where the public is not admitted.

Another suggestion is that the Beatles be taken from the airport to the city to avoid the huge traffic pileup that is expected.

Housing for the world-famous group remains one of the most pressing problems for Tokyo authorities. It seems that no hotel is willing to accomodate the Beatles for fear of property damages that might result when screaming Beatle fans over-run the hotel.

Already, Tokyo is thinking Beatle. Much of the city's male population has grown shoulder-length hair and local wigmakers are enjoying a big boom in business.

BEHIND THE SCENES
WITH THE BEATLES

You had to be hip, but hip, babe, to keep up with the Beatles' behind-the-scenes happenings during their brief California vacation and concertizing.

But BEAT reporters, covering the entire Beatlescene like go-go-ing sandflies, ferreted out the gear mop-tops and brought back a sackful of soulful saga.

Did you know, for example, that:

They were asked at the press conference how they felt about those anti-Beatles Britishers who turned in their O.B.E.'s in protest when the M.B.E. was conferred on the Four. Replied flip-lipped John Lennon: "We got ours for entertaining people. Isn't that better than getting it for killing people?"

★ ★ ★

Asked if they've changed to any extent since the awards, Paul admitted, "We're more circumspect—and there are more conflicts." To a BEAT reporter's query on how he regards his personal life while on an international tour, Paul responded simply, "I like to be quiet."

★ ★ ★

In the course of the Capitol press confeernce, the boys were presented individually with gold discs symbolizing their million-selling "HELP!" album by Capitol president Alan Livingston. Noted Livingston: "Never in its history has Capitol experienced artists' success with such speed, depth and continuity."

★ ★ ★

The boys spent two-and-a-half hours visiting Elvis Presley and manager Colonel Parker. For a couple of hours they joined Elvis in a rock session on the carload of guitars provided by the Colonel. Ever candid, Paul told Elvis bluntly that he preferred the Tupelo lad's style in Elvis' early days when it was "wild."

★ ★ ★

Walter Shenson, producer of the Beatles' flicks, spoke about their behind-the-scenes attitude toward movie making. "The boys insist on a month's rehearsal before their next picture. They say, 'Whatever we do, let's make each picture different. Another reason, of course, is I can get worried about being typed as a 'Beatle picture producer,' because every Beatle picture will be differnt. Another reason, of course, is I can get very rich. Plus the fact I like it and the pictures are rewarding and a challenge. We work to make money—and to be gratified."

★ ★ ★

The boys also disclosed at their press conference that their next flick is to be a western. They already own the story, titled "A Talent For Loving," but the completed film may have a slightly different title—one more in keeping with "A Hard Day's Night" and "HELP!" In other words, an out-of-it title. Asked if the movie is to be filmed in Hollywood, they answered negatively. The entire production, except for some interior scenes, will be made in Spain where it's cheaper —cheapest, maybe.

★ ★ ★

John Lennon was asked to explain the now popular sport of "Beatle-baiting" in Britain— popular, that is, in the same crowd who were "insulted" when they were awarded the M.B.E. "I guess," answered John with more than a touch of Lancashire wisdom, "you can't expect everyone to luv us."

BEAT photo: Robert W. Young
JOHN: BETTER THAN FOR KILLING PEOPLE . . .

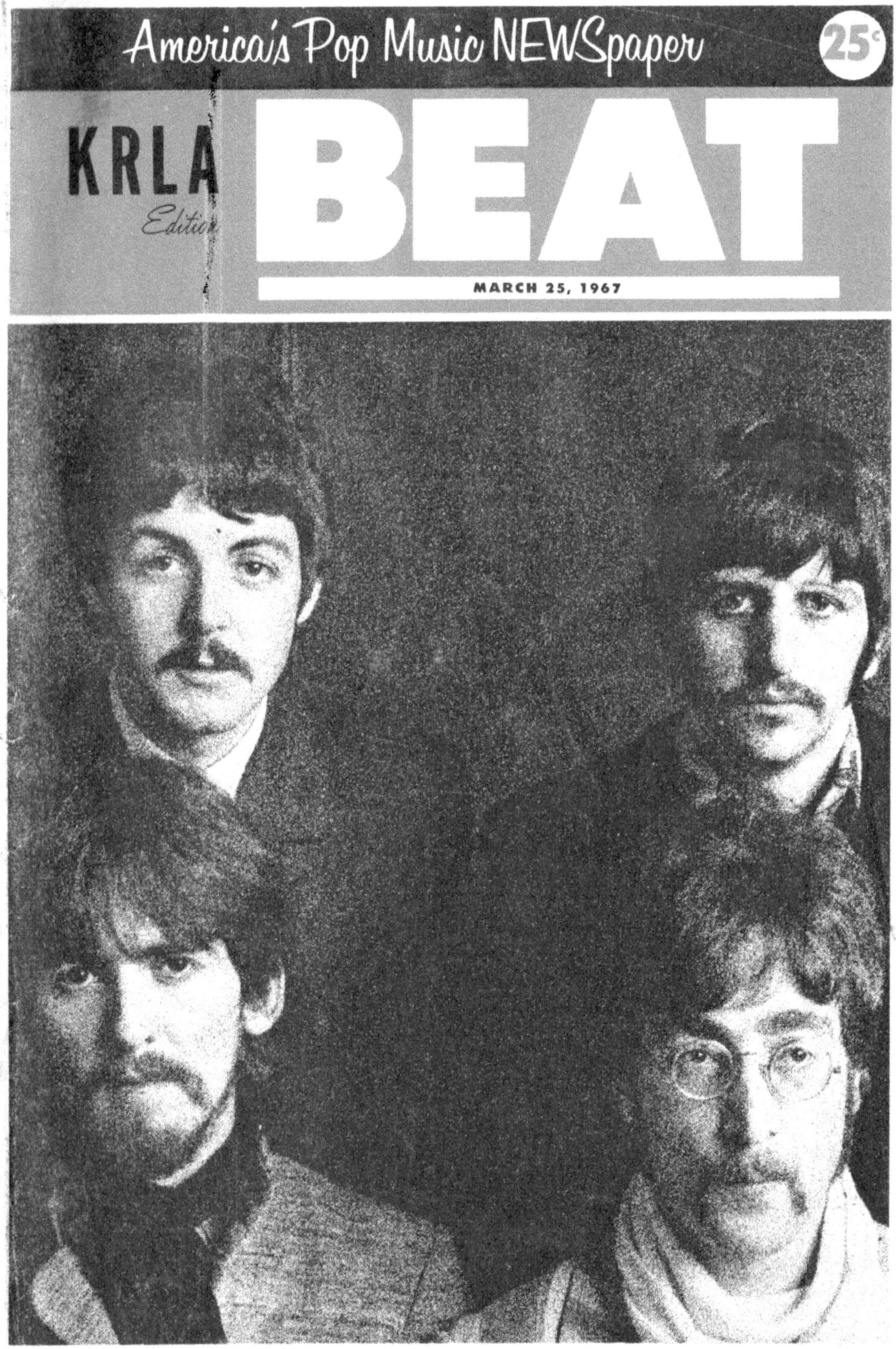

BEATLES ARCHIVES 1

America's Pop Music NEWSpaper

KRLA Edition

BEAT

MARCH 25, 1967

25¢

BEATLES ARCHIVES 1

BUT NOT SAN FRANCISCO
Beatles Say L.A. Was 'Just Great'

The Beatles are already talking of a return trip to America next year and another vacation in Southern California.

"It was tremendous," says Paul.

"Great, just great," says George.

Their only criticism of their ten-day American tour concerns the near-riot which broke out during one of their two performances at the Cow Palace in San Francisco.

At a London news conference Brian Epstein criticized the management of the Cow Palace for "providing insufficient security." During the disturbance, which forced the Beatles to cut short the second show, the fans threw rings, pens, flashlights and teddy bears onto the stage, in addition to the usual fusilade of jelly beans.

... BRIAN EPSTEIN

Underestimated Appeal

"They may have underestimated the Beatles' appeal," he said of the management. "There is a problem here. Their adulation can be underestimated."

Epstein charged that barriers were only one foot in front of the stage at the Cow Palace and that security guards were unevenly distributed.

"Although I am told that the kids in San Francisco are wilder than elsewhere, the boys and I find it difficult to believe," he said. "The second show was so bad we cut three numbers. It was the very first time the boys have had to cut their own show. It could not have been very pleasant for the boys," he said.

But speaking of their two concerts at Hollywood Bowl (sponsored by Bob Eubanks and KRLA) Epstein said: "It was well-organized as well as enthusiastic . . . the highlight of our tour."

Epstein also announced plans for a seven-city tour by the Beatles throughout Britain this autumn. He said they expected to do one-night shows at Glasgow, Newcastle, Liverpool, Manchester, Sheffield, Birmingham and London.

Screaming Welcome

The Beatles were met by a screaming mob of several hundred fans on their return to London airport. Many of them had waited throughout a chilly night for the plane's arrival.

Ringo, George, Paul and John were whisked from the airport in a private car with a police motocycle escort.

They appeared tired, but in good spirits. Glad to be home again, but cheered by the memories of huge overflow crowds and an estimated $1 million from their U.S. tour.

The Beatles' elaborate departure plans in San Francisco almost misfired. The strategy called for them to take an elevator from their eighth floor hotel rooms, descend to the second floor, cross to a fire escape at the rear of the building and climb down to the ground to a waiting ton-and-a-half truck.

Everything went smoothly until the driver, apparently anxious to speed away before fans appeared on the scene, gunned his truck and started moving away from the hotel.

Ringo was only halfway aboard the vehicle and almost fell off before he was pulled inside.

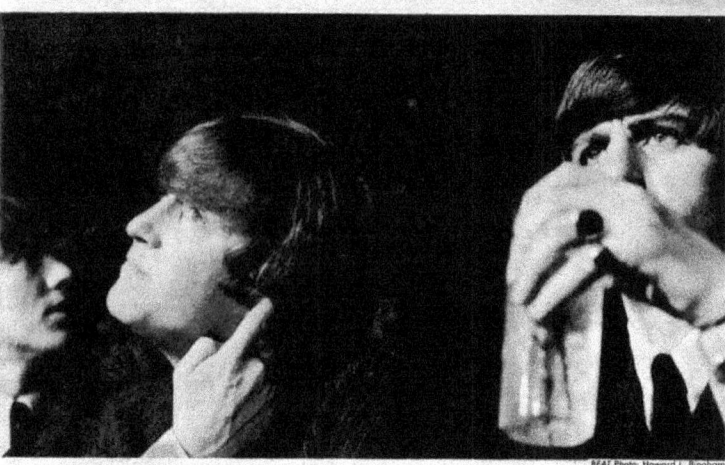
BEAT Photo: Howard L. Bingham

Boos, Jeers Greet Two Beatles At Berry Show

LONDON—John Lennon, Ringo Starr and their manager, Brian Epstein, were the object of booing and jeering from the audience at the Epstein owned Saville Theatre.

The audience, numbering over one thousand teens, booed loudly at the two Beatles and attempted to destroy the Theatre by ripping the seats, tearing down the curtains and smashing lights.

License Loss?

The rioting started when two fans jumped on stage during Chuck Berry's act. This, according to the Theatre manager, was against the Greater London Council regulations. He, therefore, ordered the safety curtain lowered. This, in turn, set off the audience who "just went wild and began tearing the place to pieces," according to a member of the audience.

Unfortunately, the two Beatles were seated in a box along with Epstein and the audience immediately turned on them with boos and jeers. Squads of police were called in and during the height of the rioting John and Ringo made a hasty exit but Epstein remained in the Seville pleading with the audience to restore order.

The police herded the outraged fans into the street near Piccadilly Circus where they chanted "we want our money back" while ripping life-size pictures of Berry which had been hanging out in front of the Saville.

The trouble, however, did not end there. Epstein announced that he sympathized with the audience and consequently fired his Saville manager, Michael Bullock. Epstein's dismissal of Bullock caused the National Association of Theatrical and Kine Employees to issue an ultimatum demanding an immediate withdrawal of what they termed Epstein's "irresponsible attack" on his staff. If not, they threatened to strike.

Safety Curtain

There is also the chance that Epstein will lose his Sunday license for the shows, but throughout all the hysteria and criticism Epstein is remaining calm. "If at any time my license is withdrawn," said the Beatles' manager, "I shall simply move the shows to another theatre."

BEATLES ARCHIVES 1

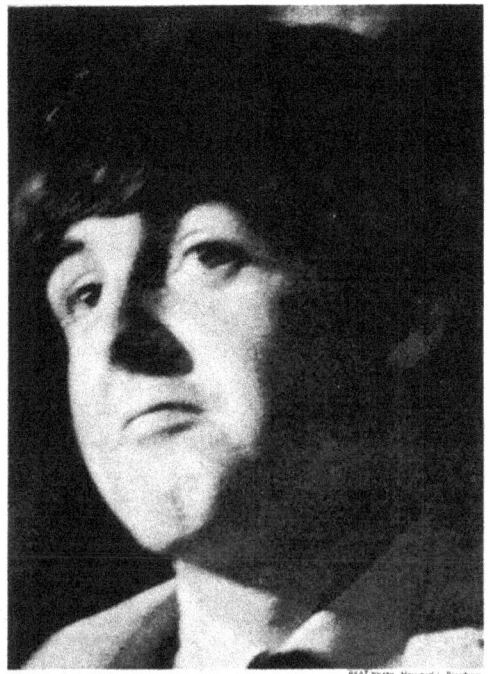

...MARTHA McCARTNEY dislikes Paul's trumpet playing.

JANE ASHER DENIES SPLIT WITH BEATLE

Whether she meant it to happen or not, Jane Asher is a well-known name today because of Paul McCartney. Perhaps she would have made it on her own talent—perhaps not. Jane is currently in the United States touring with the Bristol Old Vic Repertory Company.

Reporters don't care about that. They want to know what gives between Jane and Paul. "I'm in this country as a Shakespearean actress," said Jane, "not just a friend of a Beatle."

Word out of England is that the Asher/McCartney romance is now in the past tense. Jane obviously doesn't think so. "I love Paul very deeply and he feels the same," she declared. "I certainly should be very surprised indeed if I married anyone but Paul."

Paul did not see her off at the airport but reportedly the couple shared a candlelight dinner the night before her plane departed for the United States.

American reporters met Jane at the airport and demanded to know about McCartney, because "the public wants to know." I don't *care* what the public wants to know," sniffed Jane. "If I even said I'd had a letter from him, everybody would pounce on me and say, 'what was in it?'"

Jane, who is now 20, began her acting career when she was five playing the part of a deaf mute in the movie, "Mandy." Her father is a doctor but Jane says that both sides of her family have always been involved in the theater, if only on an amateur level.

"I think mother took her children to auditions because a neighbor said, 'with that hair, they're naturals.'" Jane, her brother Peter (one-half of the Peter & Gordon duo) and her 18 year old sister, Claire, all have an unusual shade of hair which has been described as everything from Marmalade to "just plain red." "I think 'orange' best describes the shade," said Jane. "I grew up with the nicknames 'carrots' and 'copper knob'."

Jane has done several dramatic roles in British films but is best known to U.S. moviegoers as one of the girls opposite Michael Caine in "Alfie." She has never formally studied acting, although she says "you learn new methods from each director."

With the Old Vic, Jane is playing Juliet in "Romeo and Juliet" as well as Julietta in "Measure For Measure." This is the company's first American tour and by May they will have played in Boston, Philadelphia, Washington D.C., New York, Los Angeles, San Francisco, San Diego, Denver, Dallas, Chicago, Champaign, Lafayette, Indianapolis, Bloomington, Detroit and Cleveland. They will then head to Canada to appear at the Expo 67.

"American audiences so far have been wonderfully receptive to Shakespear," Jane said. "They're so quiet. I think the English have become a bit blase."

There was quite a bit of speculation to the effect that Paul would accompany Jane on her tour. Up until press time, however, he has remained in England.

U.K. POP NEWS ROUND-UP

Beatle 'Babies' Identified

FOR ALL BEATLE PEOPLE WHO ARE STILL TRYING TO GUESS THE CORRECT IDENTITIES OF THE FOUR BABIES PICTURED ON THE CAPITOL SLEEVE WHICH CAME WITH "PENNY LANE" AND "STRAWBERRY FIELDS FOREVER" HERE'S THE RUN-DOWN THAT WINS OR LOSES SO MANY BETS! THE BABY SITTING BESIDE A TOY DOG IS JOHN LENNON. THE BABY IN THE PRAM IS PAUL McCARTNEY. THE CLOSE-UP PICTURE OF A LITTLE BOY WEARING A KNITTED JERSEY IS GEORGE HARRISON. AND THAT LEAVES RINGO STARR—HE'S THE TINY 6-MONTHS-OLD TOT SITTING ON A BIG CUSHION.

Recordings made in their pre-Monkee days by MICKY DOLENZ and DAVY JONES are being released or re-issued this month in Britain.

Davy-Solo

The Davy Jones material is in the hands of Pye Records; I understand they have enough tracks to make up an album and at least one single. The recordings, made for the Colpix label, consist of solo vocals which Davy describes as "garbage."

"Don't Do It," written and recorded by Micky Dolenz, has already hit the U.K. market on the top deck of a London single.

THE ROLLING STONES are to spend three weeks touring Europe at the end of this month and the first half of April. Included are concert dates in Norway, Denmark, Holland, Germany, Belgium and France. They'll play five nights in Athens and visit Vienna and Zurich. Other dates in Eastern Europe are to be added.

A few weeks after their return to Britain the Stones will set off on a short U.K. concert tour playing key cities in England, Scotland and Wales late April and early May.

P.J. PROBY, presumably back home in the U.S. with you by now, was given a last-minute reprieve by London's work-permit authorities so that he could plug "Niki Hoeky" on BBC Television's "Tops Of The Pops."

Before flying out of London Jim starred in a week-long cabaret presentation at Newcastle in North East England. Agent Tito Burns is hopeful that a further work permit will allow Proby to undertake a full-length cabaret and/or concert tour of Britain early this summer.

Mini-Marriage

Talking in London of his recent mini-marriage (which lasted only one week, he claimed!) Proby said: "I had known Judith Howard for 8 months before we married on my birthday last November. She didn't like my long hair and had me cut off my pony-tail. Then she didn't like my new haircut."

BARRY BENSON, once Jim Proby's hairdresser, chart-climbing here with "Cousin Jane," an off-beat ballad borrowed from The Troggs' album ... PAUL'S fast-growing dog Martha McCartney dislikes her master's trumpet playing! ... My formal congratulations to NANCY and RON on their formal announcement! ... JEFF BECK solo debut disc is "Hi Ho Silver Lining."

London journalists found SANDY POSEY a difficult interview subject ... Elektra label released self-penned DOORS single "Break On Through" in U.K. ... Have the MOTHERS OF INVENTION stopped inventing?... STEVIE WINWOOD finally quit The Spencer Davis Group to concentrate on songwriting ... Birthday telegram to GEORGE was signed "Magnets, Moscou" ... Secret Wedding Congratulations to TURTLE Mark Volman ... Ravi Shankar's brother a guest of GEORGE HARRISON at recording sessions ... BEATLES hope to acquire their own private recording studios in London's West End.

Byrd News

On their first night in town BYRDS down at London's most "in" discotheque, The Bag O' Nails, after visiting BEATLES recording session ... According to P.J. PROBY: "The Monkees will last as long as the public remains ignorant."

MONKEE MICKY's most constant London companion was "Top Of The Pops" TV deejay SAMANTHA JUSTE. Said Sammy: "He's very thoughtful, kind and generous."

From Basil Foster, boss of the Yorkshire stables where he once worked for 12 dollars a week,

DAVY JONES: album of "garbage"

BEATLES TO buy recording studio

MONKEE DAVY is buying his own race horse. Hopes to fly to Britain to see his purchase a couple of months from now.

On current ROY ORBISON/SMALL FACES U.K. concert tour, JEFF BECK'S group makes stage debut ... Will SONNY AND CHER use Trogg Reg Presley's "Our Love Will Still Be There" on next single?

B-Flat Solo

Pleased to hear PETULA CLARK confirmed for starring role (as veteran FRED ASTAIRE'S daughter) in Warner Bros. screen version of "Finian's Rainbow" ... Top Australian singer NORMIE ROWE appearing without fee throughout current GENE PITNEY/TROGGS package tour ... Top Australian group THE BEE GEES (average age of the foursome is just 17 years!) signed to management/agency contract by Brian Epstein's NEMS Enterprises ... Spring seasons at the London Palladium for FRANK IFIELD, THE SEEKERS and TOM JONES ... To be very precise that's a B Flat Piccolo Trumpet on "Penny Lane"... Will P.J. PROBY star in Western movie "Johnny Vengenace" scheduled for summer production in Spain? ... Two weeks stint at London Palladium will delay appearance of FRANK IFIELD on "The Ed Sullivan Show" until the end of April ... KEITH in London now to promote his new Hollies-penned single "Tell Me To My Face."

Because iron curtain was lowered at Saville Theatre before CHUCK BERRY had finished his Sunday concert, 1200 fans rioted doing damage estimated at a thousand dollars. As a result of the incident Saville boss BRIAN EPSTEIN fired theatre manager Michael Bullock ... BRIAN EPSTEIN now in New York prior to Mexico visit.

THE HOTTEST QUINTETTE CLUB GOING IS "THE MENDELSOHN QUINTETTE CLUB OF BOSTON"!
Irving Mendelsohn

BEATLES ARCHIVES 1

A BEATLE'S PRESS CONFERENCE
WHAT'S IT LIKE?

BEAT photo: Robert W. Young

LET'S GO SEE . . . with Louise Criscione

Hollywood — Well, gang, we are off again and this time it's to a Beatles' press conference! Wanna come?

It's about 6:30 p.m. — a half hour before the press conference is due to get underway.

The location of this press conference is a well-guarded secret, but as always happens with anything concerning the Beatles the secret has somehow managed to get out, and throngs of teenage girls are lined up outside the door.

Not a Prayer

They really don't have a prayer of gaining admittance but they wait anyway — hoping that they will get at least a glimpse of the four Beatles as they make their mad dash from the armored truck to the door of the building.

Policemen group around the parking lot and solidly line the entrance to the building. At the door a girl stands with a list of invited guests and only those people whose name is on the list are allowed past the guards.

Each guest is provided with a gold press pass, and without this pass *and* your name at the door — you are completely out of luck. This year *no one* sneaks in. Even the Beatles themselves are on the list!

As the guests are checked in they are handed a press kit which contains the Beatles' well-known biography and also a copy of their latest album, "Help."

Room a Beehive

The conference room is a beehive of activity. Television cameramen are setting up their equipment, tape recorders are being readied, reporters are chatting and officials are checking and rechecking the microphones and amplifiers.

Nothing, absolutely nothing, must go wrong tonight. It's been planned too long to have anything go wrong now at the last minute.

More people are admitted, seats are rapidly filled, the clock is moving closer and closer to the time when the Beatles are due to arrive.

It's ten minutes to seven and Tony Barrow, publicist for the Beatles, steps up to the microphone and gives the press their last minute instructions.

A Roar Outside

Then suddenly a roar is heard from the crowd gathered outside and you know that the Beatles have finally arrived!

Two policemen run up the aisle clearing the way for the Beatles who are following close behind.

And then you see them! John, the undeclared leader, arrives first followed in short order by Ringo, Paul, and bringing up the rear is George.

Immediately the flash bulbs start flashing. The four make their way to the platform on which four microphones, four stools and four small desks have been placed.

Each Beatle waves hello, chooses a seat, and the photographers move up in front of the platform to take their alloted 10 minutes of shots.

The Beatles allow themselves to be photographed individually and in a group. And then it's our turn to ask questions.

Questioning Begins

Two microphones have been set up on the floor, and as Tony points to you the microphone is brought over and you ask your question. In this way every question as well as every answer is heard by everyone in the room.

It's going very well. The veteran newsmen comment on the smoothness and organization of the conference.

The questioning lasts for a little over an hour. Some of the questions have been asked a million times before, some are brand new. The Beatles answer all of them — sometimes with a laugh, sometimes very seriously.

They field all of the questions expertly. Some reporters attempt to put them down, but they are always on-guard. And they are never without an answer. John and Paul do most of the talking, with George coming in third and Ringo remaining the quietest.

Thank the Press

After a series of short television interviews, the Beatles thank the press for coming — the press thank the Beatles for inviting them — the conference room is cleared and the Beatles jump aboard their armored truck for a quick drive to the show.

We were sorry to see the conference end so soon. But they will be back again next year (they told us so!). And we can hardly wait, can you?

BEATLES ARCHIVES 1

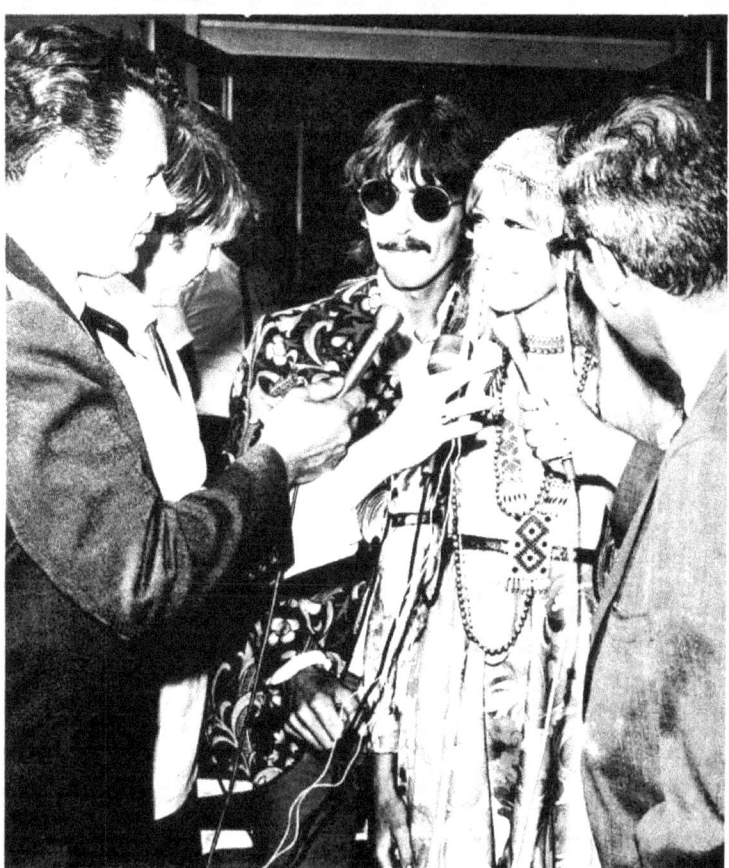

GEORGE HARRISON AND WIFE PATTI step off a Pan American jet at Los Angeles International Airport.

Harrison Arrives Stateside; Explains Controversial Ad

LOS ANGELES – Beatle George Harrison arrived at the Los Angeles International Airport for what he described as a "little bit of business and pleasure." Accompanied by his wife Patti, who was dressed in the Hippie garb reminiscent of the American Indian, the youngest Beatle was greeted by about 300 fans and a battery of the press.

George admitted that he had no plans for an extended stay in Los Angeles. "I expect to be here no longer than about five days. I have no plans, just come and try and get a bit of peace. You know, I'd like to see a few friends and a few people, that's the only thing I'm here for. And just a few things concerning business."

When asked why the Beatles have decided to give up concert tours, George answered, "It would be hard to pinpoint the problem just in a few words. There's so many different things we'd like. You see, we're all growing sort of physically and mentally and we've got to progress, and concert tours are too much in one rut. I think a lot of people realize this. We're more able to experiment with music and just generally do lots more things that we've always wanted to do.

"You know, in order to do something new, you've got to cut something out, and touring was the thing we were getting the least satisfaction from, because it was getting too big. It was too many politics being attached to it, when all we really are was a pop group coming to sing to the fans. But it was getting into big political things all related to it, that, you know, added up to the decision to stop it."

One reporter mentioned that there was a rumor that the Beatles were going to produce a new album with the "old Beatle sound." However, George denied the rumor, stating, "the Beatles have always been trying to progress with us. So all I can say is the next Beatle album is, well, we don't know. But whatever we do, we try our best."

Legalized Marijuana

Recently Harrison along with the other three Beatles signed a petition to the English Government urging the legalization of marijuana. The petition was also signed by 61 other British citizens and was addressed to the Home Secretary, Roy Jenkins. The advertisement appeared in a full-page story in the London Times. When asked about his reason for supporting the legalization of marijuana, Harrison said, "I think if somebody can go and buy a crate of Johnny Walker whiskey and drink that and be perfectly within the law then I think somebody, particularly within the privacy of his own home, should be able to smoke a marijuana cigarette. You know, I think marijuana is only as bad as ordinary cigarettes or alcohol or tea or coffee or any of those things.

"They're all drugs, all stimulants you know. The thing is to define between something that is merely a stimulant and something that makes your physical body crave for it. There's no comparison between marijuana and heroin."

Increasing Use

Harrison went on to say, "I think the use of marijuana is increasing everywhere in the world. It's not just America and Britain, but it's everywhere, and it's not just marijuana, you know, marijuana is the thing that society has picked up on, but that's not really the problem. The thing is that the young people want something more out of life than just the physically gained things that they get out of society. They're looking for something more, and it's a natural part of evolution that's taking place."

While staying in Los Angeles, Harrison is expected to attend the Ravi Shankar concert at the Hollywood Bowl.

BEATLES ARCHIVES 1

MEET TH[

BRITAIN'S "BEATLEMANIA" HAS SPREAD TO AMER[

ON TV: Jack Paar Show (Jan. 3, NBC-TV)! Ed Sullivan Show (Fe[
Feb. 16, CBS-TV)! Already seen on Walter Cronkite News (CBS-[
Huntley-Brinkley News (NBC-TV)! Featured in Time, Life, Newsv[
and newspapers everywhere! Among record buyers "Beatlema[
has proved absolutely contagious. Over 3,000,000 discs already [
in England alone. So be prepared for the kind of sales epid[
that made THE BEATLES the biggest-selling vocal group in Br[
history! CALL YOUR CAPITOL SALES REP. TODAY!

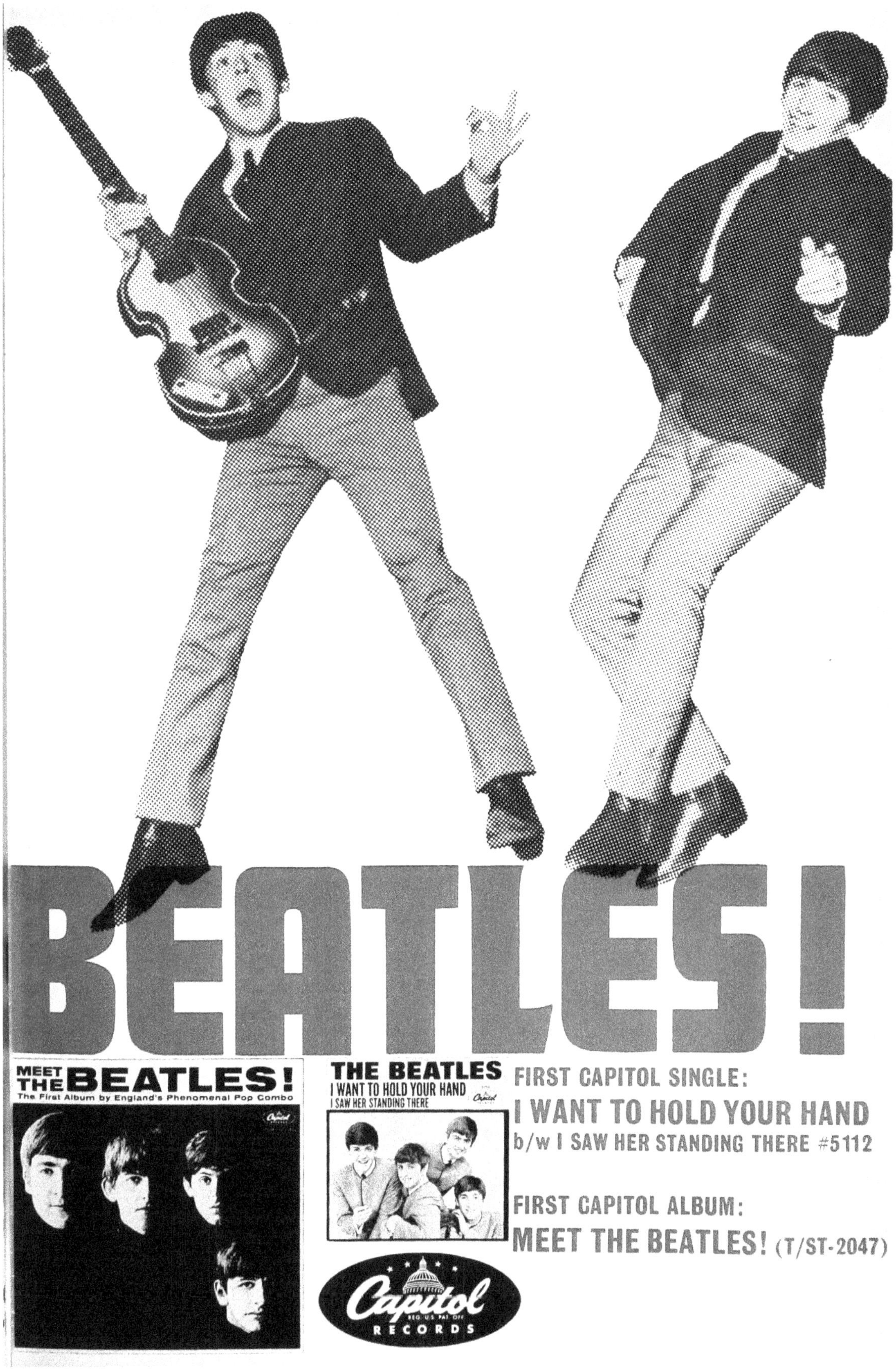

BEATLES ARCHIVES 1

FIRST CAPITOL SINGLE:
I WANT TO HOLD YOUR HAND
b/w I SAW HER STANDING THERE #5112

FIRST CAPITOL ALBUM:
MEET THE BEATLES! (T/ST-2047)

BEATLES ARCHIVES 1

The Cash Box "Sure Shots" highlight records which reports from retail dealers throughout the nation indicate are already beginning to sell quantity or else give every indication of doing so.

"PAIN IN MY HEART"
OTIS REDDING .... Volt 112

•

"A FOOL NEVER LEARNS"
ANDY WILLIAMS .... Columbia 42950

•

"TALKING ABOUT MY BABY"
IMPRESSIONS .... ABC-Paramount 10511

•

"TONIGHT YOU'RE GONNA FALL IN LOVE WITH ME"
SHIRELLES .... Scepter

•

"IF SOMEBODY TOLD ME"
ANNA KING .... Smash 1858

•

"HIS KISS"
BETTY HARRIS .... Jubilee 5465

•

"I WANT TO HOLD YOUR HAND"
BEATLES .... Capitol 5112

NEW YORK—"A Hard Day's Night" has been chosen as a title for the Beatles' new flick for United Artists. The famed British rock group selected the tag themselves.

The film is currently before the cameras in England and it will feature eight new tunes composed by Beatles John Lennon and Paul McCartney.

MGM Single Includes Beatles Sans Vocal

NEW YORK—MGM Records has the only all-instrumental showing by The Beatles on the market.

The label's follow-up to its hit Beatles single, "My Bonnie," contains the number, "Cry For A Shadow," played as an instrumental and penned by Beatleites John Lennon and George Harrison.

The other side, "Why," features a vocal, with Beatles backing, by Tony Sheridan, the songster on the "My Bonnie" date.

Like "My Bonnie," the new MGM single was obtained through a deal with Deutsche Grammophon of Germany, where the sides were recorded.

Capitol's New Beatles Single Due Around June 27

NEW YORK—The week of June 27 has been set for the release of the new Beatles single from Capitol Records, Cash Box has learned. Topside is the title tune from the group's first feature flick, "A Hard Day's Night," which will have its U.S. bow in Aug.

The release will mark Capitol's third singles offering by the crew (label has released two LP's and an EP). Their last single was "Can't Buy Me Love." The label recently tried to put over the flip side, an item called "You Can't Do That."

Meanwhile, United Artists Records is preparing its release of the soundtrack score of the Walter Shenson-produced "A Hard Day's Night." Murray Deutch, vp at UA's publishing operation, has left for England to bring back the completed tapes, after which UA will try to get the LP out as soon as possible.

Beatles' Pic A Preview Sell-Out In Toronto

NEW YORK—A preview of things to come for the upcoming Beatles flick, "A Hard Day's Night," came out of Toronto last week.

United Artists, distributor of the flick, decided to hold a preview of the effort on Aug. 11, the day before it officially opens in 11 Canadian theaters in Toronto. Scheduling the preview in four of the 11 houses, it took 90 minutes to sell a total of 3,098 tickets, which account for the entire seating of all four theaters.

This preview push got week-long UA-sponsored attention on radio, TV, in newspapers and through special movie trailers. UA plans to use a similar preview idea in other Canadian cities.

The film will open in New York on Aug. 1, and throughout the month it will get world-wide coverage.

Tollie Releases Beatles' "Love Me Do"

NEW YORK—The Beatles have added another chapter to their historic and often confusing triumph in the U.S.

Get this: Tollie Records, the affiliate of the Vee Jay label, has just released the Beatles disking of "Love Me Do," which had been available (and getting chart action) on the Capitol of Canada label.

Since it is understood that Capitol of Canada is no longer producing the "Love Me Do" side and since Vee Jay and Capitol recently settled their legal dispute over Beatles products (see last week's issue), Tollie apparently can go ahead with the release, but, under the Vee Jay-Capitol settlement, will have to dish-out royalties to Capitol on sales of the session.

BEATLES ARCHIVES 1

Breaking In All Major Markets
WHO DO YOU LOVE
THE SAPPHIRES
S-4162

CHAIN REACTION SWAN ON

The Beatles' Biggest Hit Is On Swan!
19 Weeks On England's Top 10
#3 Last Week
This Is The Record Performed On The Jack Paar Show...
SHE LOVES YOU
THE BEATLES
S-4152

Another Chartmaker!
AMAZONS AND COYOTES
THE DREAMLOVERS
S-4167

SWAN RECORDS
8th & Fitzwater Sts.
Philadelphia, Pa.
MA 7-1500

BEATLES ARCHIVES 1

Beatles Get 4th Cash Box Int'l Award

Royalty To See Beatles' Film Premiere; Transatlantic Press Conference Held In N.Y.

NEW YORK—HRH Princess Margaret and the Earl of Snowden have accepted an invitation to attend the World premiere of "A Hard Day's Night," the United Artists flick which marks the film debut of the Beatles. The first showing will be held July 6, at the London Pavilion.

During the final week of shooting of the picture, the Beatles took time out from their chores to attend a reception in their honor at Australia House where they were the guests of the Australian Consul. During their reception, the hot British group participated in an international press conference at which they fielded questions from newsmen, deejays and fans who were gathered at U.A.'s New York offices. The transatlantic hook-up was engineered by the Bell Telephone Co. and AT&T, with the questions and answers relayed over a loudspeaker system.

LONDON—The fabulous Beatles are pictured with their Cash Box International Awards presented to artists whose internationally produced recordings reached the number one spot on the Cash Box Top 100 Chart. Sir Joseph Lockwood, Chairman of EMI (third from right) attended the presentation made by George Albert (third from left) Cash Box vice president, who hosted the presentation luncheon while on a trip through Europe. The three gold awards were made for "She Loves You," "Twist And Shout" and "Can't Buy Me Love." When the Beatles were in America they received their award for "I Want To Hold Your Hand." The Beatles, (l. to r.) are Ringo Starr, George Harrison, John Lennon and Paul McCartney. The photo on right shows Sir Joseph admiring one of the gold CB International Trophies, commenting on it to Neville Marten, Cash Box's European Director.

Beatles Coming Back

(Continued from page 7)
Stadium; Aug. 23: Los Angeles' Hollywood Bowl; Aug. 24 and 25: Open; Aug. 26: Denver's Red Rocks Stadium; Aug. 27: Cincinnati's The Gardens; Aug. 28 and 29: New York's Forest Hills Stadium; Aug. 30: Atlantic City's Convention Hall; Aug. 31: Open.

Sept. 1: open; Sept. 2: Philadelphia's Convention Hall; Sept. 3: Indianapolis State Fair Grounds; Sept. 4: Milwaukee's Auditorium; Sept. 5: Chicago's International Amphitheater; Sept. 6: Detroit's Olympic Stadium; Sept. 7: Toronto's Maple Leaf Gardens; Sept. 8: Montreal's Forum; Sept. 9 and 10: open; Sept. 11: Jacksonville's The Gaitor Bowl; Sept. 12: Montgomery's Coliseum; Sept. 13: Baltimore's Civic Center; Sept. 14: Open; Sept. 15: to be scheduled; Sept. 16: New Orleans' City Park Stadium; Sept. 17: Open; Sept. 18: Dallas; Sept. 19: Houston's Colt Stadium; Sept. 20: to be announced.

SON OF A GUN!

Who'd ever think that little Vee Jay Records would have 9 out of the top 100 best selling singles?

DO YOU WANT TO KNOW A SECRET ✻ BEATLES T-9001
SHOOP SHOOP SONG ✻ BETTY EVERETT VJ-585
TWIST AND SHOUT ✻ THE BEATLES VJ-587
STAY ✻ THE FOUR SEASONS VJ-582
GIVING UP ON LOVE ✻ JERRY BUTLER VJ-588
THANK YOU GIRL ✻ THE BEATLES VJ-587
FROM ME TO YOU ✻ THE BEATLES VJ-581
THERE'S A PLACE ✻ THE BEATLES T-9001
PLEASE PLEASE ME ✻ THE BEATLES VJ-581

and with all this we're still only #8 in record sales?

BRAND NEW FROM tollie RECORDS

THE BEATLES

LOVE ME DO ✻ P.S. I LOVE YOU

T-9008

U. S. Disk Industry – The First 4 Months: British Artists Remain On Top

NEW YORK—With the first four months of the year completed, it is quite obvious that the record industry in America during the first third of 1964 was all but completely dominated by Britain's artists.

The overwhelming aspect of the first four months of 1964 has been, of course, Beatlemania. Since the beginning of the year, the top spot on the Top 100 has been held solely by the Beatles. As many as five Beatles decks have shared the top 10 at one time.

For a while, early in the year, it was feared by many manufacturers that the craze would never be anything more than a Beatle fad, funneling all teenage record dollars into one company's till. Fortunately, for the indie distribs who had the Swan, Vee Jay and Tollie lines, some Beatles dollars were reaching their registers. But there was no doubt that Capitol had come up with the hottest act the pop business had ever witnessed.

For a few weeks immediately after the Beatles arrived in the U.S., the record industry was almost completely separated into the haves and have-nots. If you had anything to do with a Beatles disk you were very much in business; but if you were in no way affiliated with Beatles goods, coming into the office was a difficult chore. Airplay on records other than Beatles product was hard to come by and many companies changed their releasing schedules, holding back on some potentially strong singles, waiting for a clearing, and perhaps issuing some non-competitive product such as country music singles, etc.

But as soon as a clearing did develop, in moved other British acts. And there is no doubt that Beatlemania was directly responsible for turning America's eyes to the British charts for other artists, sounds and hits that were replacing the Beatles in the number one spot in England.

This, of course, resulted in the present situation which sees the Beatles still very much in the driver's seat (more firmly entrenched here as the top act than they ever were in England) but with many other British acts getting considerable acceptance. The Dave Clark Five, the Searchers, the Swinging Blue Jeans, the Bachelors, Dusty Springfield, Billy J. Kramer and the Dakotas are just a few names who have met with tremendous success here since the Beatles clicked.

Fortunately for the non-Capitol distributors, this influx of British material, primarily on indie labels, spread the wealth of the British craze in many directions, permitting a number of companies to make it through the lean Beatles months.

Retailers, one-stops, rack jobbers, etc., never once complained about the British craze. There were, of course, some bad payers who had to come up with past due payments to get delivery of much needed Beatles merchandise—and these had cause for complaint from time to time. But the Beatles sensation was pulling the public into the stores like nothing had since Presley's debut, creating an excitement that hadn't been felt in years. For a while it was only Beatles product the teenager was buying, only because of the unique phenomenon of three top ten singles (and two LP's) by the group riding at one time. But it wasn't too long before appreciating the Dave Clark Five, rather than blasting them for their somewhat Beatlelike haircut, became the "in" thing among the kids, leading to the teenagers' acceptance of the exciting Clark sound as well as the hits of other groups.

The result was that dealers and racks were selling more records to a broader audience and Beatlemania had revived an interest in records which was waning since the Twist days.

Capitol Off & Running With Beatles EP

NEW YORK—Capitol Records is back in the EP business with a release b the Beatles.

Word from the label indicated tha the EP, which had not received fu distribution until week's end, woul be the largest EP seller in the firm history.

The deck, containing two tunes eac from the group's first two Capit LP's, is selling like a "very good, no Beatles' single," as one Capitol ex put it.

Selection of the tracks, the lab said, was made after a survey of portion of the fan mail Capitol h received on the Beatles, which no totals more than 2 million pieces.

In the normal singles release fiel Capitol is moving to put over the fl side of the Beatles recent number smash, "Can't Buy Me Love." T group will perform the song, "Y Can't Do That," on next Sunday's Sullivan TV'er. This confirms rumo that Capitol would have no n Beatles single until its release of t title tune of the teams upcomi flick, "A Hard Day's Night," som time before the premiere of the eff in the U.S. in Aug. This Sunda Sullivan show will include a film c from the film.

UA & Capitol To Share Beatles' Flick Date

NEW YORK—The Beatles' first feature-film, to give United Artists its first Beatles product, has just been completed in England. For the film, a United Artists release called "A Hard Day's Night," the English team's Paul McCartney and John Lennon have written nine new songs, including a main-title, which will be part of the UA disk release.

It was noted that UA only has LP rights to the score, and cannot issue any singles from the album. Capitol, however, will release a single of the title song. It's understood further that Capitol can also employ items from the soundtrack for an LP, but is prohibited from merchandising the album as a soundtrack package.

Flick gets a royal sendoff with a benefit premiere in July, sponsored by the Variety Clubs of Great Britain and attended by HRH Princess Margaret and the Earl of Snowdon. The American premiere takes place in New York in Aug. Both premieres will be attended by the Beatles, who will be in the U.S. in Aug. for a month-long tour across the country (see last week's story).

Shot in and around London, the film is a fictional account of 36 eventful hours in the lives of the boys. Also featured are Anna Quayle, star of the London and New York productions of "Stop the World . . ." and Wildfrid Brambell, British TV comedy star.

Atco Gets Beatles Single

NEW YORK—Atco Records has joined the parade of labels in on Beatles product. Label last week released "Sweet Georgia Brown" by the group with Tony Sheridan. Deck, the first American non standard available here by the group in the singles market, was originally cut by Polydor Records of Germany, the pop outlet for DGG.

Previous Beatles material cut by Polydor, including a single, "My Bonnie" and an LP, "The Beatles with Tony Sheridan," was released in the U.S. by MGM Records, which releases DGG classical product in the U.S. and has first-refusal rights on much of the Polydor catalog.

Other Beatles-sporting labels are Capitol, Vee Jay and its Tollie affiliate, and Swan.

Atco is backing the release of the single with a major nation-wide promo effort, including novel promo ideas with radio stations.

Distribs and radio stations are now being supplied with the session.

BEATLES ARCHIVES 1

When Legends Speak of Legends

By Doug Gilbert

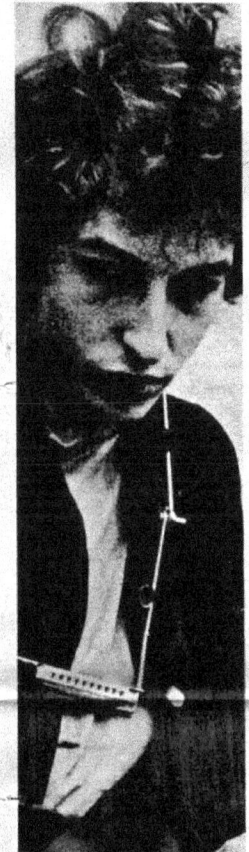

When an established performer gives his opinion on the ability of another star, the result is often a gain or loss of status for the person being discussed. Of course, this is sometimes reversed. As when Tom Jones was recently critical of the Beatles. A majority of Tom's fans considered his words to be both unwarranted and unfair. Whatever your reaction, the fact is that Tom's prestige did suffer. Though obviously it can only be a temporary loss. After all, Tom is a singer of tremendous ability, and this ability will certainly make up for anything that he might have said in the heat of the moment.

Normally stars are not too critical of other stars as it is considered unprofessional. Personally I don't agree with this idea. The Beatles are among the most outspoken of people, regardless of whether their words are courteous or not, so they can't complain about anybody else speaking his mind—and they don't.

Thanks To John

John Lennon can be both generous and ungenerous in his choice of words, but he usually makes a good point. As when he once spoke of Donovan: "I bought Donovan's 'Catch The Wind' so that I could listen to it, without having to look at him." However, when he likes something or somebody John tells the world about it. His praise of Bob Dylan was a deciding factor as to the success of Dylan's first trip to England.

When a Beatle gives an opinion it gets around faster than a declaration from the House of Windsor, so after John praised Dylan, English fans went out and bought up all the available seats for Bob's string of concerts. Before embarking on his U.K. tour Bob Dylan was comparatively unknown in the world of popular music. It is true that he was already accepted in the folk circles as a sort of demi-God, but either there are not many folk fans or else they don't buy as many records as their Rock 'n' Rolling cousins. After Bob added a beat to his music he was gradually becoming more popular but it was the U.K. trip that finally started the ball rolling.

Dylan for Dinner

John Lennon has said that he first heard of Dylan in France where Paul picked up an album by Bob, and they both spent the rest of the day running the grooves off it. Later in 1964 he met him in New York, during a Beatle tour, and they became pretty good friends. When Dylan reached England he was invited by John to stay at his Tudor Mansion in Weybridge. Dylan accepted, at least for dinner, and so he got to know Cynthia.

Neither the Mods or the Rockers are prone to believing everything that they hear, but in England John Lennon is fast becoming something of a folk leader, so the kids hear what he has to say and then test his words by checking the facts for themselves. They checked out Bob Dylan and they liked what they heard.

Even if the concerts had not been sell-outs, the people who did attend would have recognized Dylan's brilliance and put the credit where it belong. But that kind of acclamation travels much slower than the voice of Lennon.

When Dylan returned to America he found that he was the leader of a new Folk-Rock revolution that was sweeping the U.S. from a point somewhere along Madison Avenue. Months later Lennon was asked how he felt about being something of an unpaid publicity man for Bob. John replied: "If I was, I don't mind—Dylan is a great talent. Donovan has done more to promote Dylan anyway." Donovan and Dylan fans in the U.K. are still arguing as to whether Donovan is an original artist in his own right, or simply a carbon copy of Dylan.

One thing that I do feel confident in saying is that Robert Zimmerman's talent, in his particular musical sphere, is almost beyond comparison. Had he never left Hibbing for a fourth time; had he never spent his summers treading and devouring the dirt of this continent, or his winters freezing to the bone in the City of New York; had he never heard the wail of a mouth-organ or the rhythm of a guitar, he would still have emerged from the mass of talent that is America and made his presence felt.

Dylan's Success

Dylan's success has also brought problems. His major one seems to be the fanaticism of some of his fans. Donovan recalled a Dylan concert that he attended: "This fellow came up to Dylan and said that he would kill for him. He kept asking Dylan who he wanted him to kill." People like this are too far gone for persuasion, but ordinary fans should keep in mind that Dylan is a man—not a God. Indeed he is a small and seemingly frail man, but a man who has displayed a brilliant comprehension of the very soul of rhythmic music.

Beatle Single Is Minus The Sitar

By Tony Barrow

The first products of The Beatles' marathon series of April and May recording sessions will America on June 6 and in the UK on June 10. The titles are "Paperback Writer" and "Rain."

The first thing likely to surprise everyone who hears "Paperback Writer" is that the group's instrumental sounds are limited to their regular line-up of two guitars, bass guitar and drums. Most people had expected to hear all sorts of weird and wonderful innovations including, perhaps, George Harrison playing sitar. But for those special new sounds we must wait until August or September—the earliest planned release date for the album which the boys have been working on since Easter. Only seven album tracks have been completed to date. Some additional material has yet to be written.

Back to "Paperback Writer"—it's a fast-mover with a drumbeat which drives hard. The lyrics tell the story of a man who has written a novel and is trying to have it published. He's composing "Dear Sir or Madam" letters to book publishers pleading with them to read the 1,000 page work.

"Paperback Writer" opens up with a three-pronged vocal attack featuring John, Paul and George. Then Paul takes over the solo vocal side of things to be joined again by the other two for the chorus segments. Towards the end, there are some terrific guitar figures and a reverberating echo effect on the boys' voices.

Even if this deck doesn't boast an assortment of off-beat instrumental sounds it's certainly packed with technical specialties which took The Beatles and their recording manager, George Martin, plenty of thought to work out.

Mostly I find I need to hear any new Beatles' record five or six times before the tune sticks in my mind. Not so with "Paperback Writer." It has an instantly infectious tune, dominated by the much-repeated and multi-voiced title phrase.

The second side, "Rain," is a much less complex number which gives the vocal spotlight to John Lennon. Paul and George join him occasionally and contribute a se-

(Turn to Page 2)

Beatle Single—A Weather Forecast

(Continued from Page 1)

ries of ear-catching falsetto effects. "Rain" has as its theme the idea that whatever the weather is like somebody is ready to moan—if the sun shines too strongly we rush into the shade and if it rains we want the sun back again.

At the end of May, The Beatles filmed on location around London a series of television clips for "Paperback Writer" and "Rain." These will be made in colour and in black and white and are designed for TV screening on a worldwide scale.

Otherwise John, Paul, George and Ringo are finding plenty of activities to fill their days. They've been spending some time seeing top journalists from German newspapers prior to their late-June dates in Hamburg, Munich and Essen. John's place down in Weybridge, Surrey, has become the group's favorite meeting place for the moment. There all four boys gather to write or rehearse new album numbers before each new recording session. Quite frequently they give themselves a break from more serious work and shoot off some zany home movies in John's vast garden.

How London Feels About The Beatles

By Gil McDougall

Who is "in" and who is "out?" What do London's Mods and Rockers really think of the beat scene, and how do they rate the Beatles? If you would like to know the answers to these questions, as I did, then read on.

America is always being told what celebrity after celebrity thinks of the Beatles. So I thought that, for a change, I would compile an article consisting of the opinions of the people who set the style in popular music—the Mods and Rockers. I achieved this by embarking on a pub-crawl with some of London's "in" places. The various discussions were rather intermittent, as you will see, and on some occasions I never did get to hear a complete summation of the scene.

During the tour, I deliberately avoided such places as the Ad Lib, the Scotch Club and the Marquee. The reason: These places, and more, are still very much "in" but they are invariably packed with big names and I did not feel that they would represent a fair sampling of British opinion. Instead I went to these gear clubs and pubs: The Ship in Stepney; the Dragon in Hackney; the Bridge Tavern in Canning; the Rising Sun at Bethnal Green and finally, the Two Puddings. There were many more places, but this was about all I could cope with in one night. All those mentioned had Rock 'n' Roll bands, and they were all frequented by Mods (Rockers seem to be dying out.) English Mods are one up on most of their American cousins as they are allowed to enter the clubs and pubs at the age of eighteen, consequently most start when they are about sixteen.

Okay, now put everything aside, shut yourself in your room, turn up your radio, and come on a rave-up pub-crawl with me to the gear places in Big L.

"The Ship"

Beatles? They've been around too long and are getting stale . . . Ringo's down to earth and John is definitely a giggle . . . when I think about how long they've been in now, I begin to feel old . . . getting a bit too old for that stuff . . . you've got to take life more seriously when you get to nineteen . . . Well, yes, they have talent but they are dead now . . . now take the Blue Beat, it's been around for five years and only just beginning to catch on . . . it's great music . . . stiff at knee's, throw arms everywhere and make like a gospel singer . . . hips to the side four beats at a time and the rhythm is like a locomotive thumping along a track . . . sound like a drum and the words are really mad . . . it makes me laugh when people talk about Mersey music . . . Liverpool's a dead city now . . . you don't see the Beatles or Epstein living there . . . now in Manchester you can really have a rave-up . . .

"The Rising Sun"

The Rolling Stones are better—there's a really exciting sound . . . some people just can't recognize talent . . . they are brilliant . . . of course the Beatles are here to stay . . . now take my bird—she's dead potty about Paul . . . a bloke that engaged . . . Liverpool is a thing of the past now. I was up there a month ago and they're doing things that went out ages ago . . . the swim . . . the monkey . . . the huggy-bug . . . that stuff went out in Big L. a long time ago . . . the block and the bang are still "in" . . . there will always be competition between the cities . . . I like the Beatles because they make good records but I also like Tchaikovsky . . . they can't sing a note, it's just the sound . . . I'm jealous of their money though . . . that Paul's the one . . . what a bighead . . . if you see them in photographs or on Tele he's always in front fooling around and talking . . . Paul's fab . . . he's really a nice fellow too . . . he's a bighead . . . he needs someone like Lennon to tell him where it's at . . .

I think that the Merseybeats are just as good but I like the Beatles because they don't put on any fancy airs . . . the grown-ups like them too—just to get in with us . . . they are a young thing and grown-ups shouldn't try to get in with us through them . . . I like Lennon because he's pretty cool . . . did you see him last night when that interviewer asked a really stupid question . . . John just sort of looked at him once and then the bloke withered away . . . okay so I'm a Rocker . . . my boy's a Rocker and I'm proud of him . . . he's got guts . . . I'd marry him tomorrow . . . if he was agreeable . . . I have seen in some dance halls, a white line painted along one side of the dance floor . . . Rockers one side and Mods the other . . . if you ask me that's asking for trouble . . . it only makes the Rockers more mad and inclined to hate the Mods even more . . . Mods go to dance halls . . . discotheques . . . the Palais . . . the Rockers are prehistoric with Elvis-type sideburns . . . Elvis is old-fashioned now only the Rockers keep him up . . . the Mods are the smartest every time . . . people talk about them taking purple hearts but not many of us do . . . (this fellow liked to illustrate with his hands and for his final gesticulation he sent several glasses flying with his arm.)

Thinking that this was a good time to leave, I got up. As I did so I noticed that Kink Ray Davies was talking to the Rock 'n' Roll group on-stage. I attempted to make my way over there, but the place was packed and by the time that I got there he had disappeared. The lead singer told me that he had been "spirited away," and so I left it at that.

"The Dragon"

My dad thinks that the Beatles set a bad example for us teenagers . . . he thinks that they shouldn't drink and smoke so heavily but why should they pretend to be doing something that they're not . . . it's like saying that it is okay to be hyprocritical as long as you don't smoke . . . well I'm a southerner and I don't like the way all these northerners are taking over . . . Wilson is taking over the government and the Beatles are taking over everything else . . . I think that the people of today . . . the young people I mean . . . are best represented by Lennon with his mod-to-hip aggressive sort of attitude . . . but I can't say that I like him very much . . . I don't know if they are going out or not . . . they came in on Ringo's nose . . . Paul's good looks and John's personality . . . as far as I know they've still got all three things.

"The Iron Bridge"

. . . there was a time when I liked them quite a bit . . . I suppose that I still do like them . . . I buy all their records . . . they're knocking the stuffing out of the neo-Victorians . . . in the beginning they were really great, but they seem to have quieted down now . . . the Stones are the hip one's now . . . I'd hate to marry a Mod . . . my boy's a Rocker . . . his ambition in life is to do a ton down the M.I. . . . he'll do it too . . . they say Rockers are scruffy but it's not true . . . you know what Mod stands for—moderation in all things . . . what a way to carry on . . . they can say what they like about us—we know what the score really is . . . they aren't worth worrying about . . . I think that Elvis is great . . .

"The Bridge Tavern"

When they appear on a discussion show George hardly ever has anything to say . . . he's very quiet all the time . . . you couldn't say the same for John and Paul . . . their music is the greatest . . . there will never be anything like the Beatles . . . it's sort of like Churchill—that kind of thing only comes once . . . Rockers are a bunch of scruffs . . . I buy plenty of clothes . . . they call it Mod street now, not Carnaby Street.

Mods and Rockers like beat music, but they like different kinds . . . the Rockers always dig Elvis but the Mods like the groups . . . the Stones . . . Kinks . . . Yardbirds . . . Unit Four Plus Two . . . P. J. . . . and the Beatles . . . everybody has to say that the Beatles are going out, but they've been saying it for a year and a half now.

"The Two Puddings"

Mods go down to Carnaby Street with their own designs for clothes and John Stephens makes them up . . . a lot of Mods still model their clothes on the Beatles . . . trousers have seventeen inch bttoms . . . boots are made from imitation crocodile or python . . . shirts are giraffe collar—they are very high and crease up . . . three buttons on the jackets with narrow lapels and two vents in the bottom . . . I never watch Tele unless it's "Ready Steady Go" or something like that . . . I like the Yardbirds, they're really way out . . . Ringo's so easy-going it makes me wonder if the others take advantage of him.

Do you know how many cars John Lennon has got? . . . and here's me riding around on a Vespa . . . well, you bought his records . . . you've got to admit they have made some great records . . . yes, I'd buy them again if it came up I suppose . . . I think that it's John's personality makes them really you know . . . yes, that's true in a way but look at how cute Paul is . . . actually they all contribute . . . they probably wouldn't be so great if they split up . . . they'll never split, not with a combination like that . . . I don't think that any of the others can touch them really . . . not in any field . . . Time gentlemen, please.

What About Me?

What about me? I listen to Blue Beat music, but I don't dance the Blue Beat way. I dig Mod clothes and wear them, but not all the time. I dig everything a Mod raves over, but I don't hunt with the pack. I dig the Beatles and I do think that they are here to stay. England's Mods also dig the Beatles and though there are a few voices of dissent they all appreciate that rarely is such great talent grouped together in one combination. Not only do the Mods *think* that the Beatles are here to stay but they are determined to make sure that they do just that. The Beatles are Mods and the Mods are Beatles—may their tenure be as long as their talent.

Bob Dylan Touring U.S. and Canada

NEW YORK—Bob Dylan is currently embarked upon one of the most ambitious cross-country tours of the country to date. During the course of the tour, he plans to cover 14 states as well as parts of Canada.

The trip, which began the week of February 5, is one of the longest personal appearance tours of Dylan's career, and states listed on the itinerary include: New York, Tennessee, Virginia, South Carolina, Connecticut, Pennsylvania, Florida, Missouri, Nebraska, Colorado, Oklahoma, New Mexico, Oregon and Washington.

The tour will extend to parts of Canada, including Ottawa, Ontario, and Montreal, Quebec and will wind up about March 27.

BEATLES ARCHIVES 1

Nurk Twins Have Come A Long Way

By Gil McDougall

Who are the "Nurk Twins?" Long before the Beatles, the Silver Beatles, and before many other group-names were even thought of, there descended upon the city of London a musical duo who called themselves the "Nurk Twins." They were, of course, John Lennon and Paul McCartney in theatrical disguise.

John and Paul had gone south to enter a talent competition that was sponsored by the BBC. Their performance was a dud and the BBC scout just didn't want to know. Before you break-up at such an over-sight, let me remind you that this event occured almost four years ago and the boys were not the polished performers that they are today. The Nurk Twins may have thought that they were Britain's answer to the Everly Brothers, but in fact they still had a long way to go.

Talented Composers

Since this early disappointment Lennon and McCartney have emerged as two of the most talented composers that the popular music world has ever seen. When they took that first train trip to London, they were eager but inexperienced and, in fact, had little to offer "Tin Pan Alley." Today their songs are recorded by such talents as Ella Fitzgerald, Peggy Lee, Henry Mancini and many others too numerous to mention. It is interesting to note that success eluded the Beatles until they started singing Lennon and McCartney originals.

John and Paul formed the Nurk Twins through a mutual friendship and desired to become performers in the world of Rock 'n' Roll. It has been said that had Lennon and McCartney never become close friends, had they just remained working associates, then they might never have written such great songs. Evidently as friends they are able to compose on a much better working basis. Their composing sessions are part of their friendship because they enjoy working together.

Of course not all of their songs are great one's, but the few exceptions are never produced. As Paul has said: "The first song that we ever wrote was 'Too Bad About Sorrows.' We never recorded it because it was too crummy. They don't often turn out like that but when they do we just don't do them."

Dislike Covers

Sometimes they release a song later one of them wishes they hadn't done. Remember their version of "You Really Got A Hold On Me," which was originally done by the Miracles. Their recording was a success, but some months later John said: "Oh God, I can't stand that now. I never like any cover that we do, though at the time it was only a vague cover. No-one in England had ever heard of the Miracles then but it has always embarrassed me – it's me trying to do a coloured voice, and I can't do that."

Every composition by John and Paul contain contributions from both, but sometimes one will put in a bit more than the other. One example that quickly comes to mind is "Norwegian Wood." This was at first a poem by Lennon entitled, "This Bird Has Flown" and the melody was added later. When discussing the subject of who writes what, and why one of them sings a particular song Paul answered with: "This is usually decided by whoever gets the first idea for it. John had the original idea for 'I'm A Loser,' and I just helped a bit. I had the original idea for 'She's A Woman' and then John helped a bit with that. Sometimes it happens that we decide John has a better voice for a particular song – there are actually many reasons." The extent that each contributes to each song varies so much that it is difficult to be able to say that one of them wrote a particular composition. However, we do get something of an inkling when Lennon comes out with such things as: "Now,

... THE NURK TWINS

'Ticket To Ride' was three-quarters mine and Paul changed it a bit. He said let's alter the tune. It was not as commercial as most of our singles because it wasn't written as a single, it was intended to be in 'Help.' It was the first time that a song had been brought into a studio that hadn't been written for that purpose."

The amount and the variety of songs that John and Paul produce is quite phenonal. It is conceivable that such an effort would take them all of their waking time, but this just isn't the case. When Lennon and McCartney were asked about this both replies were a little hazy. John put it this way: "I usually write when there is nothing else to do. Most of the time this is at home. I just sort of sit down and do it. It is quite dry at times, but mostly the ideas come thick and fast."

On the same subject Paul said: "We get our ideas from anywhere. Sometimes it's just inspiration and sometimes it's because somebody tells us to sit down and write because we need songs for a new album. When that happens I go out to John's house and we'll just sit down for the day and try to write a couple of songs. I don't know where we get our ideas from exactly. It's a mutual thing we just sort of kick something off in each other."

Some of their composing sessions are a bit tense as they are often being urged to hurry for one thing or another. Sessions like this are interrupted only by Cynthia bringing in some tea for John and coffee for Paul. Lennon and Mc-

Cartney worked very hard on their songs for the "Rubber Soul" album. So hard in fact that right after that, when they were presented with the M.B.E. from Queen Elizabeth, John told the Queen that they had just come back from a vacation instead of saying that they had been hard at work.

A supposedly wise man once said, that if the kids can't dance to it, they will not buy it. This theory is certainly disproved when you consider the range in variety of Beatle hits. From the beat of "I Wanna Hold Your Hand" they have progressed to the soul of "Norwegian Wood," and the beauty of "Yesterday." I myself have often wondered just what type of songs Lennon and McCartney prefer to write. John cleared this up with: "I prefer writing up-tempo songs I suppose. I don't care about a song having a message – I just write a love song. Most of our hits are cheerful. I like them a bit aggressive too."

Beatle Spectacular

Whatever they may personally like, it is plain to see that popular music fans, and singers alike, enjoy anything that they can turn out. Singers and orchestras from almost every nation in the world have recorded their own versions of Beatle songs. With this thought in mind, British Television recently produced a spectacular of these artists singing their interpretations of music by Lennon and McCartney. The show featured as many artists as possible and among this distinguished gathering was Henry Mancini, who is himself one of our greatest composers.

The boys had a great many things to do and a great many places to appear when the show was in the production stage, but they agreed to participate because the thing was being produced by Johnny Hamp who risked his job by giving them a TV spot when they were still unknown. One special part of the show that Paul enjoyed was the rendition of "And I Love Him" by Ester Phillips. Paul revealed that he thought that Ester's record of the same song was really tremendous. The completed show, which was a tribute to the composing talents of the Nurk Twins, was a great success in the U.K. and will almost certainly be presented in the U.S.A.

Achievement

During the production of the show John mentioned a sense of musical progression in the music of Lennon and McCartney when he said: "We try to find a truth for ourselves, a real feeling. You can never communicate your complete emotion to other people, but if we can convey just a little of what we feel then we have achieved something."

After "Rubber Soul" you may have felt yourself a sense of participation in the feeling that John was referring to. You may even have marvelled at the constant stream of melodic ingenuity stemming from John Lennon and Paul McCartney. If you did, then when John and Paul say "there are only about one hundred people in the world who really "understand our music" you may well feel that you are one of the hundred.

BEATLES ARCHIVES 1

Two down - Now what?

...PAUL havin' "A Hard Day's Night."

WALTER SHENSON and the Beatles take time off in the Bahamas during the filming of their second motion picture together, "Help."

On a spring day in 1964, a young film producer named Walter Shenson raised a weary head from a cluttered desk and cast a wary eye at his visitor.

"You want me to produce a movie starring what?"

The visitor, a representative from United Artists, smiled patiently. "The Beatles," he repeated.

Shenson shrugged. "Who are they?"

The visitor went on to explain they were a rock and roll group that had taken England by storm, and that they appeared to be working the same magic all over the map. They had wild hair, a wild beat, and were, well... just wild.

"Sorry" said Shenson. "Not interested."

And he went on to explain that what he wasn't interested in was making an ordinary little pop musical.

While this particular scene was taking place in London, a similar discussion was being held in London.

"You want who to produce a movie starring us?" four Beatles chimed in unison.

"Walter Shenson," came the reply.

"Who's he?" chorused John, Paul, George and Ringo.

However, several weeks later, five strangers by the names of Lennon, McCartney, Harrison, Starkey and Shenson joined forces to film the most extraordinary little pop musical in motion picture history.

It was titled "A Hard Day's Night," but it wasn't one. It was ninety low-budget minutes of pure delight.

How did this manage to happen considering that not so long ago, the foursome didn't know the fifth from Adam and the feeling was mutual?

First off, there was a good reason why Walter Shenson had never head of the Beatles. It all started seven years ago.

Seven years ago, Shenson was not the creator of avant garde films. He was the bright, young European Publicity Director for Columbia Pictures. The brightest and youngest thing about him at that time being the fact that he did not intend to remain the European Publicity Director for Columbia Pictures for the remainder of his days.

Someday he would produce pictures for Columbia. Not publicize

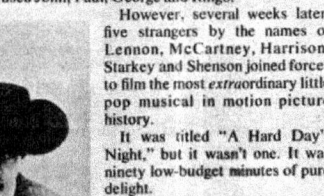

...PAUL prepares for a western?

By Tony Barrow

There is only one man in the world qualified at this time to give an up-to-date progress report about the search for a suitable script for the third movie to be made by the Beatles. He is producer WALTER SHENSON, the man who is doing all the searching.

Shenson has read scores of scripts and story ideas submitted by American and British writers. He has held extended meetings with the Beatles. As I write, he is still waiting to find the right material for the foursome's vitally important third motion picture.

Today I talked with Walter and here, to set the record straight, are the facts as they stand.

WHEN WILL THE NEW MOVIE GO INTO PRODUCTION? It will not, says Walter, until the right story is found. He goes on: "It must be a subject which we feel is dead right for the Beatles. It must be something we all have a lot of enthusiasm for. We're not going to rush into something just for the sake of getting a shooting schedule under way."

WILL THE STORY BE A WESTERN?: "Probably not. The Beatles themselves can see plenty of good comedy situations in a Western setting. So can I. Someday I'm sure they'd like to try a Western. I doubt if they'll do so just yet. Right now the subject could be anything. Writers are working on ideas but at no time have I suggested that I am especially anxious to see Western ideas. All this dates back to the period when 'A Talent For Loving' was under consideration."

WILL DICK LESTER DIRECT THE THIRD MOVIE?: "That will depend on two things – whether Dick likes the script we finally choose and whether he's available at that time to direct the picture."

WHY HAVE SO MANY STORY IDEAS BEEN TURNED DOWN?: "For a variety of reasons. For one thing, so many writers have been bas-

ing their ideas on 'A Hard Day's Night' or 'Help!' or a combination of both scripts. As first and second pictures, these were fine. Now we want to find something completely original for the third one. To repeat the same ideas would be to look backwards instead of forwards. The boys want to have four completely different parts to play in their next film. They can still be John, Paul, George and Ringo but they needn't even be the Beatles. They need not be together when the story opens. They can come together as the story progresses. What we're after is a story which will put the boys in the centre of the action but a story which is strong enough to stand up as an entertaining picture in its own right."

THIS IS HOW WALTER SHENSON SUMMED UP: "We don't have a subject. As soon as we do, we'll move forward into production as quickly as possible. I know just how many rumours and bits of false information there are in circulation but all I can do for the moment is answer with negatives. As soon as there is something positive the full details will be announced – both from me and from the Beatles' office. There's no question of holding back information."

In the meantime, the Beatles' vacation is coming to an end. Within the next few weeks they will be getting down to work on something like fifteen new compositions – material for their first new album of 1966 plus two numbers for another single.

Until now, the boys have done most of their composing at home. In the future they are anxious to put greater pressure on themselves by fixing definite working hours.

Says John: "We don't really think up new songs on the spur of the moment. We need to go into a room, sit down and decide to spend a day writing. That's the way we'll work on the new album. We'll fix dates and times and stick to them. It's like any other job of work – you've got to discipline yourself."

● ●

them. But, through a twist of fate, he found himself out of the publicity racket long before entering the producing game.

You see, there was this book. You know, one of those. Not the kind you read and think "hmmmm, would that ever make a great movie." The kind you read, and if you are Walter Shenson, think, "I will make this into a great movie, or else."

At the outset, Shenson contacted the author and purchased the movie rights. (With his own money.) Then, with a star already in mind for the lead role, he hired a screenwriter and had the book scripted. (Using what was left of his own money.)

Then he took the project to the head of Columbia Pictures.

"This is it," said Shenson, handing over the manuscript.

"No it isn't," said his employer, returning the manuscript.

A bit of fencing followed. Shenson stood his ground firmly. It was a good idea. It would make money.

His employer paried, with a no

on both counts. Then came his final thrust. In Shenson's opinion, was the idea worthy enough for him to consider resigning his present position in order to produce it?

It was, jabbed Shenson.

"Good luck, then," said his former employer. And that was that.

But what does all that have to do with Shenson's lack of Beatle knowledge?

(Turn to Page 12)

BEATLES ARCHIVES 1

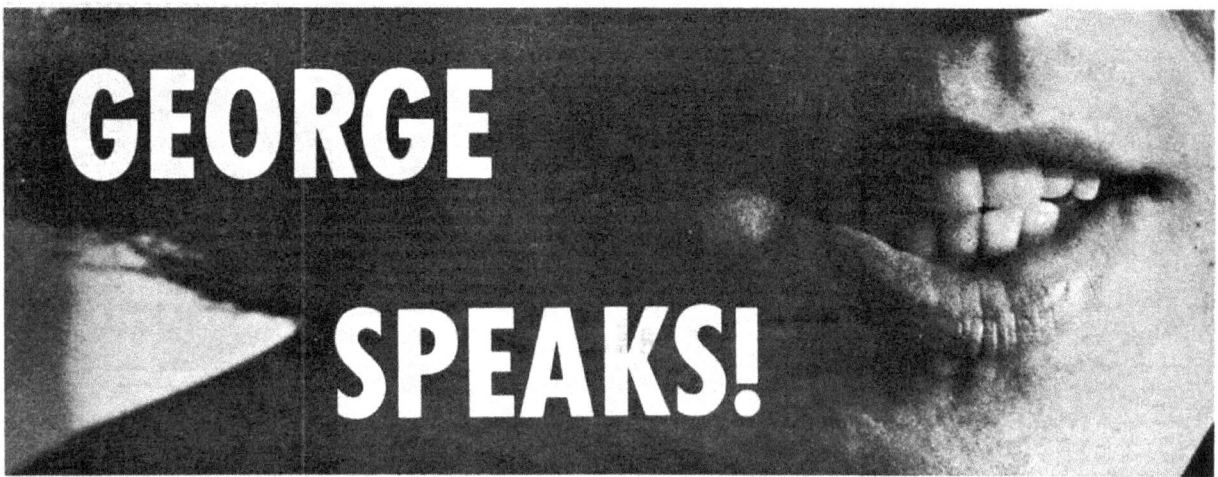

GEORGE SPEAKS!

By Gil McDougall

The quiet Beatle. The boy next door. These are some of the descriptions that reporters often apply to George Harrison. Well, I've got news for them! Mr. Harrison is sick and tired of being known as the do-nothing, know-nothing type of person.

George never was satisfied as being known as the boy next door. The idea is pretty crazy anyway. After all, how many people have such a rich and famous neighbor?

Possibly his marriage to Patti had something to do with it, but even if this is not so, George is now more determined than ever to speak his mind when he feels like it. Of course, like the other Beatles, George has always been known to speak out when the occasion called for it. Today, however, he is much more forward with his thoughts and ideas.

These new vibrations emitting from the Harrison Household tend to shatter previous conceptions of George's personality. People are now saying "maybe he isn't so quiet after all."

One particular myth that went quickly to the dogs was the much publicized "Harrison Guitar." According to his press agent, George had been steadily working on a new type of guitar that was soon to be put on the market. George killed this with: "There is no guitar. It was just a publicity thing."

Like John Lennon, George isn't particularly worried about his image. This kind of honest attitude is perhaps very seldom found among recording stars. Now, of course, George is married (sorry if I keep bringing it up) but before he and Patti took the vows he was asked if traveling with his girl hurt his image. George's answer was typical Beatle: "I don't know what you mean. We don't have an image. We don't believe in images."

Ignorant Reporters

Some people attending Beatle press conferences are not that familiar with the facts of life pertaining to the group. This irritates George very much, and he has often complained about reporters who try to interview him but are actually ignorant of facts about the Beatles. Some are so completely ignorant that they can not even tell one Beatle from another. This often results in quotes being ascribed to the wrong person.

Before getting married, George enjoyed living it up in London's great clubs. Even while on tour he enjoyed a little life now and again. He has visited the "in" places in many major cities. New York's discotheque, Arthur, did not impress him very much however. On Arthur, George said: "The discotheque in New Nork called Arthur is just a bad copy of an original. I'm talking about the Ad Lib. I was not very impressed with Arthur. They should chase out all the people who go there, turn the lights down and change the sound."

Being a married man now it will be some time before George is able to hit his favorite club again. He is more than occupied with his duties as a husband. He and Patti have done considerable redecorating in their Surrey bungalow. George has lived there for some time, of course, but as he recently said: "It was like a flat before I got married, but now it seems like a home. I'm not very hard to please when it comes to food, but Patti is a good cook anyway. She's not spectacular, but she is finding out a lot from this big cook book that she has."

Patti usually just lets her husband talk to the press, but she had plenty to say on her new way of life: "There is a lot to do in the house, and it is really a lot of fun. Sometimes it is a little bit difficult to believe that we are man and wife. We were going steady for two years."

Marriage

On the subject of going steady George revealed that he was very pleased that he and Patti had waited as long as they did. George explained: "Marriage is a very final thing and you should know about each other's peculiarities. I think that all people getting married should make a point of really knowing about their future husband or wife. Sometimes I forget that Patti and I are married. Every now and then I have to remind myself that Patti is my wife and not my girl friend."

With only one single Beatle left many people expected a lot of nasty letters to be sent to Patti and George. But as it turned out, the fans were very understanding. Patti especially hoped that there were no sore losers. She said: "I hope that we didn't break any hearts. I never think of George as a Beatle. When we are at home I just think of him as George – my husband."

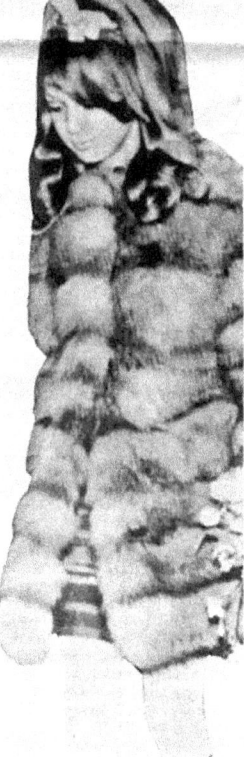

By Sue Barry

"My own tastes run to small blondes who can share a laugh with me. That sense of humor is all important to me ... Anyway, I so date as often as we get a night free or an hour off."

So it was that George Harrison once spoke of his dream girl. He hadn't found her, but dated as often as possible in hopes that one day the right one would come along. It wasn't Estelle Bennet, Sally Anne Shaw or any of the other lucky girls who found themselves on a date with the "quiet Beatle."

George was the youngest of the quartet, in no hurry to marry. He once said when asked about another marriage in the group, "I don't think one marriage has hurt us. I don't think John was wrong to marry, one marriage out of four's all right, but two marriages or three, I'm not sure. I'm inclined to think it would hurt us."

And then one day he met Patti Boyd. She was one of a group of girls chosen to be in the Beatle's first film, "A Hard Day's Night." Patricia Ann Boyd was not what you'd call a beautiful girl, but she was a typical "dolly," a person of the moment. With her 5 ft. 6 in., 34-23-35, 110 lb. frame she seemed to fit in perfectly as a "Beatle girl." She and George were attracted to each other.

Tina Williams who worked with Patti in "A Hard Day's Night" put it this way, "I found that he (George) likes to sit and have long conversations and he prefers to talk about you rather than himself."

"I think this may be what attracted Patti particularly, as she is so reserved. But I noticed they always seemed to have plenty to say to each other."

But it wasn't love at first sight. They dated often, but only because they enjoyed each other's company. Said Patti: "George is tremendous fun to be with. We want it to stay just fun without having to talk about engagements and marriage."

It was not long after that, that Patti accompanied George, John and his wife Cyn to Ireland for five days. The public began to take notice of George and his steady. Once, when they dined at the Pickwick Club, George held Patti's hand and announced, "I'm old enough to go out with girls!"

Then in May of 1964 George and Patti vacationed once again with John and Cyn, this time in Taiti where they spent twenty peaceful days on a cruise of the Polynesian Islands. On a stopover in Los Angeles George smilingly introduced Patti as his "chaperone."

It became apparent that perhaps George had found the girl he was looking for in Patti. The same girl, was, once spoke of as, "... a thoroughly nice person." They shared many interests – among them cars, watching movies and that all important sense of humor – Patti is easy to amuse.

Eventually the question of marriage popped up. George said, "Well, I can tell you I'm not going to end up like Elvis and think I'll wreck my image if I get married before I'm forty. Who will I marry? Well, that's obvious isn't it? You don't go around with a girl for months and months if you don't feel serious about her."

He went on to say, "Patti and I are not engaged. What is the use of engagements? It's just a way of telling people so they can save up for presents. And I don't want a white wedding – all that business with vicars and snivelling people."

And so it was that on January 22 of this year George married Patti in a quick simple ceremony in Epsom, Surrey.

Patti is a typical mod. She wears her blonde hair long, has blue eyes and enjoys a wonderful sense of fashion. Simple, loose-fitting dresses are her favorite.

She is, as has been said, a very quiet person which comes as a surprise for someone who lives in a world of constant excitement – she is one of the best fashion models in the London area.

Mick Curtis who has worked with her has this to say: "Patti is very quick, professional and punctual. She's very quiet, never says what her aims or ambitions are. I tried to talk to her about this once but didn't get very far. She doesn't talk about George either."

This young woman has come a long way from the farm in Kenya where she spent much of her childhood. Not only has she become a leading fashion model, but also has become one of the most envied girls in the world – wife of George Harrison, a boy from Liverpool made good.

BEATLES ARCHIVES 1

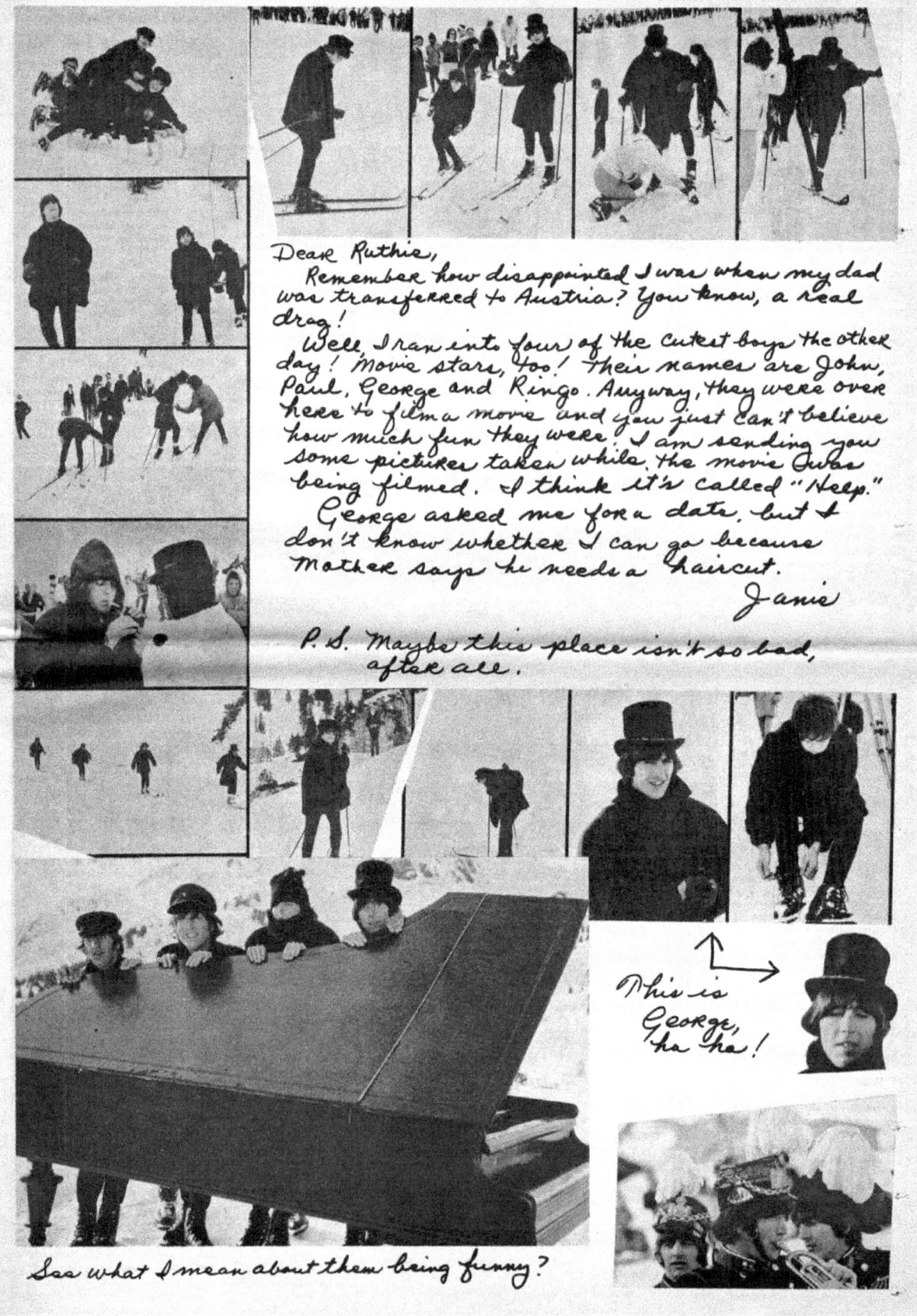

Dear Ruthie,
 Remember how disappointed I was when my dad was transferred to Austria? You know, a real drag!
 Well, I ran into four of the cutest boys the other day! Movie stars, too! Their names are John, Paul, George and Ringo. Anyway, they were over here to film a movie and you just can't believe how much fun they were. I am sending you some pictures taken while the movie was being filmed. I think it's called "Help."
 George asked me for a date, but I don't know whether I can go because Mother says he needs a haircut.
                                        Janie

P.S. Maybe this place isn't so bad, after all.

This is George, ha ha!

See what I mean about them being funny?

BEATLES ARCHIVES 1

U.S. Teenagers Welcome The Beatles: Capitol Single A Smash, Rush LP

NEW YORK—The Beatles are here on disks with a bang. The rock group, the sensation of England, shapes-up as the most important teen-market attraction ever imported into the U.S.

Capitol Records, which has obtained rights to disking by the group from EMI, its parent company, is off to a sure-fire sales run on its first offering by the group, "I Want to Hold Your Hand," a million-seller before its release in England about a month ago.

Two weeks ago, the deck made its first appearance on the Top 100 in the number 80 spot; in its second week, the date has rocketed to number 43.

Beatles' release schedules at Capitol, already altered for the "Hand" side, are being changed to rush LP and EP product to market immediately.

An album, "Meet the Beatles," originally set for release Jan. 20, initial release date for the "Hand" single, was ordered into immediate release last week by Alan Livingston, president of Capitol. In addition, Stanley M. Gortikov, vp and general manager of Capitol Records Distributing Corp., announced the release of an EP by the crew. Though intended primarily for jukebox operators, the 4-track disk will be made available to all CRDC customers.

Vito Samela, the label's singles sales manager, reported last week that the single had sold about 200,000 in the New York area, and that one-stops in such cities as Boston, St. Louis, Philadelphia, Los Angeles, Baltimore and Richmond had heralded the disks as their top seller of the week.

As for the "Meet the Beatles" album, Livingston said that Capitol had earmarked the LP for Jan. 20 release when there would be sufficient stock on hand to meet orders. As it now stands, Capitol branches, which have been stockpiling the album for two weeks, have been instructed to give all their customers a share of existing inventory. Size of shipments will be prorated on the size of the customers initial order. This system, Livingston said, will be followed until production catches up with demand, which should take a week's time.

The Beatles are due to arrive in New York on Feb. 8. The next day, they will make the first of three appearances on the Ed Sullivan Show. The second will be done "live" from Miami Beach the following week (16), with the third yet to be scheduled.

Tremendous coverage in the nation's press plus a filmed sequence of the group on a recent Jack Paar Show will have preceded the team's in-person appearance in the U.S.

"THE BEATLES' SECOND ALBUM"—Capitol ST 2080
The Beatles, with a plethora of best-selling singles and LP's running rampant on the charts, come up with their second album entry on Capitol —a package that has to top the charts in short order. The lads lash out with "Roll Over Beethoven," and follow thru with such chart-riders as "She Loves You" and "Thank You Girl." Still the hottest group around, there's loads of loot to be made with this one.

EMI's A&R manager **George (The Beatles) Martin** has paid his own tribute to the group by recording an LP entitled "From Me To You" to be released here in May on Parlophone and in the United States later this month on United Artists. With the exception of "Don't Bother Me," which was penned by Beatle **George Harrison**, all twelve tracks are **John Lennon/Paul McCartney** numbers, including "From Me To You," "I Want To Hold Your Hand," "Please Please Me," "She Loves You" and "Can't Buy Me Love." Orchestration by George Martin, who also conducts the 37-piece orchestra.

Capitol Requests RIAA OK 3rd Beatles Gold Disk Prior To Release

NEW YORK—For the third time, Capitol Records is putting in a call to the RIAA for certification of a gold disk prior to release of a date by the Beatles.

New move involves Capitol's second album by the English sensations, "The Beatles' Second Album," which is due for release this Mon. (6). Previously, the label had requested RIAA to certify gold-disk awards to the group's first album, "Meet The Beatles" and "Can't Buy Me Love," the group's current top-of-the-chart sound. Latter date was officially certified a million-seller by the RIAA last week (31).

Capitol contends that "Can't Buy Me Love" eclipses the Beatles first single, "I Want To Hold Your Hand," as the fastest selling record in the industry's history. On the initial day of its release (Mar. 16), "Buy" missed the million mark by less than 60,000 when it sold 940,225. "Hand" had orders for over one million during its first week of release and is currently hovering around the 4 million mark in sales.

"Can't Buy Me Love" broke into the charts within a week after its release and climbed rapidly towards the number one spot.

According to Voyle Gilmore, A&R vice president of Capitol, "Can't Buy Me Love" had nearly consumed Capitol's initial press-run of 2 million when it sold 1.5 million copies in 10 days. In addition to Capitol's own facilities, at least three outside plants were pressing the hit single and its flip side, "You Can't Do That."

Both sides were written by Beatles John Lennon and Paul McCartney during their stay in this country.
(Continued on page 43)

Beatles & Riaat Gold
(Continued from page 7)

"You Can't Do That" will be included in the Beatles' second album along with "She Loves You" and "Roll Over Beethoven," already released as a single by Capitol of Canada.

Meanwhile, Capitol's first **Beatles** album, "Meet The Beatles," is the top album seller for the 10th straight week. It was released 11 weeks ago.

BEATLES ARCHIVES 1

LEGALMANIA OVER BEATLEMANIA

NEW YORK—As The Beatles continued on their sensational way up the Top 100 chart, legal suits developed last week over rights to their recordings.

New York and Chicago were the scenes of legal action by Capitol Records and Vee Jay Records, both labels of which have Beatles product, with Capitol receiving Court decisions in its favor in both cities.

In New York, a Federal Court ordered Vee Jay to stop manufacturing and selling "in the State of New York and elsewhere" an LP, "Introducing the Beatles." Also affected was Malverne Distributors, Vee Jay's distrib in Gotham.

[At deadline, it was learned that a Vee Jay suit against Capitol Records, Swan Records (which also has a Beatles single) and Transglobal, Inc., agent for England's EMI had been instituted in New York. A hearing was set last Fri. (at press time) before Judge Saul Streit in the Supreme Court of New York.]

New York ruling was handed down after Beechwood Music, a subsid of Capitol Records, and Ardmore and Beechwood Ltd. of England filed suit last week against Vee Jay. Suit charges the label with copyright infringement involving two selections in the album. Restraining order was issued by U.S. District Judge Dudley L. Bonsall.

In Chicago, a Capitol Records suit against Vee Jay resulted in an injunction, handed down by Cook County circuit Judge Cornelius J. Harrington, restraining Vee Jay, its "agents, attorney or servants from manufacturing, selling, distributing or otherwise disposing of . . . any and all recordings by The Beatles. Vee Jay failed to answer Capitol's complaint at a scheduled hearing last Wed. (15).

In its actions, Capitol contends that any rights Vee Jay to issue recordings by The Beatles ceased to exist last Aug. 8. At that time, the actions claim, Transglobal, Inc., which deals in foreign disk rights, notified Vee Jay that U. S. rights to The Beatles which it had held since Jan. 10, 1963, were being cancelled for breach of contract (Transglobal alleges non-payment from Vee Jay). Transglobal, the suit charges, subsequently relinquished its rights to Electric & Musical Industries, Ltd. of England, to which The Beatles are under contract. EMI gave exclusive U. S. rights to Beatles recordings to Capitol Records last Nov.

Specifically in the New York action, Ardmore and Beechwood say that Vee Jay did not request permission to include the two selections in the LP until after it had been manufactured and distributed. The selections involve "Love Me Do" and "P.S. I Love You," included in Vee Jay's album, "Introducing the Beatles."

Besides the LP, Vee Jay also has a Beatles' single, "Please, Please Me." Capitol is represented with an album, "Meet The Beatles" and a single, "I Want To Hold Your Hand," which is the nation's top singles seller, moving on the Top 100 from the number 43 spot to no. 1 this week.

A third label entered the Beatles sales race late last week. MGM Records issued a single called "My Bonnie," backed with "The Saints (When The Saints Go Marching In)."

The Beatles As Seen Thru The Eyes Of An American

LONDON — While in England last

1 Day Out, Capitol's 2nd Beatles LP Sells $1 Million

HOLLYWOOD—"The Beatles' Second Album," issued nationally last Monday (6), accounted for over one million dollars' worth of business (calculated at manufacturer's price) on the very first day of release, according to Stan Gortikov, vice president & general manager of Capitol Records Distributing Corp. The Album thus becomes the fastest-selling LP in the history of the Capitol label.

Capitol has already applied to the Record Industry Association of America (RIAA) for official certification of the album's Gold Record status. The RIAA's independent audit of Capitol's sales books will be conducted at the label's Billing Center in Scranton, Pa., on Friday (10).

According to RIAA executive secretary Henry Brief, the time between release of "The Beatles' Second Album" and Capitol's application for Gold Record certification is the shortest in RIAA history.

Beatles Invite Murray "The K" To London

NEW YORK—Murray "The K" Kaufman will plane to London this week (21) for a series of personal appearances throughout England, at a special invitation from the Beatles.

The bid for the WINS deejay's British debut was tendered as a result of his connection with the Beatles during their recent stay in the U.S. The group considered Kaufman to be the foremost exponent of their kind of music, and through their manager Brian Epstein, arranged a series of theater, radio and TV appearances to introduce him to Britain's younger set.

Kaufman, who recently concluded a 10-day Easter show at Brooklyn's Fox Theater, became so friendly with the Beatles during their stay here that he accompanied them on their trip to Miami. The friendship has continued via transatlantic phone calls.

BEATLES ARCHIVES 1

THE BEATLES
On MGM Records With A Smash

MY BONNIE

b/w

THE SAINTS
(When The Saints Go Marching In)

K-13213

MGM Records is a division of
Metro-Goldwyn-Mayer, Inc.

BEATLES ARCHIVES 1

Cash Box
FEBRUARY 8, 1964

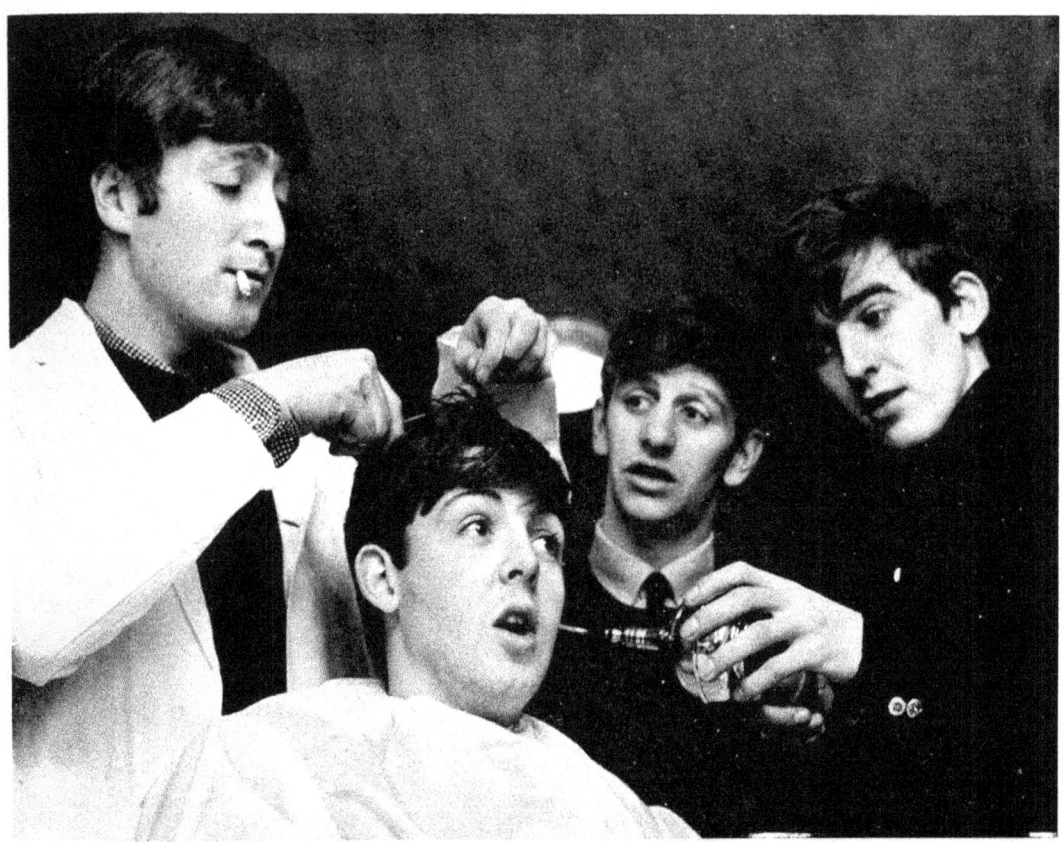

Barbers have figured prominently in the music world. One from Seville is still world famous. Another named Como ranks with music history greats. A third whose name should be entered into the disk industry's Who's Who is the designer who styled the hair of the lads seen above. For, there is little doubt their wild hair style in combination with their refreshing sound and powerful teen material has made the quartet the hottest act to hit the teen public since Elvis Presley. If you haven't already guessed, the four British youngsters are the Beatles. Although the Beatles disks recorded on EMI in England were released on varied American labels during the past two years, it wasn't until Capitol Records in the U.S. got behind the group that their fabulous potential became a reality. In the short span of little more than a month, the Beatles have climbed to the #1 spots on both the singles and LP charts with "I Want To Hold Your Hand" and "Meet The Beatles." In addition, everything with the Beatles' name on it is on the best seller list. Their Swan disk of "She Loves You" is also top ten. Two of their early dates on Vee Jay are Top 100, as is a Vee Jay LP "Introducing The Beatles." Even an early Beatles' single recently issued by MGM is now on the charts. The four Liverpool lads, including l. to r. in top photo John Lennon, Paul McCartney, Ringo Starr, and George Harrison, arrive in the U.S. this week for appearances on the Ed Sullivan TV'er this weekend as well as a big Carnegie Hall one-nighter February 12.

BEATLES ARCHIVES 1

VJ is only #~~12~~ #1 in sales
...but here is why
you should go with us

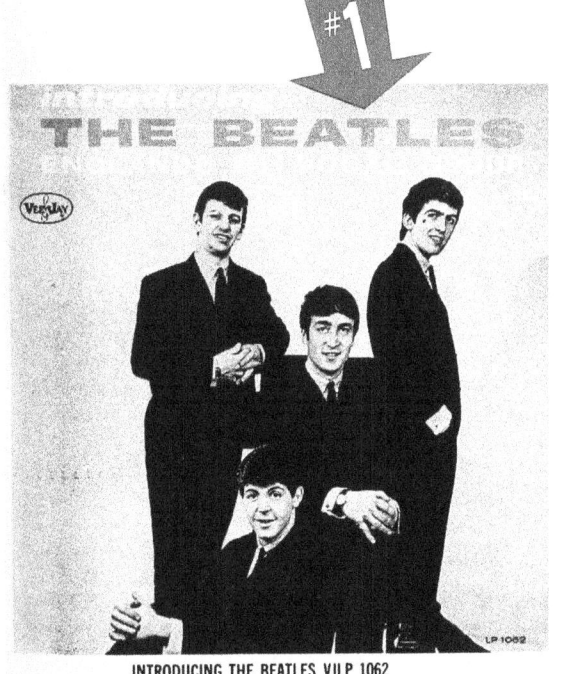
INTRODUCING THE BEATLES VJLP 1062

THE BEATLES & FRANK IFIELD VJLP 1085

& THE HOTTEST SINGLE VJ 581
#3 PLEASE, PLEASE ME
& FROM ME TO YOU

 V-J's NEW HOME · 9056 SANTA MONICA BLVD. · LOS ANGELES 69, CALIFORNIA · CR 3-5800

BEATLES ARCHIVES 1

IF YOU CAN'T BEAT 'EM... JOIN 'EM
THE BEATLES
Jump on the PROFIT BANDWAGON
SELL THE NEW 40-PAGE BEATLE MAGAZINE
With 8 Full Color Pages

Packed 100 to Shipping Carton Weight 31 lbs. FOB New York or Miami

50¢ RETAIL Also Available 2 FULL COLOR PHOTOS 8 X 10 EACH SUITABLE FOR FRAMING Retailing at 10¢ Each Packed 100 to a Shipping Carton

RIGHT NOW: PHONE YOUR LOCAL RECORD DISTRIBUTOR OR CONTACT THE EXCLUSIVE NATIONAL DISTRIBUTORS

New York Record Distributors, Inc.
15 West 20th Street
New York 11, New York
Phone: 212 989-2255

Sunshine State Record Distributors, Inc.
8170 N.W. 36 Avenue
Miami, Florida
Phone: 305 696-4951

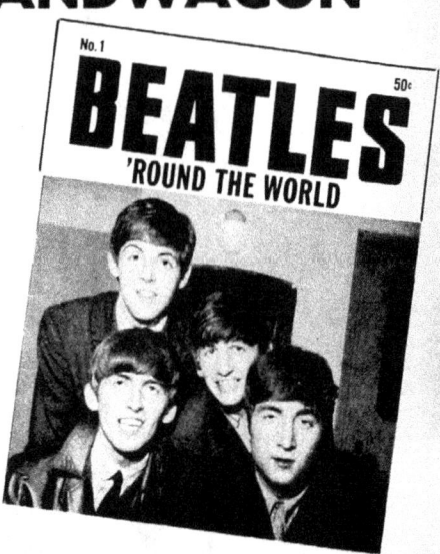

SIZE: 3½" and 4"

ONLY
OFFICIAL
LICENSED Nems Ent. Ltd. '64
BEATLE BOOSTER BUTTON IN COLOR
AVAILABLE AT ONCE!

Use For:
prizes
beatle parties
fan clubs
promotions
souvenirs

39¢ suggested Retail Price   Weight: 100 pins—7 lbs.

100 per display box with card and window banner
F.O.B. Chicago, Illinois
F.O.B. Philadelphia, Pa.

AREA DISTRIBUTORSHIPS NOW AVAILABLE:

ACT NOW...... Phone your local Record
Merchandiser or Distributor or contact the National
Selling Agent...

Beatle Booster Button Company
care of Musical Isle Record Corp.
2429 W. Fonddulac Ave.
Milwaukee 6, Wisconsin. Tel. 414-2644940

or

Beatle Booster Button Company
care of M.S. Distributing Co.
1700 So. Michigan
Chicago 16, Illinois Tel. 312-3460865

BEATLES ARCHIVES 1

BEATLES WIN OVER AMERICA

NEW YORK—The Beatles have completely upset the United States. And it will be weeks before the police force in New York City recovers from the effect of the Beatles week-long stay in the big town.

Although the group was big on disks for only five or six weeks prior to their appearance on the Ed Sullivan CBS TV'er, their stint on the show ignited a series of explosions unprecedented in the record industry.

The Sullivan TV show itself set a precedent by doubling its usual rating in the New York area the night the Beatles appeared. The Nielsen rating for the show was 58.8, meaning the percentage of television homes that were tuned to the Sullivan show. Nielsen said that this was the highest rating for an entertainment program in the New York area since it established its instantaneous rating service in 1959.

Beatles In Florida

MIAMI—The Beatles, who left New York last week (13) amid the shouts and screams of thousands of teenagers, got a brief respite during their plane ride to Miami and were then met by an estimated crowd of 10,000 teenagers including 5,000 members of WFUN's 'Beatle Fan Club.' The British rock and roll envoys reportedly turned International Airport into a seething madhouse.

Dade County's Port Authority called the turnout, which tied up traffic in a five-mile radius, the Greatest in Miami history. The mop-haired singers were met by WFUN's "Good Guys" led by Dick Starr, originator of the fan club.

The effect of the TV appearance sent Beatles records (which were already topping the chart) skyrocketing in sales as though they were new records never before available. According to Vito Samela, Capitol's national single sales and promo manager, the Beatles "I Want To Hold Your Hand" will easily exceed the three million unit mark and could top the 4,000,000 figure. The company will not be surprised if the single exceeds 5,000,000 units. According to Brown Meggs, the label's eastern operations manager, the single is currently back ordered quite heavily. The Capitol LP "Meet The Beatles," said Meggs, is well over the 2,000,000 unit mark and as of last Thursday was back-ordered to the tune of 270,000 pieces.

Bernie Binnick and Tony Mamarella of Swan Records which has the Beatles "She Loves You" single, expressed disbelief at last week's orders for the disk. Binnick said last week that orders for his disk during the five business days of last week exceeded 600,000 records. He expects the disk to reach the 3 to 3½ million mark. He is already approaching the two million figure.

The Vee Jay album dubbed "Introducing The Beatles" is back-ordered more than 200,000 according to Randy Wood, president of Vee Jay Records. Both the Vee Jay single of "Please, Please Me" and the MGM single which bills the Beatles with Tony Sheridan on "My Bonnie" are also zooming up the charts.

As far as personal appearances go, the Beatles have been playing to packed-plus houses everywhere they turn. At the Sullivan show thousands were turned away. In Washington, D.C., the nation's capital, the Beatles played to 8,900 people in the Coliseum. Their two Carnegie Hall appearances the same night last Wednesday saw full houses both shows with hundreds of people sitting on stage enjoying a rear view of the Beatles "live."

Audiences for these appearances were absolutely wild. For their first few numbers on stage the screams were shattering. They were so high pitched and unanimous that you could actually feel the air waves hit you. You had to squint to soften the blow. From then on it was only mildly impossible to hear anything the boys were singing.

The press has hopped on Beatlemania with all its linotype machines. Almost every New York newspaper has been carrying daily front page photos of the boys. Many have been running daily features covering a different Beatle each day.

Visiting the Beatles in the sedate Plaza Hotel was truly a courageous feat. Police were everywhere. Inside the Hotel. On horseback outside the Hotel holding back crowds of youngsters with wooden barricades. As the boys moved through the lobby you could hear the distant shrieks coming closer and as the boys came into view with body-guards protecting them, frenzied youngsters with talons exposed, clawed at the boys. It was literally dangerous to be a Beatle or be near one.

It was also interesting watching the hardened trade people's reaction to meeting the Beatles at a cocktail party in their honor. Everyone, it seemed, wanted the boys' autographs, some even expressing embarrassment at asking for autographs, never having done so before. Dee jays waited in lines to get personal interviews with the boys and throughout the party there was an atmosphere of excitement that we have never seen at any N.Y. cocktail party. It was also packed with hundreds of people.

Although retailers are very happy about the Beatles craze, manufacturers not handling Beatles disks are not so happy. Most previous crazes, not as big as Beatlemania, created traffic resulting in extra sales of disks other than the big hit. But with so much Beatle merchandise available and the frenzy so hot, other big records in many cases have to wait until the youngsters complete their Beatles collection.

Manufacturers also have commented on the tremendous air time devoted to Beatles product, cutting into the time available for new releases.

What has happened to date is really difficult to believe or comprehend. And this may still be in its early stages. The Beatles, at this writing, have yet to make two more appearances on Sullivan's show. One was scheduled for last Sunday, February 16th and another this coming weekend, Feb. 23rd. Can it be bigger than it is now?

Chi Court Stays Capitol's Temporary Injunction On Vee Jay's Beatle Decks

CHICAGO—The effect of a temporary injunction against the sale of Beatles product on the Vee Jay label has been stayed by the Appellate Court in Chicago.

This new development in Capitol action against Vee Jay in the Windy City lifts one of two court orders involving Vee Jay sessions by The Beatles (see below).

The stay, signed by Judges Burk, Bryant and Friend, was initially entered on Feb. 5. Capitol petitioned for a re-hearing, but on Feb. 7 the Court re-affirmed its issuance of stay. An appeal by Vee Jay on the Capitol suit was set to be filed last Fri. (14).

In New York, where Capitol's publishing affiliate, Ardmore & Beechwood, has obtained a preliminary injunction against the sale of the Vee Jay album, "Introducing The Beatles," over two selections in the LP a hearing is scheduled this Wed. (19) in the Circuit Court of Appeals. The Court has given the matter preference by having established a special panel to hear the case.

Thus, while the Chicago action lets Vee Jay move its Beatles dates, preliminary injunction in New York prevents the label from marketing the LP as long as it contains the two songs in question.

"Fly Columbia" Promo Boosts New Album Sales

NEW YORK—Strong sales activity on albums featured in the "Fly Columbia Records" ad program from the label was reported last week by Mort Hoffman, general manager of Columbia Records Sales Corp.

The campaign, which involved two-month LP release, is aimed directly at local newspapers with full color in-store promo material to support the local ads.

"Dealers from all over the country have been calling our offices," Hoffman noted, "telling us about the additional customer traffic attracted by the unique Columbia displays in the windows."

Promo material includes full-color window, counter and wall units, mobiles, posters, counter cards and browser box dividers, as well as specially designed consumer brochure featuring Columbia's Jan. and Feb. product for use by local retailers as counter give-aways.

New albums by Andy Williams, Tony Bennett, Ray Conniff, Percy Faith, Eydie Gorme, Barbra Streisand and Jerry Vale are among the LP's that have benefited from the program, the label said.

Capitol's Gold Single And Album

NEW YORK—The Beatles are pictured with Alan Livingston, president of Capitol Records, after having received RIAA gold disks for the sale of one million copies of the single, "I Want To Hold Your Hand," and sales totaling $1 million for their album, "Meet The Beatles."

CB International Award

NEW YORK—The Beatles are shown accepting the Cash Box International Award presented to international artists whose recordings reach the number one spot on the Cash Box Top 100. Making the presentation were Marty Ostrow, CB Editor in Chief (left) and Bob McKeage of Cash Box. George Martin, the group's A&R producer, holds up the award.

Swan Gold Disk For "She Loves You"

NEW YORK—Swan Records awarded the Beatles a gold record for their "She Loves You" deck. Standing (left to right) at the recent presentation ceremonies were Bob McKeage of Cash Box, Paul McCartney, John Lennon, Swan co-topper Tony Mamarella, Ringo Starr, Bernie Bernick, and another Swan topper, George Harrison, Bill Shockett of Malverne Distributors (Swan's Gotham area distrib), and Steve Harris of Malverne. Standing off-camera were Al Hirsch, Shockett's partner in Malverne and Roland Rennie, president of Transglobal, which licensed the record to Swan.

BEATLES ARCHIVES 1

The Beatles: The Top 4 On The Top 100

NEW YORK—The first four artists on the Top 100 are the Beatles, the Beatles, the Beatles and the Beatles.

Thus, the English rockstars have made Top 100 history by becoming the first disk attraction to hold down the first four positions on the listing.

The disks are "She Loves You" (Swan), which moves into the number 1 spot, replacing "I Want to Hold Your Hand" (Capitol), second after nine weeks at the top, "Please, Please Me" (Vee Jay) and "Twist & Shout" (Tollie).

Accompanying the four sides on the Top 100 are "My Bonnie" (MGM), number 37, "From Me to You" (Vee Jay), number 57, and "Roll Over Beethoven" (Capitol of Canada), number 75.

The amazing Beatles singles story will continue this week with the release of two other singles. Capitol is offering "Can't Buy My Love" and "You Can't Do That," which the label hopes to have certified as a million seller shortly after its release, and Vee Jay is releasing "Do You Want to Know a Secret" and "Thank You." In addition, Vee Jay is releasing a Beatles EP with four songs, "Misery," "Taste of Honey," "Ask Me Why" and "Anna."

There was also a rumor that Capitol of Canada would re-release its Beatles single, "All My Lovin'," the hot number in the Beatles' Capitol debut LP but never made available in the U.S. as a single. However, this information could not be confirmed by deadline.

Beatles Get Six Pages In Sat. Evening Post

HOLLYWOOD—New issue of the Saturday Evening Post (cover dated Mar. 21) wraps up in a grand manner major national press coverage of The Beatles' American tour last month.

In addition to featuring John, Paul, Ringo and George on the cover, the Post carries a six-page article (by Al Aronowitz), a one-page think-piece by Vance Richard, two and a half pages of far-out fiction by Beatle John Lennon, a cartoon, and wraps it all up with an editorial (the Post approves). The cover is the Beatles second major-magazine cover here; when Newsweek front-paged them last month, the book enjoyed one of its biggest news-stand sales in history.

In his article on the Beatles, Post contributing writer Aronowitz quotes Capitol A&R vice president Voyle Gilmore on Capitol's promo campaign for the group; "Sure there was a lot of hype. But all the hype in the world isn't going to sell a bad product."

Beatles Leave Chart Smashes Behind As They Return Home

NEW YORK—The Beatles, back in England after their historic confrontation with the U.S. public, are still knocking 'em dead on disks.

In keeping with their remarkable success here, strange things are happening, as comic Red Buttons used to say.

For instance, Cash Box has received action on the retail level of a disk that has not been released in the U.S. as yet. Evidentally, a Beatles cut, "Roll Over Beethoven," has made its way here from Canada, where it is on issue. It was believed for a while that Capitol Records had released the side, but this was denied by company execs.

Meanwhile, a new single by the group is out and is already making sure-fire headway on the Top 100. Vee Jay Records, in the Top 10 with the group's "Please, Please Me," released "Twist & Shout" from its LP, "Introducing the Beatles." The deck, which appears under the Vee Jay-handled Tollie label, is number 64 in its initial stand on the chart. Label's Randy Wood reported last week that the deck had a five-day order total of 400,000.

Older Beatles' dates, including "Please, Please Me," number 4, are still blanketing the listing. For the seventh straight week, Capitol's "I Want To Hold Your Hand" is in the top spot, followed by Swan's "She Loves You." MGM's "My Bonnie" is number 32 and Vee Jay's "From Me To You" re-appears on the chart as number 89.

The group is still to make its fourth & fifth appearances on the Ed Sullivan Show, whose Nielsen ratings have zoomed up since the boys initial guest-shot.

The survey for the Feb. 23 show put it in fourth place among network offerings. It was noted that the program could have placed number 1 if the survey were compiled on a weekly basis instead of covering a two-week period.

Beatles In Closed-Circuit Theater TV'er Mar. 13-14

NEW YORK—A closed-circuit theater telecast of a show featuring The Beatles is set for the weekend of Mar. 13 & 14.

Along with The Beatles, the show will also feature hot teen performers Lesley Gore and The Beach Boys.

Sponsor of the event is National General Corp., a division of Concerts, Inc. The Hollywood-based theater chain-flick producer has set out to use about 100 theaters as a medium for the showing of ballet, concerts and Broadway productions on closed circuit color TV, employing a new process.

The show, which was taped at the Washington Coliseum in the nation's capitol, will be presented four times, two performances each day.

Beatlemania runs riot on both sides of the Atlantic as "B" day approaches for the release of the Group's next single, "Can't Buy Me Love." With the British advance expected to top the million mark and a possible two million advance in the United States, the fabulous Beatles look like they'll get their hands on three gold disks before their fans get their hands on the record. "Can't Buy Me Love" also got the Royal assent recently from H.R.H. The Duke of Edinburgh, when he toured the EMI factory at Hayes and watched

John Lennon, who with Paul McCartney, writes all the Beatles' hits and those of many other groups as well, this week emerges as an author "In His Own Write," the title of his book published by Jonathan Cape. Music publishers Francis, Day and Hunter have pulled for a scoop by securing exclusive world distribution rights outside the book trade, excluding the U.S. and the Philippines. A brilliant, original and highly amusing collection of stories, anecdotes and poems "In His Own Write," is illustrated with 24 full page 'off beat' drawings by the author. A potential best seller by any standards by John Lennon of the Beatles, it will sell a million, and probably win the Nobel Prize.

BEATLES ARCHIVES 1

THE BEATLES

CAN'T BUY ME LOVE b/w YOU CAN'T DO THAT #5150

COMING MONDAY, MARCH 16! A brand-new single just recorded in England for simultaneous release throughout the world! Two great sides written by Beatles John Lennon & Paul McCartney! Never before available anywhere, on any other label! Bound to follow "I WANT TO HOLD YOUR HAND" into the #1 spot! 1 million pressed before release! Don't get caught short, call your Capitol Sales Rep NOW! P.S. "Roll Over Beethoven" will appear in The Beatles' next Capitol album, now in preparation.

The Beatles' #1 album

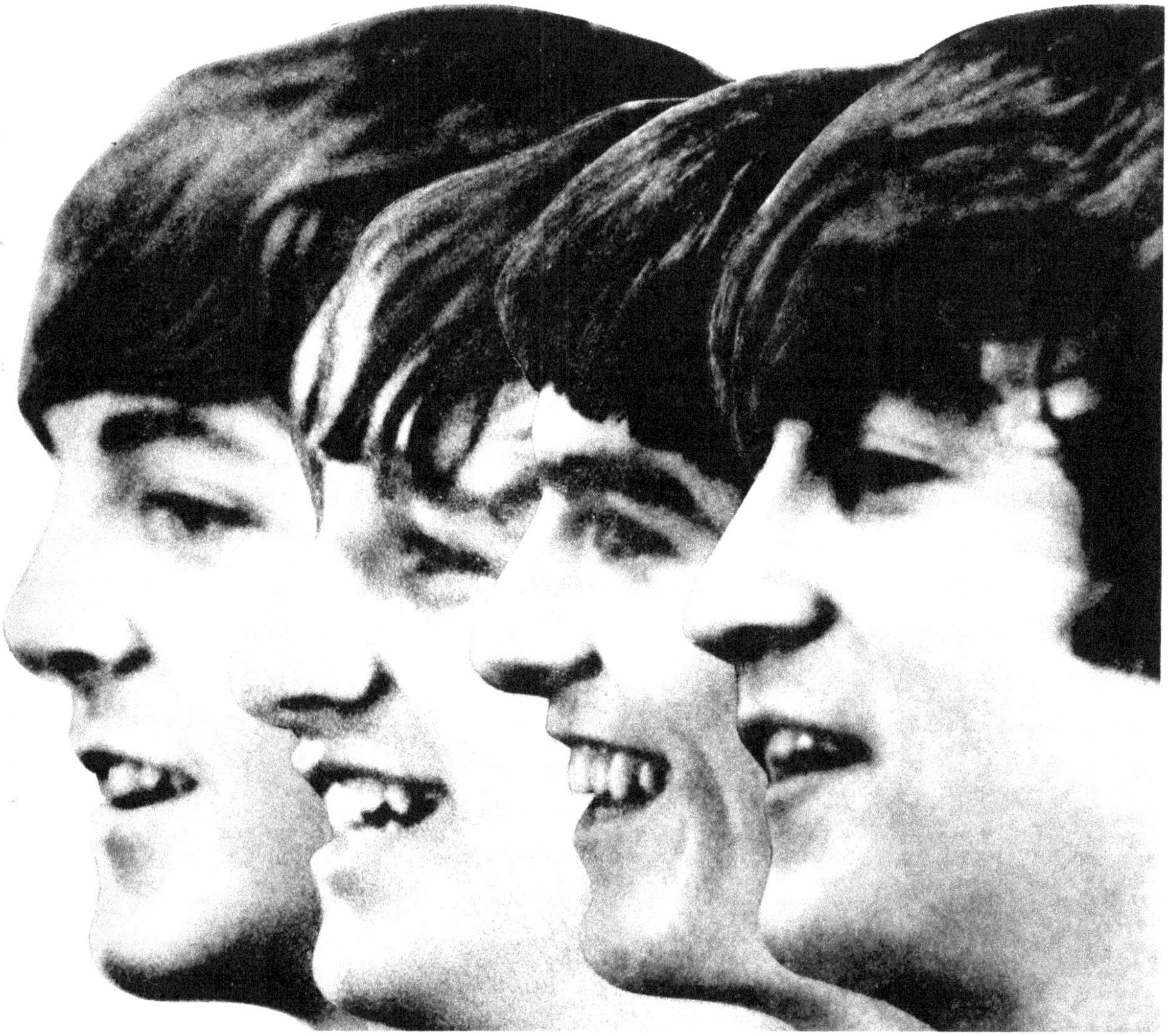

BEATLES ARCHIVES 1

Capitol's New Beatles Single, Tunes Unheard Passes Million Mark Prior To Mar. 16 Release; "Beethoven" In New LP

NEW YORK—Within hours after its release of a new single by The Beatles next week (16), Capitol Records plans to request the RIAA to start the ball rolling on its million-seller certifying audit.

There was, of course, little doubt that the label's second singles appearance by the group would get a million-selling response to its release. Still topping the Top 100, for the eighth straight week, is "I Want to Hold Your Hand," on which the label reports a sale of 3.4 million in 10 weeks.

Capitol Records Distributing Corp. has been taking orders on the new disk without even disclosing the titles, which happen to be "Can't Buy Me Love" and "You Can't Do That," cut in London shortly after the group's return to England from the U.S. Songs, however, were written by Beatleites Paul McCartney and John Lennon during the quartet's Miami Beach sojourn two weeks ago.

By last Wed. (3), the label admitted that some 1,700,000 orders were already on the books. EMI will release the single in England and Europe on Mar. 20.

Explaining its non-rush release of the single, Capitol said it decided to hold back release until the deck reached its initial press-run goal of 2 million copies.

To reach this mark, at least three outside plants, in addition to Capitol's own two facilities, will be pressing the single.

The label also cleared up confusion over another Beatles side, "Roll Over Beethoven," which has been getting retail reaction in the U.S. via the import of the side from Capitol of Canada.

Voyle Gilmore, A&R vp, said that "Beethoven" would be included in the Beatles next Capitol LP, now being prepared.

"There was tremendous pressure on us to release the 'Beethoven' side as a single," he said, "but we and the Beatles agreed that the new tunes would be far better."

Will Beatles Bring Back 78's?

NEW YORK—Anything can happen when the Beatles are involved. This isn't earth-shattering news, but the LP, "Meet The Beatles," Capitol's top-of-the-chart success, is now the only mono pre-recorded tape issue currently on release by a major firm. The label has just released a mono tape version along with a regular 4-track edition.

Reason for the mono entry was explained by Oris Boucler, special products manager of Capitol Records Distributing Corp.: "The fantastic sales of our Beatles disk albums, combined with the fact that there are some 2,800,000 monophonic tape machines in the country should make this the biggest selling pre-recorded tape ever released."

Also a departure from standard pre-recorded tapes is the smaller reel size (five-inch) and speed (3¾ ips), which enabled CRDC to lower the list price ($4.98) and dealer cost ($3.08).

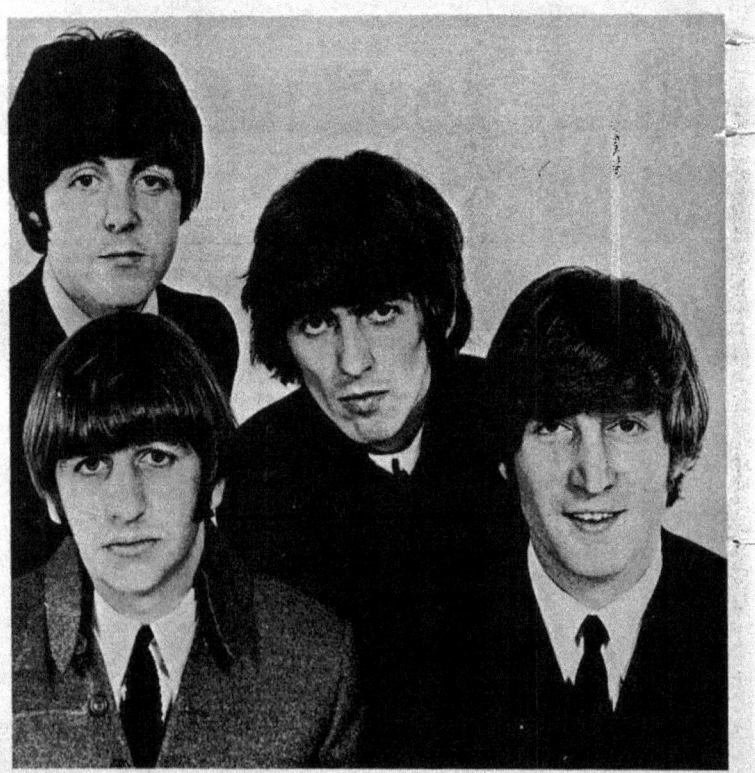

THE BEATLES' first concert date of '66 has been announced by their press agent and **BEAT** writer Tony Barrow. It will be played on May 1 at the Wembley Empire Pool just outside of London. On the show with them will be the Stones, Herman's Hermits, Tom Jones, the Fortunes, Dusty Springfield and at least 10 other acts.

BEATLES ARCHIVES 1

RINGO STARR   **PAUL McCARTNEY**   **JOHN LENNON**   **GEORGE HARRISON**

US VEE-JAY PEOPLE WOULD RATHER FIGHT ...THAN ADMIT WE ARE ONLY #9 IN SALES

2 NEW BEATLES RELEASES

NEW BEATLES SINGLE

IN SPECIAL SLEEVE
VJ 587

DO YOU WANT TO KNOW A SECRET
AND
THANK YOU GIRL

NEW BEATLES E.P.

Beautiful new four color Beatle paintings front and back. Four Great Songs never released as singles. Each a Hit in its own right.

MISERY
TASTE OF HONEY
ASK ME WHY
ANNA

THE E.P. (ECONOMY PACKAGE) OF THE CENTURY

VJ EP 1-903

BEATLES ARCHIVES 1

It's Here!
It's on Capitol!!
and It's ALL Beatles!!!

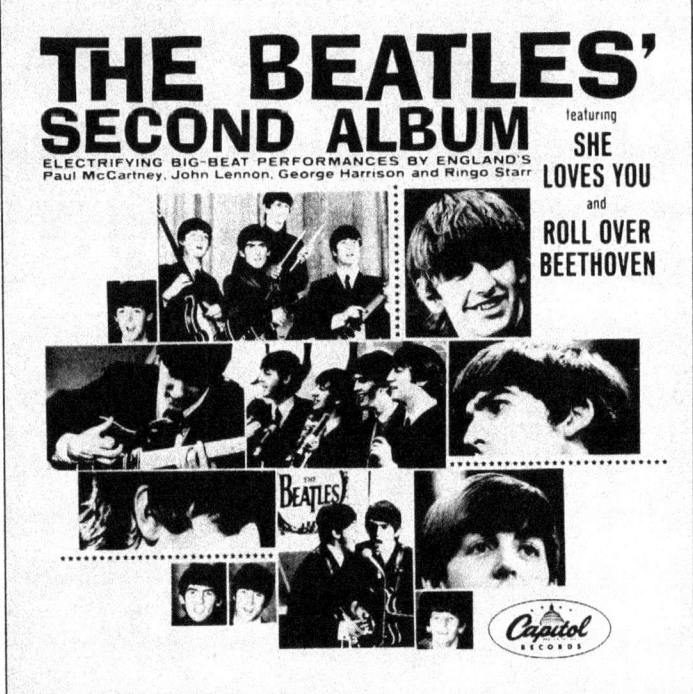

(S) T 2080

For the first time on any album their smash, number one single "She Loves You" and "Roll Over Beethoven." PLUS other great tunes ALL by the fantastic Beatles. Their first Capitol Album broke all sales records everywhere. And this one's going to break even THOSE records. THE Beatles albums are on Capitol.

And THE Beatles singles are too. "Can't Buy Me Love" b/w "You Can't Do That" (#5150) is an unprecedented hit, just released on Capitol. Within 2 weeks of release "Can't Buy Me Love" was #1 on the Billboard Chart — and your #1 money maker!

#5150

HAVE YOUR BUYER CALL CRDC AND ORDER IMMEDIATELY.

BEATLES ARCHIVES 1

America's Largest Teen NEWSpaper 25¢

KRLA Edition BEAT
AUGUST 27, 1966

ARE BEATLES MORE POPULAR THAN JESUS?

'Burn The Beatles' — Ku Klux Klan
'Misinterpreted' — Author of Article
'Stay Out of Pennsylvania' — Sen. Fleming
'Perhaps They Are' — The Rev. Pritchard

KRLA BEAT

Volume 2, Number 22   August 27, 1966

'More Popular Than Jesus'

JOHN 8:4

What seemed to be a harmless interview at the time has touched off one of the most heated controversies of the modern generation. The following is an exert from the explosive text of Maureen Cleave's article on John Lennon that has caused the heated blasts against the Beatles.

Miss Cleave quoted Lennon as saying:

"Christianity will go. It will vanish and shrink. I needn't argue about that. I am right and will be proved right.

"We're more popular than Jesus right now. I don't know which will go first—rock 'n roll or Christianity. Jesus was all right, but his disciples were thick and ordinary. It's them twisting it that ruins it for me."

In the article, Miss Cleave said of Lennon, "Not that his mind is closed, but it's closed round whatever he's thinking at the time." She said Lennon had been conducting a thorough religious investigation for some time.

Beatles 'Ban-Wagon' Rolls!

John Goes Solo For New Film

With the Beatles stymied at the stormiest, most closely watched point in their careers, John Lennon quietly announced he is going on his own—at least temporarily.

The BEAT has learned that John, the brash focal point of the Beatles, plans to act in a movie—without the other Beatles—for the first time since the origin of the group.

A spokesman insists, however, that Lennon's single act will not involve a permanent split among the group. Lennon will be back with the other Beatles for the next group movie in January.

And, of course, it does not affect recording sessions or the Beatles' U.S. tour in August.

The Beatles are believed to have been disenchanted with the rigors of their singing routine for some time. Those close to the Beatles say the boys want to start doing more things individually.

Two Animals Leave Group

The BEAT has learned that at least two and maybe three members of the original Animals will be leaving the group. Both Hilton Valentine and Chas Chandler have said they will now concentrate on record production.

Drummer Barry Jenkins is expected to continue working with Eric Burdon, but the future of jazz organist Dave Rowberry is still unknown.

Inside the BEAT
Letters To The Editor 2
On The Beat 3
People Are Talking About 4
Herman's Low Guarantee 5
Rock On The Road 6
Pictures In The News 7
Johnny Rivers 9
Kinks—Musical Rebels 10
Open Letter To Mick Jagger ... 11
Is Dylan Weird? 15
Yardbirds "Over, Under, Sideways, Down" 19
Temptin' Temptations 21
The Beat Goes To The Movies . . . 23

The BEAT is published bi-weekly by BEAT Publications, Inc., editorial and advertising offices at 6290 Sunset Blvd., Suite 504, Hollywood, California 90028. U.S. bureaus in Hollywood, San Francisco, New York, Chicago and Nashville; overseas correspondents in London, Liverpool and Manchester, England. Sale price, 15 cents. Subscription price: U.S. and possessions, $5 per year; Canada and foreign rates, $9 per year. Second class postage prepaid at Los Angeles, California.

JOHN — Storm Center

BEAT MEDIATES
Eureka—a Solution!

The BEAT is proud to announce "The Great Compromise."

Acting as a voluntary mediator in the dispute which has strained relations with our closest ally and turned brother against brother and daughter against mother in America, *The BEAT* has successfully negotiated a reciprocal agreement with the Beatles.

After exhaustive negotiations they have agreed—in return for similar concessions on our part—that they will not attempt to interfere with our rights to freedom of speech or freedom of religion.

Nor will the Beatles try to force any Americans to praise England, provided we don't ask them to praise America. Most important of all, perhaps, the Beatles have unanimously agreed not to ban any American radio stations.

Thus, now that this really vital crisis has been settled, the world can return to less pressing problems such as Viet Nam, disarmament and starvation.

Epstein Fears Security Dangers During U.S. Tour

Embroiled in a controvesy which produced more mass reaction than the Viet Nam war or big-city race riots, the Beatles launched their third American tour prepared for an uncertain reception.

Manager Brian Epstein, trying desperately to soothe ruffled feelings, openly expressed fears of security dangers while denying rumors that some of the 14 scheduled concerts might be cancelled.

Still unresolved was the intent of John Lennon's statement that the Beatles are "more popular than Jesus." The writer whose interview created the furore claimed the statement was taken out of context, and John quickly followed suit.

But many Americans were still dissatisfied and dozens of radio stations across the U.S. continued to ban Beatle records and organized mass burnings of Beatle records and photographs.

Subsequent statements by two other Beatles merely aggravated the situation.

Columnist Maureen Cleave appeared to ease hostile feelings when she stated that her article

READERS REACT TO BEATLE BAN PAGE 2

had been "completely misinterpreted and that Americans have the story entirely wrong."

Lennon Christian
Miss Cleave said that Lennon, whom she termed a "Christian with a young son who has also been Christened," deplored the lack of interest in the Christian Church.

Lennon, according to Miss Cleave, observed that the "power of Christianity was on the decline in the modern world and that things had reached such a ridiculous state that human beings (such as the Beatles) could be worshipped more religiously than religious figures."

She said that Lennon, far from approving this type of worship, was appalled by it.

But if Miss Cleave's explanation of the article eased feelings, ensuing statements by the other Beatles rekindled anti-Beatle sentiment.

Beatles Paul McCartney and George Harrison got in on the act while Manager Epstein was in New York City attempting to clarify Lennon's statements. McCartney said he found the American people's pursuit of money "sort of frightening," and Harrison said he wasn't really looking forward to the Beatles' current U.S. tour.

Doesn't Like U.S.
McCartney said he liked England better than the United States chiefly because of "the attitude of the people in America." He said, "They seem to think that money is everything.

"And this applies especially to the kind of people we meet — agents and corporation people. You get the feeling everybody's after it—money—and it's sort of frightening," Paul declared in a BBC radio interview.

Harrison, who earlier said the Beatles were "coming to America to get beaten up," eased his blast against the United States only when he spoke of California—where the Beatles finish their tour in late August.

"At least there," he said, "we
(Turn to Page 16)

GEORGE — Dreads Tour

PAUL — dislikes U.S.

BEATLES ARCHIVES 1

Win A Life Size Yellow Submarine

With the Beatles top new record, "Yellow Submarine" gurgling its way to the top of the charts, KRLA *BEAT* makes possible for its readers the ultimate in one-upsmanship. Be the first kid on your block to actually own a life-size "honest to goodness really works" yellow submarine six feet long, four feet wide, weighing 108 pounds.

This two-man sub is pedal operated and can navigate under water at three to four knots. (You never know when the Los Angeles riverbed will flood again and if there's a tie-up on the freeway, this sub will be the envy of your neighbors).

Because Paramount's great new mid-Atlantic action thriller "Assault on a Queen" is all about how some crazy mixed up kids (Frank Sinatra, Virna Lisi, Tony Franciosa and Richard Conte) float a German sub from the bottom of the ocean and hi-jack the Queen Mary, we thought we'd make a contribution to ending juvenile delinquency in their name — and the Beatles, of course. One thing is sure — a yellow submarine will really keep the kids off the streets.

See the contest blank on this page for details or listen to KRLA for contest details. Contest closes August 31, 1966.

Well, everything's back to normal again with the Beatles in the midst of controversy and the Stone fans camped outside of the RCA Studios in Hollywood waiting for a glimpse of the fab five. Phoenix fans are up-in-arms over the Dave Clark Five appearance in their city and "I Saw Her Again," "Along Comes Mary," "Sweet Pea" and several other American hits are being recorded in Swedish and Norwegian. Other than that, nothing much is happening — except maybe Fire And Ice.

Something strange is definitely going on in the Beatle camp and no one in the business is quite sure what. Reports filtering out of England seem to indicate that Epstein is losing his control over John Lennon. Up until the last few months, all Beatle comments to the press were guarded. And now within the span of a month, John has told the world that he didn't even know the Philippines had a president and that "we're (the Beatles) more popular than Jesus now."

...JOHN LENNON

And, on top of his statements to the press, John is going to make "How I Won The War" minus Paul, George and Ringo. The whole mess adds up to "something wrong somewhere." People who know John (or who know those who do) are not in the least bit surprised about John's views on Christianity but they *are* surprised that Epstein would let John go ahead and make them public. John, naturally, has the right to his opinions but Epstein is a shrewd businessman, one who is well aware what adverse effects John's views would have in the U.S.

That is the fact which makes people wonder if Epstein isn't perhaps losing his control over John and I, for one, would give anything to find out what is *really* going on with the Beatles.

The Stones had their share of trouble this week too, thanks to the air strike. They had booked studio time at RCA but missed three entire days because they couldn't get a flight into Los Angeles. No small matter, you say? Well, it is when you're paying $40 an hour for a studio to sit empty!

Jesus—'OK, But...'

(Continued from Page 1)
can swim and get a bite to eat."

Immediately after the statements by McCartney and Harrison, the Beatle management attempted to silence the outspoken singers. A London spokesman said the Beatles would refrain from comment to "avoid further confusion and misinterpretation."

The statement by Lennon has been construed into countless meanings and explanations by everybody from American Nazi party leaders to clergymen.

Statement True?

Could there, in actuality, be truth in Lennon's allegations? A Madison, Wis., minister thinks there is.

"There is much validity in what Lennon said," commented The Rev. Richard Pritchard of the Westminster Presbyterian Church. "To many people today, the golf course is also more popular than Jesus Christ."

The "Beatle Boycott" was begun in Birmingham, Ala., by two disc jockeys who took issue with Lennon's remarks in the Datebook Magazine article.

The disc jockeys asked listeners to send in their Beatle records, pictures, souvenirs and mop-top wigs for a huge "Beatle Bonfire." The burning was scheduled for Aug. 19 — the night the Beatles were slated to appear in Memphis, Tennessee.

Even the Ku Klux Klan is jumping on the Beatle "Ban Wagon."

In Tupelo, Miss., Dale Walton, Imperial Wizard of the Knights of the Green Forest, Inc., urged teenagers to "Cut their locks off" and send them to a "Beatle Burning" by the Ku Klux Klan on Aug. 15.

Similar bonfires have occurred across the nation, and the West Coast is no exception.

In Los Angeles, an angry mother and a number of teenagers lit the Beatle torch by publicly destroying Beatles' albums and records. A bonfire protesting Lennon's statements also burned in San Francisco.

But while the radio boycott of the Beatles was spreading — especially in the Midwest and the South — Station WSAC at Fort Knox, Kentucky, in the heart of the Bible Belt, started playing Beatle records for the first time.

"Perhaps the Beatles could be more popular than Jesus," a WSAC editorial said. "Perhaps that is what is wrong with society. And if they are, dear friend, you made them so. Not Jesus, not John Lennon and not the Beatles."

A few miles away, in Louisville, Station WAKY sided with the growing anti-Beatle forces. It provided ten seconds of silent prayer for it's listeners every hour, explaining that it replaced a Beatles' record.

Beatle Laws

But in Pennsylvania, an even sterner anti-Beatle movement is afoot.

State Senator Robert Fleming says he intends to file a resolution calling on talent agents in the state to refuse to book the British singing group and to cancel engagements already made.

Fleming said his resolution will also ask radio and television stations to stop playing Beatles' records and ask juke box operators to remove them from their machines.

As expected, the most heated resentment toward the Beatles occurred in the South and Midwest. And while there were a few isolated "Beatle Burnings" on the West Coast, California teens, for the most part, still supported the Beatles and resented banning of their records.

In sampling a cross section of West Coast youth, *The BEAT* found that 93 per cent of those questioned favored the continued airing of Beatles' records by radio stations.

Guilty Feelings

Several teens commented that Lennon's critics might "just have guilty feelings because maybe they don't go to church."

Others argued that the intellectual Beatle is perfectly within his rights — as granted in the American constitution — and besides, "What he said is very true."

There is, however, a moderate-sized group of California youth who took offense at Lennon's remarks. And they are just as staunch in their beliefs — if not more so — than the larger percentage of teens defending the Britons.

One youth in his late teens thought Lennon "should be punished for what he said." Another teenager, citing the Beatles' "Yesterday and Today" album as an example, said, "John Lennon has become too much of an authority on religion and not enough of one on music."

Many of the complaints against Lennon's comments were religious in nature. "Then let them die for us," quipped one youth.

Second Incident

Lennon's statement set off the second international controversy involving the Beatles in less than a month. The group was recently shoved, kicked and cursed at the Manila International Airport after the singers failed to keep a luncheon date with the Philippine's first lady.

But even that incident didn't have the effect of the statements made by Lennon.

It's beginning to look as though it's in vogue to be in questionable opinion. The Beatles — once again — are the pacesetters.

Beatles in Nassau

ANOTHER BEATLE PHOTO from the dream vacation of Susan Frazer. The teener, from Palos Verdes Estates (near Redondo Beach) spent her vacation in the Bahamas — at the same time as the fabulous BEATLES were filming their second movie on location. Imagine waking up every morning — and knowing that you'll spend the day with the BEATLES! Susan's big problem now is how to ever top that wonderful vacation she took at Nassau.

BEATLES ARCHIVES 1

GEORGE HARRISON is the last Beatle to attempt a solo venture. He will write the entire score for an English movie, "Wonder Wall." The film will have its London premiere in the late Spring or early Summer.

UPI Photo
BEATLE RINGO STARR and his wife, Maureen, make a colorful departure from the Rome airport. Ringo had just finished several weeks of filming on "Candy" in which he plays the role of a Mexican gardener.

O STARR lived on such a road until well-meaning excited fans coming round at all hours drove EATLES' drummer off to another hideaway somewhere in England.

The Beatles Own Gold 'Revolver'

The Beatles have done it again — earned a Gold Record for their "Revolver" album on the day of its release! This marks the tenth consecutive Beatle LP to receive a Gold Record on the day of release.

The "Revolver" album cover was designed by Klaus Voorman and does not have any meat or decapitated dolls anywhere in sight. Instead, it contains a montage of Beatle caricatures and pictures, both full-length and head shots. Hidden in one corner of the cover is a picture of Voorman. The album cover has been described by a student of art as the newest development in the arts — "Beatles Art" to be exact.

"Revolver" includes 11 Beatle-penned tunes, including the group's current single, "Yellow Submarine" b/w "Eleanor Rigby." The single is also expected to sell the necessary million dollars worth of copies to insure yet another Gold Record for the Beatles, who have made a habit out of collecting Goldies.

The songs, composers and soloists on "Revolver" are "Taxman," written and sung by George Harrison; "Eleanor Rigby," written by John and Paul and sung by Paul; "Love You To," written and sung by George Harrison; "Here, There and Everywhere," written by John and Paul and sung by Paul; "Yellow Submarine," written by John and Paul and sung by Ringo Starr; "She Said She Said," written by John and Paul and sung by John Lennon; "Good Day Sunshine," written by John and Paul and sung by Paul; "For No One," written by John and Paul and sung by Paul; "I Want To Tell You," written and sung by George; "Got To Get You Into My Life," written by John and Paul and sung by Paul; "Tomorrow Never Knows," written by John and Paul and sung by John.

BEATLES ARCHIVES 1

KRLA BEAT

Volume 1, Number 24   LOS ANGELES, CALIFORNIA   15 Cents   August 28, 1965

Southland Premiere! KRLA Presents—
THE BEATLES in 'HELP!'

KRLA BEAT

Los Angeles, California — August 28, 1965

A BEAT EDITORIAL

NO CENSORSHIP

In the music world, this is the age of the protest. As an old Latin proverb observes, "It's What's Happening, Baby."

Bob Dylan was the first to break the sound-off barrier when his "Like a Rolling Stone" jumped overnight from no place to top place on the sales charts. Dylan has been protesting against various things for years, of course, but the masses are just beginning to listen.

But the real ding-dong daddy of protest songs is Barry McGuire's "Eve of Destruction," a rousing ditty talking up The Bomb — which also became an overnight sales hit and is unquestionably the most talked-about and controversial record of recent times.

But McGuire's protests about modern suicidal warfare were nothing compared with the protests which quickly came pouring in from those who were offended by the song, particularly conservative and right-wing groups.

Ashcanned

As a result, many radio stations throughout the country — and even ABC Television — have banned the record. Despite "Eve of Destruction's" huge popularity and heavy public demand for it on the airwaves, these stations absolutely refuse to play it.

But in spite of the heated controversy surrounding it KRLA is still playing the record, refusing to join the ranks of those who yanked it from their turntables.

KRLA Station Manager John Barrett, a long-time advocate of giving the public what it wants to hear, sums it up this way:

"Regardless of our own personal feelings about the record — pro or con — we don't feel KRLA has the right to tell our listeners what they can and cannot hear. KRLA doesn't believe in censorship and we will bend over backwards to play any record or form of music which is in public demand."

And he added: "Our listeners set the music policy. KRLA plays whatever records they indicate a preference for — so long as they are not distasteful or morally offensive — and the public can accept or reject each one on the basis of personal taste.

"If they decide they want to hear Chinese music, then that's what KRLA will play."

The BEAT echoes a hearty "Amen." But who knows — at this very moment someone may be penning a Chinese protest song.

BEATLE MOVIE REVIEW

'HELP' Fab Film, But Poor Ringo!

It is quite obvious to the BEAT that the Beatles' second movie will need no financial "help." It's sure to be a box-office smash. The photography, the color, the production and the direction are fabulous.

Walter Shenson and Richard Lester are again teamed as the producer and director of the film. These two talented Americans, of course, fulfilled the same two jobs in the Beatles' first, "Hard Day's Night." They did such a great job that a reporter from the London Evening Standard said: "If the Beatles were awarded the MBE for what they did for Britain, Walter Shenson and Richard Lester ought to get life peerages for what they have done for the Beatles."

And as for the Beatles, they are delightfully and tremendously the Beatles. They were even more relaxed and sure of themselves this time, and it shows.

Missing Ring

The movie opens in the Far Eastern temple of the Goddess Kaili. A human victim is about to be sacrificed to the Goddess when Ahme (Eleanor Bron) makes the starling discovery that the intended victim is not wearing the sacrificial ring.

The ring is, of course, in the possession of one Mr. Ringo Starr who is at that very moment banging away on his drums. Ringo, extremely attached to rings anyway, is especially attached to this special ring, a gift from a fan, because it has somehow become stuck on his finger!

The High Priest, one Clang, (Leo McKern) and his gang of

TURN TO PAGE 10

WADING THROUGH THE SURF AT NASSAU, John, Paul, George and Ringo complete the Bahamas' segment of their new film ("HELP!") and prepare to fly to the frozen alps of Austria for more scenes from the fabulous movie. KRLA will present a special advance screening of the long-awaited Beatle movie on Aug. 23. Huge turnouts are expected when the film begins its city-wide showing on Sept. 1.

KRLA HAS PREVIEW OF NEW BEATLE FILM

KRLA will present the Beatles in another first next Monday (August 23).

The first Southern California showing of their exciting new movie ("HELP!").

And the timing couldn't be more perfect.

KRLA's special advance showing of the United Artists film is timed to celebrate the long-awaited arrival of the Beatles in Southern California on the same day.

It will be a special treat for 500 lucky Beatle fans who will not only be the first in this area to see "HELP!" but will be able to see it without charge. Every seat for the special advance screening is being given away free.

It will be shown at the Carthay Circle Theatre, 6316 W. San Vicente, starting at 10:30 a.m. All is not lost, however, for those who miss the KRLA preview of "HELP!" The movie opens its regular city-wide run on Sept. 1, and huge crowds are again expected — equal to the turnouts for the Beatles' first movie, "A Hard Day's Night."

The movie climaxes a frantic week of Beatle activity in Southern California.

Begins Monday

It begins Monday when the Fabulous Four arrive in the Los Angeles area for a six-day vacation.

Saturday night they are to travel by plane or helicopter to San Diego for a performance at Balboa Stadium, returning to their guest home in Los Angeles after the show.

Sunday and Monday they will perform for Bob Eubanks and KRLA at Hollywood Bowl, two performances which have been sold out since mail order ticket

TURN TO PAGE 10

Beatles Lease House In Benedict Canyon

When the Beatles tour the U.S.—and particularly California—they don't stay at just any ordinary hotel. Why should they when they can live in plush private homes surrounded by movie stars?

During their eight days in California The Beatles will lease a mansion-type house in picturesque Benedict Canyon outside Hollywood.

Their sanctuary even comes equipped with a drawbridge and moat. However, the moat is not as hazardous as the real kind, for it contains no animals of the man-eating variety.

For the pleasure of living in this drawbridged mansion, the boys paid the mere sum of $3,500, plus an additional $2,000 for insurance to cover any damage which might be caused by their overly-enthusiastic fans.

But since they are receiving approximately $45,000 per concert this will not take quite their last cent.

The Beatles hope the insurance precaution will not prove to have been necessary. Last year thousands of fans found their hiding place in Bel-Air, but the boys didn't mind because nobody tried to mob the house, break windows or steal souvenirs.

They deserve the same courtesy this year.

BEATLES ARCHIVES 1

BEATLES FIND MUSIC AND FUN

"ALL SOME TEACHERS EVER THINK OF IS HOME WORK"

"I'LL TAKE THE LEAD, GEORGE"

"YOU ALWAYS TAKE THE LEAD, DARN IT!"

BEATLES ARCHIVES 1

BEATLES IN TV CONTROVERSY

By Tony Barrow

A violent storm of controversy surrounded the London unveiling of "Magical Mystery Tour," the Beatles' first self-made TV movie. When the show was screened by the BBC on December 26, the switchboard at the TV company's London headquarters was jammed with calls from baffled viewers who didn't understand what "Magical Mystery Tour" was all about.

General reactions were unexpectedly varied and amongst the press critics opinion was sharply divided.

In *The Sunday Times*, Hunter Davies described the film as "excellent entertainment, funny, clever and very professional looking." He went on: "They went into it all with their eyes closed to all the traditions, ignorant of all the ridiculous conventions which have ham-strung almost every British film director who ever wanted to make a film exactly as he wanted."

Too Chaotic

In the *Daily Mirror*, Mary Malone's view was that "it was chaotic." She wrote: "Too Toot Tootsie John, Paul, George and Ringo as film makers. It's hello—and goodbye."

In the *Sun*, Richard Last called it "a bore based on the proposition that improvisation and random selection are a valid substitute for organized art."

In the *New Musical Express*, Norrie Drummond hailed it as "a most entertaining film" with "extremely clever" sequences for the musical numbers. He went on: "They break many of the rules which established directors stick to but this only seems to add to the delightful, free and easy atmosphere."

The rest of the musical trade press was just as enthusiastic as the *New Musical Express*, "Ringo emerges in this hour-long fairytale as a delightful comedian with a real touch of brilliance" decided Penny Balentine in *Disc and Music Echo*.

Record Mirror reviewer Derek Boltwood wrote that "there was comedy, pathos and some beautiful fantasy scenes—all held together by the multi-colored magical mystery bus."

Must Be Color

It is worth nothing here that the more favorable press reviews of the show were written by critics who saw "Magical Mystery Tour" in color. Inevitably special color effects play a major part in the show's fantasy sequences.

In television and newspaper interviews the following day, Paul McCartney attempted to clarify the situation. "The show was made up of a lot of different scenes we like the look of" he said. "If people were looking for a plot they were bound to be disappointed. We used the excuse of a Mystery Tour to string together all the bits of Magic. We thought people would understand. We thought the title itself was explanation enough.

The trouble is if people don't understand they say 'A lot of rubbish' and switch off. We will make another film. We learned a lot and making another film will be a challenge."

By the end of December two and a half million copies of the Beatles' "Magical Mystery Tour" record and book package had been sold in Britain and America. The cartoon version of the "Magical Mystery Tour" story in the book which accompanies the album differs from the TV movie version in various minor ways. For one thing the scenes are in a different sequence and the book includes a couple of scenes which had to be excluded from the film to bring the screening time down to fit a one-hour program schedule. The main deletion is the "What a Marvelous Lunch!" segment including "Happy Nat's Happy Dream."

Despite the mixed reaction to the initial screening, "Magical Mystery Tour" had a repeat BBC showing in color on January 5 throughout the U.K.

My own feeling is that some viewers were looking for too much reality in a film which relied upon the magic of fantasy, the mystery of unfamiliar happenings. Maybe some folk were a little afraid of the unfamiliar. At any rate "Magical Mystery Tour" is being accepted all over the world as an important and successful experiment in TV moviemaking. And where experiments are concerned you'll always encounter opposition.

Starr Checks Cues

RINGO STARR CHECKS SCREENPLAY — As crucial scene is set for cameras in a few minutes, BEATLE RINGO reads the "bible," the script for the film, which outlines camera angles and actors' lines, as well as directions for action. Photo shows how close lucky Susan Frazer of Palos Verdes came **each day** to THE BEATLES. Susan spent her whole vacation in the Bahamas watching the Fab Four.

BEATLES' SOLO CAREERS DETRACTING FROM GROUP?

With the Beatles all going separate, solo ways these days, Brian Epstein has announced the group may not release a customary disc during the Christmas season.

If they do not, it will be the first time since 1962 the Beatles haven't had a record at the top of the charts.

Epstein also announced Paul McCartney will soon be going the solo route. "It is not an acting role," the Beatles manager clued, "and an announcement can be expected soon."

The Beatles are also not expected to make a group appearance in England for the remainder of the year. Their last appearance there was in May.

Their failure to release a Christmas Season disc is the first major intimation that the boys' solo careers are detracting from their effectiveness as a group.

"We would naturally like to have another Beatles single before the end of the year," said an EMI spokesman, "but they have nothing in the can, so it is entirely dependent on whether they record again in time."

The Beatles are, however, expected to enter the recording studios in November to record songs and incidental music for their next film. The film is tentatively scheduled to begin production in January.

'HELP' PACKED WITH THRILLS

(Continued from Page 2)

applications were first accepted back in May.

Favored Hollywood

Last year the Beatles stated publically that their Hollywood Bowl Concert was the highlight of their tour. This was not only because they loved the Bowl, the weather, the well-behaved crowds and their first sight of the movie capital of the world, but because of the smoothness in which the concert was handled by KRLA and Bob Eubanks.

Fans who were lucky enough to obtain tickets for the Hollywood Bowl concerts are requested to follow three general rules:

(1) Scream as loud as you like, but remain seated.
(2) Do what the police and security men say so that no one will get hurt.
(3) Treat the Beatles as nicely as you would wish people to treat you. Remember, they are coming to Southern California to entertain us, and they are here as our guests.

'Help' Fab Film, But Poor Ringo

(Continued from Page 2)

no-gooders, set out to find Ringo, and all sorts of strange things begin happening. When Ringo is asleep, a weird "thing" comes through the wall and attempts to recapture the ring, but Ringo wakes up only to find himself on the floor and the ring still on his finger.

Enter Foot

Being extremely clever, the Beatles pay a visit to Professor

BEATLES ARCHIVES 1

WHEN NOT OFF HUNTING RINGO

... WHO NEEDS AN AUDIENCE?

... "PLEASE DON'T TAKE MY TAMBOURINE, SIR"

BEATLES ARCHIVES 1

Beatles Are Not Breaking Up!

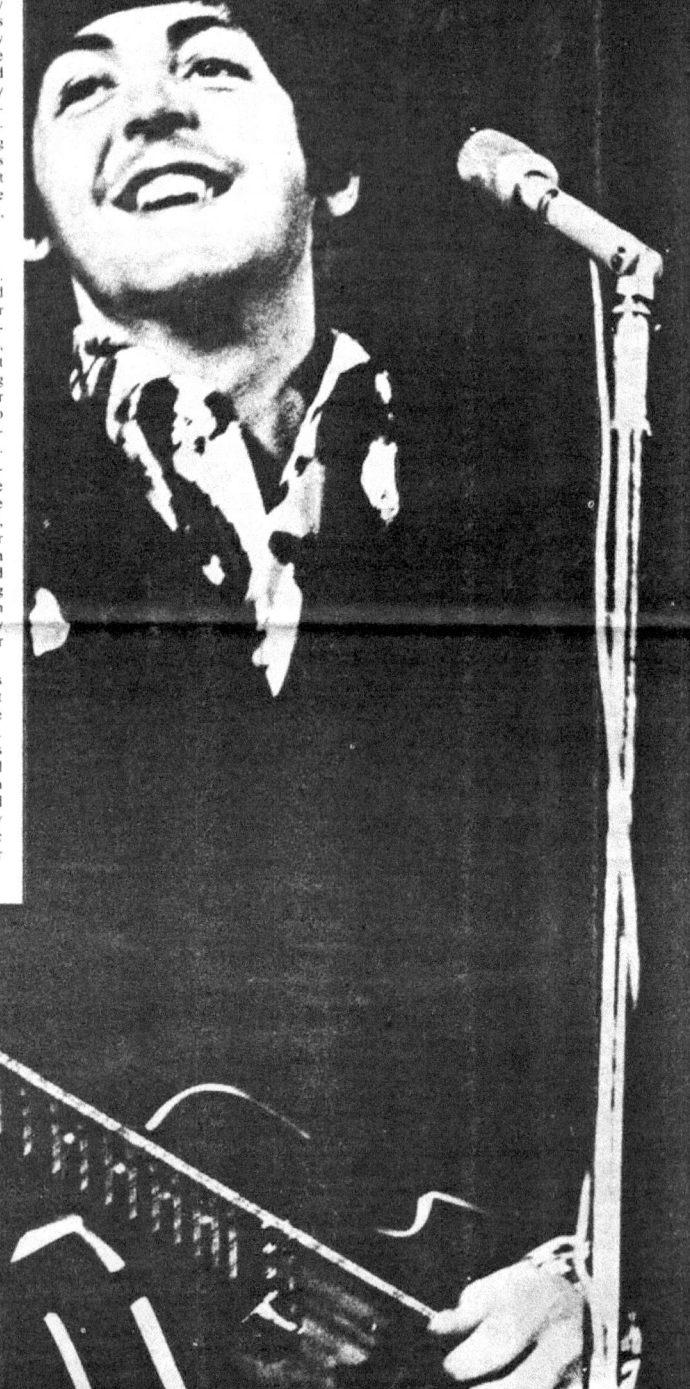

By Louise Criscione

Let's cut out the hysteria and the sobbing and the rumors. The Beatles are not splitting up! At least, not literally. It's true that individually each Beatle is pursuing his own goals and, in time, a break-up will inevitably rear its head. But right now, today, both Paul McCartney and Ringo Starr have emphatically denied that a split is anywhere near imminent.

Naturally, when the announcement of no more personal appearances was handed down, speculation spread that it was finis for the Beatles as a group. And John Lennon didn't help matters much when he told a reporter that his years as a Beatle "had been fun." By using the past tense, John's statement was taken to mean that those Beatle years were over.

The End?

And, at the time, those years certainly appeared to be coming to a definite end. John was off filming his movie, Paul was busy writing the music for "The Family Way," George was in India learning sitar techniques and Ringo was getting bored and looking around for a solo movie stint for himself. "Revolver" was the newest piece of Beatle material issued and there was no official word on a script for the Beatles third movie.

During this lull in group activity, reporters and gossips, who for lack of anything better to occupy their time and available space, began a long string of rumors and insinuations. None of which were flattering to the Beatles and none of which caused rejoicing in their fans' ranks.

Probably the most popular "news" was the hot rumor that jealousy existed between the Beatles. Reporters claiming a "scoop" added wood to the already burning fire by gleefully pointing to the fact that Ringo was jealous of the others because they collected writer's royalties and he didn't . . . that George was mad because John picked off a juicy movie role . . . that Paul was breaking the famous and successful Lennon-McCartney team by writing the music for a Hayley Mills movie . . . that John was furious at Paul for not asking his assistance in composing the music. And on, and on and on.

"Isn't Any"

Until enough was just enough. Tired of picking up papers and magazines to read about their alleged jealousy, Paul finally declared: "There isn't any." Fact is, continued Paul, by doing different things each Beatle can pass along his new information to the other three. Thus, allowing the group to progress and maintain their tremendous popularity and influence.

Remaining delightfully unpredictable, in the very midst of the break-up and jealousy rumors, the Beatles congregated in London, cut a Christmas message for their fans, started work on a new album and a new single and told the world that, while they were still having script difficulties, a story had been selected and if all went well they would begin filming in March or April.

So, with personal appearances definitely out and a third movie not definitely in, what *is* in the future for the Beatles? Better records. Without the pressure of tour dates to confine them, the Beatles will be able to progress musically with no trouble at all. And they intend to do just that. They are not ready to be counted out of the music business just yet—and you better bet your life they won't be!

BEATLES ARCHIVES 1

Beatles Good Even When They're Not

BEAT Photo: Robert W. Young

If you're a Beatle fan, there's a good chance that you almost left home on January 3, 1966.

Why? Because the following is a good example of what happened on that particular date. In homes all across the nation, and especially in California, the number one Beatle stronghold in America.

The time was 7:30 p.m. The scene, your living room. The cast of characters, your family.

Mum and Dad looking bored on the sofa. Little Brother draped over a chair. You sitting cross-legged in front of the telly.

The event? Something you'd been waiting for all day, all month, practically forever.

The Beatles' debut on "Hullabaloo".

When you heard the familiar theme song, you started holding your breath. But host Roger Smith was first on the bill.

You like Roger Smith. He's a nice guy. Cute, too. But you seriously wondered if he would *ever* finish the opening number.

Finally, he finished. And finally, the Beatles began.

George and Ringo came on the screen first. Kidding around before the start of their first song. Then they were joined by Paul and John and "Day Tripper" filled the room.

But, after a line or two, a new sound was added. Somewhere behind you, Little Brother was *talking*.

You turned around, aghast. "*Shhhhh*," you hissed.

But Little Brother does not give up easily.

No Color

"Why aren't they in color?" he hissed back.

"They just *told* you why," you snapped in a stage whisper, trying to speak and concentrate on the Beatles at the same time. "This is a *film* clip from *London*!"

That shut him down for the moment, but just as you turned your rapt attention back to the foursome, Mum piped up.

"Ringo isn't really playing the drums," she announced.

You sighed wearily. "I know. They aren't really singing either."

Dad snorted. "That's for sure," he announced.

"*Dad*," you wailed. "I mean they're lip-syncing their record!"

Then you returned to George, who was flirting into the camera and flexing his long fingers as they flew about the neck of the guitar.

"Wow," you breathed. "Look at *that*."

"He isn't really playing," Mum reminded patiently.

"Amen," amended Dad.

"He *is so*," you quivered. "You do play and sing when you lip-sync. What I meant was that no one *hears* you."

"We should be so lucky," offered your little brother, but before you had a chance to throw something at him, the song was over.

Unfortunately, the conversation was not.

"Why didn't they wiggle?" inquired Mum.

"They *never* wiggle," you answered, shocked.

"I suppose they never stomp or scream either," remarked Dad.

"*No*, they *don't*!"

"That hair is terrible," continued Little Brother. "John looks like a camel."

Well, that did it. That's when you decided to leave home. Right *after* the Beatles' second number.

All was silent in the living room until Paul was two bars into their encore.

Then, Mum spoke. "What's a day tripper?"

"*Mother*!"

Then, Dad spoke. "Do not address your mother in that tone of voice."

"*Please*! I'm *trying* to watch the *Beatles*!"

Then, Little Brother spoke. "You're trying all right. *Very*."

Then, when you were about to burst into tears, Mum, Dad and Little Brother burst into laughter. And you joined them.

No one talked during the rest of the song, and you made a swift and solemn promise to luv John Lennon for the rest of your life.

"They aren't *too* bad," Dad admitted when you snapped off the telly. "And that what's-his-name, the guy at the piano. He's funny."

You smiled fondly and decided not to start packing after all.

Those Beatles were really something, you thought to yourself. In the short time it had taken to sing "We Can Work It Out," they had done exactly that.

You were right.

Close To Bad

The Beatles had once again proven why they are the most powerful and popular stars in history. Because they are the best even when they're at their worst.

If they weren't at their worst on "Hullabaloo," they came close. For several reasons.

Being live performers, they aren't used to the lip-sync process, and this caused a few mistakes. The process was used only because the production of a sound tape would have been too expensive and too time consuming. But, after a goof, the Beatles just forged ahead and most viewers didn't even notice the errors.

During "Day Tripper", the photography left a lot to be desired. They appeared to be on two separate spliced-together films, with George and Ringo on one and Paul and John on the other. This may not have been the case, but whatever was, in order to get all four Beatles on the screen at once, the camera had to pull back so far, it was difficult to see any of them clearly.

However, this mattered little, thanks to a series of breath-taking closeups. The two-part clip contained some of the finest footage ever shot of Paul McCartney. He looked so adorable, he probably heard the screams all the way to London.

And George Harrison fans surely must have come apart at the seams. He looked more handsome than ever before.

The perfect balance of the appearance was supplied by Ringo and John.

Frosted Cake

Ringo's dead-panning and konky antics were jolly good fun. John's mugging into the camera was the frosting on the cake, and the ice-breaker.

In some living rooms, the scene was more hectic than in the one we "visited." A Beatle fan's reaction to the foursome depends upon her degree of involvement.

If you just *luv* the Beatles, you watched in fascination. But, if you really *love* Paul or George or John or Ringo, there's panic intermingled with your fascination. A panic that stems from caring about someone who's so close and so far away.

A lot of tears were shed in front of TV sets that night. And a lot of worried parents looked on with a mixture of amazement and concern.

John dried many of those tears and quelled a lot of fears. His wry humor changed the mood by saying "Surely you don't think we take ourselves *seriously*." It also helped many parents realize that Beatlemania is not an unnatural or unhealthy thing.

That it is, instead, a perfectly natural reaction to four totally irresistable individuals.

For a group which had none of the technical elements on their side that night, the Beatles accomplished a lot.

But the most important thing they did was agree to appear. Accepting what payment the show could afford to give us a mid-term boost, and making it a little easier for us to wait until summer for the real thing.

Yeah, yeah, yeah.

BEATLES ARCHIVES 1

Ringo Starr—Oldest And Most Unchanged Beatle

By Jacoba Atlas

Controversy and change seems to characterize the Beatles these days, yet one member of the group has remained astonishingly quiet and unchanged. He is the oldest Beatle, the one with the sad-blue eyes, Ringo Starr.

Whereas John and Paul have been creating controversy with their outspoken statements; and George's passion for Indian music and near-Eastern philosophy denotes the enormous change in his thinking, Ringo has said little that would indicate the ways in which his mind has been moving.

This does not mean, however, that Ringo has stayed the same. It would be virtually impossible for him to remain the same person that he was in 1963, when the Beatles first burst onto the scene. It only indicates that Ringo's growth has been less public.

Stand-Out

Ringo has always been a stand-out member of the group. Even in the early days when people were having great difficulty in determining which Beatle was which, Ringo stood out because of his height and his rings.

He joined the group after they had achieved fame in their hometown of Liverpool, and were already established under the banner of the Beatles. Originally Ringo was not the Beatles' drummer, but rather played with another Liverpool group led by Rorry Storm. In those early days, Peter Best was the Beatles' drummer, but due to a controversy still not cleared up today, George and Paul wanted Peter out and Ringo in. Brian Epstein, following the wishes of the majority, arranged for the change.

Least Affected

Ringo immediately became one of the most popular members of the group. Many reasons were given for his personal popularity. He seemed to convey to fans a closeness and a familiarity somewhat lacking in the others. Many felt that Ringo was the easiest to talk to and the least affected by stardom.

With the film "A Hard Day's Night," critics were singling out Ringo as a fine comic actor. In America during those first years, Ringo won the popularity polls and was the most talked about Beatle. Indeed, Brian Epstein states, "America discovered Ringo."

But it was difficult to determine just where Ringo was going, although the direction of the Beatles as a group became evident. Paul and John were writing song after song and each one was receiving more critical acclaim than the last. George also joined the composing field, but Ringo never ventured in to that end of the business.

John stunned the world with his widely misquoted statement concerning the relative popularity of Jesus and the Beatles, George went off to India to study with famed musician Ravi Shankar, John soloed in a movie, and Paul scored a film. Most recently, Paul followed in John's footsteps by shocking the world with his views on LSD. With all this going on, Ringo seemed strangely quiet.

While the others have been revolutionizing the pop world with their music and their unconventional ideas, Ringo has remained for the most part, silent. Perhaps, this is the clearest key to his personality. Ringo is simply the quietest, most uncomplicated Beatle of the lot.

It is unnecessary to draw conclusions concerning the Beatles on the basis of comparisons, for they are nothing if not individuals. Therefore, what is Ringo like apart from his famous friends?

Most Mature

He would appear to be very much like his public "image." The oldest, and many believe, the most mature, he has coped admirably with the strains of success. A devoted husband and father, he takes special pride in protecting his young wife, the former Maureen Cox, from the glare of publicity. He delights in telling friends that when they got married her parents "signed her over to me" because Maureen was still a minor.

He is equally concerned over the welfare of their son, Zak, who will be two at the end of the summer. He echos John's statements about a son not owing his father anything, and plans to let the child live his own life, without parental domination. "I will never send my child to boarding school. And I'll never push him. If he passes tests and gets diplomas and everything, well and good, but I'll never say 'you won't get this bike unless you go to college.' And I'll let him decide as he grows up what he wants to be."

He and Maureen spend a good deal of their time with their son, and look forward to the birth of their second child in late August. Another boy? "I do want another boy, but it doesn't matter as much this time. We'll both be very happy whether it's a girl or a boy."

Ringo lives in Surrey in an enormous Tudor house not far from the homes of John and George. The house, which has undergone extensive re-decorating under the close watch of Ringo, has become the gathering point for the Beatles and their friends. For some unknown or unexplained reason, Ringo's home and not Paul's in London or George's and John's in Surrey has become the center for most Beatle activity.

Ringo has always been an avid collector, first of antique guns (Burt Lancaster once sent Ringo a set of pistols) and now of Beatle regalia. He hopes one day to have a thorough collection of souvenirs, photos, articles and other such remembrances tracing the careers of the Beatles from their early days in Liverpool to their present success.

Home Movies

Perhaps borrowing some enthusiasm from Paul, Ringo has also become quite involved with making tapes and home movies. Whether the results of these endeavors will be shown publicly is doubtful, but the interest is there.

Ringo has never claimed to be the world's greatest drummer, and indeed, many music critics have placed him rather low on that achievement ladder, yet his sound is an integral part of the entire Beatle scheme. He seems to know instinctively what the others want, and how to play it. Norman Smith, who has worked on many a Beatle recording session states, "Ringo will start off with one sort of rythmn, then be enlightened by John and Paul as to the particular way they 'hear' it in their original song. Ringo then comes up with it. It's fantastic, the closeness of the group—the way they're all on the save wave length and read each others thoughts."

Many people seem concerned over what Ringo will do if the group breaks up. They need not worry. He is an interested and interesting individual with many directions open to him.

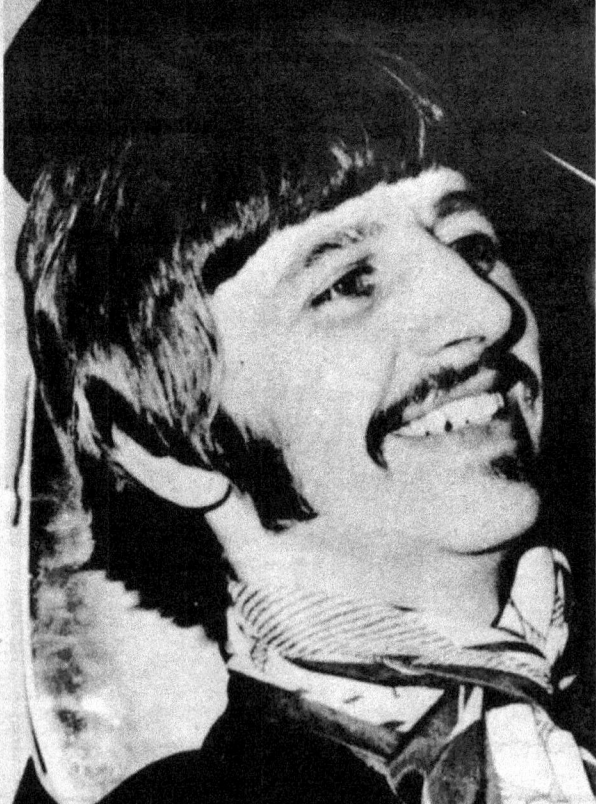

"While the others have been revolutionizing the pop world with their music and unconventional ideas, Ringo has remained strangely silent."

BEATLES ARCHIVES 1

BEAT EXCLUSIVE

George: A Different Face, New Life

By Rochelle Reed

He's a member of Sgt. Pepper's Lonely Hearts Club Band resplendent in an orange braided uniform and flowing hair, with a mustache that somehow grows across his upper lip and drops down on his cheeks to form a beard.

It's been a long time since the days of a silent, sulking George, least obvious of all the Beatles, on the stage of Ed Sullivan.

He's a new George, a different George. A George who no longer spends his free moments "polishing his bottle green Ferrari" as John once put it, but instead packs himself and his wife off to Bombay for six weeks to don Indian garb and master the sitar.

Back in London, he seems aloof, mysterious and introverted. Driving a shiny new Jaguar, he meets his sitar instructor, Ravi Shankar, at the London airport. George, in Indian attire, opens the door for Shankar, dressed in a Western business suit.

Step Back

George, everyone discovered, in 1964, was considered the third Beatle, before Ringo but after writers John and Paul. He was the youngest of the group and news of his 21st birthday traveled around the world from South Africa to Japan.

Onstage, everyone noticed, he had the shortest hair, the shyest smile and the fewest words. He seldom danced around like John and Paul, but stood very still and appeared to be concentrating on his guitar, though those who know him say he was actually eyeing girls in the front row!

He wasn't quoted very much, but reporters managed to discover that he loved cars, hated flying, (he said he was scared of it) and that his favorite dinner – or the food he ate most often in publicity pictures anyway – was eggs, bacon and toast with strawberry jam. He also ate it for lunch.

Meets Patti

Then came "Hard Day's Night" when he met wife-to-be, Patti Boyd, who had a small walk-on part in the movie. She admitted she didn't even like the Beatles until then. So immediately rumors spread that obviously they had married.

George got very angry at newspapermen over the story. But then, he had a reputation for that. Back in 1964, when the Beatles had a few days off in Los Angeles, a photographer nearly received George's version of Waterloo.

Joins Jayne

The Beatles had always wanted to meet Jayne Mansfield and they arranged to join her in a local club where presumably most of the press wouldn't expect them to appear.

However, after a few minutes, the scene turned into a menagerie of fans, press and gawkers. George, particularly annoyed, tossed a few ice cubes towards a photographer. The press, though, stated that it was more like a whole drink.

At the end of the year, he summed up the whole situation and sent out a very personalized Christmas card. The cover bore a picture of George himself, scowling at a cameraman.

But that seems like a long time ago. George hasn't been known to throw anything at a reporter or photographer since. In fact, he waved and smiled to them at his wedding and did the same in Bombay.

So, the question is, what has he been doing lately?

A Lot

Quite a lot, apparently. He was seen at a party by one American pop star who described him as "friendly and talkative. George, along with everyone else, just sat on the floor and discussed all sorts of things and ate a lot and when everyone was quite full, we all went home."

Others have seen him around town – at movies, clubs and his own discotheque, Sibylla's. If he's been traveling (there were rumors that he slipped into the U.S. last month), very few have seen him.

Concepts

Then there is "Within You, Without You," the song George composed for the new Beatle album. Perhaps all the time he was silently staring at the audience back on the Ed Sullivan Show, he was formulating the concepts and ideas he wrote into the song.

In "Within You, Without You" there is the plea for all of us to look within ourselves to find the meaning and the beauty of life. George also re-affirms his belief that all the world can be united through awareness of self. He speaks of going beyond the single person to encompass all living things and people. "We're all one, and life flows on within you and without you."

A DIFFERENT GEORGE — it's been a long time since the Ed Sullivan Show.

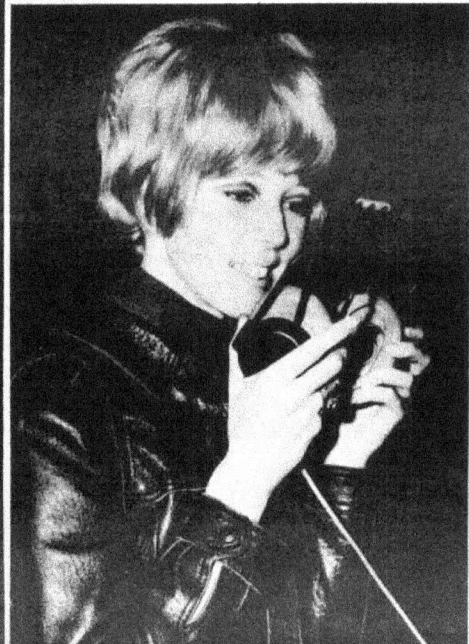

PATTI ATTENDED a Beatle session in jeans and leather jacket.

AT THE SAME session, George unsmilingly posed for the camera.

BEATLES ARCHIVES 1

Beatles Sell Out

Beatles, Paul McCartney and John Lennon, know as much about handling large amounts of money as they do about writing fantastic material, since they're experienced in both.

Quite some time ago, Brian Epstein formed Lenmac Enterprises, Ltd. with John and Paul holding 40 per cent each and Epstein holding the remaining 20 per cent. The company was formed to receive the composers' share of the royalties from the songs which Lennon and McCartney wrote which included "From Me To You," "She Loves You" and "All My Loving."

Since its formation the Lenmac company has been doing landslide business. Its income last year was more than a half million dollars and this year it will net well over one million dollars. Next year, unfortunately, it will drop to only about $200,000 as the royalties decrease.

Now, John and Paul as well as Epstein have sold their shares in Lenmac to its sister company, Northern Songs Limited. Each Beatle received a nice $408,000 and Epstein sold out for $204,000.

Lennon and McCartney will continue to derive a hefty profit from Northern Songs which collects royalties on their songs as publishers. They own about 30 per cent of Northern Songs — worth one and a half million dollars.

What the whole thing boils down to is the fact that it will be a long, long time (would you believe about a century and a half) before John and Paul will be forced to scrub floors for a living.

Brand New Beatle Album Out Soon?

Beatle fans in America and Great Britain are anxiously awaiting the new Beatle album, scheduled for release sometime this summer.

Although no title has been definitely decided upon as yet, Paul McCartney says some suggestions currently under consideration include "Magic Circles," "Beatles On Safari," and "Revolver" — which is John's favorite at the moment.

Some of the titles included on the new track will include a new sitar number written and performed by George, "Love You To," while Paul will be singing a rather sad new tune entitled "For No One," on which he will be accompanied by French horns.

Paul will also take vocal honors on the new tune, "Good Day Sunshine" which will feature the Beatles recording manager, George Martin, on honky-tonk piano in the background.

The Beatles have also made several references in the last few weeks to the idea of using some jazz musicians on these new tracks — an idea which has met with mixed reactions from members of several other top British groups.

All in all, it promises to be another fantastic album from The Beatles destined to chalk up still another smash summer success for the quartet.

Release of the long-awaited LP in this country may be scheduled to coincide with The Beatles' upcoming U.S. tour, which begins in Chicago on August 12.

Beatles Score With Germans

First reports in on the recent German tour made by The Beatles indicate nothing but a smash success. German sales representatives are reporting the tour to be a classic in the history of record sales promotion, explaining that there has never been such an effective tie-in with a tour and a sales promotion as was achieved on the "Bravo Beatles Blitz-Tournee" — the German tag for the tour.

The tour was sponsored by "Bravo," a German magazine for young people in that country, which reports that the tour was a sales success even before the Beatles arrived in Essen for their debut German performance.

The record sales on Beatle discs increased by approximately 500 per cent in Essen, Hamburg, and Munich — all three cities where the Beatles were booked for performances, and the increase soared to an astronomical and unprecedented 1,000 per cent before the end of the tour.

Final tabulations on the overall results of the tour are still in the process of completion, however trade officials in that country are already saying that there is little doubt that the tour will send Beatle record sales sky-rocketing to an all-time high in Germany.

The German tour was also one of sentimental — as well as financial — value to the Phenomenal Foursome.

Here They Come!

By Louise Criscione

The Beatles have announced the schedule for their August tour of America and Tony Barrow cabled *The BEAT* the information immediately so that you would be the first to know what dates and cities will be featuring Beatle concerts this year.

Fourteen cities are now certain for the Beatle tour which will open in Chicago on August 12 and then rapidly move on to Detroit (13), Louisville (14), Washington (15), Philadelphia (16), Toronto, Canada (17), Boston (18), Memphis (19), Cincinnati (20) and St. Louis on August 21.

The Beatles will then take a slight breathing spell before hitting New York City on August 23. The 24th of August will be a free traveling day and then John, Paul, George and Ringo appear in Seattle on the 25th.

Los Angeles will definitely be a Beatle stop this year despite some initial talk that the Beatles would by-pass the city this year. August 28 is the date firmly set for the Beatles appearance in L.A. which leaves them a full two days rest between Seattle and Los Angeles. On both of their former cross-country tours, the Beatles chose to spend time-off in L.A. just lazing about.

Seclusion?

In 1964 they spent their free time in supposed seclusion among the movie star colony in Bel Air. However, as always happens, their fans discovered their hideaway and the Bel Air Patrol was forced to work extra long shifts to keep fans from overrunning not only the Beatles' house but all homes in the vicinity.

August of '65 found the Beatles hoping for a little peace and quiet again up in the hills, but this time in Benedict Canyon. Once more their faithful and diligent fans discovered their house and camped out all up and down the street until police cleared them out. At which time the persistent fans found hiding places in trash cans, behind bushes and anything else that was handy.

And so it went in every single city where the Beatles spent more than a few hours. It bothered everyone but the Beatles. Paul once told *The BEAT* that the Beatles weren't at all disturbed because they saw what they wanted to see and went where they wanted to go. And they did too. They popped up at recording sessions, night clubs and Elvis Presley's house. The people who the Beatles wanted to meet or old friends who they wanted to see again were merely invited to wherever the Beatles were staying.

After Los Angeles the Beatles will make one more stop, closing their tour in San Francisco — where they chose to end their tour last year, too. The San Francisco Beatle appearance will be on August 29 and as of now it is not known whether the Beatles will immediately head back for England following their concert or if they will remain in San Francisco for a few days to rest, relax and see the famous San Francisco sights.

Speaking with the various promoters along the Beatle route, *The BEAT* has discovered that if at all possible, the Beatles would rather skip the prestige spots such as the Cow Palace and the Hollywood Bowl and instead play the bigger auditoriums where more of their fans will be able to see them.

Sullivan, Too?

It is highly probable that somewhere on their hectic tour, the Beatles will take time out to appear on "Ed Sullivan," the show which first introduced them to America in February of 1964. But as of yet their appearance is not definite.

If you are lucky enough to live in any of the 14 chosen cities you have only to save up your ticket money. However if you don't, *The BEAT* suggests that you really start penny-pinching in order to have enough money for not only your concert ticket but your plane fare as well!

And if you can't possibly come up with enough money to attend one of the 14 Beatle concerts yourself, don't fret. *The BEAT* will follow the tour along from the time it begins in Chicago until it winds up in San Francisco letting you in on all of the highlights of the entire tour.

...RINGO AND PAUL STEPPIN' DOWN STATESIDE

Inside the BEAT

On The Beat	3
The Mama's And Papa's	4-5
Proby – The Man And The Boy	7
Teen Panel Discussion	10
Adventures of Robin Boyd	12
Where The Real Action Is	13
For Girls Only	14
Winners of Beat Poll	15

The BEAT is published weekly by BEAT Publications, Inc., editorial and advertising offices at 6290 Sunset Blvd., Suite 504, Hollywood, California 90028. U.S. bureaus in Hollywood, San Francisco, New York, Chicago and Nashville; overseas correspondents in London, Liverpool and Manchester, England. Sale price, 15 cents. Subscription price: U.S. and possessions, $5 per year; Canada and foreign rates, $9 per year. Second class postage prepaid at Los Angeles, California.

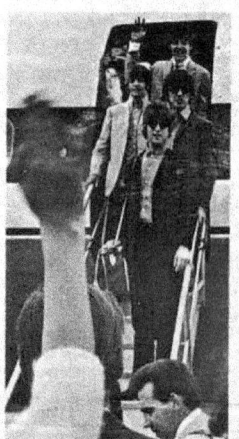

...ARRIVING AUGUST 12

BEATLES ARCHIVES 1

Christmas Is A Happening...

Thanks To

THE BEATLES

JIMI HENDRIX

THE BEACH BOYS

and Capitol Records

AVAILABLE AT

BEATLES ARCHIVES 1

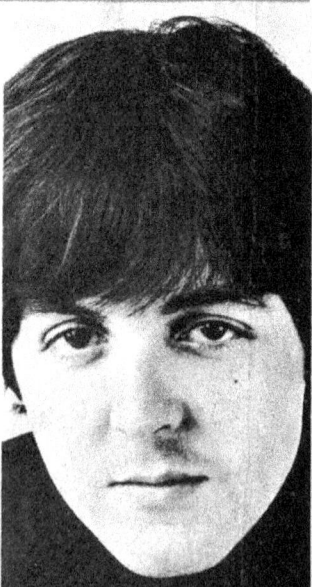

America's Largest Teen NEWSpaper — 15¢

KRLA Edition **BEAT**

JULY 30, 1966

Beatles Mauled — PAGE 1

Stone Hold On Beatles — PAGE 4-5

BEATLES ARCHIVES 1

Regarding the black eye given him in New Delhi: "I got it from a policeman's baton in New Delhi and he was on our side!"

"We're going to have a couple of weeks to recuperate before we go and get beaten up by the Americans."

"We didn't even know about the invitation, must less receive it, until it was too late."

And John Lennon had this to say, "I didn't even know they had a President."

Beatles Mauled
(Continued from page 1)

port, was touched off when the Manila press reported the group deliberately snubbed Mrs. Marcos by not appearing at the designated time.

Manilan government officials, who issued an official apology over the incident, are now saying the group knew nothing of the appointment until it was too late.

The promoters of the Beatles' appearance in Manila lost their shirts over the concert. The Beatles played two shows in an auditorium which holds 100,000 but each night they drew only 40,000 to their concerts. Consequently, their promoters are now out of business.

President Marcos, who issued the statement, said, "There was no intention on the part of the Beatles to slight the First Lady or the government of the Republic of the Philippines." Marcos called the airport demonstration a "breach of Filipino hospitality."

The Beatles' unexpected encounter with the Manila mob at the airport was a nightmare for the group. "I just don't understand," said a stunned Paul McCartney as he pushed his way through the mob.

Almost all police protection and special considerations for the Beatles were cancelled and the Philippine tax bureau threatened for a time to hold up their departure until they made a declaration of their earnings as required by law.

The Beatles were forced to go through all the ordinary procedures required of departing passengers instead of being hustled through customs and immigration formalities.

As they stood inside the terminal waiting their turn, they were surrounded and harassed by an angry crowd who pushed, shoved and cursed the Beatles and their companions.

An unidentified member of the Beatle party was kicked to the ground. Shouts of "Scram," "Get out of our Country," and unprintable curses were hurled at the quartet as the boys tried to push their way through the jeering mob.

The raucous departure debacle was in sharp contrast to the rip-roaring welcome extended the Beatles on their arrival the previous Sunday by thousands of fans and a massive security cordon.

Only about 100 die-hard Beatle fans turned out Tuesday to cheer their idols but they were outnumbered and out-shouted by the newly organized Beatle-haters.

George, sitting alone and dejected afterwards, probably best summed up the new fears of the Beatles when he said, "Now I guess we can go to America and really get beaten up."

... BOBBY HATFIELD CONGRATULATES JACKIE

Beatles Cursed, Shoved By Mobs...America Next?

A barrage of apologies and clarifications has followed the shocking incident in Manila recently where the Beatles received the first maltreatment of their careers, but it looks as though the group may not be able to forget its alleged "snub" of Manila's First Lady for a long, long time.

Reports of the incident were heard around the world and the Beatles were victims of similar mob action in India, where Paul suffered a black eye.

Paul said he received the black eye when he was struck by the baton of a policeman who was attempting to protect the boys during the Indian riot.

The group's sudden unpopularity came about after the boys failed to keep a scheduled luncheon date with Mrs. Ferdinand Marcos, wife of the Filipino president. The Beatles denied they knew anything about the appointment.

Paul, speaking on behalf of his companions, apologized for standing Mrs. Marcos up, but said he and his companions simply knew nothing of the schedule.

At the time of the luncheon, Paul said he was sightseeing around Manila and the other three Beatles were sleeping in their hotel suite.

An angered John Lennon wasn't nearly so calm and apologetic as spokesman Paul. "I didn't even know the country had a president," he quipped.

The Manila incident, a harassing, violent send-off of the group at the Manila International Air-
(Turn to page 6)

Inside the BEAT
Letters To The Editor 2
Herman's New Movie Contract 3
Obscenity In Pop Music 4
Beatle Fans Turning To Stones 4-5
The Soul Of Jackie Wilson 6
Herman's Pop Satire 7
Adventures Of Robin Boyd 10
Righteous Brothers On Stage 11
Noel Harrison — Secret Agent 12
Spoon Of The Lovin' 13
Cyrkle Around The World 14

The BEAT is published weekly by BEAT Publications, Inc., editorial and advertising offices at 6290 Sunset Blvd., Suite 504, Hollywood, California 90028. U.S. bureaus in Hollywood, San Francisco, New York, Chicago and Nashville; overseas correspondents in London, Liverpool and Manchester, England. Sale price, 15 cents. Subscription price, U.S. and possessions, $5 per year, Canada and foreign rates, $9 per year. Second class postage prepaid at Los Angeles, California.

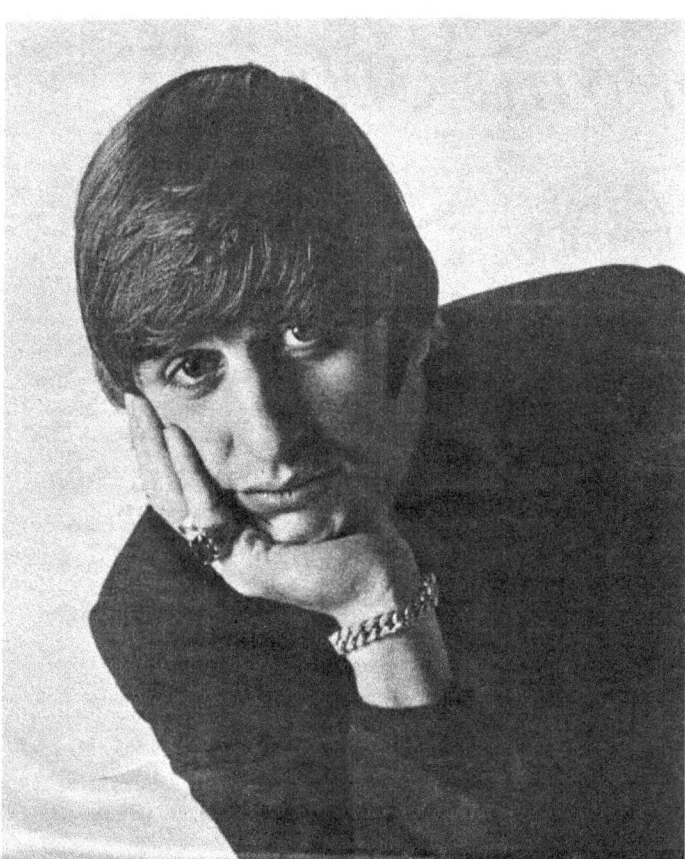

THE BEST QUOTE OF THE WEEK comes from Ringo Starr, who says wisely, "Once you are deaf to your public, you might as well retire because you'll give them nothing,. Judging from that quote, Ringo and the other Beatles plan to be in business for quite a while

BEATLES ARCHIVES 1

A New Look For Paul - WOW!

PHOTOGRAPHED IN AUSTRIA during filming of "Help," Paul's familiar cherub face appears to have hardened and matured, giving him a rugged, handsome, adventurous look. Wonder if he'll look that way at Hollywood Bowl?

BATTLE OVER MEDALS
Beatles Blasted!

Great Britain is involved in a major controversy, and the Beatles are right in the middle of it!

It began quite innocently when John, Paul, George and Ringo were recently accorded one of England's highest honors by Her Majesty, Queen Elizabeth II. She bestowed upon them the Order of the British Empire.

But no sooner had the prized honor been announced than a storm of protest was aroused.

A least four holders of the coveted M. B. E. have sent back their medals, claiming they were debased and cheapened because the Beatles were given the same honor.

"Nincompoops"

One of them announced he was sending his back because "English royalty wants to place me on the same level as those vulgar nincompoops." Another a war hero declared he did not want to be in the same order "that recognizes such stupidity and hysteria as that long-haired Mersey group exhibits." And another charged the Queen's recognition of the Beatles had made the award a "farce".

The BEAT has learned that Prime Minister Harold Wilson has received a number of other complaints — some from high sources — about the decorations given to the Beatles.

But John, Paul, George and Ringo have not been left speechless by the furor.

"Duffy-Duddies"

George promptly called them complaining "Duffy - Duddies" and said if they don't like their medals they should turn them over to the foursome so they can give one to their manager, Brian Epstein.

Declared Ringo: "People are being childish. They can eat their medals for all I care."

Ringo added, "We never asked for the award. For once young people get an award. What's wrong with that?"

BEATLES AGAIN PROVE THEY'RE STRONG AS EVER

For approximately 18 months now, the Beatles have been going around setting precedents and breaking records like nobody's business. One of the toughest precedents they have set for themselves is selling enough copies to insure a gold record for each of their albums. In order to receive this coveted gold record, one million copies must be sold. To date, every single Beatle album released by Capitol Records has sold the necessary million.

The newest Beatle album, "Beatle VI", is not deviating one inch from the established Beatle tradition. After only five days of taking orders, the half-million mark was reached. And by the time the album was finally released on June 14, it had qualified for a gold record!

Who says the Beatles are losing popularity?

Best For Beatles

The Beatles are the best and they demand the best to go with them.

For their upcoming December special on BBC they have signed two of the top entertainers in the world. And they don't stick strictly to English entertainers either.

For this special they have signed an American, Henry Mancini, and an Englishman, Peter Sellers.

You always know that you're getting the best if it's a Beatle production.

PAUL McCARTNEY AND HIS FELLOW BEATLES haven't been doing any group work since their last U.S. tour but individually all but Ringo are keeping themselves quite busy. John is, of course, making a movie; George is growing a mustache and learning to play sitar; Ringo is playing with his baby boy. And Paul? Rumor has it he is the voice behind Donovan in "Mellow Yellow."

BEATLES ARCHIVES 1

BEATLES ARCHIVES 1

Making A Gold Record

By Derek Taylor

St. John's Wood is very much London. Solid and a little old. But nice and comfortable, and not yet shabby. The buildings have dignity and an elderly charm. And people still clean their windows.

If a horse-drawn cab clattered up Abbey Road, it wouldn't seem too unusual. Somewhere far away there is still a faint rustling of crinoline.

It is 2 o'clock in the afternoon in Abbey Road in St. John's Wood. The leaves are flickering from the sycamore trees, and George Harrison is late.

John Lennon's Rolls-Royce glides by and the blue uniformed doorman straightens his tie.

Teenagers Gather

Around the wrought-iron gates of the EMI Studios in St. John's Wood, flushed and flustered knots of teenagers gather, clutching ballpoint pens and rolled-up drawings, newspapers, magazines and autograph books.

Paul McCartney's Astin-Martin is snaking its way through the lunch-hour traffic of London's cholled West End. Paul is still battling his way. He isn't worried because he knows he won't be late. He never is.

And miles away, deep in the heart of the Surry countryside, George Harrison is trying to buy a swimming pool.

Ringo To Reality

Ringo Starr has just this minute passed his driving test and Bert, the Beatles' general chauffeur, is waiting by the huge black Austin Princess to take Ringo away from his dreams of Italian cars to the realities of the studio.

Another Beatle recording session is about to begin. Around the corner and only a few weeks away, lie a brace of golden discs, hundreds of thousands of dollars, and fresh glory in the perilous world of recordings.

Paul and John are usually early. Particularly Paul. He is the eager Beatle and, in any case, he has neither wife nor domestic involvements to hold him back.

Midnight Deadline

In the No. 2 Studio in St. John's Wood, the thin, stooping figure of George Martin is hunched over the control panel. He knows the Beatles may be a few minutes late, but he knows, too, that as an "A" side must be recorded by midnight, then an "A" side will be recorded by midnight.

Also, he knows it will be a worldwide hit. And this helps him to relax.

The doorman salutes John, who steps from his Rolls-Royce, says goodbye to his chauffeur — John doesn't drive yet — and walks with that curious, swift loping Beatle walk up the steps into the hallway of the cream-painted building.

"John," the fans wail plaintively, waving and dropping their pens and books, their pictures and magazines.

Professional Fans

Neil Aspinall, the taciturn Beatles road manager waves back. "He'll be back later, he assures them. Neil doesn't worry because he knows that these fans have three or four dozen sets of autographs already. They are the professional hunters—they have kept a vigil outside the studio and outside the Beatles' homes for the past eighteen months.

It is now 2:20 p.m., and George is still talking swimming pools in Surrey. Little Ringo bustles in from his Princess and joins John and Paul in the control room.

John tells him, "We've got the single, Ring."

And Ringo says, "Great." Which is the optimum in Beatle enthusiasm.

"It's Gear"

The single is called "I Feel Fine," and John says, "It's gear, except for one thing. We've got the phrase 'diamond ring' in again. But we can always change that."

I'm there, too, smoking and a little worried because a nervous photographer is waiting to take arty pictures of the Beatles' hands for a way-out European magazine.

The Beatles want to get on with their music, and I want them for pictures. Not a new dilemma.

How?

Curious how the Beatles get away with it. As someone once said of a great politician, "He can charm the birds out of the trees and yet remain, himself, totally unmoved."

George Martin knows the session must start soon and the Beatles, being basically diciplined people, get down to business. George has still not arrived but John and Paul have to get together on "I Feel Fine" because Paul has never heard the tune and there is no middle eight'.

Within minutes the two of them are leaping about the studio in delight. Paul says he is quite happy for "She's A Woman" to go on the "B" side. "I Feel Fine," he agrees, is a far more commercial number.

Where's George?

"Okay, Beatles," says George Martin amiably. "Let's have something on tape. Where's George?"

"Here, Mr. Martin," says George, unwrapping himself from a gigantic black wollen scarf. "I've got a gear swimming pool."

The four most expensive artists in the world are now in position in the spot where they first stood two-and-a-bit years ago to play the first tentative bars of a song called "Love Me Do." Which is where they and we all came in.

John Thrilled

One hour later, without studio musicians, without benefit of tricks or gimmicks, the next Beatle single is on tape. John is thrilled, because not only has a song—born that morning—grown into a fully developed recording, but he has achieved a unique effect on the first note.

Paul, it seems, has stepped between two pieces of equipment to produce a weird twanging sound. John, with his odd, off-beat view of life, thinks this is great. A hit with a differential, he says ?????.

And, of course, a few weeks later that twang will become world famous. And because the Beatles are exceptional, they were able to reproduce this sound on stage as well.

Beatles Happy

So, with an "A" side of a new single in the bag and the "B" established as "She's A Woman," the Beatles are now completely happy. Any other group would have settled for any one of the four or five songs already recorded "No Reply," "Eight Days A Week," "I Don't Want to Spoil the Party," or "I'm A Loser."

But the Beatles are not any other group, and their aim is to make every track on an album a potential single.

This is why they are great. This is why they are different. This is why they are millionaires.

Professionals

The atmosphere in the studio is marvelous. To watch the Beatles at work is to watch great sportsmen in an arena. It is — without overstating the case — like sitting in on a group of scientists talking about space, or time. They are total professionals and they could, no doubt, produce hits in somebodys back kitchen.

George Martin is thrilled with them, but because he is an austere Englishman, he plays it very cool. "Would the great and famous Beatles," he asks, "run through 'I Feel Fine' once again?"

Tea Time

"Yes," says John, "If the great and famous George Martin would let us have a cup of bloody tea."

The faithful Neil Aspinall shoots off for tea and for cheese sandwiches. And sitting in a corner, mending guitar strings and reading a detective novel, massive Mal Evans, the Beatles' equipment manager, smiles to himself. He turns to me and says, "This is when you get proud of them. They can be difficult but when you see how good they are, you forgive them everything."

You do!

BEATLES ARCHIVES 1

Beatles Split?... Epstein Mum

Three years after instigating an entire era, the Beatles are breaking up.

At least, that's the concensus among London music observers and those close to the princes of pop. The word came as a whisper at first, but subsequent statements by Brian Epstein and the Beatles themselves have given the speculation certainty.

National wire services broke the story last week, and when no one in the Beatles' organization denied it, more than 200 angry Beatles' fans picketed Epstein's London home in protest.

But not even the Beatles' manager, who probably hasn't seen his group en masse in nearly four months, could deny the story.

Instead, he pointed to the Beatles' forthcoming film as an indication the foursome would remain intact. John and Paul are writing the entire music score for the 1967 film, he pointed out.

But even the film will have a strange irony to it. Not once do all four Beatles appear simultaneously in the film.

Asked bluntly if the Beatles are breaking up, Epstein was quoted by an English newspaper as saying he'd have to call a special meeting with the Beatles to discuss their futures.

"That's silly," said a press spokesman, "he sees them all the time, he doesn't need to have a special meeting to discuss their future."

Epstein's ambiguous statements suddenly bore new significance as speculations of a Beatles break-up increased. His strangely worded refusal of an invitation for the Beatles to appear in a two-hour television spectacular to aid victims of the Aberfan slag-heap disaster was seen in a new light.

Although everyone from the Rolling Stones to Richard Burton and Elizabeth Taylor agreed to appear, Epstein refused, saying: "I know without consulting them the boys would feel unable to make an appearance of this sort for too many reasons to enumerate."

The following day, Epstein twisted out another ambiguous statement to the press. "The Beatles have changed their thoughts as their career has been *(Turn to Page 5)*

...THE BEATLES IN THE GOOD OLD DAYS WHEN THEY STILL WORKED TOGETHER!

BEATLES SPLIT..?

(Continued from Page 1)

altered by their attitudes in the past," he said. "Naturally, this pattern will continue.

"I'd be a fool to forecast exactly how it will be."

To anyone familiar with the Beatles' schedule during the past four months, the alleged break up will come as no surprise.

John has been in Spain filming his first effort without the other three Beatles. George was in India learning to play the sitar, his favorite instrument now. Ringo has been in and out of London and Paul is now taking a vacation abroad.

The four have kept it no secret in the last few months that they were disenchanted with group work and wanted to expand their individual talents. None of the Beatles would apparently be without a new field when the group splits.

John expresses distaste for the Beatles earlier, harder recordings. "Songs like 'Eight Days A Week' and 'She Loves You' sound like big drags to me now," he told an interviewer recently.

BEATLE COMMENTS:

JOHN LENNON: "I suppose we've got to go on being the four mop-tops. We've no intention of splitting up. We will go on recording."

GEORGE HARRISON: "We've had four years of doing what everybody else wants us to do. Everything the Beatles have done so far has been rubbish as I see it today. We're not kidding ourselves."

RINGO STARR sports a movie-type beard as he leaves London Airport for a vacation in the Caribbean. "It's just that I haven't been working and I haven't had to shave," he explained. "I hate shaving anyway." His wife, Maureen, and Mr. and Mrs. John Lennon were also on the trip.

Beatles Loafing Through First Six Months of Year

LONDON -- The Beatles are in such a high tax bracket they will practically loaf the first half of this year, according to *BEAT* informants.

George Harrison disclosed part of the story behind the relaxed schedule, stating that the famous foursome has not a single date fixed for all of 1966.

But friends explain that this is only because some details, now being negotiated, have not been completed. Manager Brian Epstein is now abroad arranging an American tour for late summer, although all details are not yet known.

However, *The BEAT* has learned that the Beatles are tentatively scheduled for concert dates in Los Angeles and San Francisco in August—approximately the same dates as last year's concerts.

PROPOSED BEATLE FILM 'NOT ABOUT POP GROUP'

Don't look for the Beatles' forthcoming movie to change their new image.

Because, once again, the Beatles won't be acting like Beatles.

Film Producer Walter Shenson arrived in California last week and though reluctant to talk about the long-awaited flick, admitted "it's not about a pop group."

"For over a year I've looked at ideas from distinguished writers and playwrights, but Owen Holder's two-page idea was the only one I—and the boys—liked," Shenson said.

Shenson said filming would "hopefully" begin in February.

BEATLES ARCHIVES 1

John Lennon–Then And Now

25¢

KRLA *Edition* **BEAT**

JUNE 3, 1967

BEATLES ARCHIVES 1

THE BEATLES POSE WITH ROAD MANAGERS, Neil Aspinall and Mal Evans, during recording of "Sgt. Pepper." For the full and exclusive details on how each track of the album was recorded. See Tony Barrow's report on page three and discover how John Lennon's young son helped his famous dad come-up with a song title.

THE TELEPHONE NEVER STOPS RINGING FOR THE BEATLES, even in remote areas such as this one where they filmed a portion of "HELP." Paul doesn't seem a bit surprised to find a ringing telephone hidden in the tall undergrowth — but he was a little peeved to discover the call was for someone else.

BEATLES ARCHIVES 1

BEAT EXCLUSIVE
A Behind The Scenes Story Of Beatles' 'Sgt. Pepper'

By Tony Barrow

LONDON—On the first day of February THE BEATLES began to record a song called "SGT. PEPPER'S LONELY HEARTS CLUB BAND." Paul had contributed the basic ideas for the number so Paul was assigned to handle the main vocal action—with the others joining him for the chorus segments. To add instrumental effect an actual "Lonely Hearts Club Band" was formed—for one time only! It consisted of four horn players, all true and tried session musicians.

Centerpiece

At that point "Sgt. Pepper" was just one of twelve new compositions in line for inclusion on The Beatles' first album of 1967. A couple of weeks later the group began to think of tentative program titles for the finished production. Gradually they began to talk in terms of making "Sgt. Pepper" the centrepiece of the whole thing—a sort of *Lonely Hearts Club Band Show* which would open up with the "Sgt. Pepper" number and, eventually, get back to the same song towards the end.

From here on everything was based on this theme. Instead of being "banded" or broken up into individual tracks, the album would be virtually continuous with no more than a split second of silence between the end of one item and the beginning of the next one. In fact "Sgt. Pepper" runs straight thru into Ringo's solo vocal called "With A Little Help From My Friends," the instrumental link being provided by producer George Martin playing the organ!

Repeat

"Audience reaction" noises were put in behind the "Sgt. Pepper" number, giving an effect resembling that of a live show recording. And before the very last number on Side Two there's a repeat performance of "Sgt. Pepper's Lonely Hearts Club Band" with the same tune, different words, no horn quartet but everyone joining in the vocal and more audience sounds superimposed upon the finished recording.

Before I go any further let me give you an exclusive pre-release run-down on all the other items. After Ringo's specialty number comes "Lucy In The Sky With Diamonds," a title suggested to John by his own son, Julian, who came home from school with a painting he'd just done and claimed that it represented precisely that! John is lead singer and you can hear Paul playing Hammond organ.

Other numbers in which John takes the lead vocal are "Being For The Benefit Of Mr. Kite" (includes quartet of harmonicas played by Ringo, George, Neil Aspinall and Mal Evans), "Good Morning, Good Morning" (which has saxophones, trombones and French horn played by Sounds Inc.) and "A Day In The Life" (in which Paul looks after the solo singing in the middle segment and a 41-piece orchestra provides the series of three fantastic instrumental climax points).

John and Paul are jointly involved in the vocal for "She's Leaving Home" (in which harps and strings form the accompaniment and The Beatles are not heard at all instrumentally).

George Alone

George has a typically off-beat item all to himself—he wrote "Within You, Without You" and he sings it. The other Beatles are not featured at all and the instrumental backing is of strongly Indian influence featuring three tambouras, a dilruba, a tabla, a zither-like Indian table-harp, three cellos and eight violins. George brought a bunch of Indian friends into the session to play the colourful assortment of instruments—and, of course, George himself is featured as solo sitarist as well as tamboura player!

Items in which Paul plays the main role so far as singing is concerned are "Sgt. Pepper's Lonely Hearts Club Band," "Getting Better" (where George plays tamboura), "Fixing A Hole" (with Paul on harpsichord), "When I'm 64" and "Lovely Rita" (Paul plays piano; John, Paul and George add special effects with combs and paper).

Incidentally Paul got the idea for "Lovely Rita, Meter Maid" from an American visitor who pointed out to him that the young women we call female traffic wardens are known as meter maids on your side of the Atlantic!

So there are twelve new numbers in all—with one of them being heard twice. The longest performances—each just over five minutes—are "A Day In The Life" and "Within You, Without You."

The creation of the very elaborate album cover shows just as much imaginative thinking as the music contained within it. The cover is one of those spectacular open-out jobs with a giant 24-inch by 12-inch colour photograph spread across the inside. For the album cover photographs The Beatles wore specially tailored "Sgt. Pepper" uniforms made up from vivid personally selected satin materials—with lavish braid, equally bright hats and orange and yellow patent leather shoes.

What about the FRONT of the album cover? That's quite amazing in its own way too but you'll see what I mean when Capitol issues "Sgt. Pepper's Lonely Hearts Club Band." For once I understand that every detail of the recordings and the cover will be duplicated precisely by Parlophone in Britain and Capitol in America.

One particularly welcome feature of the cover so far as album collectors are concerned will be the reproduction of all the lyrics in full on the back space. This means that Beatle People wanting the words of all the new songs but NOT the actual music will have the information without paying separately for copies of the sheet music.

More personal effort by The Beatles has gone into the preparation and production of "Sgt. Pepper" than any previous album they've recorded. On other occasions, even if just as much concentration has gone into the music content, there hasn't been the opportunity for John, Paul, George and Ringo to follow thru and take such a close interest in the album cover and other details. Usually they've finished their recording sessions to meet a deadline and gone away on a concert tour. This time they stayed in London and supervised all stages of the album's preparation prior to release.

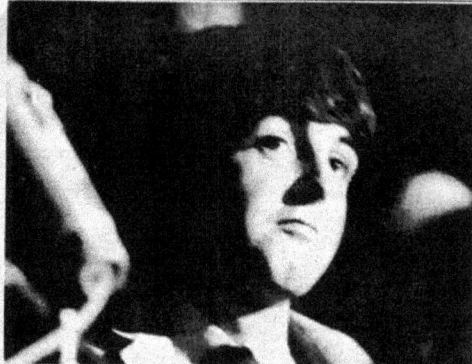

PAUL McCARTNEY — On the Pop Festival Board of Governors.

KRLA Helps Present Monterey Pop Festival

Radio KRLA, along with Lou Adler, Donovan, Paul McCartney, Terry Melcher, Brian Wilson, Mick Jagger, Jim McGuinn, Johnny Rivers, Paul Simon, Abe Somer, Smokey Robinson, Andrew Oldham and Alan Pariser will present the Monterey International Pop Festival on June 16, 17 and 18.

To be held on the Monterey County Fairgrounds, the Festival will include a number of exhibits, booths and workshops in addition to the concert.

Prices range from $6.50 to $3.00 (See page 16), and accommodations can be obtained by writing to the Monterey Peninsula Chamber of Commerce, Box 489, Monterey, California or phoning (408) 375-2252.

June 16, with a concert featuring The Association, Buffalo Springfield, Grateful Dead, Jimi Hendrix Experience, Laura Nyro, Lou Rawls and Simon & Garfunkel. Saturday afternoon, at 1:30 p.m., the following acts will perform: Big Brother & The Holding Company, The Mike Bloomfield Thing, Paul Butterfield Blues Band, Canned Heat, Country Joe And The Fish, Hugh Masekela, Steve Miller Blues Band, and the Quicksilver Messenger Service.

Saturday evening will feature The Beach Boys, Booker T and the MG's, The Byrds, Jefferson Airplane, Hugh Masekela, Moby Grape and Otis Redding.

Sunday afternoon Ravi Shankar will give a special performance.

Sunday night, the concert will include The Blues Project, The Impressions, The Mamas & Papas, Johnny Rivers, Dionne Warwick and The Who.

The Beatles' English tour was a smashing success but their fans have definitely changed. They don't seem to scream so much anymore. Instead they listen.

When the Beatles staged their triumphant return to Liverpool they got the shock of their lives. Naturally, their concert was a complete sell-out but when they appeared on stage they were *not* greeted with screaming hysteria.

No, even The 'Pool has matured. The overflow audience welcomed the Beatles home with thunderous *applause*. The Beatles didn't quite know what to make of it but after a few songs they came to the conclusion that the fans still loved 'em. Only now they want to hear them as well as see them! Think that will ever happen Stateside?

Speaking of the Beatles, their father-figure Brian Epstein has been confined to bed for three weeks suffering from yellow jaundice. The illness forced Epstein to cancel a visit to the U.S. to negotiate the sale of the taped Beatles' show at Shea Stadium.

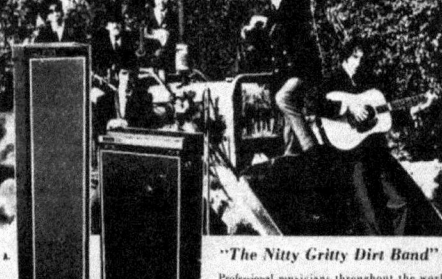

...JOHN LENNON

BEATLES ARCHIVES 1

BEAT EXCLUSIVE

The Chief Beatle – Thru His

By Louise Criscione

John Lennon is the head Beatle. Make no mistake about that. The only question is whether Lennon is best known for his talent or for the quotes he has given the press. And since we're a press-oriented society, the answer is probably the latter.

Lennon was the first Beatle to have his name connected with his face in the minds of fans when the Beatles first appeared on "Ed Sullivan" and the message flashed across Lennon's televised figure: "Sorry, girls, he's married."

Hidden Wife

What American fans didn't know was that while the Beatles were climbing up the elusive ladder of success in England, Lennon's wife, Cynthia, had been carefully hidden.

"I haven't deliberately hidden her from the public," declared John when the "secret" was out. "But I have tried to keep her away from the press. I don't see why they should treat her like a freak just because she married a Beatle."

Perhaps even then the press knew Lennon was a man to be reckoned with. At any rate, neither Cynthia nor the Lennon's baby son were ever treated as "freaks."

As a matter of fact, the press and fans alike thought Lennon and the Beatles could do no wrong. Their careers went jubilently along with more broken sales and attendance records than possibly any entertainer has ever or will ever again be able to achieve.

Lennon was anything but silent during this period, but his statements then did not cause bonfires. On the subject of fan letters, Lennon commented: "You want to see the letters the Japanese write us. You wouldn't believe it. Better than the ones we get from America. You wouldn't believe them either! A lot of American fans are just plain illiterate. You can hardly make out what they're all about."

It wasn't until the Beatles were awarded MBE's that the first hint of uproar reared its head. Beatle fans, were, of course, delighted that their idols had been chosen for MBE's. But some of their fellow award-holders were verbally horrified. Said one war hero: "English royalty wants *me* on the same level as those vulgar nincompoops."

"Better Than Killing"

To which, Lennon answered: "We got ours for entertaining people. Isn't that better than getting it for killing people? But I guess you can't expect everyone to luv us."

Lennon refused to remain undaunted by the uproar, however, and let his wit shine through when he said: "I don't think we got ours for rock 'n' roll. On that basis, we'd have got OBE's (a higher award) and the Rolling Stones MBE's. I reckon we got them for exports and the citation ought to have said that!"

Asked what he planned to do with his MBE, John replied: "I think I'll have mine made into a bell push so that people have to press it when they come to the house."

The first major batch of "Beatlemania dying" rumors were caused by the "greeting" the Beatles received at the Roman airport in July, 1965. One hundred and 50 policemen turned up to protect the Beatles from their enthusiastic fans – the hitch being that only nine fans showed up to greet the Beatles, all of whom were British! The news media had great fun with that one and couldn't refrain from speculating as to the future of the Beatles.

Mob Scene

The fun died a few days later on July 29, 1965 when the Royal premiere of the Beatles' second movie, "Help," was held at the London Palladium in Picadilly Circus. The Beatles were almost mobbed by a 10,000-strong guard of fans. Fourteen ambulances had to be called to carry the injured to hospitals for first aid.

Rumors die hard but by August most people had forgotten that they had only weeks earlier predicted the "end of Beatlemania" and the Beatles were once again "as hot as ever!"

Especially when they arrived on U.S. soil for their cross-country tour in August of '65. Press conferences were held at the Beatle stop-offs and it was Lennon again who received the most attention from inquiring reporters. And again, Lennon let the world in on his quick wit and sometimes-cutting, sometimes-acid, but mostly marvelous humor.

Someone asked him what he thought of Sid Bernstein, the promoter of the Beatles' New York shows, and Lennon replied: "I think 'West Side Story' is his best work."

On the subject of his newly-acquired contact lenses, John quipped: "They're marvelous! I can see things like bus stops and garden gates!"

Serious Lennon

John did, however, become serious when asked about the Beatles' music and about the wave of protest songs which were then hitting the charts.

"There are only about 100 people in the world who really understand what our music is all about," said Lennon. "We try to find a truth for ourselves, a real feeling. You can never communicate your complete emotion to other people but if we can convey just a little of what we feel, then we have achieved something."

On protest songs Lennon spoke frankly: "If there is anything I hate it is labels such as this (protest). The 'protest' label in particular means absolutely nothing – it's just something that the press has latched onto and as usual is flogged to death. Some of the songs which appear to come under this heading are simply good songs – some are not. But, personally, I have no time for the 'Eve Of Destruction' songs."

Stands Straight

Throughout the Beatles' 1965 U.S. visit, Lennon refused to bend to the Establishment whenever he felt they were wrong or out of place. At a Chicago press conference, a distinguished gentleman approached Lennon and haughtily informed him: "I am the acting British Consul General. Are you doing a good job for your country?" "Yes," snapped Lennon. "Are you?"

Returning to England following a highly successful U.S. tour, John Lennon remarked on it only by saying: "The weather's too hot and someone's pinched three of me shirts!"

The Bad Year

No doubt the Beatles will never forget 1966. The first six months of the year were great for them. Their first working date was not until May 1 when they appeared at Wembley Empire Pool outside of London.

After that all hell broke loose. The first thing to go wrong was the original cover of "Yesterday And Today." The Beatles posed in butchers' outfits with decapitated doll heads and raw meat surrounding them. Advance reaction was highly unfavorable and Capitol quickly changed covers at a reported cost of $250,000.

But instead of getting better, thing's got decidely worse. The Beatles visited Manila in July of '66 and received the first physical maltreatment of their careers. They failed to show up for a luncheon appointment with the First Lady of the country and furious Filipinos sent them off at the airport with kicks, curses and shouts of "get out of our country." Practically all police protection and special considerations were cancelled and the tax bureau threatened for a time to hold up the group's departure.

Apology

The Beatles declared that they had not received the invitation in time to attend but nevertheless Paul, on behalf of the group, apologized. Lennon was not so polite as he told the press: "I didn't even know they had a President." And George let the cat out of the bag when he said: "We're going to have a couple of weeks to recuperate before we go and get beaten up by the Americans."

The Beatles had no way of knowing then that the worse was yet to come. It came in the form of a comment from John Lennon that "The Beatles are more

Controversies

popular than Jesus." The uproar that ensued in America could be heard around the world as a wave of Beatle bonfires, radio station bannings of Beatle records and whispered warnings that the Beatles were certain to get hurt if they tried to make their scheduled tour of America broke out across the country.

Hurried Flight

Epstein made a hurried flight to the U.S. to attempt to calm the roar. Lennon made a formal announcement that the quote had been taken completely out of context, which it had. However, when the Beatles arrived in the U.S. Lennon publically apologized—repeatedly. Still, reporters seemed to get some sort of twisted satisfaction out of making him explain and apologize again and again and again.

When the Beatles held a press conference in L.A., it was the first question asked. "I've explained it 800 times and I think it should be clear," said a tired and disgusted Lennon.

"Well, you made an apology before," snapped the reporter, "can't you say it again?"

"No," answered John, "I can't because I can't remember what I said. Look, I could have used television or anything else. I used the Beatles because that's what I know the best."

Thru the Fire

They dragged Lennon through the fire and they just wouldn't let him go. A middle-aged lady stood up and demanded to know if John was really and truly sorry he had said such a thing, even if he was only using the Beatles as an example.

"I am, yes," said John in an almost-whisper. "Even though I didn't mean it that way, I'm sorry I ever opened my mouth."

But back in England, John snapped out of it and announced: "I hope to get to see more of America because it's the kind of place that might blow up someday by itself, or with the help of some other country."

So, Lennon was still Lennon—despite all the controversy. And thank God he is. Can you imagine what a world it would be if everyone was afraid to open his or her mouth and express their opinions and ideas?

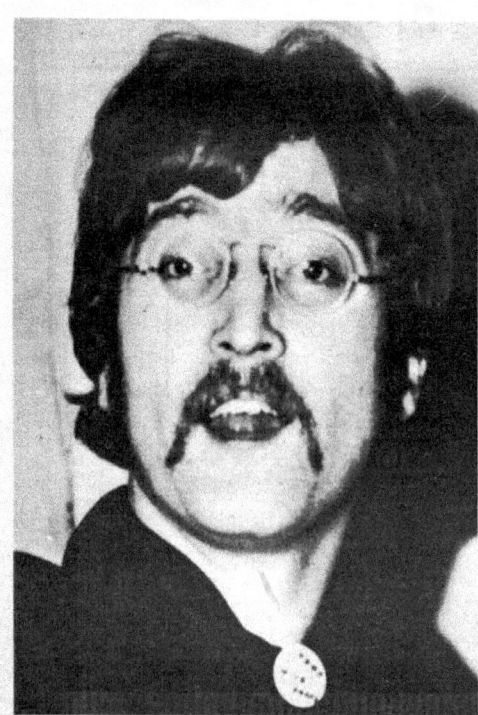

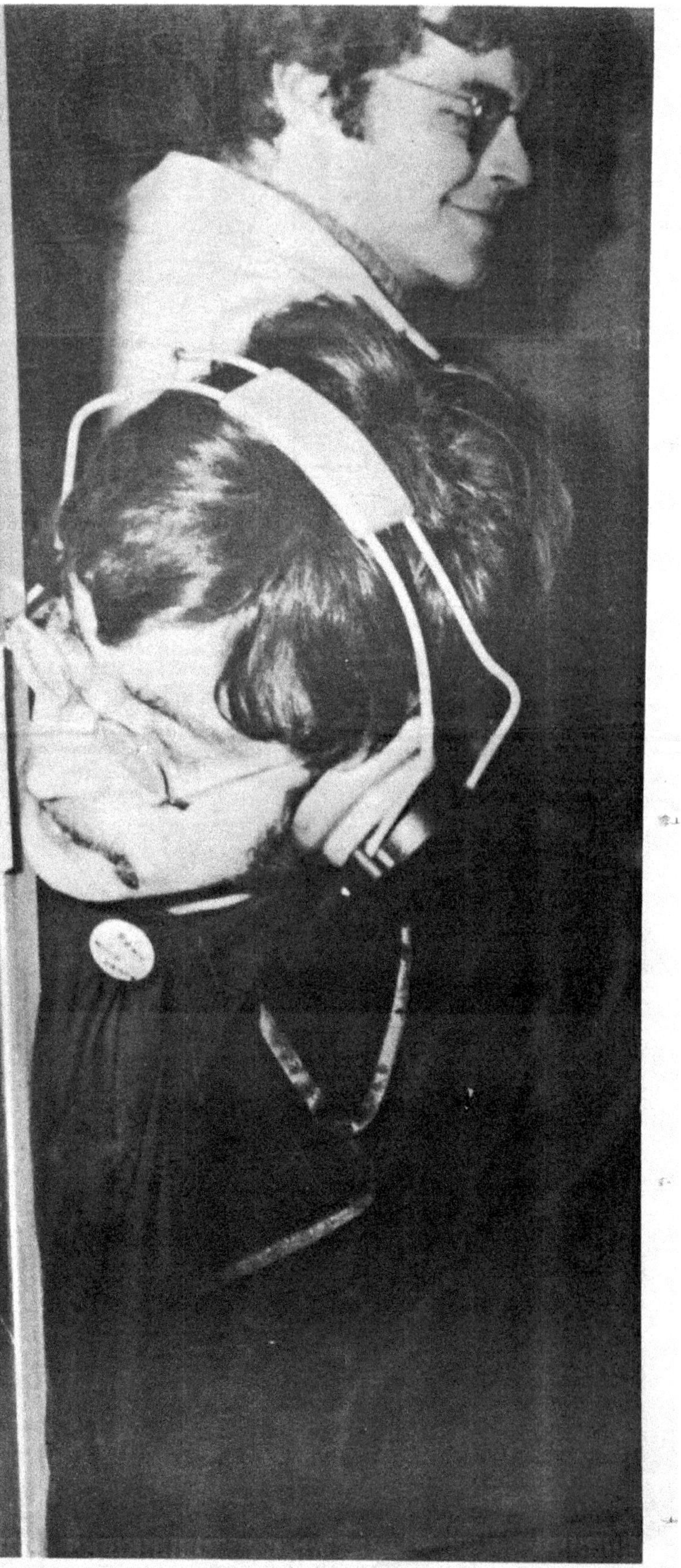

BEATLES ARCHIVES 1

Paul McCartney With 48 Per Cent

By Shirley Poston

The Beatles Survey compiled by April Orcutt of Tustin, Calif. and printed in Shirley Poston's "For Girls Only" column shows Paul to be the most popular Beatle.

He received almost 50% of the votes, followed by George with less than 25%, then John and finally Ringo.

"Yesterday" proved to be the most popular Beatle song with "Mr. Moonlight" the least popular and "Help" showed up as more popular than "Hard Day's Night."

From comments received over 80% of the readers who responded feel the Beatles will last "forever."

Following are the questions and answers along with many of the comments received.

The opinions found in the parentheses are those of April's and not necessarily either Shirley's or *The BEAT'S*.

1. Who is your favorite Beatle and why?

PAUL — 48%. Reasons: cute - friendly - sweet - enjoys life - sense of humor - has that "something" - bouncy - his looks at John - sad and sexy voice - witty - big, droopy eyes.

GEORGE — 24%. Reasons: mysterious - good looking - polite - takes music seriously - accent - lonely eyes - tall, thin, sexy body - thick, tousled mop - big feet.

JOHN — 21%. Reasons: Handsome - warm - fascinating - wit - sexy - clever - mature - humorous - can feel it from head to toe when you look at him.

RINGO — 7%. Reasons: cute, especially his nose - funny - serious - sad blue eyes - neat smile - lifts our spirits.

2. What is your favorite Beatle song?

Winners were (1) "Yesterday," (2) "And I Love Her," (3) "Michelle," (4) "She Loves You," (5) "We Can Work It Out."

(Turn to Page Fourteen)

BEATLES BACK TWIGGY FILM

LONDON — Twiggy is venturing forth into new areas of exploration. Deciding that modeling was too limiting for the slender 18 year old, her friend and mentor, Justin de Villneuve announced that Twiggy is embarking on a movie career.

Her first film will be a fairy tale based on Nobel Prize winner William Faulkner's short stories called *The Wishing Tree*. In the film, Twiggy is reported to be playing a very young boy. The film is being produced by the Beatles new corporation, Apple.

Beatle Poll Shows Paul The Favorite

(Continued from Page 1)

3. What is your least favorite Beatle song?

Losers were (1) "Mr. Moonlight," (2) "Act Naturally," (3) "Matchbox."

4. Why do you like the Beatles?

Continually original - not phonies - fab composers - very talented - lovable - entertaining - care about fans - warm - witty - magnetic - cheer us up - enjoy themselves - deserving - great performers and people - little things they do - faith to stick with it when all was against them - "make you feel great just being alive" - something in their eyes that says "I care" - "They don't go around shouting 'I can't get no girlie action'" (*I love that answer*) - "I'd have been so much the poorer had I never known the ecstasy, warmth and magic of loving a Beatle" (how true!!!!).

5. What other groups do you like?

Winners in the order of their appearance were Herman's Hermits, the Rolling Stones, the Byrds the Animals and Sonny & Cher.

6. What is your opinion of the movie "A Hard Day's Night?"

The majority loved it; 9% liked it better than "Help," 6% didn't like it and 3% didn't see it. Comments: fantastic - sheer magic - new and fresh - one of a kind - full of charm and quick wit - no plot but certainly sufficient for us Beatlemaniacs - more emotional than "Help" - showed their true greatness - "rapid transport to utter bliss" - a photographic masterpiece - "stunk" (that's sure not *my* opinion.)

7. What is your opinion of the movie "Help?"

Again, the majority loved the film. 26% liked it better than "HDN" and only 5% of those who replied hadn't seen it.

Comments: exciting - imaginative - original - thrilling - marv - wild - great hidden lines - never knew what would come next - better acting and photography - "fantastic when you see it, but you can't quite believe it when it's over."

8. Which Beatle do you think is the best actor?

John — 40%, Ringo — 29%, Paul — 25%, George — 6%.

9. Which Beatle do you think has the best singing voice?

Paul — 49%, John — 31%, George — 16%, Ringo — 4%.

10. Do you think you'll still like the Beatles when and if Paul and George get married? (At the time the survey started, George was still a bachelor.)

Yes — 97%, maybe — 2%, no — 1%.

11. Why or why not?

"They've made us so happy we can't deny them happiness — impossible to stop loving them and to ignore their talent — we'll be happy if they're happy — marriage won't change their looks, personalities, songs, voices or humor ... only the last names of their fave girls — John and Ringo are married and are still number one — it's their business, not ours — we can't all marry them — "why let some other girl spoil all MY fun?"

12. Do you think the Beatles will last?

FOREVER! — 85%, For A Few Years — 10%, No — 5%.

13. Why or why not?

Always original and a bit ahead of the rest — versatile — totally unique — talent always lasts — their records keep improving — their music has made a lasting impression — "they've lasted this long ... why not longer?" — are loved by so many — entertainers in the true sense of the word — have an enduring quality — not always on top but will be around — "In MY heart they'll last" — "Who wants to worship a person 50 years old?" (*I do!!!!*) — "Everything has to end ... too bad, that's life."

14. What do your parents think of the Beatles?

39% like them, 25% tolerate them, 12% dislike them. In 24% of the cases, the mother likes them but the father doesn't.

Comments: "They try not to like them" — "My parents don't appreciate good music" — "Dad knew they'd go far" — like them more than Elvis — don't like their screaming fans.

Parents' Comments: "They're okay if you can hear them" — "George has a needs-to-be-mothered look" — "I wish they'd go back to England and stay there" — "Give me a pair of scissors and five minutes."

15. Which Beatle is the you-know-whattiest?

JOHN — UNANIMOUSLY!!!!

BEATLES ARCHIVES 1

Here Come The British!

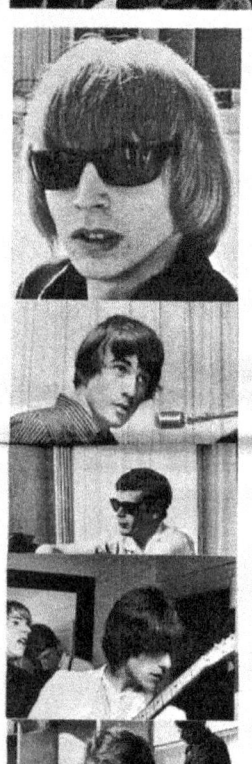

By Louise Criscione

Better get ready, the second tidal wave of British recording artists is set to hit Stateside throughout the summer months. One after the other (and sometimes together) the English groups will be landing on American soil to the delight of their fans and the terror of their parents.

Leading the parade will be the Yardbirds — *if* they can get into the country, that is! Last time around the Yardbirds almost succeeded in getting themselves deported and were then told not to count on coming Stateside again. However, they hope things will be straightened out enough to allow them into the country for a mammoth show at Yankee Stadium on June 10.

The Dave Clark Five kick off their *fifth* U.S. tour on June 12 with yet another appearance on "Ed Sullivan," followed by a cross-country string of personal appearances.

Stoned In June

The first of the big Three, the Rolling Stones, invade the U.S. on June 29 for a tour scheduled to last 20 days. Dates already set, include Los Angeles, New York, San Francisco, Chicago and Detroit. As usually happens when the Stones reach L.A., they will utilize the RCA Studios in Hollywood for recording sessions.

Herman's Hermits and the Animals will be making a joint tour of the U.S., arriving shortly after the Stones. The double-headlined bill starts its run in Hawaii on July 1 and as of now winds up on August 8 (for a complete itinerary of the tour see last week's *BEAT*.)

It should be interesting to see which tour will draw the biggest crowds and the most publicity — Herman/Animals or the Rolling Stones? Judging from past tours, one would have to give the edge to the Stones, who seem to have a natural talent for making headlines, evoking riots and smashing attendance records. *But* Herman certainly hasn't done badly for himself either — on his last tour, he broke attendance records in twelve cities.

The Animals, on the other hand, have enjoyed neither wide publicity nor a long string of broken gate records. I can't imagine why the press hasn't paid more attention to Eric Burdon. He is one of the most controversial and outspoken entertainers today and can certainly provide some of the most interesting interviews ever read.

Bent Minds In July

Arriving Stateside the same day as Herman and company will be the Mindbenders, those "Groovy Kind Of Love" guys. To begin their five week U.S. tour on July 1 with the majority of their dates set for colleges and state fairs. It's rather a novel concept in summertime tours but that's the way the Mindbenders obviously want it — so that's the way it's going to be. It stands to either set a new trend in tours or prove to be the biggest bomb of the summer. The month of July will provide the verdict.

While the Stones, DC5, Herman, the Animals and the Mindbenders are thinking of winding up their respective tours, the Hollies will be embarking upon their second major U.S. tour July 28.

When the Hollies landed in London last week from their just-completed U.S. tour (which was plagued with problems from the minute they set foot in the country until they boarded their London-bound jet at Los Angeles International Airport) they discovered that they have been set to return Stateside for over a month.

The Hollies will remain in the U.S. until September 4 with their time spent here in concerts, ballroom appearances, club dates and television shows. We at *The BEAT* heard the Holly news with decidedly mixed reactions. We've only just managed to get things back to normal around here — and now they're coming back!

Beatles In August

Two short weeks after the Hollies arrive, the Beatles' plane will touch down in Chicago spilling out John, Paul, George and Ringo for their third American summer tour beginning August 12.

Cities to be hit by the Beatles this time around include Detroit, Washington, Philadelphia, Boston, Memphis, New York, San Francisco and Los Angeles.

September is the month set aside for your recuperation — but it's also the month you should again replenish your supply of cash for a quick trip to Las Vegas in October.

And just who is going to be in Vegas in October? Tom Jones — the office hero!! Tom is set for a four week stint at Caesar's Palace beginning the end of October (how's that for clarity?) If you can't possibly swing a Vegas trip in October, don't worry. Tom will play two more month-long engagements at Caesar's during the next year.

You may now consider yourself duly warned of what is in store for you this summer — a fantastic time! Never have so many top British groups played the States in so short a time span — it ought to drive your parents out of their minds!

BEATLES ARCHIVES 1

Like And Dislike About Americans

..."IS MY HEARING OFF, or are these reporters soft?"

..."AFTER ALL, they're paying the money."

..."WELL, it's cold in London."

By Gil McDougall

The Beatle press conference was going very well. It was already half over and both the press and the Beatles seemed pleased and in good humour. So far all of the reporters except one had stuck to asking sensible questions. The one exception seemed to have suicidal tendencies as all of his somewhat absurd questions were directed at John Lennon.

The reporter asked John one foolish question after another. Usually John made an attempt to answer, but it was obvious that his temper was becoming frayed at the edges and his answers were becoming very sarcastic indeed. Paul McCartney tried to help out by jumping in and answering some of the questions that the man directed at Lennon.

A reporter that the Beatles respected then stood up and asked John: "Are you writing a book at this time?" John grinned and answered: "No, not right at the moment, I'm talking to you."

"You"

Everybody laughed, and then the man with the suicidal tendencies stood up and said to Lennon: "What is it that you dislike most about America?" Quick as a wink John flashed back the answer: "YOU."

People like this, who apparently find it impossible to believe that Beatle fans could be interested in anything other than what kind of toothpaste the boys use, are very high on the four Liverpool lads list of dislikes.

During a press conference the press usually assumes that the Beatles are too busy answering queries to notice one individual reporter. The truth is that the four actually get a kick out of singling out the reporters that they consider to be intelligent enough to warrant a fair answer.

There are many things that the Beatles like about America and most of their problems during a tour are very minor. When you attend a Beatle concert you most probably go there and scream your lungs out. The Beatles consider this situation from two viewpoints.

Without Screams

In the first place they couldn't care less how much you scream or yell. They feel that if this indicates your enjoyment, then their visit to your town has been more than worthwhile. Paul was asked about the noise during a performance and he said: "The fans pay their money to come in and if they want to scream then that's their perogative. We don't mind if they scream. Why should we. The only thing that counts is that they are having a good time for their money." Paul continued: "Anyway five years ago we were playing without the screams, and friend, it wasn't half as nice. I mean the bread is important too y'know."

All of the other Beatles concurred with Paul, and John had something to say on the other view point of the fantastic noise that happens at all Beatle performances: "We can be heard if there is a decent mike system. Most of the people responsible for the concerts just don't want to spend the money necessary. In Atlanta they had a real good system. The fans screamed just as loudly, but they also heard us because of the superior equipment. We don't mind the screaming at all if it's what the fans want. After all they are paying the money, but it *is* possible for the kids to hear us and scream at us at the same time. Atlanta was great. Our best American concert yet."

The Beatles really get a kick out of seeing how loyal their fans are, but there are some things about the scene that they wouldn't be sorry to see go. Perhaps number one would be the objects fanatical fans chuck at the stage. The boys don't mind you crowding around the stage (providing that nobody gets hurt as so often happened during the 1965 tour) but they really would appreciate it if you would stop throwing things at them. Those items that you chuck so lovingly could cause one of the group a permanent injury.

Mostly though the Beatles love America as much as America loves the Beatles—and that is really going some! Before starting their 1965 trip they were a little concerned about rumours that they were dead in the U.S. However, the way in which these false stories were quickly dispelled pleased them very much. It is doubtful that there will be a reoccurance of the same situation. The Beatles have proved that they are here to stay and in 1966 the rumours will never get off the ground.

Meeting El

They all really enjoyed their stay in California. One big spot during their stay in Los Angeles was their meeting with Elvis Presley. All four got a kick out of that. Even though they were supposed to be resting up in L.A., Paul and George took time out to visit a recording session that the Byrds were doing. One funny part of the tour was that the Beatles met more fans than anyone had ever expected.

These are the kind of incidents that made the Beatles like America. Fans and stars alike, all were welcomed into the Beatles' house if it was at all possible. They enjoyed just meeting Americans because this was the best way possible to get to know America. And Americans enjoyed meeting the Beatles, even if they had to do it in a concert hall. It was as if four of the greatest friends of their life had just come to make their annual visit to town. And they were, and they did, and they will again this year.

KRLA BEAT

Volume 1, Number 25   LOS ANGELES, CALIFORNIA   15 Cents   September 4, 1965

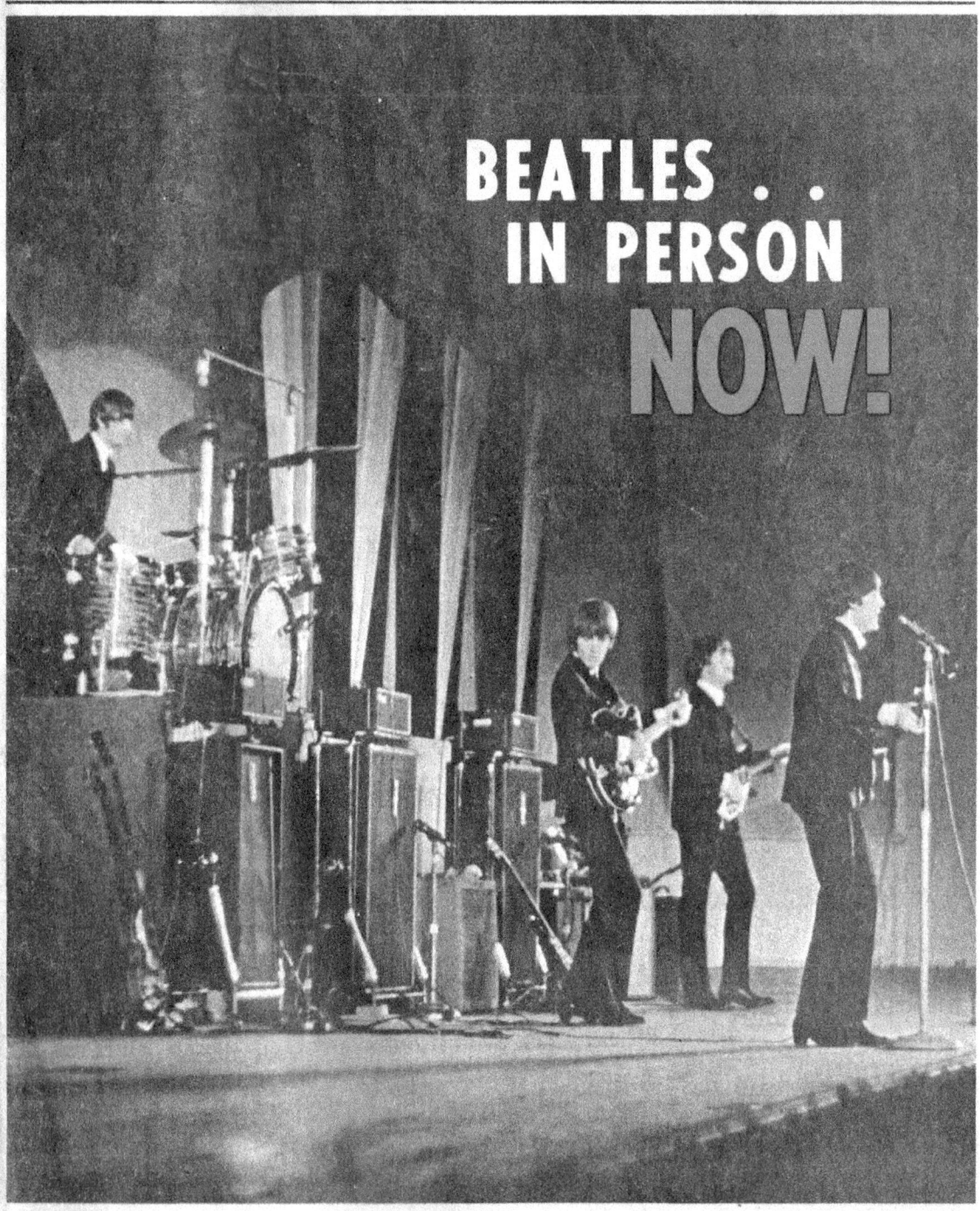

BEATLES..
IN PERSON
NOW!

BEATLES ARCHIVES 1

"HELLLLPP" . . . RINGO GETS A CHARGE OUT OF MOVIE ROLE

NEIGHBORS UPSET
George Has Problems With His Home Life

By LOUISE CRISCIONE

Those of you planning on traipsing to England to visit George Harrison had better beware — George's neighbors are furious!

Too many of George's devoted fans have been driving, walking, or hitch-hiking out to his house in hopes of at least capturing a fleeting glimpse of the distinguished Mr. Harrison M.B.E.

That was all fine and good (at least from the fans' standpoint) but in the process of tracking down George, his fans have also been trampling down all of his neighbors' petunias, chysanthemums and daisies.

All in all, since George's advent there has been nothing but trouble in that particular corner of the once quiet and reserved Surrey countryside.

His patient neighbors stood the noise, the trampled flowers and the wailing girls for quite awhile. They didn't dig it, but they they hoped that maybe if they just avoided it, it would go away.

Neighbors Explode

So they gritted their teeth and waited and waited AND waited. But each day only brought another horde of fans and another patch of trampled petunias.

It was inevitable — the spark finally reached the dynamite and the neighbors exploded. They held a kind of block meeting to chart their course of action.

Everyone spoke his piece and after hours of deliberation a decision was reached: War was officially declared on all George Harrison fans!

Neighbors' Union

Near-by neighbors banded together in a sort of Neighbors' Union which organized complete with by-laws and the whole thing. And the very first by-law instructed all to summon the police at the first sign of anything which looked suspiciously like it might be a Beatle fan.

Anyway, we just thought we'd warn you. The Neighbors Union is now in full operation — so don't visit George. And if you're abroad and determined to visit him anyway, then at least make sure that you don't look to much like a Beatle fan.

Oh, and one more thing — please be careful about trampling George's neighbors' petunias, chrysanthmums and daisies.

LOOKING AHEAD
Will Beatles Return? They Came This Year

Beatlemania is made up of many things. One of them is anticipation.

We wait breathlessly for them to come to America. When they arrive we're overjoyed to see them, but we start waiting for them to come back again long before they even leave our country.

The Beatles have just arrived in California, and we are already wondering when we'll get to see them again. And some of us aren't just wondering when. We're wondering IF.

The arguments against a third tour are reasonably sound. Beatlemania has become permanent. The Beatles need never worry about their popularity dying, and no longer have to work so inhumanly hard at being the world's star attraction.

It makes sense. The Beatles have every right to stop rushing all over the globe, and nothing to lose if they choose to take a well-deserved rest on their laurels.

But if this possibility is worrying you, stop and remember how long ago the concrete of Beatlemania hardened.

Was it before plans for this present tour were cemented? Or was it after?

It was before. When the Beatles returned from America in 1964, they had our country in the palms of their hands. And they still do.

The Beatles don't have to be here next year. But don't let it keep you up nights. They don't have to be here this year either.

If you want to start waiting for Beatles 1966, feel free to. We started weeks ago!

FLANKED BY PROFILES of John (left) and Paul (right), Beatles' manager Brian Epstein (facing camera) and KRLA's Bob Eubanks iron out final details in preparations for the Beatles' eagerly-awaited concerts at The Hollywood Bowl.

Huge Crowds Expected At Beatle Film

"Help," a most unsuitable term for the Beatles' second movie financially speaking, has opened in theatres across the United States to rave reviews and bulging box office registers.

From the initial box office returns in both the U.S. and England, "Help" is running way ahead of the Beatles' first movie, "A Hard Day's Night," so far as the gross intake is concerned.

KRLA Scoops

The technicolor Beatles opened their citywide engagement on September 1 — but, of course, KRLA helped 500 of you Beatle fans drool at the Fab Four at an exclusive premiere at the Carthay Circle Theatre on August 23 — thus scooping everyone else in Los Angeles by a full nine days!

By giving KRLA the Los Angeles premiere of "Help"; and by allowing us to present them at the Hollywood Bowl for two years in a row (despite many other offers), it looks as though the Beatles are trying to tell us something — like KRLA is the number one Beatle station in the whole world!

BEATLES ARCHIVES 1

WE GOT YOU BACK AGAIN!

BEATLES ARCHIVES 1

McCallum to Record Lennon's Poems

Hey, it's finally happened — The Beatles have joined U.N.C.L.E.! Now, don't go getting excited — no, John, Paul, George and Ringo aren't coming over here to film an episode of our favorite television show.

In fact, one of the men from U.N.C.L.E. is going over there to pull off a deal with John Lennon. David "Illya" McCallum is going to England to cut an album for Capitol of, are you ready for this, John Lennon's poetry.

The album was originally set to be cut here in America but it was switched to London so McCallum can do it at the same time he's filming "Three Bites of the Apple."

Done By June

The filming starts March 23 and has to be completed by June, when he returns to film more U.N.C.L.E.

This really shows the impact of John's writing on the world. Everyone's been talking lately about Bob Dylan but no one has ever made an album reading Dylan's poetry, unless that's what you consider Dylan's own albums.

And as for whether or not John's writings are any easier to comprehend than Dylan's, well that's up to you.

David McCallum reading John Lennon's poems — this could be better than Charlton Heston reading the Bible.

What more could we ask for, fans?

Lennon's Legend

By Gil McDougall

Such is the impact of John Lennon upon people who come into contact with him that the Lennon attitude is fast becoming a cult. That aggressive humour that we link so easily with the Beatles is an integral part of John's character. His acid wit has withered many a stuffed shirt you may be sure.

When Lennon was the guest of honor at a rather pompous luncheon, held as a tribute to the success of his first book, he rose to answer a toast with: "Thank you very much, you've got a lucky face."

John was criticized severely for this, as many thought that he should have given a speech. He later answered the criticism with: "Give me another fifteen years and I might make a speech, not yet."

None of the Beatles suffer fools easily but John refuses to suffer them at all. His remarks have often been described as cruel. But undeserving sources will rarely feel the acidity of his tongue. He delights in deflating officials who are full of their own self-importance.

At a Chicago press conference, a rather somber looking gentleman stood up and said: "I am the acting British Consul General (at which point all the Beatles stood up and saluted). Are you doing a good job for your country?"

"Yes," answered John, "Are you?"

The original Beatle Fan Club President, Roberta Brown, had this to say of John: "His humour is very intelligent, half of the time I couldn't understand his jokes. He's very comical but a serious person really. I think he's very shy and to cover up this shyness he has this way of being funny." This is not an opinion that many would agree with — but then few have been as close to John as Roberta has.

When Lennon does make a friend he seems to stick with them. Witness his long-standing friendship with McCartney. Most people credit John as having the dominant voice in the group. It has been suggested by many that Paul relies heavily on his mate's judgment and friendship.

Even so, McCartney is no robot. He has very strong opinions and ideas of his own. Sometimes it takes Paul to get John and the others out of touchy situations. As Lennon has said many times, Paul has the Mary-Sunshine approach to life and usually soothes over any upheavals that Beatle talk sometimes arouses.

In his book, "A Cellar Full Of Noise," Epstein has this to say of Lennon: "John Lennon is, in my opinion, a most exceptional man. Had there been no Beatles and no Epstein participation John would have emerged from the mass of the population as a man to reckon with.

"He may not have been a singer or a guitarist, a writer or an artist but he would most certainly have been a something. You cannot control a talent like this. There is in the set of his head a controlled aggression that demands respect."

Beatle Movie Plot

The Beatles are off on another series of European concerts after completing three months of difficult filming for their second movie.

Back in London, the 90-minute film spectacular is being edited, dubbed and prepared for release later this year.

Now that "8 Arms to Hold You" has been scrapped as the title (See Derek Taylor's column) everyone connected with the film is competing to see who will be the first to dream up an acceptable new title.

For those of you who missed the exclusive Beatle interviews by KRLA's Dave Hull and Derek Taylor — in which most of the plot was revealed — here's a recap:

Opens With Song

The beginning of the movie starts with a song penned by Paul McCartney. The opening scene shows the preparation of a priestess for sacrifice to the gods of a Far-Eastern temple.

Careful attention is given to the fact that she is wearing the ceremonial ring, a precious collection of exotic stones carrying a high religious and financial value.

As could only be expected, the ring slips from the priestess' finger . . . and into the hands of Ringo Starr.

From this point on the movie is filled with high comedy and un-Beatle-like chases, as our "fearless foursome" speed back to England, pursued by ruthless-looking hired gangsters.

Beatles Disguised

Throughout the movie, John, Paul, George and Ringo wear different disguises in an effort to elude their pursuers.

Somehow The Beatles manage to escape to Austria, where they are seen in some comical daring-do as they speed down a mountain slope, with the crooks hot on their heels!

Through scenes that the viewer can hardly believe, our intrepid do-gooders make their way back to England, where Ringo finally manages to get the ring off his finger.

As fate would have it, the ring then falls into the hands of a very unlucky young man. As the Beatles un-knowingly walk away whistling, he is seen running like mad from the ever-present crooks intent on retrieving the ring.

It all shapes us as exciting entertainment for millions of Beatle fans around the world.

BEATLES ARCHIVES 1

KRLA Beat Exclusive -- Portrait of a Beatle

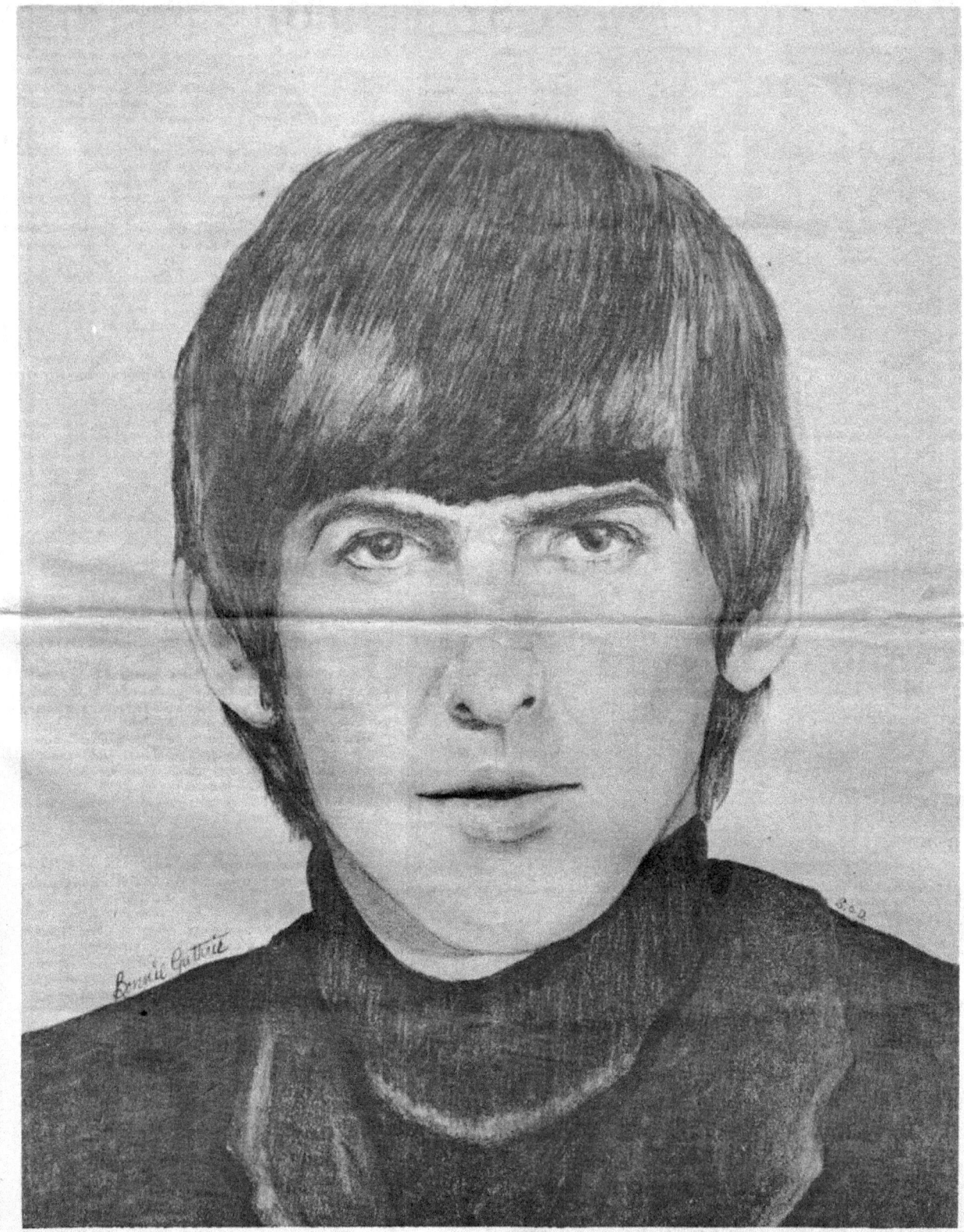

THIS MAGNIFICENT PENCIL DRAWING OF GEORGE HARRISON is the work of BONNIE GUTHRIE, 16-year-old San Diego high school girl, who has already presented several of her drawings to other leading world artists. She is planning to take up art as a career. In December, Bonnie presented a splendid drawing to a famous man — a portrait of BRIAN EPSTEIN. It was handed over to the BEATLES' manager when he was here with his singer TOMMY QUICKLY. Bonnie does not trace over a photograph — she draws from models or just simply recollection, and has produced some startling results. In addition to Bonnie's obvious talent as an artist, she also sings rhythm and blues, and has done some work in that field. But her first love is her work with art. Watch for other impressive exhibitions of Bonnie Guthrie's work, coming soon in the KRLA BEAT.

BEATLES ARCHIVES 1

Paul To Score Movie — Without John?

BEAT has learned that Paul McCartney may write the musical score for "Wedlocked Or All In Good Time," a film starring Hayley Mills. He will not work with John Lennon on the project.

If Paul actually does do the music for the picture, and indications are the he has already consented to the task, it will be the first time Paul has composed officially without the help of John.

It is also rumored that George Martin, Beatles A&R man, will help produce the soundtrack recording.

Paul's Mum

Paul is mum about the solo undertaking, as are other officials connected with the project.

Tony Barrow, Beatles Senior Press Officer, said: "No announcement is being made for some time."

Boulting Brother, the film company making "Wedlocked," stated: "It is premature to say anything." This probably means Paul has verbally agreed to do the musical score, but has not yet signed the papers.

Both Paul and John are under contract to their music company, and Dick James, Beatle publisher, said: "Any music writeen by either Paul or John must be published by Northern Songs."

The movie, "Wedlocked Or All In Good Time," is based on the play, "All In Good Time," written by Bill Naughton, author of "Alfie." Paul is believed to have seen the play when it was staged in the West End section of London.

Hayley's First

The picture will be a first for Hayley Mills, as well as for Paul McCartney. Hayley will play a married woman for the first time in her screen career.

In the film, she and her screen husband, Hywell Bennett, are forced to spend their honeymoon with her parents after an unscrupulous travel agent absconds with their money. The color picture has already been shot at the Shepperton Studios, with a few scenes filmed on location in northern England. It is set to premiere early next year.

...WHILE JOHN'S AWAY, Paul will probably score a film.

Beatle Rumor

Most absurd American Beatle rumour of the month must be the one about Ringo planning a series of solo appearances at cafes in Europe!

BEATLES must have paid more than 60,000 dollars in recording studio rental charges to make "Sgt. Pepper's Lonely Hearts Club Band" album . . . Big

Beatles Need Help on Their Third Movie

What's happening with the Beatle's third movie?

"Hard Day's Night" and "Help" were both huge smashes and the world is waiting for a third. But there's a lot of confusion over what their third movie will be or where it will be filmed.

They were originally set to start filming one called "A Talent For Loving" in Spain as soon as they returned from their last American tour.

That was postponed and the reason given was that the weather in Spain was unreliable at that time of year. But reports from London say that the weather had nothing to do with the postponement and the real problem was that the Beatles didn't like the script as it stood then. It was reported that as soon as some script changes had been made that filming would start.

Then later there were reports that an American movie company had offered the Beatles $50,000 and 50% of the profits to do a movie here. There has been no confirmation or denial on this offer.

And now there's a rumor floating around that Walter Shenson has commissioned Max Wilk to write a picture for them to be filmed here. It's reported to be set in America during the American revolution against England.

So what goes fellows? We loved the first two movies and we're anxiously awaiting the third. So let's get the contracts straightened out, get a good script, decide where to film it and get going. We're waiting.

Paul McCartney In America; Beatles Finish 'Sgt. Pepper'

By Tony Barrow

On Monday, April 3, Paul McCartney flew from London to the West Coast of America, via Paris, accompanied by Mal Evans who is one of The Beatles' two remaining road managers. It was Mal who acted as Paul's traveling companion late last year when the Beatle took off for an unplanned vacation, driving down through France into Spain and, finally, making an on-the-spot decision to visit North Africa for a breif cine'-safari in Kenya.

With Jane

The simple but important motive behind Paul's trip to America was to spend time with Jane Asher before and on her 21st birthday. His travel plans were cloaked in utter secrecy since Paul made it clear that he wanted to avoid publicity.

So that he could get away from London on time, The Beatles worked to an April 2 deadline on the final recording sessions for their next LP album. They didn't quite make it – while Paul was away extra orchestral accompaniment was added to a ballad track entitled "She's Leaving Home."

Otherwise the main work remaining unfinished was that of re-balancing and finally mixing all the recordings, a long and intricate job involving a series of tape playback meetings between producer George Martin and The Beatles themselves.

Named

Now everything has been worked out and the album has a title ("Sgt. Pepper's Lonely Hearts Club Band") and a U.K. release date (early June). What's more, there is to be a most elaborate open-out album cover carrying, in addition to much highly decorative artwork, colorful new photographs of John, Paul, George and Ringo. For the photo session they hired an assortment of military gear from a theatrical costume agency in London!

The album takes its title from the song which will be heard on Side One Band One. As this issue of BEAT goes to press The Beatles have yet to decide the precise running order of the rest of the tracks but I can reveal exclusive details of at least a few recordings involved.

Ringo's track, one of the last to be written and recorded, started out with the title "Bad Finger Boogie" but this has been amended to "A Little Help From My Friends."

Two For George

George wrote and recorded two of his own original items during the 4-month series of sessions. One is to be held in the can for future use but the other, called "Within You And Without You," is amongst the "Sgt. Pepper" selections. Other tracks include "A Day In The Life" (which has full orchestral accompaniment supplied by no less than 41 top musicians), "Good Morning, Good Morning" (for which brass men from Sounds Inc. were brought in to produce the beefy R & B backing), "Being For The Benefit Of Mr. Kite" (with lyrics which John based upon the wording of an old theatrical poster he bought at an antique shop), "Rita" (all about a female traffic warden) and "When I'm Sixty-Four" (Paul's novelty specialty with a Vaudeville influence).

BEATLE PLANS REVEALED

KRLA BEAT

April 7, 1965 — Los Angeles, California — Ten Cents

More of Hull-Tayor Interview Tells About Beatles' Life

The recent Beatle interviews by Derek Taylor and Dave Hull — broadcast over KRLA — have attracted widespread interest and enthusiasm.

Because of the close friendship between Dave and Derek and The Beatles, they were able to obtain intimate, personal insights into the lives and personalities of the four lads from Liverpool who have become the most popular entainers in history.

Radio stations across the nation have requested tape recordings of the exclusive interviews. The Beat has also been beseiged by requests to print them in their entirety.

This is the second in a four-part series. The subject this week is George Harrison. The setting is Nassau, the Bahamas, where the Beatles were filming a segment of their second movie — "Eight Arms to Hold You." Derek begins the interview:

DEREK: With the gentle swish of the Caribbean behind me, this is Derek Taylor sitting thankfully in the sun on the beach of Nassau with George Harrison, who's wearing a straw hat and blue jeans, and looks extremely well. His long, dark hair is curly. He's, of course, one of the two single Beatles and I think the first to buy a house. He bought a house in Surrey which he takes considerable interest in. Anyway, George, let's say first it's nice to see you after about three months away.

GEORGE: Nice to see you again, Derek.

DEREK: How do you like it here?

GEORGE: I like it fine except that we're up at 7:00 in the morning every day on the set filming. It's good really because

—MORE ON PAGE 2

Derek Taylor Reports

Freddie & the Dreamers' success in America, though late, comes as no surprise.

What had amazed me was that he hadn't made it earlier over here for he has been a very big act in England for two years or more.

Beatles Share

The Beatles themselves chose Freddie and his lively friends for their recent three-week Chrismas Show in London.

Also — and this is more important, since the Beatles are very careful about sharing their humor — they included Freddie in a number of their skits on stage.

The hit song the States have just discovered — "I'm Telling You Now" — was released in England more than eighteen months ago and was a very big seller. Deservedly so.

Freddie is not as light-hearted off stage as on. He takes his work pretty seriously. Like many other pop stars, he wants to expand and become more than just a teenage idol. Unlike many other pop stars, however, he may well do it because he is an able dancer and a very good comedian. As I say, like a lot of clowns, a little melancholy at times.

"I'm Telling You Now" should pass the million mark over here. I'm very glad.

Freddie lives a couple of miles from my old home in Manchester and I used to see a lot of him and the Dreamers in days gone by. Nice to see them again when they were in Hollywood a month ago.

Potential

And Chubby Checker has a disc out called "Let's Do the Freddie." Mr. Checker is very fast to see potential in a new craze.

Had a marvelous phone call last week from an American who said his name was Chuck, and he was

—MORE ON PAGE 4

BEATLE BITS
by Dick Moreland

It's time for those Beatle bits again!

George has lost so much weight that his doctors are putting him on a special diet! The poor boy only weighs 118 pounds! Don't worry, George, that's the same number of pounds carried by Miss America!

"I Feel Fine / She's A Woman" (you can't say just one title, since both are number one!) sold three quarters of a million records before it was even released! I'll bet it took all of two days to become a million seller!

John and Paul are very serious about writing a Broadway-type musical! The two are even writing plot outlines! They won't quit the Beatles if they become successful playwrites, but as John said, "It's always nice to be well rounded!"

John's new book, tentatively titled "A Spaniard In the Works" will be out in February or March. They're saying it's even better than John's first one!

Yes, it's true that Ringo was evicted from his apartment! But for a very funny reason! His fans wanted to wish him good luck before he went into the hospital, and they all congregated outside Ringo's apartment to do it! The noise was so great that the apartment manager politely asked the Beatle to move.

That catches you up on the latest... I'll be back in two weeks with more Beatle Bits!

Hang Len?

While on the subject of new singles I think Len Barry (who is a doll of a guy) should be hung at half-mast for his latest release. Or, at least, he should have titled it "1-2-3 Revisited."

Everyone's getting into the act. John Lennon's father, Alfred Lennon, has just been signed to a recording contract! What next? The Senior Lennon's record debut is set to be "That's My Life," a self-penned song.

Rumor has it that Mr. Lennon has been on the down-and-out for a long time now. I suppose he finally decided to swallow his pride and make some money off his famous son. Don't blame him too much — you don't know the full story. And neither do I.

Probably the only two who know are John and his father. And they aren't talking... yet.

BEATLES TO DO SIX NEW SONGS

LONDON — If you want to get in touch with the Beatles... by phone, that is, get ready to place a call to London on February 16th! That's the date the four groovy guys will be recording six songs for their upcoming movie. The recording session will take place in studio two at EMI, starting at 3:00, London time. The six songs were written by, of course, John and Paul. And here's a little scoop... a lot of you have been wondering which part Paul writes and which part John writes. Here's the lowdown... Paul writes the words and John writes the melody! Walter Shenson, the producer of the film, said that there is no title or release date yet, but the film will definitely be in color. Shenson was also the producer of "Hard Day's Night."

BEATLES ARCHIVES 1

More Beatle Answers

FROM PAGE ONE

if you're off work there's nothing much to do. It gets boring just sitting in the sun, and we'd all prefer to be up and working.

DEREK: I asked you because it may seem like a paradise to people who can't get into the sun to think of spending two or three weeks in the Bahamas. But of course you are working very hard all day.

GEORGE: Yeah, that's right. Well, we get up at 7:00 and we usually start about 8:00 or 8:30, right through and then have lunch for about a half hour, and then we work right through until the sun goes and there's no more light, which is usually about 5:30.

DEREK: The pattern of your life now seems to be with not so much touring. Now that you can record 11 numbers in five days you can have an awful lot of leisure. Do you have too much leisure, do you find?

GEORGE: No. We haven't had a great deal, really. This year, maybe, because after the film I'm not too sure what we're doing. I think we may have a week or so and then we go to Europe for about a week.

DEREK: Are you touring Europe?

GEORGE: I think we're doing six concerts — two in France and two in Italy and two in Spain.

DEREK: You've been in France. You haven't been to the other places before?

GEORGE: We've been to Spain — Paul, Ringo and I went.

DEREK: You didn't play there, though.

GEORGE: No.

DEREK: When that tour is over you presumably will then have a lot of time before visiting America.

GEORGE: That's August. I think in the meantime we'll have a new record out, doing TV and things in England. And then with a bit of luck the film will probably be out around about that time. So then we'll have the film songs out to plug and we'll have a premiere. And then I think it'll be the American trip. Or maybe the premiere will be after the American trip, which is in August.

DEREK: So in fact the pace in life seems to be almost as hot as it was. It appears deceptive.

GEORGE: We can't tell, really, because we haven't really been told exactly what's happening. We just vaguely know that it's America, and then for all we know we may start on our third film after the American trip, in which case, you know, we'll be . . .

DEREK: I notice that . . . you seem to be doing two films in one year.

GEORGE: We're trying to. I hope so because we enjoy it so much more than anything else.

DEREK: You prefer films?

GEORGE: Yeah, it's great. And when the film's finished you get more satisfaction from it. You feel as though you've done something worthwhile more so than a tour.

DEREK: Brian Epstein did say once — I don't want to commit you to anything that you don't want to talk about — but he did say once that it might be you'd go more and more into filming, and into isolated shows. Is this going to be sooner than we expected?

GEORGE: I don't know. This depends on when we expected it.

DEREK: He means in terms, I think, of next year.

GEORGE: We'd like to do more films and naturally a little less touring because . . .

DEREK: Touring's tiring.

GEORGE: Yes, it is. People don't realize that each day you jump

out of bed onto an airplane and fly two thousand miles to do a show . . . You know that's not much fun, really.

DEREK: The American trip destroyed almost everybody. Everybody was a bit off their heads when it was over.

GEORGE: Yeah.

DEREK: Now going back to leisure, how do you spend your free time when you're home? Like spend a Sunday off?

GEORGE: On Sunday I have a lie-in, I suppose, and then . . .

DEREK: You're a great sleeper . . . a sleep worshipper, really.

GEORGE: Yeah, but I do like it if I can. It's just trying to get up. Since I've gotten my house I used to just lie around in the backyard last summer when it was quite hot. But now, as it's sort of freezing cold in England, on a Sunday I just get up and have a late breakfast about 12 o'clock.

DEREK: Have you got help in the house?

GEORGE: I've got a woman who comes in each day. She cooks dinner for me and keeps the place tidy.

DEREK: What's her name?

GEORGE: Margaret. Mrs. Walker. I read the Sunday papers and go out for a drive, and sometimes go out for lunch with some people.

DEREK: Do you eat more out than you do in?

GEORGE: Uh . . . I think so because I usually just eat in on the weekends. I usually, on a Sunday, have friends over and just stay in and have dinner and watch TV.

DEREK: You've got a pretty good garden. You don't do it yourself, do you?

GEORGE: No.

DEREK: Do you like gardening?

GEORGE: Well, I like a sort of nice garden but it's too much trouble really. But the good thing about my garden is that most of it just lawn. It's just lots of big lawn with trees and things.

DEREK: It's a new house though?

GEORGE: It's a bungalow, actually, just a big long bungalow.

DEREK: Bungalow is what we call a one-level house, I think.

GEORGE: Anyway, originally the fellow who built it is the fellow I bought it from was an Australian. He built it like an Australian ranch bungalow. It's about ten years old. Two years ago he had a new part built on the end so it's ten and two years old.

DEREK: Do you take an interest in the house in improving it or is it simply a place to live?

GEORGE: I like it.

DEREK: Are you a house-proud man? Do you talk about your house to other people?

GEORGE: Well, to friends and things I suppose. I like the idea of it looking great in the way I like it.

DEREK: Are your tastes in interior decorating simple?

GEORGE: Really being the first house ever of mine I've just tried to get it so that it pleases me. At first I got some fellow to get some furniture and he bought a lot of rubbish. Since then I decided I didn't really like it. He just bought odd stuff just so I could move in straight away. Since then I've changed it around a lot. Things I'd like to do if ever I buy another house is stay in this one until I get the new one furnished just how I like it and then move. I'm not a great believer in interior design and all that because it ends up you're living in the designer's house and I'd much rather do it myself.

DEREK: Yes, I quite agree. You were going to have a pool put in, I think, the last time I saw you. Is that still happening?

GEORGE: They started about two weeks before we left England, and actually the morning we left the airport there was a massive great hole dug out and mud all over the place, and one of these big diggers in the backyard. The workmen have got sheds built up. Everytime I go out there I just hear music in the little shed and they're all playing cards and singing. They never seem to do any work. I'm hoping by the time I get back most of the mess will be gone.

DEREK: Have you spent a lot of money on the house since you got it?

GEORGE: Uh . . . not really, no.

DEREK: What's it called, by the way, has it a name or a number or what?

GEORGE: It has a name but somebody pinched it.

DEREK: The fans know where it is, do they?

GEORGE: Well, some of them do. Actually there's a girls' school right next to it but the head mistress was good and she told the kids to give me a bit of privacy.

DEREK: Pursuing the point of leisure but now forgetting about the house, it has for a long time been quite easy for you in certain places to move around London as a normal human being in your own car. Can you explain how you've been able to do this because I've never never known how you managed it, how you park and how you get from the car to the theatre?

GEORGE: The thing is, if we're doing a show then that's the only time there is going to be thousands of people, really. If we're not doing a show and just going out for the night somewhere, there's not liable to be millions of people waiting for you to arrive at the restaurant

—MORE ON PAGE 3

BEATLES ARCHIVES 1

Best Man Soon A Groom?

FROM PAGE TWO

because they don't know where you're going.

DEREK: But you still have the autograph books.

GEORGE: Oh, yeah.

DEREK: How do you avoid that? Do you go to selected places?

GEORGE: Now, you know, through experience, you just do it by . . . if you go to a place and have quite a good time and you're treated all right, then naturally you go back again. And usually the managers of places like you to go there so it's in their own interest, really, to make sure you're having quite a good time. But generally in London it's quite good.

DEREK: You're very fond of London, I think?

GEORGE: Yeah, I thing it's fabulous.

DEREK: Do you go home very often?

GEORGE: To Liverpool? I went there about three weeks ago. I was up there for a week . . . my brother got married.

DEREK: I saw the picture in the paper.

GEORGE: Yes. Really, there are so many people and friends to see in the short time I was there.

DEREK: You're like most people you left the place you were born and you've grown very fond of London. It happens in most countries of the world. You probably grow away from places and grow up a bit. Never been any suggestion of your living outside England?

GEORGE: No.

DEREK: This is a good place to live here, of course.

GEORGE: Thing is, with a place like, say this beach, we're sitting on now, I think it's marvelous and I'd love a house . . . but probably after two or three weeks of this I'd get fed up. I wouldn't mind living in a place like this . . . nice beach, nice sea, and sort of hot climate. But it's so boring after two weeks. But still I wouldn't mind a place like this say . . . every time I got fed up with the cold in England you could just fly out here. But still I prefer to live in a place like London anytime.

DEREK: Well, there's an awful lot happening in London and in Los Angeles, where your voice will be heard pretty soon — as soon as Dave Hull and I get back there. Los Angeles has a climate similar to this only cooler in winter and always much drier. Well, George, I won't keep you any more because I know you have to get on the set. It's been nice to see you and I'll see you later on today. I'll turn you over to Dave Hull now.

GEORGE: Okay, see you, Derek. Bye, Bye.

DAVE: How're you, George?

GEORGE: Hello, Dave, how're you?

DAVE: Good. You look comfortable, you've got on a pair of faded blue Levi's and an old straw hat . . .

GEORGE: They're not Levi's.

DAVE: Well they're jeans. In America we call them Levi's. That's what we call anything that's blue and faded. You got a straw hat on. Where'd you find that straw hat?

GEORGE: Just bought it here.

DAVE: I see you stole my dark glasses.

GEORGE: They're yours, are they?

DAVE: Yeah.

GEORGE: No they're not . . . I bought them.

DAVE: No you didn't, you just stole them from me. I just set them on the sand.

GEORGE: No you didn't, they're mine.

DAVE: No they're not.

GEORGE: They're not . . . I've had these on for days.

DAVE: Listen . . .

GEORGE: Don't believe this man . . . they're mine.

DAVE: Listen, this idol out there in the water that we're watching, is going to be a one-shot take, and it comes up and it's got ten arms. What has this got to do with the movie?

GEORGE: This is Kali, and . . . it's the sacrificial god or something. It's a bit involved. I'll wait until they finish making the film and then I'll go and see it and then I'll know what's happening.

DAVE: How come it has to be a one-shot take?

GEORGE: This thing is 20-foot high and it's taken them two hours to submerge it under the water. They can do it again but they'll have to wait another two hours before they can get the thing down on the bottom again. It's a lot of work, so if they can do it in one take it saves a lot of time and trouble.

DAVE: How do you feel about this movie compared to "A Hard Day's Night." Is the script different? Is there a lot of spontaneity?

GEORGE: The only thing, really, that's the same as "Hard Day's Night" is the fact that we're still playing ourselves. But I mean, this has got a story line to it whereas "Hard Day's Night" didn't, really. It was more or less like a documentary.

DAVE: You mean this one's got a plot?

GEORGE: Yeah, this one's got a plot.

DAVE: Are you ad-libbing a lot of lines? A lot of scenes that were in "A Hard Day's Night" were spontaneous and when you had to go back and cut the scene came out completely different from the way it was before. Is this happening now or not?

GEORGE: Yeah, there's lots of things that if we think of on the actual day of shooting — if the director can think of something or we can — that will make it a little bit better, then we'll change it a little bit. But, you know, so far we seem to be sticking to the script.

DAVE: I didn't ask John or Paul or anyone about the songs in the movie, but can you give me an idea . . . You have seven new ones, is that correct?

GEORGE: Well, we recorded 11 the last week before we left England.

DAVE: But you're only using seven, are you?

GEORGE: We'll only use about seven in the film, but even if we use only about five in the film, we'll still have about 10 or 12 tracks on the L.P.

DAVE: Can you tell me what the titles are . . . I bet you can't, can you?

GEORGE: I can't, no.

DAVE: Can you give us a hint, then, what they're like?

GEORGE: It's so hard, really, because when you record eleven all in one week, you just work on one until you've finished it then completely disregard that and go on to something else. By the time the week's over, you've forgotten, really, what you've done. You know vaguely, but not until we start doing

—MORE ON PAGE 4

BEATLES ARCHIVES 1

At Deadline

BRIAN JONES of the ROLLING STONES is hosting JOEY PAIGE at his home in England.

The Stones invited Joey to visit them while they were here recently. To quote Joey's letter to the Beat: "I'm living with Brian. He has a groovey place. It's a little house. All the boys are fine and are getting ready to go on tour for two weeks. Saw a few of their shows here in England and they were just great. They did a live album that should be out in America in a month or so. They're the hottest act going here (London) right now."

Joey has been mobbed in London since his arrival there. He will no doubt be a top artist in England by the time he returns to the U.S.

The BEAU BRUMMELS were in town recently to appear at the Cinnamon Cinders. While there, photographers and writers from Look Magazine saw their show, photographed and interviewed them. The June 1 issue of Look will have the full story. Their new record is really great. It is taken from their first album, "Introducing the Beau Brummels," which will be available very soon and includes 10 original songs.

The BEATLES will play their August 15 concert in New York to nearly 60,000 fans. ED SULLIVAN will introduce them and the event will be filmed for release throughout the world within days. Of course we expect to see them in person in Los Angeles soon after.

ROGER MILLER who is nearing the million record mark with *King of the Road* is in Europe to appear on several TV shows and make personal appearances in England and France.

FREDDIE AND THE DREAMERS will join Dick Clark's "Caravan of Stars," a tour which begins on April 30. Also, they will appear on Ed Sullivan's show on April 25.

PETER AND GORDON were in the U.S. during the last week of March to tape for "Hullabaloo." They begin a six day visit to Japan on April 19.

Also scheduled for a tour of Japan by way of California are THE ANIMALS. They will arrive in the U.S. on May 19 and be in California a few days after.

The DAVE CLARK FIVE's film will be released this summer. To assure all the fans which film is theirs, the title selected was "The Dave Clark Five Runs Wild."

WAYNE FONTANA and the MINDBENDERS will appear on "Hullabaloo" on April 20. Their first American release, "Game of Love" keeps on a steady climb toward the top of the charts.

DEL SHANNON is drawing capacity crowds in England. He will return to the U.S. in mid-April.

BOBBY SHERMAN who is a regular on "Shindig" is on a cross-country tour. Bobby is a very handsome and talented artist and should gain a lot of fans by making personal appearances.

BEATLE JOHN LENNON ordered *contact sunglasses*, while filming on sunny snowslopes in Alpine segs of *Eight Arms To Hold You*.

FAN CLUB INFORMATION

BOBBY SHERMAN
c/o Barbara Schare
P.O. Box 3187
Hollywood, California
(Dues — $1.25. Members receive a fact sheet, 8"x10" picture and a monthly call from Bobby)

BEATLES
Judy Doctor, Vice President
401 S. Barrington Avenue,
Apt. 116
West Los Angeles 90049
(Dues — $2.00. Members receive quarterly newsletter, picture and exclusive Beatle book)

ROLLING STONES
c/o Debbie Kelley
11360 Harvard Drive
Norwalk, California

BEATLE BOBBIES, INC.
11122 S. Corley Drive
Whittier, California 90604
(Members must be over 13)

BOB EUBANKS
c/o Janet Wolfe
7839 Beckett St.
Sunland, Calif. 91040

READER'S NOTE
So that you could read every word of the GEORGE HARRISON interview as it was recorded, Louise Criscione's column ON THE BEAT has taken a vacation for one week, because of space limitations.

More Derek Taylor

FROM PAGE ONE

with one of the Animals, the drummer John Steele.

They were, he said, stranded without money at Los Angeles International Airport. He added, "Eric Easton (Rolling Stones' manager) and Brian Epstein flew off in a private plane taking all our money and passports with them to the Bahamas."

"Oh," said I. "That means you want money."

He muttered, "Yes," and put 'John Steele' on the line.

"Hello, John," I said.

In what he believed to be a North British accent he grunted, "Hello there."

And I said, "Where are you from, John?"

He replied, "From Liverpool."

I asked him what part of Liverpool and he said, "Near where John Lennon lives."

I said, "Now listen, the Animals, as you should have known, come from Newcastle-on-Tyne, which is a very tough seaport 170 miles from Liverpool, another very tough seaport. And no Newcastle man would ever say he came from Liverpool, or vice versa."

I advised him to go off, rehearse his accent, check his facts, and then try the trick somewhere else.

Nice to see the success of "Red Roses For A Blue Lady." There are three versions in the national top 20 — proof that a good song can always stand revival by any number of artists. It was a great hit fifteen years ago when melody was in fashion, long before the days of rock 'n roll and big beat.

The Righteous Bros. had a successful tour with the Beau Brummels. More than that, it has been a happy, friendly tour. The Bros., after their experience on the Beatle tour, take great pains to make all the other artists on the bill feel happy and comfortable.

You may remember that the Righteous Bros. left the Beatle tour in the east because Beatlemaniacs refused to give them a chance. The Beatles themselves were fine to the California twosome, but the fans weren't. Now that the Righteous Bros. are at the top, they always go on stage at the opening of the show and apeal for a fair hearing for the other artists.

Watch for "Cast Your Fate to the Wind." This is a beautiful instrumental with a dominant piano. It leapt up the British charts without warning, with little promotion, and is in direct contrast to the pounding beat of most chart-toppers.

The pianist, by the way, is Johnny Pearson, musical arranger for Cilla Black. The record will be a big hit.

That's all for now. Keep smiling.

Beatles Booty Bag

WATERPROOF—WASHABLE—STRONG

TOTES-ALL
—YEAR ROUND—

"*Stylishly Carries*"

- SHOPPING
- OVERNIGHTING
- PICNICKING
- BEACHING
- BALL GAMING
- BOATING
- TRAVELING
- CAMPING
- BOWLING
- SPORTING

Foods and Drinks • Toiletries • Swim Suits • Towels • P.J.'s • Records • Blankets • Books • Gym Clothes • Cameras • Radios • Tennis Shoes • Tennis Balls • Raincoats • Art Supplies

CARRIES THREE WAYS

DETACH AND SEND

TO: BEATLES, BOX C, CULVER CITY, CALIFORNIA
PLEASE RUSH . . . Beatles Booty Bag at $1.00 ea., incl. tax OR 4 Beatles Booty Bags for only $3.00, incl. tax.
ENCLOSED FIND $_____
NAME_____ ADDRESS_____
CITY_____ STATE_____

More Beatle Answers

FROM PAGE THREE

the songs do we remember them one at a time. It's a mixture.

DAVE: I want to ask you a question about your mother and father, if I may for a moment. They had planned on coming to America and to Hollywood. Do you know if your mother and father have continued with their plans?

GEORGE: I don't know... don't think so. I think they'd like to go for a holiday. They've mentioned to me that they may go. I don't think they've made any sort of definite plans.

DAVE: You probably haven't seen them for some time anyway.

GEORGE: I saw them three weeks ago when I went to Liverpool for my brother's wedding.

DAVE: Oh, that's right. Your brother Peter, is it not?

GEORGE: That's right.

DAVE: You were best man?

GEORGE: That's right.

DAVE: When did that all take place?

GEORGE: It was January.

DAVE: Well, you've been a best man now. What about your plans? Do you have any plans for the future as far as Pattie Boyd or anything like that, can you say?

GEORGE: Well, you know, I wouldn't make sort of long arrangements long before hand. At the moment I have nothing in mind at all.

DAVE: Have you talked to Pattie recently?

GEORGE: Not since I was in England.

DAVE: You haven't called her then?

GEORGE: No, not yet.

DAVE: We'll be seeing you tonight. I see you've got your feet buried in the sand. It'll cool you off a bit.

GEORGE: Okay, see you then, Dave.

DAVE: Thank you very much.

BEATLES ARCHIVES 1

   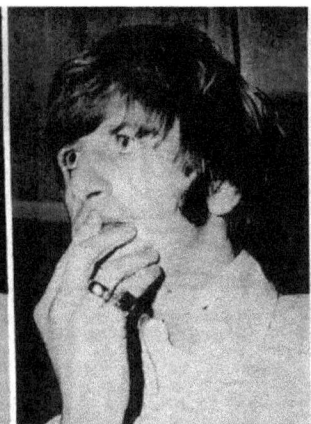

... JOHN ... PAUL ... GEORGE ... RINGO

IS BEATLEMANIA DYING?

Beatle rumors are flying again, and it's the same old story. According to the latest rumblings from the grapevine, "the Beatles are slipping in popularity."

These rumors are no doubt being manufactured by the same people who said "Elvis will never last", and the Beatle gossip is no more fact than the Presley predictions were.

Rumors aren't completely fabricated out of thin air. They usually spring from acorns of doubt and grow into towering oaks of confusion.

One of the reasons behind the most recent crop of rumors is the fact that concert tickets have not yet been sold out in all the cities on the Beatle itinerary. Tickets are still available for concerts in Portland, Oregon and Kansas City, Missouri and one or two other cities.

This is causing a bit of speculative whispering, but no matter what is being said, the availability of tickets in some areas does not mean the 1965 American tour will be the Beatles' swan song.

Tickets for some Beatle concerts have always sold out in a matter of hours, but this has not always been the case throughout all of the country. During the last Beatle tour, tickets were available in some cities as late as the day of the concert, but were always sold out by the time the great moment arrived.

Beatled Areas

Some areas are simply more Beatled than others, causing tickets to be sold at a faster and more furious pace. Last year many California Beatlemaniacs got to see John, Paul, George and Ringo only because it was still possible, at the last minute, to purchase tickets for the Las Vegas concert at Convention Hall.

The availability of tickets in some places is only an acorn, but because the situation is being looked at through misinformed eyes, the rumor-bearing oak is already beginning to take root.

It needn't bother. The tickets will be sold. They always *have*, and the chances are good that they *always will!*

As always, the proof is in the pudding. If the Beatles were in any sort of slump, their latest album wouldn't be the number one LP in the nation, and "Beatles VI" wouldn't have climbed to this spot in three short weeks when it often takes as long as three months for an album to rise to the top.

Beatle Albums

Where other Beatle records are concerned, "Beatles 65" is still the number twenty-five best-seller in the country, after seven months on the charts. Another Beatle album, "The Early Beatles" is also selling well (number fifty-three after three months on the charts), in spite of the fact that it includes no new Beatle songs and is a re-issue of early album tunes like "Anna."

The most recent Beatle single, "Ticket To Ride" has finally dropped off the national American charts, after reaching the number one slot, but is still riding high on many foreign charts. To mention a few, "Ticket" is number one in Holland, number four in Hong Kong and number seven in Malaysia.

The new Beatle single was released on July 19, and a world of loyal Beatlemaniacs eagerly awaited its arrival. (Don't have to tell you where you heard it first, do we?) (Hardly!!)

Illegal in Indonesia

There is only one place we can think of where the Beatles may be having a problem, and that's in Indonesia. The Indonesian government has outlawed the sale of rock and roll music and recently staged a raid on a black market storehouse of rock tapes. Many Beatle tunes were confiscated in the raid, which proves that the foursome is popular even in places where it's against the law to be a Beatlemaniac!

Now that you know the whole truth and nothing else but, you will have something to fight those rumors with, and don't hesitate to quote the BEAT when you're standing up for John, Paul, George and Ringo. The information printed in this article isn't just our opinion. It's fact!

And so is the fact that the Beatles are here to stay!

BEATLES ARCHIVES 1

... NEW SOUNDS IN A NEW STUDIO?

HOTLINE LONDON SPECIAL
Beatle Rumor Half True

By Tony Barrow

Just about half of those widespread rumours about THE BEATLES' plans for a U.S. recording session were true. What I mean is that John, Paul, George and Ringo would like to go into an American recording studio although there are no concrete plans in hand for them to do so at this time.

The rumours started when Brian Epstein visited Memphis after bringing Cilla Black to New York for your Ed Sullivan and Johnny Carson TV shows. In fact, the main purpose of Brian's trip to Memphis was to make various routine checks in connection with The Beatles' August concert at the Memphis Coliseum. While he was in the area, he looked into one or two aspects of the local recording situation and, immediately, a lot of people decided that The Beatles would be traveling to Memphis very soon.

There would be no possibility of The Beatles recording in Memphis during their 1966 concert tour. The night before they're scheduled to play in Boston and the night afterwards they'll be in Cincinnati.

I talked to George about the general idea of having some recording sessions in America. He told me: "If we ever did I'd like us to go to a good place – not just any American recording studio. People like Otis Redding, Wilson Pickett and a lot of others who are amongst our personal fave-rave artists make their records in Memphis. The recording engineers there are specialists. It's not just a job to them. They love our kind of music. There'd be this great atmosphere."

Paul added: "It would be interesting to discover what new sounds we could get by using a different studio."

Recording manager George Martin would go along with the boys wherever they planned to have sessions. "If we ever do go out of London for sessions," George Martin told me, "it would be experimental. It's true that different local musical environments could have a strong affect on The Beatles. We wouldn't know what to expect in the way of results but it would be a new experience for all of us."

Meantime, The Beatles are right in the middle of an extended series of sessions with George Martin at the EMI studios, St. John's Wood, London. Sessions will continue until nearly twenty new numbers are on tape – enough material for a fresh album plus a single.

The complete list of August U.S. concert dates for The Beatles has now been announced. The series will kick off with two performances at the mighty International Amphitheatre in Chicago on Friday, August 12. All told, fourteen cities are included with a grand total of something like twenty concerts.

Last year there was a week-long stop-over in L.A. when The Beatles lazed in the sun beside their inviting pool up in Benedict Canyon. This time they won't be in California for quite so long. After playing New York City's Shea Stadium (August 23), they move to Seattle (August 25) before coming into Los Angeles for their Dodger Stadium date on August 28. The tour finishes on August 29 in San Francisco.

The 1965 tour took in 10 cities. Places like Washington, Philadelphia, Boston, Memphis, St. Louis and Seattle appear in the '66 schedule and did not show on last year's list. The idea is to take in new cities which were missed last time. The Beatles return to New York, Los Angeles, San Francisco and Toronto but a number of '65 cities like Atlanta, Houston, Minneapolis, Portland and San Diego are not lined up for repeat visits this summer.

In 1965, the group's charter aircraft covered something like 10,000 miles during the tour and the boys played to 350,000 Beatle People. This year's audience total is estimated at over 400,000.

* * *

THE YARDBIRDS, on their way up your charts with their U.K. best-seller, "Shapes Of Things," recorded the instrumental backing for their current money-spinner before the lyrics were even written! *(Turn to Page 5)*

Good news for you Beatle fans. The Beatle concert filmed at Shea Stadium last year will most probably be shown to American audiences right before the Beatles arrive Stateside in August.

John says the Beatles think it's "a fabulous film. In color it's great because all our faces look blue and brown under the flood lighting. It starts with Paul doing 'I'm Down' and we all look very sweaty because it's hot in New York in August and, in any case, 'I'm Down' was at the very end of our act and we'd been on stage over half an hour by the time that bit was filmed."

Of course, the film was shown in England not too long ago and everyone flipped out over it. The reviews were very favorable and Ringo would just like you all to know that those badges the Beatles were wearing at Shea are genuine Wells Fargo Agent badges which were given to them while riding in a Fargo van on the way to the concert.

... JOHN LENNON

BEATLES SET FOR WORLD TELEVISION

BEATLES postpone Indian trip

By Tony Barrow
LONDON — The Beatles have postponed their Odyssey To India in order to complete an hour-long color television special. They will not leave for the Orient before the first week in October.

The boys expect to return to England a few weeks before Christmas after a period of meditation studies under Maharishi Mahesh Yogi.

The theme song for the special, "Magical Mystery Tour," has already been written by John and Paul, and they are currently composing at least four other songs for the show.

Reports indicate that the music will be released either as a series of singles or as an EP disc and not on a full-length LP.

The Beatles are anxious that the special be screened during the Christmas period on a world-wide basis.

The Magical Mystery Tour is a replacement for a previously planned special which was to center around the "Sgt. Pepper" album. There is a possibility that some of the "Sgt. Pepper" material will be included in sequences of the "Mystery Tour."

BEATLES ARCHIVES 1

By Tony Barrow

An important concert marked the arrival in the U.K. of Indian instrumental virtuoso and classical sitar expert RAVI SHANKAR. GEORGE HARRISON attended Shankar's opening performance in London's famous Royal Festival Hall, home of the capital's finest symphony concerts. To be there the Beatle left his three colleagues in the middle of a recording session at E.M.I.'s North London studios! With him to watch the Shankar recital went George's wife Patti.

Immediately afterwards George returned to E.M.I. and the recording session continued until nearly three o'clock the following morning. By that time one of the final tracks for the group's forthcoming album had been completed. Now the boys have still got to rehearse and record four further titles and the 14 numbers for their August U.K. album will be ready.

Beatle Comfort

Six years ago during their first visits to Germany, THE BEATLES slept alongside members of two or three other beat groups in one large room of an unfurnished attic apartment in Hamburg. This month when John, Paul, George and Ringo round off their three-day six-show German tour in Hamburg, their accommodation will be somewhat less cramped. They will stay for two nights in a huge, ancient and very historical German castle built high on a hill 20 miles to the north of Hamburg.

On the second day of the tour the group will use its own special train to move between Munich, Essen and Hamburg. The party will spend twelve hours in the luxuriously equipped Pullman rail carriages which will have a television lounge, restaurant section and sleeping quarters.

It goes without saying that The Beatles will not be playing Hamburg's Star Club this trip. That's where they gained some of their first major success. Now they'll play a considerably larger venue holding more than 12,000 people.

Spencer Tops

Meanwhile the Star Club continues to flourish. Latest favorite there is our SPENCER DAVIS GROUP who drew a record-splintering crowd of two and a half thousand fans just a couple of weeks ago. The club announced that the Davis' attendance was the biggest since the Beatle days of '61 and '62 when the Star Club had just opened.

This summer Spencer Davis tours Norway and Sweden before making a return visit to Germany. The group hopes to finalize details of a full-scale U.S. tour for the month of October but this may depend upon the success of "Somebody Help Me" on your side of the Atlantic.

French Spurn Beatles

If there's anywhere in the world that the Beatles need help, it's in France only.

In spite of their return tour of this country, the Beatles have not been able to crack the almost impenetrable French charts.

Their "Help!" disc has been a powerful international hit elsewhere. At present it has claimed top honors in both America and Britain, and also been at the head of the sales list in Canada, Ireland, Hong Kong, New Zealand, Australia and South Africa.

The Beatles have also registered on the charts of late in Argentina and Singapore, but the only two foreign groups to win recent slots in France are the Rolling Stones ("Satisfaction") and Sam The Sham & The Pharoahs ("Wooly Bully").

Could it be that the French just don't parlez-vous where the Beatles are concerned? It's beginning to look that way.

Just goes to show that fifty million Frenchman *can* be wrong after all.

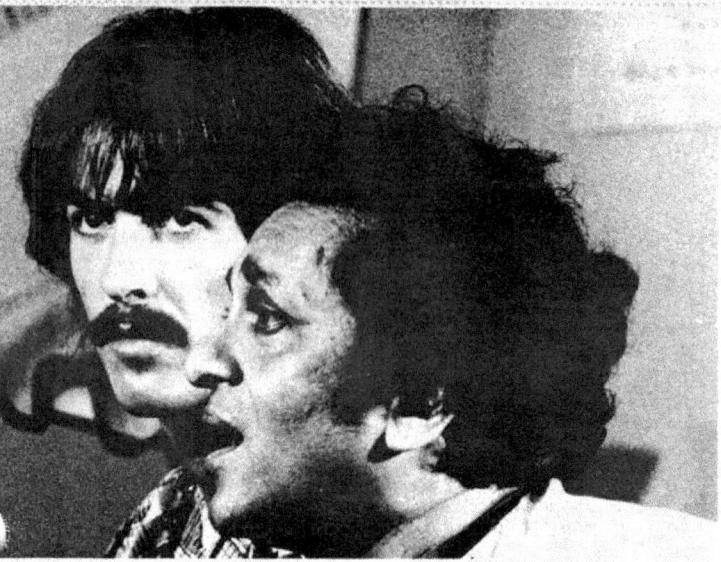

GEORGE HARRISON DRESSES rather like a hippie but says that "they're hypocrites."

Beatle George States Hippies 'Hypocrites'

LONDON — George Harrison's recent trip to the hippie homeland of Haight-Ashbury has left the Beatle with a surprising and unexpected bitter taste. In an interview shortly after his journey to San Francisco, George described many of the Hippies he met as hypocrites who were too hung up on LSD and other drugs to really be hip.

George revealed that he was continually being offered LSD and STP during his short stay in Haight, but refused to take any of it.

"LSD isn't the answer. It doesn't give you anything," he said. "It enables you to see a lot of possibilities that you might never have noticed before, but it isn't the answer."

George described the true hippie as one who knows what's going on and doesn't need LSD or other drugs.

"There was the bit where people were so out of their minds trying to shove STP on me and acid, but I didn't want to know about it. I want to get high and you can't get high on LSD."

Harrison added that he could, and would rather, get high from the practice of yoga and meditation, which he has taken up along with the other Beatles.

In an unusual disclosure, George said he had never deliberately taken acid, but one day before LSD became the subject of everyday conversation someone slipped the drug in the Beatles coffee. "I'm not embarrassed. It makes no difference because I didn't actually go out and try to get some."

Haight-Ashbury is a lot like the Bowery, George said, largely because of the great number of beggars who inhabit the hippie haven.

"These people are hypocrites," George said. "They are making fun of tourists and all that, and at the same time, they are holding their hands out begging off them. That's what I don't like."

Turn to page 11

What Causes Beatlemania?

By Eden

You've seen it hundreds of times before—in mob scenes at airports, in screaming crowds of fans at concerts, even in one's and two's sitting 'round the television set when "they" were on.

Yes, you've seen it all before. The girls who scream, the girls who faint—the girls who cry.

Why Do They Cry?

Time and again parents and teachers and other concerned adults ask the same old question—why? Why do they act this way? Why do they cry?

The most obvious and most frequently seen example of this teary problem is to be found in anything even remotely connected with the Beatles.

Beatlemania, as it were, has indeed taken over the world. Members of every age group have found themselves succumbing to this delightful disease, and the main symptom is sheer happiness!

But, what of the young—and *not-so-young*—girls who scream, faint, and cry at the slightest mention of the Four Fabulous Fellows from Blightyland?

Intensive Research

Psychiatrists, psychologists, and sociologists the world over are among many who have done, and are still doing, intensive research in this area in order to answer this question. As yet, there seems to be no one who has been able to find *the* answer; perhaps no one ever will.

This reporter does not profess to be a psychiatrist or even an expert in the field of human behavior. But I am a female and I am a Beatlemaniac—and very proud of it. Beatlemania is one of the happiest states of mind conceivable and there is no greater group of people in all the globe as the one we label "Beatlemaniacs."

Through my own personal encounters and experiences with Beatlemania, I have been able to draw some conclusions and form a few answers of my own. Per-

BEATLES-EYE VIEW OF BEATLEMANIA — NATURE PROVIDES A SAFEGUARD

BEATLES ARCHIVES 1

BEATLES' MAGIC MYSTERY TOUR

By Tony Barrow

There was a little bit of private and personal nostalgia for The Beatles when they set off in their chartered bus to begin shooting "Magical Mystery Tour," their created, self-scripted, self-directed and self-produced color TV special.

The bus, a grand looking yellow and blue vehicle with luminous posters glaring out from its sides and rear, departed from Allsop-place, a little side street close to London's famous Baker-street, Tussaud's Waxworks and the Planetarium. Allsop1place is, by tradition, the departure point for groups setting out on one-night-stand pop tours. It must be all of four years since The Beatles traveled the roads and motorways of Britain in a bus—but way back in the early part of 1963 when they went out on concert tours with stars like Tommy Roe, Chris Montez and Roy Orbison, it was at the Allsop-place that the whole show assembled on the first morning.

The Beatles have been thinking about the "Magical Mystery Tour" project for the best part of five months. As far back as April 25 they began recording the title number for the show. It was their first session since the competition of the last "Sgt. Pepper" album track.

Beatles TV Special

"Magical Mystery Tour" will contain at least three new Beatle compositions apart from the title song. One of the others may well be George Harrison's "Blue Jay Way" a piece written in Los Angeles a few weeks ago when George made his August trip to California for Ravi Shankar's Hollywood Bowl concert.

The entire hour-long TV special will be completed no later than the first week of October. The Beatles have set themselves this deadline in order to leave for India prior to John's 27th birthday on October 9. They will be in the East for two months returning to London shortly before Christmas—the time when "Magical Mystery Tour" is likely to have its first screening on British television.

Flower Wedding

Jimi Hendrix wrote "The Burning of the Midnight Lamp" in flight between New York and Los Angeles . . . Mike Jagger and Keith Ricard have written a 16-minute track for The Stones' next album . . . Englebert Humperdinck (Number One in the U.S. with "The Last Waltz") is to star in "Robinson Crusoe," the London Palladium's four-month pantomime production opening December 19 . . . Expect U.S. release of two new singles by The Bee Gees in quick succession . . . "London's First Wedding of the Flower Children"—that's how the press described the Caxton Hall register office marriage of Eric Burdon and model Angie King on Thursday, September 7 . . . Pre-Monkee singles out in U.K. from Micky Dolenz "Huff Pull" and Davy Jones ("Theme for a New Love").

Every teen mag in the world carries 'gossip' and 'scoop' items about the Beatles. So does this page of The Beat. The difference is that only the true facts appear here. Far too many magazines rely upon building up and then knocking down their own fictitious Beatle rumors—which makes for a lot of sensational copy-selling headlines but leaves the reader confused by such a made mass of unreliable stories!

Keith West, star of the London-based group called Tomorrow, has had fantastic chart success in the U.K. and all thru Europe with his self-penned "Excerpt From a Teen-age Opera." West hopes to promote this and the follow-up via a brief visit to America at the of October.

"Davy and I often giggle about them", said Australian songstress Lynne Randell when required to comment on newspaper romance stories linking her with the name of Davy Jones. She went on: "I'm honestly surprised Day is still such a nice, straight-forward person. He's so friendly he immediately puts people at ease. The first time we met I felt I'd known him for ages."

Ringo Solo

Their own London recording studio to be built and furnished for the Beatles . . . Ringo Starr has said many times that he is interested in the idea of making a solo movie appearance if the right screen-play is presented to him. Most interesting offer yet is under his consideration right now . . . "Gettin' Hungry" by Brian Wilson and Mike Love out in U.K. via Capitol label.

John Lennon's younger fans cannot attend public showings of "How I Won The War" in U.K. because movie has an "X" certificate barring all under-sixteens. So Official Fan Club, trying to find a loophole in the law, wants to organize private screenings for holder of membership cards regardless of their age.

"Top of the Pops" TV girl Samantha Juste away from program because of illness for an extra two weeks after her return from California . . . Prime Minister Harold Wilson has, in effect, given the Move more national newspaper publicity than any PRO could have mustered — by suing the group for alleged libel over a postcard which showed a drawing of Wilson in the nude!

Mothers Appearance

For only U.K. concert appearance of Mothers of Invention — on September 23 at London's Royal Albert Hall—top ticket price less than 4 dollars and lowest around 75 cents. In Melody Maker 1967 Pop Poll award for Musician of the Year to Cream's Eric Clapton, Single of the Year to Procol Harum's "A Whiter Shade of Pale", Album of the Year to "Sgt. Pepper's Lonely Hearts Club Band" . . . Offspring of Paul McCartney's cat Thisby named Jesus, Joseph and Mary.

A Peek At Young John And George

By Jamie McCluskey III

If you are a loyal Beatlemaniac, you have undoubtedly wondered, at some time in your life, just exactly what our Fab Four were like as children. Anyways, I know I have, so I have begun a BEAT scrapbook of "Beatle Snapshots;" little flashbacks into the childhood adventures of the Mersey Mop-Tops. I'd like to share some of them with you, so if you're ready—

Let's begin with John. John was raised by his aunt, Mimi Smith, from the age of five, and her recollections of him provide a very clear picture for our BEAT scrapbook.

"He was a loveable rebel; he hated any kind of conformity and those who wanted to make him conform, especially his school masters. He was always the leader of his little gang, and insisted on being the Indian and never the Cowboy. His word was law; if he said, 'You're dead,' than his friend had better accept the fact that he was dead!"

John is now world famous for his off-beat writing and Aunt Mimi tells us of the early beginnings of some of John's literary endeavors.

"He had this little house built in a tree, in our back garden. From the spring onwards it was impossible to see through the leaves, and he used to hide in there for hours. He called it his 'den' and used to sit there drawing and making up rhymes, just like those in his books. I used to get annoyed because he kept stealing all my clothes lines to make alterations to his tree-house."

Now that we've seen a little of John's childhood, let's turn the page and glance briefly at some snaps of George.

George's mother tells of George's early interest in performing for people: "He has always been fond of entertaining other people. When he was ten years old, his Dad gave him some hand-puppets for Christmas. From then on, whenever we had visitors, he always insisted on giving a little show kneeling behind the settee. The first time he ever got a big urge to play the guitar was when he was 13 years old. His brother Peter bought one and George promptly tried to learn to play it. Eventually, he formed a small group with some friends and they went along for an audition at the Speke British Legion Hall. The main act did not turn up, so George's group played instead. They only knew two songs and once they had done both of them, they started again with the first and went on playing the same two over and over again!"

Even as a child, George was concerned about the clothes he wore. Today he designs much of his own clothing and then has them made up for him. But a few years ago, George had to take matters into his own hands. His father explains that he and his wife used to emcee some of the local old-time dances, and George used to get quite a big chuckle out of the wide-bottomed trousers that most of the dancers were wearing. "He decided to do something about his own because he said he did not want to be old-fashioned, so one day, when I bought him a new pair of flannels for school, he sat up till late at night and altered them on his mother's sewing machine until they were narrowed to his satisfaction."

These are just a few of the many little Beatle snapshots which are in our BEAT scrapbook, but it's time to put the book away for now.

If you will join us again next week, we'll re-open our scrapbook and take a look back into the childhood of one Mr. Paul Beatle, MBE as well as his three long-haired companions.

See ya then, luvs. Cheerio!

BEATLES ARCHIVES 1

Beatles No. 1 – Again!

The Beatles have again proved that their vast audience is definitely not limited to teenagers only.

Students from forty-four American colleges named the foursome the "Top Group On Campus" in a recent music poll. Runners-up to the title included the Stones, Supremes, Beach Boys, Lettermen, Righteous Brothers, Four Seasons, Dave Clark Five, Chad & Jeremy, Lovin' Spoonful, Herman's Hermits and the Miracles.

"Best In-Person Show" honors went to Peter, Paul & Mary, who also won the title of "Favorite Folk Group."

Bob Dylan and Joan Baez were crowned king and queen of folk, with Andy Williams and Barbra Streisand reigning as top pop artists.

Among the others who registered on the pop portion of the poll were Elvis, James Brown, Pet Clark, Bobby Vinton, Roger Miller, Cher Bono, Mick Jagger, Paul McCartney and Len Barry.

Other recent surveys have proved that many of the record buyers who purchase "teenage music" are past college level and well into the 25-30 age bracket.

Our music just isn't "teenage" any more. If anything, it's "ageless." But whatever you choose to call it, it's certainly here to stay.

THE BEATLES

Welcome back, Beatles!

After too long a time of reading about what the "fab foursome" *wasn't* doing, their hard-earned holiday is over and they're back in the headlines.

Biggest news of all was their tour announcement. The Beatles will definitely return to the States next August for a three-week, 14-city personal appearance trek.

Meanwhile, back at the record rack, the Beatles continue to rule. Their "Nowhere Man" came on the national charts like gangbusters, at #24 the first week. Destined to be the next Beatle goldie, this disc sold 744,000 during its first eight days of release!

Ringo Scores

And, just as there are two sides to every story, there are two sides to every Beatle 45. Ringo's "What Goes On Here" was a slow starter, hitting the charts a week later than the flip and coming on then at #89. But it's moving hard and fast now, so chalk up another double-barrelled Beatle bulls-eye.

The long arm of Liverpool has finally touched the contemporary folk fan. The Kingston Trio's "Norwegian Wood" single is a national pick to click and it's quite possible that this segment of the market may also find itself held gently but firmly in the palm of the powerful Beatle hand.

Album-wise, "Rubber Soul" has dropped out of the number one slot, but is still in the top five. This LP is well past the two-million-copies-sold mark and is expected to remain on the charts indefinitely. Three other Beatle albums are still best-sellers. Namely, "Help" (#30 after 29 weeks on the charts), "Beatles VI" (#62 after 104 weeks) and "Beatles 65" (#104 after 62 weeks).

Three albums headlining Beatle compositions are also listed. Bud Shank's "Michelle" rates at #71, Billy Vaughn's "Michelle" at #84 and "The Baroque Beatles Book" at #93.

Coming up fast is the Hollyridge Strings new longie titled "The New Beatles Songbook."

Stereo Business

Additionally, the Beatles have now gone into the stereo tape business. All the songs from "Rubber Soul" and "The Beatles Second Album" will be featured on a package containing eight other reels.

Elsewhere in the world, the Beatles have once again cracked the hard-shelled record market in France. "Michelle" (released there as an EP) has parlayed to the number one spot and "Rubber Soul" is number two on the French LP charts.

Beatle discs (singles, EPs and albums) are also top-tenning it in thirteen other countries.

Since there doesn't seem to be anything the Beatles can't accomplish, perhaps they can do something about the fact that August is almost six whole months away!

Let's hope so.

...JOHN AND RINGO COMIN' BACK.

The Beatles are definitely coming! Brian Epstein has announced that the Beatles will make their third tour of America in late August or early September.

Tony Barrow sent a telegram to *The BEAT* saying, "Beatles playing 14 cities including New York, Chicago and San Francisco plus probably Washington. No other cities and no venues named at this time."

The Beatles' New York appearance will be at Shea Stadium which was the scene of last year's Beatle triumph. It was also at Shea that their entire concert was filmed and shown throughout England where it met with rave reviews from everyone.

Announcement of the Beatles' forthcoming American tour came as a slight surprise to people in the business because of the trouble the Beatles seem to be having getting started on their third movie. Beatle spokesmen hinted at the possibility of keeping the Beatles out of the U.S. until their movie is completed. There was even talk making the rounds that their movie would not even *begin* filming until late summer which would have, of course, kept the Beatles from an extensive U.S. tour before, at least, October or possibly November.

The fact that the Beatles have not firmed contracts to appear in Los Angeles is rather upsetting to all Beatle fans living in Southern California. On their previous tours the Beatles have played the Hollywood Bowl selling out within 24 hours after tickets went on sale.

It is highly conceivable that John, Paul, George and Ringo will skip San Diego this time around because last August when they played San Diego's Balboa Stadium they only managed to half fill the stadium.

San Francisco was the scene of the wildest Beatle audience ever. The Beatles' appearance at the Cow Palace was the most riotous performance by an audience that the Beatles ever witnessed in America. When it was over Brian Epstein stated that the Beatles would *never* play San Francisco again.

And yet San Francisco was one of the first cities the Beatles agreed to play on their third tour! Fans in Los Angeles are furious over the fact that they have faithfully supported the Beatles in record sales and especially in personal appearances and instead of showing their gratitude to L.A. they have decided to play San Francisco first!

The BEAT would like to caution Southern California Beatle fans not to panic just yet. The Beatles are negotiating at this very moment for a return to L.A. so it is more than likely that they *will* be playing the Hollywood Bowl once again.

Beatles Order Lookalikes

George Harrison's special custom-built "Millionaire's Mini" is ready for delivery. The tiny but powerful little car has a Mini-Cooper tuned engine, seats which are in the Rolls Royce class, power-operated windows which have dark-tinted glass, luxurious lambswool carpets and a load of other plushy extras. Cost of the finished product is in excess of 4,000 dollars and three other similar vehicles are being prepared for the other Beatles.

The boys were very specific about their requirements for the fleet of Beatle-Minis. They gave exact details of what they wanted in the way of special fittings and the cars were ordered late last year. Each one will have minor differences inside, according to individual requests from the boys.

It goes without saying that the outsides will be painted black, the all-time favorite color of The Beatles.

BEATLES ARCHIVES 1

DEREK TAYLOR'S LIFE WITH THE BEATLES
Recalls First Meeting When He Marveled At Their Magnetism

AS BEATLE PRESS OFFICER

By DEREK TAYLOR

On May 30, 1962, I telephoned the manager of the Odeon Cinema in Manchester, and told him that I was interested in a touring show due at his cinema that night.

The manager — a gloomy, pessimistic man like a lot of his kind in England — was not impressed because he knew that newspapermen working for daily publications were of no use to him so far as 1-night stands were concerned.

The reason for this is that by the time the journalist's report on the show is published, the show has moved to another town and the publicity is, therefore, of no help to his cinema.

KRLA BEAT

The KRLA BEAT is published weekly by Prestige Publishing Company; editorial and advertising offices at 6290 Sunset Boulevard, Suite 504, Hollywood, California 90028.

Single copy price, 10 cents.

Subscription price: U.S. and possessions, and Canada, $3 per year or $5 for two years. Foreign rates upon request.

So he merely grunted when I asked for a couple of tickets. He said, "There are no free ones for the press." Journalists, such as their temperament, detest paying for admission to anything, whether to a cinema, theatre or a nightclub.

But as this was to be no ordinary show, I said, "Well, how are you fixed for tickets if I pay?"

He grunted a bit more and left the telephone for a moment or two. Then he returned and said, "You can have a couple on the front row for a guinea each."

"Right," I said. "I'll pick them up at the box-office for the first show."

Turning Point

That telephone call was the turning point of my life, for the stars of the show were the Beatles.

I phoned my wife and said, "You know that group your sister told us about — the Beatles. Well, they're in Manchester tonight and I've got a couple of tickets."

She hustled about, found some babysitters, and at five minutes to 6:00 we were in our seats among the most nervous audience I'd ever seen.

I had been to pop shows before — not many, for the popular music scene in England up to that time had held little appeal for anyone above teen age — but I had neevr sensed such urgency and excitement in any audience.

There were banners everywhere. Everyone was sitting on the edge of his seat, and I said to my wife, "There's something happening in this theatre and whatever it is, it's new to me. Can you feel it?"

Like Sinatra

She said she could, and we both agreed the nearest we had come to it was in the early 1950s when Sinatra — during his fall from grace — had toured England, playing in old-fashioned vauderville shows with the top seat price less than a dollar. But neither Sinatra, nor Danny Kaye in the wild days of 1949, had caused such extraordinary tension in any theatre.

On the bill with the Beatles were Roy Orbison, Gerry and the Pacemakers, and a few other acts whose names I have now forgotten.

The show opened with the lesser-known acts and then, to a storm of applause, little Gerry Marsden burst onto the stage in a tight suit and pounding into the first bars of "How Do You Do It."

His reception was enormous and I remember thinking that if the Beatles were going to top it, they had better be pretty good.

Gerry was a delightful artist and his personality and energy were something completely new in popular music, which had become very jaded and static.

Remember that at that time the major recording stars of England were Cliff Richard and the Shadows who, though experienced and established, were hardly electrifying on stage.

Teen Idols

The Beatles by then had a huge teenage following but were scarcely known to adults. This was not the fault of the Beatles, for they had already made three records — "Love Me Do," which had reached No. 17 in the British charts, "Please Please Me" and "From Me To You," both of which had made No. 1.

It was simply that most adults didn't concern themselves with the teenage world or its idols.

Perspiring and obviously delighted by his reception, Gerry finished his act in a hailstorm of jelly babies and I slipped out for a drink during the intermission.

After the break, the extraordinary Orbison strolled up to the microphone to a hushed, almost reverent reception.

—MORE ON PAGE 6

More About:

Derek's Start With Beatles

(Continued From Page 2)

I must confess that I had never heard of him, and his appearance was, not to put too fine a point on it, unconventional for a pop star.

He wore his tinted glasses, and that smooth white face was surrounded by a halo of lacquered hair. Also, he was plump. But, of course, any early doubts were scattered by the man's enormous skill with a song and by his repose at the microphone. He was the perfect antidote to the wilderness of Gerry and the Pacemakers. And to give the audience their due, they applauded him as if he were the top-of-the-bill act.

New Era

By this time I realized that popular music had improved beyond belief. And when the emcee came from the wings and started to say, "John, Paul . . ." the auditorium exploded in a massive scream from 3,000 throats.

It was the Beatles.

From the right-hand side of the stage came George Harrison and Paul McCartney. It was my first sight of the choir-boy countenance of Paul. Little had been written about them in newspapers, and not too much in magazines. And neither my wife nor I could identify them on sight.

But I had noticed the strong and cynical features of John Lennon on television a few days earlier and also the homeliness of Ringo Starr who, with John, pranced in from the stage-left.

By now the scream was permanent and I felt my ears would explode.

What a show! The Beatles sang ten songs and it was clear to me that we were in the presence of something quite outside normal experience.

My recollection of that first night is so clear and my assessment of the Beatles' quality was so immediate that I still see red when someone attempts to knock the Beatles' talent or personality with one of those dead-pan questions like, "What's so special about them?"

(Derek Taylor's nostalgis account of his introduction to the Beatles and of his later employment as their press officer will be continued next week.)

BEATLES' MOVIE
(Continued From Page 5)

tions are so explosive that to give out even an inkling of their content might spoil the impact when the film is shown.

Broke Up

On more than one occasion during the making of "Help!" notoriously blase film technicians had to leave the set because their vainly suppressed laughter during the shooting was coming through on the sound track.

"Help!" is essentially a holiday picture," says Producer Shenson. "It was made in two totally contrasting holiday resorts. We travelled from calypso to yodel with a lot of yeah-yeah thrown in besides. It will be released in August both in England and the States— holiday time for most people — and we hope the movie itself will be something of a holiday for everyone who sees it."

Dick Lester describes "Help!" as an adventure comedy. "The boys will play themselves again but in a completely fictitional situation, unlike 'A Hard Day's Night' which could be described best as cinema journalism."

Filmed in Eastman's Colour, Walter Shenson's and Dick Lester's second movie starring the Beatles will once again be released throughout the world by United Artists.

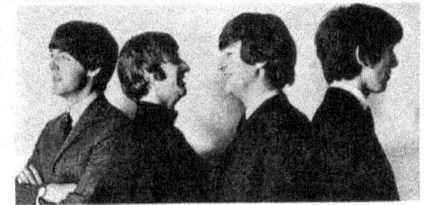

FREE BEATLE PIN-UPS

(Regular 50¢ Each)

TO EVERY CUSTOMER WHO PRESENTS

THIS AD AT:

HOLLYWOOD WAX MUSEUM

HOLLYWOOD BLVD. AT HIGHLAND AVE.

BEATLES ARCHIVES 1

RINGO TO ENTER HOSPITAL; OPERATION

(Story in Col. 1)

OPERATION FOR BEATLE.....

NEW YORK—Ringo Starr has announced that he will enter the hospital later this fall for his much talked about throat operation. He made the announcement at a press conference in New York just before the four fabulous Beatles left this country to return to England.

RUMOR CONFIRMED

For months, there have been rumors that Ringo intended to have the operation, but it was finally confirmed when he made his statement to the press. Ringo does not know at this date just when he is to enter the hospital.

The operation will only take a few hours, but the famous drummer said that he expected to be in the hospital at least three days to catch up on some much needed rest. It is rumored that the three days will be sometime when the group does not have other pressing committments, and will give John, George, and Paul a short vacation.

CONFIDED IN DAVE

Ringo didn't disclose the name of the hospital he is planning for his operation, however, when the group was in Los Angeles, Ringo confided to Dave Hull that it will be the University College Hospital where he was taken after his collapse last spring. The operation itself is very simple. Since Ringo never had his tonsils or adenoids removed, the main purpose of the operation will be to remove them, along with several small growths which cause our boy to get frequent attacks of tonsillitis, and sometimes cause Ringo to come down with very bad colds.

ASKS FOR TONSILS

Other than his throat, Ringo is in excellent condition. One fan has already asked for the tonsils to be preserved for her, but Ringo doesn't know yet whether he will answer her request. Everyone in the world joins KRLA in wishing him a speedy recovery.

Pen Pals Write, "Hi, Hullabalooer"

KRLA'S DAVE HULL received an autographed photo this week from four friends in England. Perhaps you'll recognize some of them. It's one of their favorite pictures and was taken as Dave and Derek Taylor interviewed the boys during filming of "Help." The photo may look familiar, since it was published earlier — without the autographs — as a KRLA BEAT world-wide exclusive.

BEATLES ARCHIVES 1

Beatle Meets Stateside Press

George Harrison flew to Los Angeles recently to take in a concert by Ravi Shankar at the Hollywood Bowl. The visit by the Beatle, who has been taking sitar lessons from the famed Indian musician, prompted a press conference at Shankar's school of music in Hollywood.

Sitting cross-legged by his musical mentor, George told reporters he started playing sitar because "I just happened to like this instrument. One obvious reason is because it's a stringed instrument."

"Indian music," George said, makes God come through in a spiritual way. It makes one more aware God can be put into sound. Sitar music is 100 percent spiritual."

Sitar Doubts

With incense burning and sitar music gently playing in the background, George expressed doubts about his chances of mastering the 19-stringed instrument.

"I want to learn a little Indian music and use it in our medium, but I'm not an expert sitar player. If I could sit down and play sitar properly I would. I don't expect to be a brilliant sitarist. I would have to concentrate on playing sitar, but there are so many other things to do, and I want to do them."

The press meeting inevitably got away from the sitar and on to more controversial subjects such as:

The draft. "The draft is diabolical. Anything to do with arms is terrible—a waste of time. If a person wants to volunteer, it's all right but nobody should be forceably made to kill."

Lucy?

Are the initials to "Lucy Is A Sky of Diamonds" an obvious reference to LSD? "It means LSD if you want it to be. Everybody interprets everything in his own way. That's the problem with the world. We didn't realize it could mean LSD until someone mentioned it to us."

George went on to say the song was inspired by something John Lennon's young son said about a girl he knew at school. Then he started speculating about his future.

"All I know is I'm going to carry on being me—I don't know where I'm going. Something else in life has more control over me."

Getting more down to earth, George said the Beatles will be putting out another movie sometime. "We've got a contract to make another movie, but when or how is completely up to us."

'It Depends'

When someone asked George what the Beatles felt about narcotics—a reference to their endorsement of the legalization of marijuana—he answered simply, "It depends on what you call a narcotic."

George put down, however, the idea that the Beatles should watch what they endorse since they influence so many people. "This stuff about the Beatles influencing people is a lot of bull," George said. "It's up to the person if he wants to be influenced—it's their choice."

On the subject of whether he or the Beatles would ever change, George said "Some people think it is a sin to at all. The whole point of life is change. Success has given me every material thing I need, and I realize I need something not material."

Non-Material

George indicated that his interest in Indian music and culture is a part of his effort to delve into the non-material aspects of life.

A day later Harrison flew to San Francisco unannounced and was discovered by some hippies strolling in Golden Gate Park with his wife, Patti. In a short time, several hundred fans were showering the Harrisons with peace buttons, posters, and flowers.

While in the park George picked up a guitar offered to him and performed a short, impromptu concert next to a small lake. He then headed down Haight Street followed like a pied piper by the orderly crowd.

George's reaction to it all? "Wow! It's really great if its all like this."

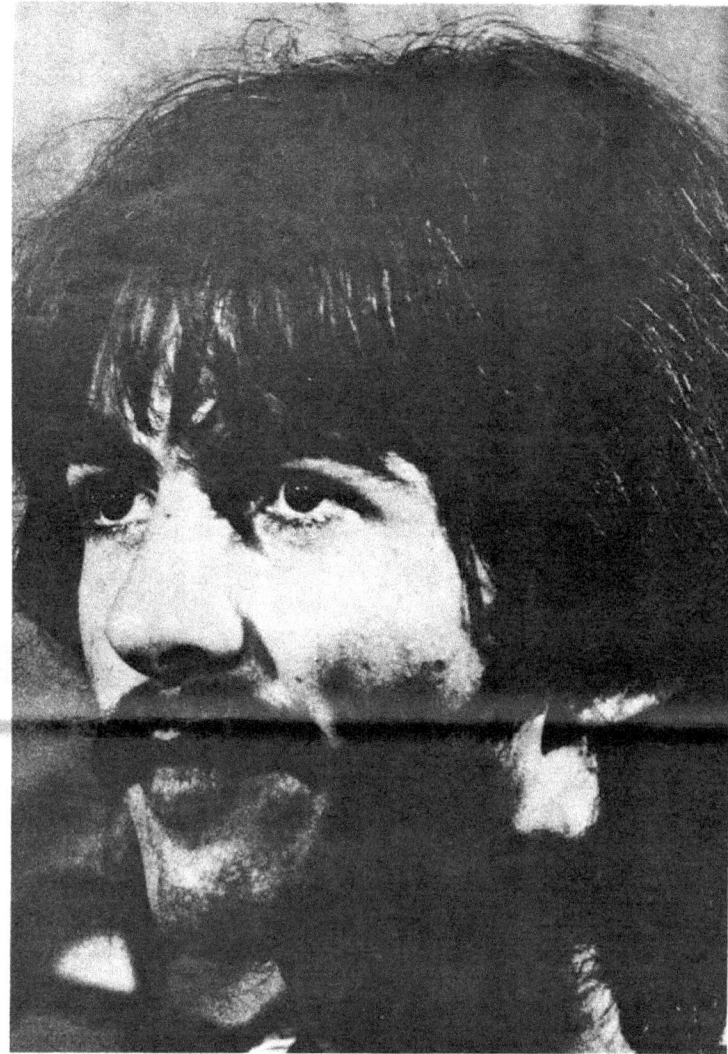

BEAT Photos: Ed Caraeff

"THE DRAFT IS DIABOLICAL," Harrison told Los Angeles reporters.

"I DON'T know where I'm going."

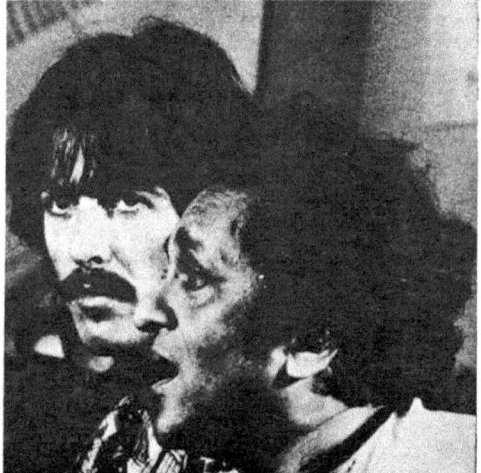
HARRISON SITS with his sitar teacher, Ravi Shankar.

BEATLES ARCHIVES 1

HI, I'M BOB EUBANKS! Here is your own personal minute-by-minute guide of the Beatles' stay in Los Angeles. KRLA newsmen and photographers were there every minute to give all our listeners a guided tour through Beatle-land! (And that's the same as K*R*L*A*N*D) The boys were so much fun to be with that I wish you all could have been with me. But since you weren't, here's the next best thing! Before they left, they asked me to give you their personal thanks for the groovy way they were treated in Los Angeles. So, from the Beatles . . . and from me . . . Thanks!

3:30 PM . . . THE BEATLES ARRIVE! Without telling a soul (except KRLA) the idols of millions land in Los Angeles to be cleared through customs. Derrick Taylor looks around to see if the coast is clear . . .

3:40 PM . . . It is, and so the boys slowly step down the ramp pausing for the KRLA photographer as they come down. The first they said was "Hey, it's sunny . . . we can go swimming!"

4:40 AM The boys are whisked into a security car and driven to the home in Bel Air where they will stay while they are in town. Ringo, in the back seat, is already half asleep. P.S.: He got to sleep later!

6:00 PM Press conference time! Out at Bob Eubanks' Cinnamon Cinder, he and Reb Foster introduce the Beatles and tell members of the press that they can start asking questions . . . and they started asking!

"WHAT ABOUT JANE ASHER, PAUL?" "W and all, but we certainly aren't married. found her yet, but I'm having a blast loo

"YOU WANTED TO SAY SOMETHING, RINGO?" "Uh . . . yes. Can I have a drink of water? Thanks. Now tell me, when do we get to ask all YOU people some questions?" Bob Eubanks handed Ringo the glass, but didn't save it!

8:00 PM 'B DAY' IS HERE! The Bowl started filling at 3:00 in the afternoon! Everyone hoped to catch a glimpse of their beloved Beatles, but the boys were secretly brought in only a few minutes before the show.

9:00 PM The other acts have performe Dave Hull, Reb Foster, Bob Eubanks is a moment of silence . . . and then

Ringo's hair is flying. His hands are going so fast that they're just a blur in the air. Every time he moves his head, the screams grow louder. Will anyone ever be able to forget 'B Day'? We doubt it!

Photography by ROBYN HILL

Too soon, the boys take their final bow. By the time the screams have stopped, they are halfway to Bel Air for a three day vacation in Los Angeles before resuming their cross country tour.

2:00 PM It's over. The Beatles are lea the weather knew how sad Los Ange them at the airport to say a last fina

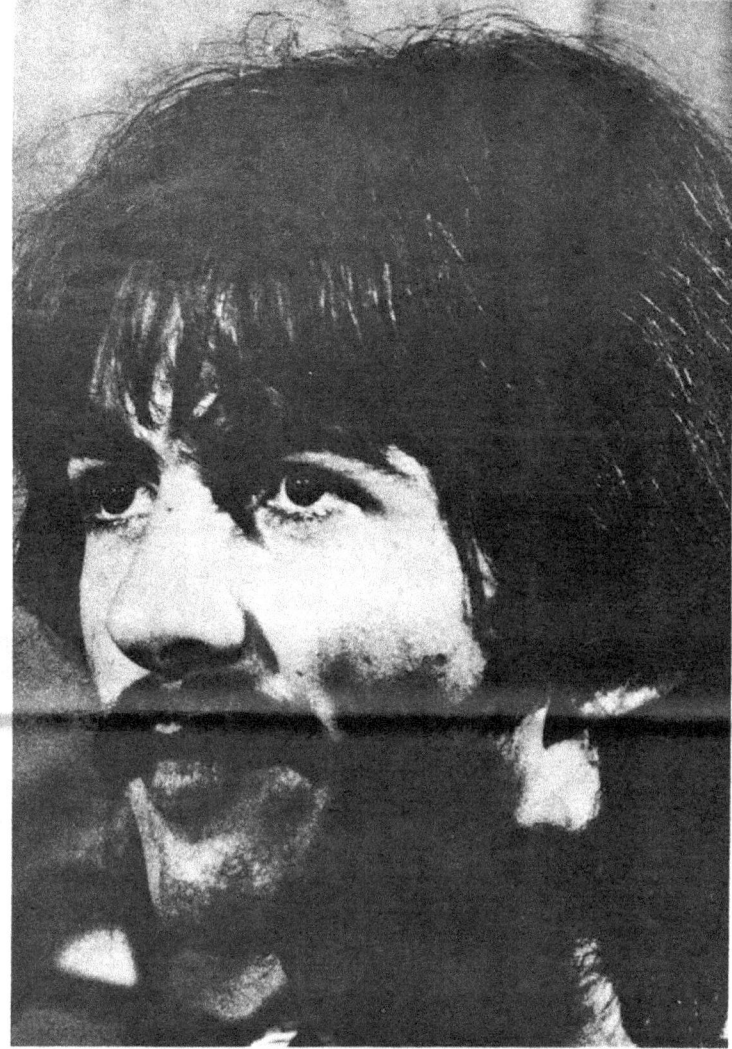

BEATLES ARCHIVES 1

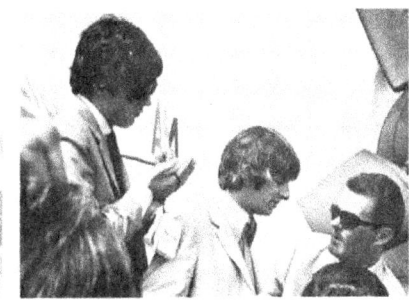

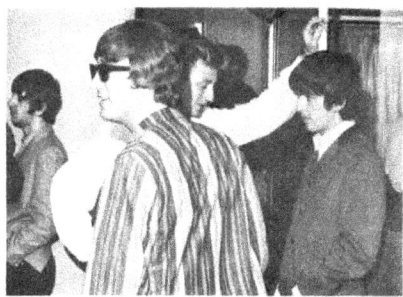

3:42 PM KRLA's newsman, Jim Steck, was right there to tape exclusive interviews with all four Beatles . . . something no one else was able to do. Then the boys took off for San Francisco's Cow Palace.

4:10 PM Finally, the Beatles arrive back in L.A. for their performance. Again, they land secretly so that crowds wouldn't mob them. Again, KRLA is first on the scene! The boys were groggy and half asleep . . .

4:25 PM . . . But they still were able to smile and talk with KRLA newsmen. The only thing they could talk about, though, was getting some sleep before the long, hard day's night ahead of them.

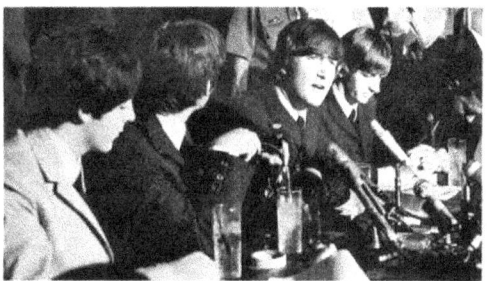

at about her? Oh, we're good friends . . . I'm looking for the perfect girl. Haven't I king!"

"WHAT DO YOU THINK OF AMERICAN GIRLS, GEORGE?" "THEY ARE JUST TOO MUCH! I really dig them! Never saw a country before where EVERY ONE of the girls were truly gear, but I haven't seen one here that missed yet!

"JOHN, ARE YOU LEAVING THE GROUP?" "Rubbish! Wouldn't have anyone to pick on if I did. Besides, if I left these poor clods, they wouldn't know what to do. I'm the only one they listen to!" (Paul laughed)

. . . the KRLA D.J.'s walk on stage . . . the audience grows quiet . . . there . . . "HERE THEY ARE . . . THE BEATLES!!!!!"

They look at Ringo . . . he adjusts his drums. Paul tunes his guitar. The audience screams louder and louder . . . finally, Ringo is ready. He gives the signal. The boys turn and face the stage . . . and sing.

"I want to hold your hand . . ." The girls let him know by their screams that they want to hold his, too! The screams go on . . . and the Beatles sing . . . and sing . . . and sing. There's never been anything like it!

ing. The day is cloudy, almost as though was to see them go. Jim Steck meets goodbye . . .

2:10 PM . . . BUT WAIT! WHAT'S THIS? WHY THE SURPRISED LOOK ON JOHN AND GEORGE'S FACES? COULD IT BE . . . YES, BY GUM, IT IS! THE BEATLES MAY BE LEAVING K*R*L*A*N*D BUT KRLA ISN'T LEAVING THE BEATLES!

2:13 PM With the KRLA 'hookey-players' safely tucked inside, the doors are closed, and the plane takes off. Yes, they're gone. But don't cry too hard . . . because they'll soon be back!

KRLA BEAT

Edition

Volume 1, Number 30   LOS ANGELES CALIFORNIA   15 Cents   October 9, 1965

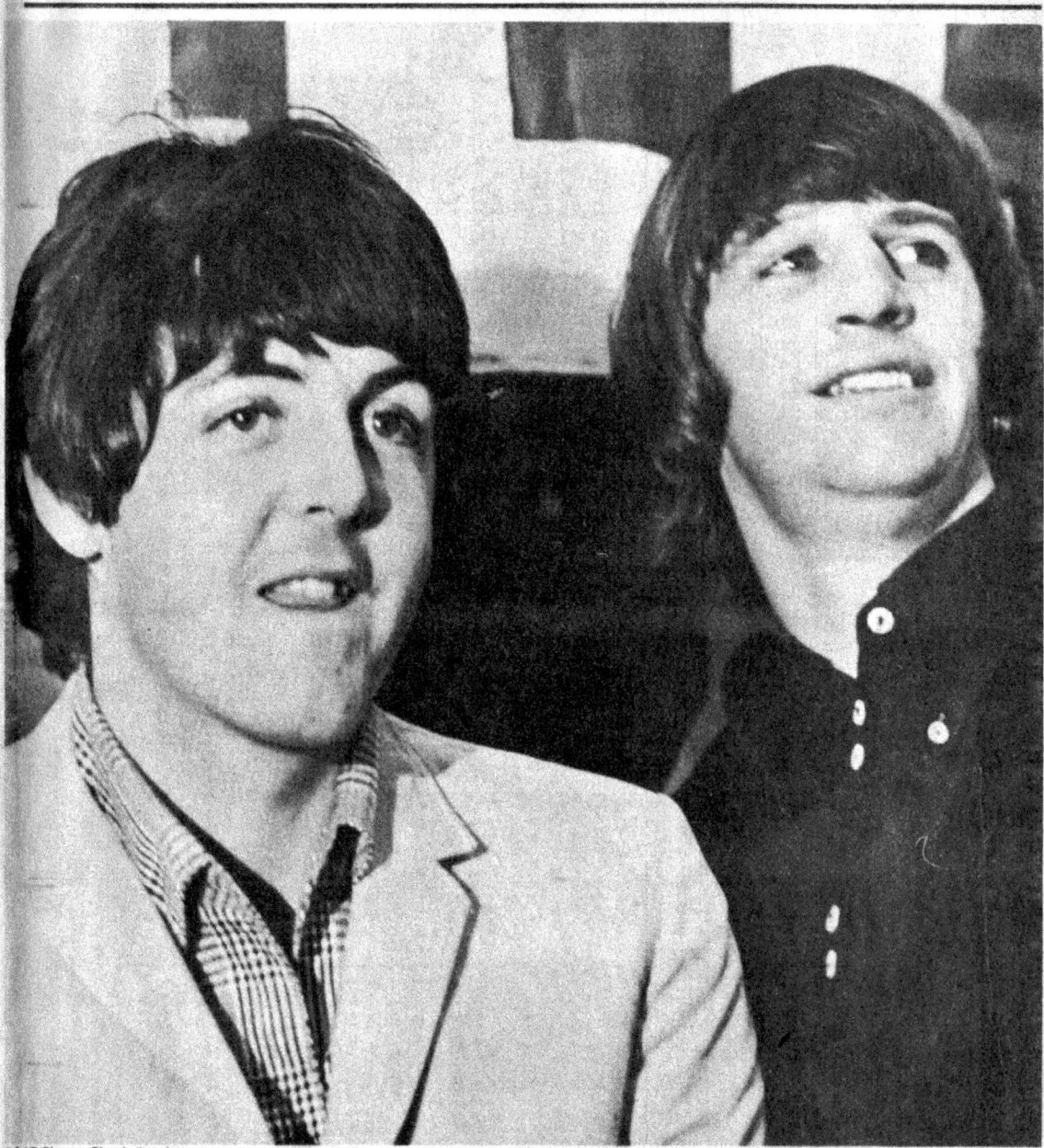

BEAT Photo: Chuck Boyd

Why Are Paul & Ringo Now Soloing? (Story Inside)

BEATLES ARCHIVES 1

THEY HOPE WE HAVE ENJOYED THE SHOW

Two Part Beatle History

By Jacoba Atlas

Once upon a time in the not so mythical sea-coast city of Liverpool, four young men emerged to carry the world along with their music. As in a fairy-tale, they were adored by all and fans eager for personal identification with their heroes clung to their clearly defined public images.

John with his glasses, books and caustic remarks was called the "clever one," he played the role well. Paul with his handsome face and charming manner was called the "sweet one" and fans who found the name Paul a bit too distant endearingly called him "Paulie." George with his high cheek bones and somber demeanor was dubbed the "quiet one," and Ringo with his puppy dog, soft eyes was called the "sad one." They wrote and played songs and called their corporate image – The Beatles.

They broke into the pop scene when it was floundering in poor songs and tired faces. Their songs were better than the other marketable offerings, and their charm and energy completely won over half the world – the younger half.

They wrote simply and sang with a driving beat accompaniment. "I Want To Hold Your Hand," "Please, Please Me," and "I Saw Her Standing There" all set the tone for the fairy-tale to unfold.

Comments

The adult population debated over their long hair, held their ears to the sound of their songs, and more or less generally ignored the Beatles except for condescending comments. Of course they were successes – never before, not even with Elvis – had there been such hysteria, but the charisma would not last; the craze would pass.

With their first movie, originally planned by United Artists to exploit the Beatles' recording popularity with a UA released soundtrack album, the powers-that-be began to take their first serious look at the Beatles and their music.

Such Establishment singers as Ella Fitzgerald and Peggy Lee sang tunes from the movie, "A Hard Day's Night;" and movie critics hailed it as a classic of its kind, likening the Beatles to the Marx Brothers.

As the critics dissected the film, they strengthened the image. John pulled off the wise cracks, Paul looked adorable, George stayed his quiet self, and Ringo emerged as a fine comic actor.

Cinematic Innovators

The film's significance to the motion picture industry was duly noted and Richard Lester, their director, was given an honored place in film hierarchy as a cinematic innovator. The fans, who knew the Beatles were marvelous all along, just enjoyed the exuberance and the honesty of the Beatles – no questions asked.

After "A Hard Day's Night" came a period which although important at the time, emerges in retrospect only as a bridge during which time the Beatles were finding their musical and emotional way. Certainly some interesting songs came out of this time – "I Feel Fine" with that prophetic opening chord, "She's A Woman" with its unique tempo, and "I'll Follow the Sun" with its folk quality; but most of their songs – although streets ahead of their contemporaries – are best kept in our memories.

John himself dismisses this period by saying, "the period I dislike in our career was 'Eight Days A Week' time . . . we weren't ashamed of it, and I suppose it was right at the time, but something told me it wasn't us . . . looking back we weren't in full control of the music. It was good at the time . . . but it was something written for a period – a period of our growth."

Their search for their own musical identity led them to new experimentation and creativity – but they were still hampered somewhat by their image.

More Satire

They made another film, "Help," much more advanced and satirical than "A Hard Day's Night," but still tied to the fairy-tale image of the Beatles. John was again the "clever one," Paul charming, George progressing to an air of mystery and Ringo the comic foil.

The music had gotten better with the lyrics of the title song being especially interesting. With "Ticket To Ride," the Beatles produced a completely new combination of divergent rhythms.

Also the satire of "Help" was a little more subtle and irrelevent than in "A Hard Day's Night." Scotland Yard, religion, drugs, the State, medicine and various social orders all came under the attack of the Beatles, again with the help of Richard Lester. Perhaps their more sophisticated story and use of classical music to underscore the humor of the picture were indications of what was to come.

About this time Paul came up with a lovely-sad ballad "Yesterday," which brought the Beatles firmly into the established "adult" popular scene. Andy Williams, Nancy Wilson, and Perry Como – to name but a few – all recorded "Yesterday." Beatle fans throughout the world fell in love with Paul all over again as he sang solo to the accompaniment of cello and violins.

Eroding Image

Then came the album to end all albums – "Rubber Soul." With this exceptional offering the fairy-tale image of the Beatles was beginning to erode and more mature, more realistic characteristics appeared in their music. Paul's famous quote about not writing fifteen year old songs at twenty, was finally coming true.

Sophistication was beginning to set in. At twenty-five and twenty-three respectively, John and Paul were no longer writing "I'm Happy Just To Dance With You" or "She Loves You." Replacing them were such songs as "Girl" which John wrote after reading a book called *Pain and Pleasure* basing its theme on the Protestant Ethnic of work.

Electronic manipulation of sound in its most simple form could be heard in the simulation of a percussion instrument in the huge intake of breath as John sings the word "girl."

The repetitious rhythms gave way, as they had in "Ticket To Ride," to the more diverse tempos in "I'm Looking Through You" and "You Won't See Me" both of which also contain fine lyrics.

The ballads were well represented with "In My Life," a lovely ode to a present love, borrowing for its bridge from the 17th century baroque period of music, and "Michelle" which like its sister song, "Yesterday" has become a standard.

"Rubber Soul" brought the Beatles the intellectual recognition so often denied them before – despite the books and the movies. It also brought them into a controversy over the meaning of one of their songs, something which had not happened before.

There could be little debate over the message in "I Saw Her Standing There" – unless you want to take exception to the words "she was just seventeen, you know what I mean" – but the protectors of teen-age morality seemed to question just what was really going on in that room made of "Norwegian Wood." One critic went so far as to say it was about a man trying to seduce a lesbian.

When asked about "Norwegian Wood" both John and Paul said that it was simply about a girl who worked in the morning and a man who didn't.

Fidelity & Revenge

Whether that explanation satisfied anyone is doubtful, but the Beatle fairy-tale image of those four jolly lads from Liverpool was beginning to change – at long last. Add to that "Run For Your Life," a contemporary song about fidelity and revenge, and the world had the foundations for the new and brilliant work to come.

(To Be Continued)

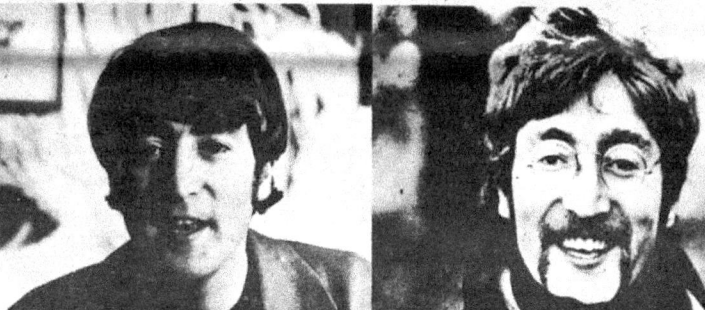

LENNON: Unchanged by success?

READY FOR the long ride to success . . .

THE BEATLES in 1964, with one movie behind them and the world at their feet.

BEATLES ARCHIVES 1

U.K. Pop News Round-Up

Stones, Beatles Closer

By Tony Barrow

"We love you all for the help from our friends to a happier end" is the slogan which accompanied the unexpectedly early arrival of a new single from THE ROLLING STONES, issued by Decca in the U.K. on August 18. My first striking impression after listening to "Dandelion" and "We Love You," the two Mick Jagger/Keith Richard compositions, is that the musical paths of The Stones and The Beatles have never been closer. It's common knowledge that Stones drop in to watch Beatle make records and Beatles take an equally close interest in the studio activities of Stones. Of course, we are unlikely to see the two groups named alongside one another on a record label since each holds a long-term contract with a different company. But the togetherness of feeling and direction is clear.

We Love You

"We Love You" is the gimmick deck and has the sound of a prison warder's footsteps, the clanky grind of keys turning in a cell-door lock. Of the two sides this is musically more in keeping with previous Stones' records. It features a wild lumpy backing, not a beautiful thing but certainly powerful in its impact. At the end there's a snatch of "Dandelion" played backwards.

Mini-Choir

On "We Love You" the theme of the lyrics runs parallel to that of The Beatles' most recent single. On "Dandelion" the actual presentation moves towards that of John, Paul, George and Ringo in that The Stones form themselves into some sort of mini-choir to provide vast high harmony effects behind Mick's simple, cleanly-delivered solo work. Of the two I prefer "Dandelion" with its brief, repetitive, familiar tune—one of the most commercial productions the group has made since "Get Off Of My Cloud" or even earlier.

The first LP album by THE PROCOL HARUM is on sale in America but *NOT* in Britain! Before the group issues an album in the U.K. a number of the original tracks will be scrapped and fresh material substituted. But a new single will be released on both sides of the Atlantic within the next few weeks. Probably title on the main side of the record will be the Gary Brooker/Keith Reid number "Homburg Hat" which has a fantastic piano theme to create much the same sort of hypnotic effect which organ playing gave to "Whiter Shade Of Pale."

Carrie To King

JULIET PROWSE stars in the West End stage production of "Sweet Charity" opening at London's Prince of Wales theatre in October . . . Under the new management of their record producer Ron Richards and publicity man Robin Britten THE HOLLIES now plan a three-week October trip to America to include college concert dates and several major television appearances. Group's "Carrie Anne" follow-up single is to be "King Midas" an original Hollie composition . . . Randy Newman's "So Long Dad" is latest MANFRED MANN single . . . British vocal group and backing band will accompany BRENDA LEE during U.K. cabaret dates in November. ENGELBERT HUMPERDINCK (latest single — "The Last Waltz") goes out on a 40-day U.K. concert tour lasting from the final week of October to the early part of December. Songstress LULU will be a special guest star on most of the dates.

Airplane Movie

At Brian Epstein's Saville Theatre JIMI HENDRIX EXPERIENCE presenting precisely the same act which was considered "too wild" for MONKEES' U.S. tour . . . During October visit to Britain JEFFERSON AIRPLANE may appear in Terence Cooper movie entitled "Freak Out" . . . Agent VIC LEWIS who promoted THE MONKEES' London concerts earlier this summer off to Russia to discuss the first-ever East-West exchange of pop talent.

Prior to September cabaret dates in Tokyo DUSTY SPRINGFIELD vacationing in California with her manager Vic Billings . . . Many TV and radio interviews by BRUCE JOHNSTON in London timed neatly to coincide with Capitol's release of "Heroes And Villains" single in U.K. . . . Very last record broadcast by RADIO LONDON before it went off the air forever was THE BEATLES' "A Day In The Life" . . . GEORGE AND PATTI HARRISON flew from London to Los Angeles as "Mr. & Mrs. Weiss" but didn't escape battery of press cameramen. They borrowed their flight name from NAT WEISS, co-manager of THE CYRKLE, who looked after the couple in California.

Answer To Lucy?

JOHN LENNON'S fave new single of the moment is "Hole In My Shoe" created by former Spencer Davis star STEVIE WINWOOD for his new group TRAFFIC. You might say this is Stevie's answer to "Lucy In The Sky" . . . Revolutionary new concept of pop concert presentation planned by THE PINK FLOYD who will operate circus-style in a mammoth tent and put on a light show. Meanwhile the group is having remarkable success with their first U.K. LP album called "The Piper At The Gates of Dawn" . . . SPENCER DAVIS had stitches in his knee after falling from the stage of New York's Cheetah Club.

Week-long October stint for THE MOVE at San Francisco's Avalon Ballroom. By then you'll have heard their latest single "Flowers In The Rain" . . . Quote from NEW VAUDEVILLE BAND'S MICK WILSHER: "Hip groups sneer at us but we're more hip than they'll ever be!" . . . Once Britain's top teenage songstress HELEN SHAPIRO, now 21, marries in a few weeks time . . . From Fontana label the new SPENCER DAVIS GROUP moving to United Artists . . . Says ERIC BURDEN: "San Francisco will be the cultural center of the world in a couple of years. Liverpool was a fallacy — there was only one group, one center of energy. What Frisco is doing where Liverpool failed is to make the scene come to them."

Flower Festival

"Festival of the Flower Children" at Woburn Abbey, one of Britain's most famous stately homes, over August Bank Holiday weekend stars a host of top pop units including THE KINKS, THE ALAN PRICE SET and THE BEE GEES . . . One of the very last commercials broadcast by the now-dead RADIO LONDON advertised special mail-order records featuring the station's jingles! . . . Capitol just issued SCOTT McKENZIE'S recording of the Mike Hurst number "Look In Your Eyes" as a U.K. single.

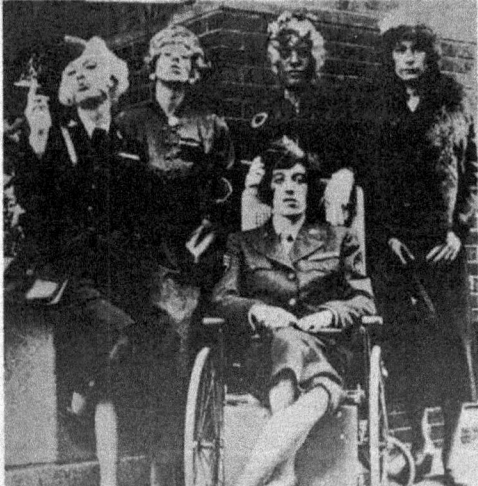

THE ROLLING STONES — sounding more and more like the Beatles.

BEATLE FIRM'S PROFITS SOAR

LONDON — Northern Songs, the firm owning copyright to 99 of the tunes composed by John Lennon and Paul McCartney and seven others by George Harrison, doubled profits for the last half year. Pre-tax earnings went soaring up to 422,000 pounds against 204,000 pounds.

Share holders prospering include John and Paul whose stake in the company runs about one million pounds. George and Ringo Starr own 40,000 shares each which would fetch up 56,000 pounds on the stock market. Is there anywhere to go but up?

BEAT Photo: Howard L. Bingham

...PAUL McCARTNEY

What Causes Beatlemania?

(Continued from page 2)

haps one of these will satisfy this question for someone else.

In America, during the summer of 1964, Beatlemania grew to a mighty peak. For months beforehand, the radio and television stations were flooded with Beatle music and Beatle programs, and every publication of any import in the nation carried news and pictures of the four lads from Liverpool.

Not Close Enough

But all during those preliminary months, the closest source of communication which the Beatlemaniacs in Uncle Samland had with their idols were the radios, television and magazines, and that just wasn't close enough.

Then suddenly — the Beatles had arrived. They were actually *here* on American soil. For the very first time after all those months of waiting, they were close enough to touch, to reach out and touch; they were no longer ten thousand miles away.

And then, the big night of the Beatle concert — a scene which was to be repeated in cities all across the nation. Hundreds and thousands of loyal Beatlemaniacs poured into theatres, stadiums, and amphitheatres around the country for their very first, live Beatle performance. It was an evening which would never be forgotten.

The lights went up, the introductions were made, and then — there they were: THE BEATLES!

The Waiting Girls

And in front of the Beatles were the girls; the girls who had waited for countless days, and weeks, and months. What were they to do now? Their beloved Beatles were now within feet, within *inches* of their grasp, and yet — they could not touch. The Beatles were there — and yet they weren't. For the moment, they were live, in person, singing their hearts out to their many screaming fans. For that one brief moment — they were *real*. They were no longer a dream. But all too soon that newly-found reality would be shattered. The Beatles would finish their performance and leave, and once again would be but a beautiful fantasy from a far-off land.

And so — happy to see them in reality at long, long last, and yet sad in the knowledge that all too soon they would be gone again — thousands of girls cried. They *wanted* to smile; they wanted to laugh, and smile, and shout, and scream, and cry. They wanted to do *all* of these things at once, because they *felt* all of these things at once. But in their confusion, they could do nothing but cry.

A Good Cry

Whenever the emotions are confused, whenever tension has been built up inside until it reaches the bursting point — the natural reaction is to cry. This is one of Nature's greatest safeguards for the human being who is the product of his own emotions.

Yes, they cry. The foregoing is just one of the many reasons for these tears, but it is also one of the most important.

Beatlemaniacs aren't really so very odd — they are just very human.

The Mothers —Soon

Enter Zak Starr

Congratulations to the Ringo Starrs on the birth of their son, Zak. Ringo has already given the idea of being a father plenty of thought and he has decided: "I will never send my child to boarding school. And I'll never push him. If he passes tests and gets diplomas and everything, all well and good, but I'll never say, 'You won't get this bike unless you go to college.' And I'll let him decide as he grows up, what he wants to be."

BEATLES ARCHIVES 1

KRLA + BEATLES = WOW!

BOB EUBANKS PLAYS STRAIGHT MAN for RINGO

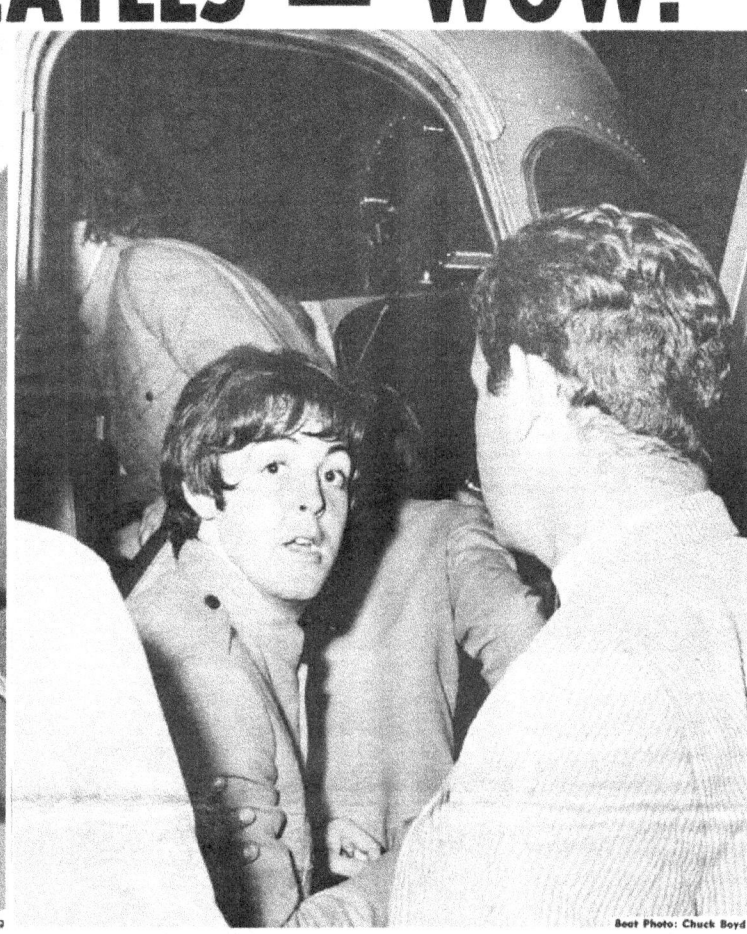

KRLA'S JIM STECK HELPS BEATLES INTO ARMORED CAR FOR GETAWAY

FLANKED BY BRIAN EPSTEIN, BOB EUBANKS AND TONY BARROW, BEATLES LAUGH AT DAVE HULL DURING THEIR PRESS CONFERENCE.

BEATLES ARCHIVES 1

HARD WORK, DANGER FOR BEATLES IN 'HELP'
Press Officer Tells Of Problems Encounted In Filming Movie

(Editor's note: Seldom if ever has any movie caused such world-wide excitement as the second Beatles film. Tony Howard was in charge of publicity, and press relations and travelled with the film company from the sunny Bahamas to the frozen Alps. Howard, a friend of KRLA's Derek Taylor, has written the following account for the KRLA BEAT.)

BY TONY HOWARD

The size of the ten-armed image of the terrible Goddess of Kaili looming above the high walls surrounding London's Twickenham Film Studios was such that, as each of her giant arms was dismantled by crane one chilly February morning of this year, rumour had it that the Beatles' second movie had been scrapped.

If it was a bad day for the local fans, for Producer Walter Shenson it was not. After many a hard day's night — preparations for his second Beatles film — this Sphinx-like idol was merely being "disarmed" for transportation to the Bahamas in order to be "re-armed" on arrival there for the astounding finale.

Producer Shenson chartered a BOAC Boeing 707 to transport the cast, unit and very piece of equipment to the Bahamas, but there was the extra passenger with more room than any first class traveller — it was Kaili, whose dismembered body, adorned in white sheets, was stored in every free corner of the plane. Her torso, however, was too big for any luggage rack or spare seat, so Kaili made the trip along the gangway, much to the chagrin of the stewards carrying their trays through the plane.

From Icebox to Oven

Artists and crew, muffled in coats and scarves to combat the wintry February weather in London, landed in Nassau to the temperature of 90 degrees in the shade.

For weeks before, Shenson's location manager had been battling with the accommodation problem which confronted him in this popular resort.

BEATLES IN SCENE FROM NASSAU LOCATION

How were 700-odd extra people going to be housed in Nassau, which was already bulging at the seems with its usual influx of high season tourists? That his efforts met with success was largely due to the enthusiastic cooperation of American Bob Rowley, chief of the Bahamas Tourist Board.

Next day was spent unpacking and getting ready for shooting. Nearly everyone assembled on the magnificent beach outside the Balmoral Club Hotel. Julie Harris, the costume designer, set about giving the Beatles their final costume fittings. The immense generator was moved into position and Director Richard Lester roamed about, deep in thought, picking the best spots for the next day's filming.

All this activity was accompanied by the cries of fans spotting their

TURN TO PAGE 9

Beatles All Pretending They're Single Artists

The Beatles have never been able to stand still — musically, personally or any other way. They're always on the go, always moving and coming up with something just a little different and unique.

After conquering the world as a quartet — becoming more popular in more countries than any other entertainers in history — they have now proven themselves as top singing stars individually.

JOHN — ALSO A SINGLE

GEORGE — SOLO CONTRACT

All four have recently become equally renowned as soloists, and it looks like this may be just the beginning.

It is reflected in their albums and the singles which are released from their albums. Instead of John and Paul doing almost all the singing together we now have Ringo warbling "Act Naturally," — and singing the western tune as naturally as a hillbilly singer from Tennessee — and Paul with his warmly intimate style reminiscing about "Yesterday."

Those two numbers, on the same 45 r.p.m. disc, have made it the hottest single record on the market.

John again displays his delightful ability as a soloist with a record of his own, "You've Got to Hide Your Love Away." George, who recently signed a separate solo contract with the McCartney-Lennon music publishing firm, turns in a great single performance on "I Need You."

Of course each of these solo efforts still has the great Beatle musical backing but their fans are wondering about the significance of this new trend.

Are they doing it for amusement?...as a challenge?...or perhaps just to help lead the pop trend away from the old "one lead singer and the rest of the group in the background" concept. It may even be a combination of these reasons, but whatever their motive there is no talk or even speculation that any of them is considering leaving the group.

And regardless of motive, it also seems like a very healthy development. It adds a touch of variety which seems certain to keep the group scene alive and interesting for years to come.

John And Paul Sign Up George

It took George Harrison a little longer than John and Paul, but he has finally arrived in the songwriting business in a very big way.

Of course, George has been contributing more and more to the Beatle's original recordings — his latest effort being "I Need You" from their movie, "Help."

So naturally, being enterprising young businessmen, John and Paul have enticed George to sign an exclusive songwriting contract for their publishing company, Northern Songs, Ltd.

Smart bunch of boys, those Beatles!

BEATLES ARCHIVES 1

DREAM VACATION

For Sandra Frazer of Palos Verdes it was a dream vacation - a dream come true. A trip to Nassau where the Beatles were on location shooting the tropical segment of their new movie. As you can see from these pictures she made the most of the opportunity - and became the envy of every other girl in the world.

PAUL looks up to say goodbye to Sandra before driving back to the Balmoval Club after a long day of filming.

JOHN looks like a typical beachcomber sitting on the White Sandy beach.

HERE'S SANDRA IN PAUL McCARTNEY'S SPORTS CAR

MORE ON BEATLES MOVIE

Days Spent Filming - But Nights Delightful

CONTINUED FROM PAGE 2

favorite Beatle, tourists taking photographs, a 50-strong group of pressmen and photographers from all over the world, plus a small army of extra policemen. It looked like unbelievable chaos. How could anyone hope to make a film under those conditions? But next day's shooting commenced without a hitch, although the number of fans and spectators had doubled.

Queen Mother Passes

During the days that followed, over 40 sequences were filmed in public places in and around Nassau, and — although most of the Island and tourist population were there at one time or another — there were very few interruptions of any consequence. The most notable incident that held up shooting for a while was when her Majesty the Queen Mother came into shot as she and her entourage of cars and outriders passed by on their way to the airport, homeward bound after her Jamaican tour.

At night, most of the unit took advantage of the delights available in this picturesque spot — the calypsos, the steel bands for moonlight dancing, the exotic menus and the inate gaiety of the native population. Most members of the unit had to take their swims at night since there was never time for bathing in the famous blue waters during the day.

The Beatles would dodge the fans congregating outside their luxurious beach bungalow, and race to the capital in their open sports cars to live it up for awhile after the gruelling day's work under the burning sun. But most of the time they would stay at home and continue working on the musical score for the picture, music and lyrics by Beatles Paul McCartney and John Lennon — seven new numbers in all.

The last sequences to be shot in the Bahamas were to take place on Paradise Island, by kind permission of Huntington Hartford, who owns the island. While Director Lester supervised the crew on the beach, further activity was going on under the sea a few hundred yards out.

Almost every skindiver in the vicinity, whether they were treasure hunters or underwater guides, were operating from the sea bed, trying to stage the dramatic rising out of the water of the great Image of the Goddess of Kaili — now complete again. Richard Lester was in constant touch by radio with the divers handling the air tanks and pressure bombs needed to make the slow appearance of the 40-foot high idol.

Mr. Huntington Hartford, with his entourage, watched the scene with great interst. His beautiful wife, Diane, was even persuaded to play a small part in the movie.

Kaili Finally Filmed

It took three whole weary days to get Kaili to come out of the water at the right time, at exactly the right place, and by that time the entire unit was glad to see the back of her as she was towed away by a specially hired Navy salvage vessel.

But with the disappearance of the Goddess, an airborne, monster-shaped object became an equally startling sight to the islands. It was the famous Goodyear blimp which was transported from Florida for a spectacular scene in the film.

By now most of the unit was in various stages of sun tan and sun burn, except for the Beatles who had to keep out of the sun throughout the location. Since the Bahamas sequences were actually the last scenes in the completed film, audiences would find it rather odd to watch the boys in varying skin colours without explanation. However, the run on sun tan products and the sale of soft drinks was formidable. It was estimated that some 700 bottles of soft iced drinks were consumed by the unit each day.

When artists and crew finally said goodbye to the Bahamas, unwillingly sweltering in their London clothes, they were given a rousing sendoff by the Bahamanians, for these islands are new ground for film producers and it may well be that Walter Shenson has started up a new profit sideline for them. Indeed, shorter afterwards a 150-strong film unit arrived in Nassau to film exteriors for United Artists' fourth James Bond film, "Thunderball."

London was cold but the unit hadn't much time to notice it because, before two days had passed, they were on their way once again by chartered plane to another extreme of climate — the Austrian Alps!

(In next week's KRLA BEAT, Tony Howard tells of the complications and dangers of filming in the avalanche-threatened Austrian Alps, of the night the Beatles surprised everyone with a performance and of the assault by Beatle fans upon their return to London.)

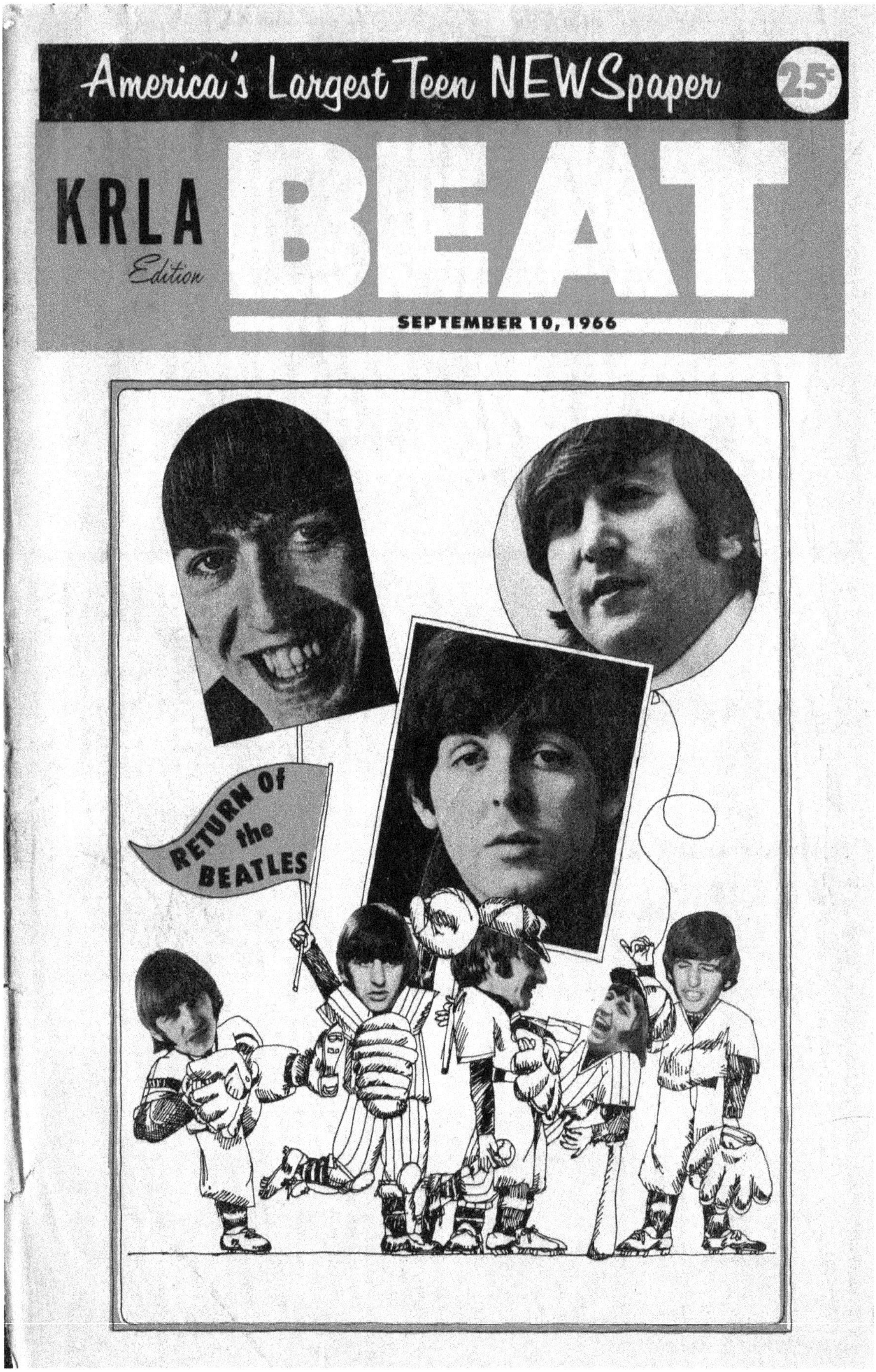

BEATLES ARCHIVES 1

BEATLES ARCHIVES 1

BEATLES ARCHIVES 1

BEATLES ARCHIVES 1

BEAT EXCLUSIVE
Reader Spends A Day With Beatle Family In England

(Editor's note: If you're lucky enough, it can be done. Beatle fan, Patty Juliono, spent a fantastic day at the home of Mr. & Mrs. Harrison. A surprise twosome greeted Patty inside the house and the following is Patty's story of the day she'll never forget. We hope you'll enjoy it as much as we did.)

By Patty Juliono

I've been writing to Mrs. Harrison ever since I got her address a few years ago and I have always gotten an answer from her. Last February I went to Paris with my father. Before I left I wrote Mrs. Harrison a letter telling her I was coming to Europe and if I ever came to England, I would love to see her. When I got to Paris I was surprised to find a letter from her. She said she would love to see me and gave me directions on how to get to her house.

Phone Call

I called her the day we were going to Germany. She sounded so nice. I told her about coming to see her. I asked what would be the best day, Saturday or Sunday. She said either so I picked Sunday. I had to hang up then because we had to hurry to the airport.

My dad asked me to call Mrs. Harrison and ask if we could come on Saturday instead of Sunday because we had to leave Sunday so we could go to Switzerland on Monday because I had to start school.

When I called, she wasn't home, so my father called later and asked her. She said it was just fine and that she was looking forward to meeting me. So on Friday, March 4, we landed in London, England. I was so excited I couldn't believe I was in England! All Friday we went sightseeing. I even had lunch in an English pub!

The next morning we got up at eight, had breakfast and then took a bus to the London airport. We had to fly from London to Manchester and then take a train from Manchester to Warrington. When we got to Manchester, my dad decided to take a taxi to Warrington. When we got to Warrington, we had to stop at the train station so we could call Mrs. Harrison and ask how to get to her house from the station.

George Answers

My dad called and when he got off the phone he had a smile on his face. I asked him why he was smiling—he didn't say anything. What he was smiling about was that George had answered the phone and he was just thinking of what would happen if I had called and George answered the phone. All the way to her house I kept saying wouldn't that be neat if George was there.

Finally we turned down the road to Mrs. Harrison's house. Mrs. Harrison was out in the front waiting. I got out of the taxi and gave Mrs. Harrison a box of candy I had bought her. We walked into the house. The door leading to the living room is made of glass. I looked through and saw someone sitting in there. Then Mrs. Harrison opened the door and who should be sitting there but Patti—she is so pretty in person.

Mrs. Harrison introduced us and we sat and talked. Then my dad came in and I introduced them. Then Mr. Harrison came in and we all started talking. I asked Patti if she got a lot of mean letters from girls after she married George. She said she got a few saying "I hate you so much." After awhile, my dad looked up and smiled and then said: "Well, here's our boy." I turned around and there stood George with a big smile on his face!

He came over and shook my hand and sat in the chair next to me. He offered everyone a cigarette—even me! I joked and started to take one. He laughed and said: "Aren't you too young?" I never did get one.

My dad and George started to talk about Vietnam. Patti and I just sat and listened and threw in our two-cents once in awhile. Then George started talking about the police protection they get when they're in America. He said the English police were better. He told me how he's seen policemen take kids and hit them with their clubs. He said English policemen don't do that.

Then Mrs. Harrison called us in for a small lunch. We had tea sausages, cheese and bread. I sat between Mrs. Harrison and Patti and George sat across from me. Mrs. Harrison showed me a scrapbook of fans from all over the world. I found a lot of pictures of kids from the United States. I even found a picture of me!

After we ate, I cleared off the table and helped Mrs. Harrison with the dishes. Then my dad suggested we take pictures before the sun went down. We took six pictures outside. After we took the pictures, George's two brothers, Peter and Henry, came with their wives and George's little niece and nephew, Janet and Paul. We got one picture of Janet. She was very shy. We started talking about cars because George just got a new car which was out in front. I think it was a GTO. George started talking about the Munsters' car.

Good-Byes

Around five o'clock, my dad said it was time to go. I didn't want to but we had to catch a train at 5:30. Mr. Harrison drove us to the train station. I really hated to say good-bye. George and Patti stood in the doorway holding hands. George's brothers all shook my hand and said they enjoyed meeting me. I told Mrs. Harrison I really had a wonderful time. She was glad.

I got in the car and as we drove out the driveway, I turned around and saw Mrs. Harrison standing there waving good-bye. I'll never forget that day. I really couldn't believe I had met one of the Beatles!

I did learn one thing about George—he is supposed to be a real good cook, his father told me. Well, I still write to Mrs. Harrison and she writes to me. Maybe someday I'll meet her again.

PATTY POSES with George and Patti and Mr. & Mrs. Harrison.

BEATLES ARCHIVES 1

WERE JAGGER AND RICHARDS SCAPEGOATS? 25¢

KRLA BEAT
Edition

JULY 29, 1967

EXCLUSIVE RAVI SHANKAR Interview

ZAL leaves SPOONFUL

HARRISON & STARR *from the beginning*

SUPREMES ON STAGE

ERIC BURDON GIVES his views on U.S.

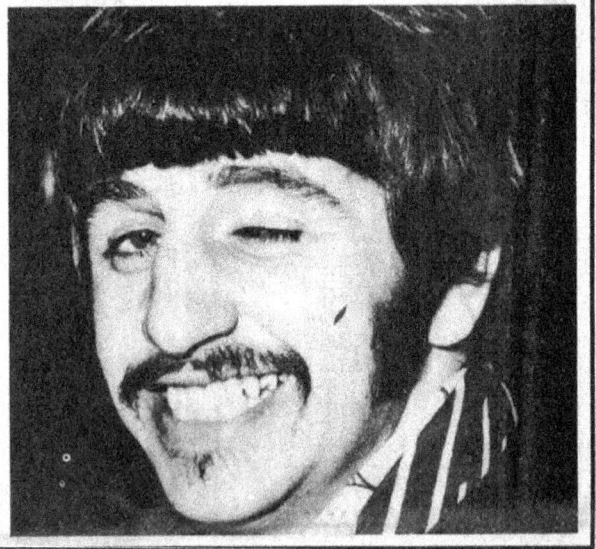

BEATLES ARCHIVES 1

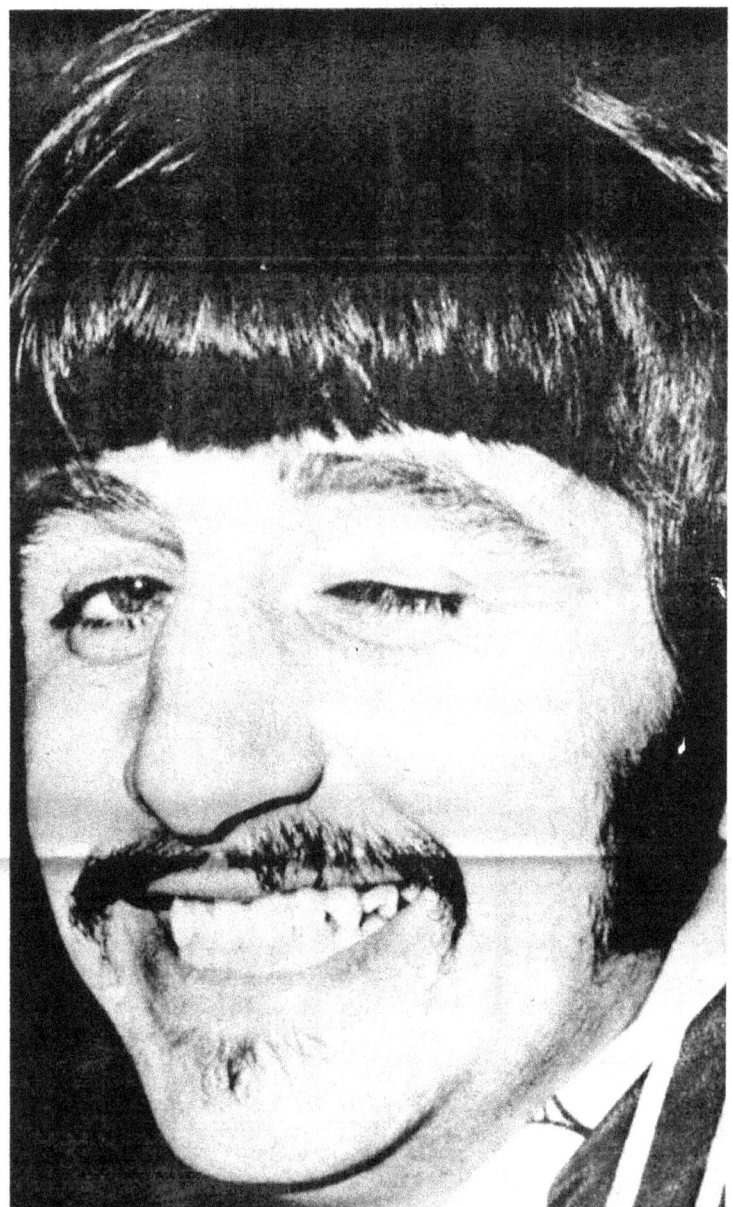

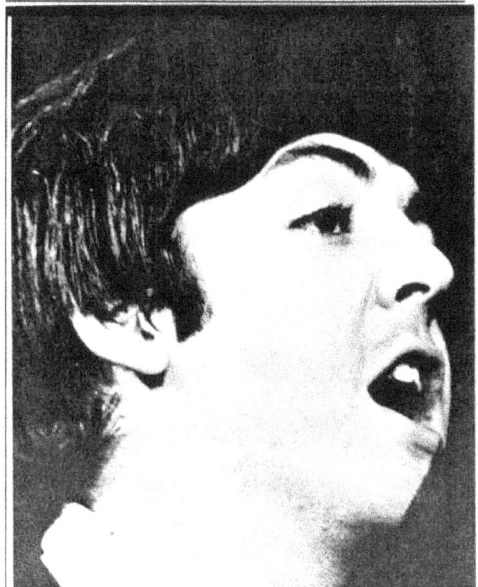

... PAUL McCARTNEY — MOST POPULAR.

Beatle Fans

By Eden

We build them up — we idolize them — we lay the physical manifestations of adulation, worship, and success at their feet.

And then we tear them down and destroy them. Pretend they never existed at all, and walk away to seek a new idol. These are the "teen idols" — the "pop stars" — the people who rise to fantastic heights because we tell them that we care.

But they are also people destined to plunge to the very bottom of failure if just once they fall out of favor with the public, their "fans" — the people who "put them where they are."

We sometimes speak a little harshly of our pop idols, criticizing them for not paying more attention to us. We say that they have gotten too big for their own good, and accuse them of forgetting their fans and all the other people who have supported them.

Ringo Lands Role In 'Candy'

By Tony Barrow

LONDON—Just over a year ago John Lennon accepted his first solo screen role, playing Private Gripweed of the Third Troop of the Fourth Muskateers in the Dick Lester picture "How I Won The War." At that time Ringo admitted that he'd be willing to consider following in his fellow Beatle's footsteps if and when he was presented with a suitable film script.

Candy Role

A month ago (October 7 issue of The BEAT) I indicated that the most interesting solo movie appearance yet received for Ringo was under consideration in London. Now the big news has broken—Ringo Starr has been signed to play alongside Richard Burton, Marlon Brando and a number of other important screen names in "Candy" which is based upon the sex-stacked satirical novel by Terry Southern and Mason Hoffenberg. "Candy," first published as long ago as 1958, is banned in many countries and the book is still unobtainable via normal retail sources in London.

Ringo will appear in the cameo role of Emmanuel, the Mexican gardener boy employed by Candy Christian's father to mow the lawn each Saturday.

Apart from the currently uncast title role, all the parts in "Candy" are little more than brief guest appearances, characters who move briskly in and out of Candy's teenage life.

Indian Trip

Ringo's acceptance of the part will cut short his visit to India. There is still no certain departure date for the Beatles' much-postponed trip to the East as the guests and pupils of Maharishi Mahesh Yogi but, in any event, Ringo will be unable to spend more than a few November weeks studying Transcendental Meditation with the others. After that he will be due to spend between two and three pre-Christmas weeks shooting his "Candy" sequences. It is most unlikely that Ringo would be called upon to visit Hollywood or any other part of America in connection with the making of this picture.

In London, Ringo told me: "This is exactly the type of part I have been hoping somebody would offer me. It's a part with a lot of scope for turning Emmanuel into an interesting screen personality. It's also a very small part which is all I want to consider at the moment.

(Continued on Page 4)

... BEATLES — BEATEN IN AMERICA?

BEATLES ARCHIVES 1

Harrison & Lennon Discuss Religion

By Tony Barrow

Before departing for India and the beginning of a two to three month meditation study course under the guidance of Maharishi Mahesh Yogi, Beatles John Lennon and George Harrison talked at length about the value and meaning of Transcendental Meditation.

After appearing with David Frost in the television discussion show, "The Frost Program," John commented: "If just one in every thousand viewers who watched the program was encouraged to look into Transcendental Meditation then it was well worth doing. We want to get the message across to as many people as possible that meditation can help everyone. Not just a special few, or brainy people or cranks but everyone."

The following is an abbreviated transcript of the views and explanations given in London by John and George before they left for India:

JOHN: Through meditation I've learned how to tap energy that I've had in me all the time. Before I could only reach this extra energy on good days when things were going well. With meditation I find that if it's not too good a day I can still get the same amount of energy going for me. It means I am more used to myself and to others. Put it another way—the worst days I had without meditation were much worse than the bad days I have now, days when it's difficult to get going.

Latent Energy

GEORGE: The energy is latent within everybody. It's there anyway. Meditation is a natural process of being able to contact that energy each day and give yourself a little more. You're able to do whatever you normally do with a little bit more happiness, maybe.

Each individual's life sort of pulsates in a certain rhythm. They give you a word or a sound which pulsates with that rhythm. The idea is to transcend to the most subtle level of thought, to replace your ordinary thought with the word or sound. Finally you lose even that and you're at a level of pure consciousness.

GEORGE HARRISON AND JOHN LENNON DISCUSS TRANSCENDENTAL MEDITATION WITH TV HOST, DAVID FROST (left).

GUESS HAS BEATLES AT OVER $70 MIL.

LONDON — An "uneducated guess" by Northern Songs executive, Dick James, points to the fact that the Beatles during the past five years have earned from $70 to $86 million dollars!

James made the statement while accepting an award for the Beatles' "Sgt. Pepper" album and although admitting that his guess "may be a conservative one" he pointed up the fact that he did not have sufficient information to make a truly accurate estimate on the group's earnings during the last five years.

James' calculation was made on the basis of the around-$14 million figure which the Beatles have earned for their songs. Of course, added to that would be their earnings from films, records, artists' fees and fees from the endorsement of goods. All of which may add up to as much as $114 million!

JOHN: You sit there and let your mind go. You introduce the word, the sound, the vibration to take over from your thoughts. You don't will thoughts away.

GEORGE: When your mind is a complete blank it's beyond all previous experience. That level is timeless, spaceless. You can be there for five minutes or much longer. You don't actually know how long when you come out of it and back to the everyday, the gross level of thinking.

JOHN: It's like sleeping. You don't know you've been sleeping until you're awake again. It seems as though no time has gone at all.

GEORGE: You can't really tell anybody exactly what it is. The teaching of Transcendental Meditation is all based on the individual. If you want to do it you get instruction. That leads to some sort of experience. Upon that experience you're taught the next part, you're told how you can go on from there to the next stage.

Impossible Description

JOHN: It's like asking someone to say what chocolate tastes like. It's impossible to describe.

GEORGE: Or to tell somebody how it is to be drunk. They've got to be drunk themselves before they know what it is.

JOHN: You don't feel you have more actual knowledge — or at least I don't — but you feel more energetic. You come out of it and it's just a sort of "let's get going" feeling about whatever work you've got to tackle.

GEORGE: It takes a lot of practice to arrive at a point where you can remain in that frame of mind, that attitude to life, permanently. I've had definite proof after only 6 or 7 weeks that this is something that really works. It'll take a long time to arrive at a state where I can hold the level of pure consciousness and bring it back with me into everyday levels of activity and thinking. That's the eventual aim.

Gold Cloth

JOHN: One of the Maharishi's analogies is that it's like dipping a cloth in and out of gold. If you leave it in it gets soggy. If you leave it out the sun will fade it. So you keep dipping it in and bringing it out and, eventually, there's the same amount of gold in the cloth whether it's in or out. So you don't meditate ALL the time but you DO meditate regularly if you want to get anywhere with it. Twenty minutes a day—something like that.

GEORGE: Drugs don't really get to the true you, the real self. The way to approach the real you is through meditation or some form of Yoga. We're not saying that this particular form — Transcendental Meditation—is the only answer. Yoga incorporates lots of different techniques but the whole point is that each soul is potentially divine and Yoga is a technique of manifesting it to arrive at that point which is divine.

JOHN: Meditation doesn't actually change you, make you different in any way. It's just something beneficial which you can add to yourself, add to your routine. When you add to your religion you don't change your religion. Whatever you are—you carry on. If you ask any of the Maharishi's people to give you a few laws for living by they'd be virtually the same as Christianity. Christianity is the answer as much as this is.

GEORGE: Christianity as I was taught it was a demand that I should believe in Jesus and in God but they didn't actually show me any way of experiencing God or Jesus.

Directly Related

JOHN: The bit about "The Kingdom Of Heaven Is Within You" seems to relate directly to meditation. Have a peep inside. Find out. I still am a Christian but had I been taught meditation at 15, well now I'd be pretty groovy.

GEORGE: The word God means all sorts of things to me. The first concept I had of a man in the sky, well, I kicked that one a few years ago but I'm coming back to that now because, yes, it's a man in the sky as well if you like, it's just every aspect of creation, all a part of God.

JOHN: I think of God as a big piece of energy, like electricity, a big powerhouse.

GEORGE: Or the energy which runs through everything and makes everything one.

JOHN: Everything you read about, all the religions, are all the same basically. It's just a matter of people opening their minds up. I don't know how divine or superhuman Maharishi is. He was probably born quite ordinary but he's working at it.

In Order

GEORGE: If everybody took up meditation it would help them to sort out their own problems, put their houses in order, if you like. People cause all the world's problems. So if people fix up their personal problems that's it, we're well on the way aren't we. It's up to each individual, every person, to make his own move.

JOHN: The main thing is it's simple. All you've got to do is to be interested. If you don't believe in meditation and you're cynical about it there's still no reason why you shouldn't try to find out what you're so cynical about. And the only way to find out is to learn about meditation and give it a try. Then you'll have the right to condemn or otherwise.

"The Standel Sound"

"The Grass Roots"

Professional musicians throughout the world choose the "Standel Sound," the accepted standard for professional musicians who demand professional performance.

Standel
Solid State Music Systems
4918 DOUBLE DRIVE • EL MONTE, CALIF. 91731

BEATLES ARCHIVES 1

RINGO SIGNS FOR 'CANDY'

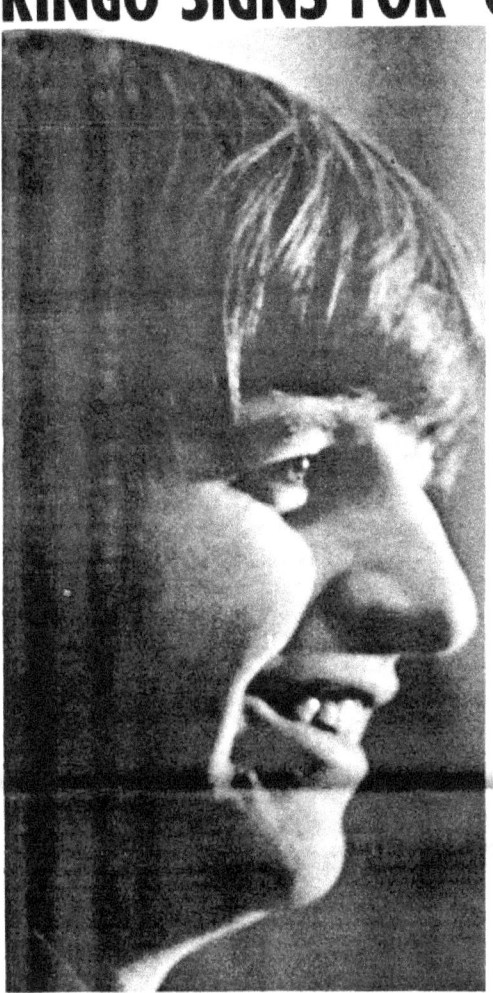

WILL RINGO STARR be forced to look like this again for "Candy?"

(Continued from Page 1)

"Apart from anything else I don't want to be away from the Beatles for too long. The timing is fine because the others will be having a break in November and December so I am not holding up any group work by taking the part. I wouldn't want a bigger film role. I have no idea whether I'm even capable of tackling a really big part.

"This is a major production with a lot of big people in it and a lot of big money behind it. I'll just be one of various names taking part. John didn't have a very large part in 'How I Won The War.' My part in 'Candy' is not as big but that doesn't mean it is anything less than an important step for me to take. I'm looking forward to this very much indeed.

Straight Acting

"In the new year the Beatles will be getting together another film. That's another reason why I wouldn't accept any solo work which would get me too involved over a long period. The 'Candy' part is a straight acting role. There's no question of turning Emmanuel into a drummer or anything like that and neither I nor the other Beatles will be involved in any soundtrack music."

The news of Ringo's signing for "Candy" came almost upon the eve of the London premiere of 'How I Won The War" at the West End's London Pavilion Theatre. A record-splintering number of pop personalities attended the star-studded premiere with United Artists announcing a virtual 100 per cent acceptance level for invitations sent out to recording and other celebrities. Apart from the Beatles, the list of attending stars included members of the Rolling Stones, the Who, Procol Harum and a score of other groups plus Cilla Black, Sandie Shaw, Anita Harris, Marianne Faithfull and numerous movie stars.

BEATLES' RELEASE

A new Beatles' Album has been released this Christmas. This is the surprise outcome of talks which have taken place in London between Capitol Records executive Voyle Gilmore and the Beatles. Gilmore met with the group to discuss the American presentation format for the six new recordings featured on the soundtrack of the Beatles upcoming color television film "Magical Mystery Tour."

One side of the new album features the six soundtrack numbers, while the other cintains five tracks that have previously been released as singles. Side two includes "Penny Lane," "Strawberry Fields Forever," and "All You Need Is Love."

Capitol is using all the cartoons and photographs from the original U.K. book but the American version will have much larger pages. However, there will be no extra charge for the "book" and the album will sell at regular album prices.